MW01039705

AIRBORNE
COMBAT

0 11557 00808 1

The Stackpole Military History Series

THE AMERICAN CIVIL WAR
Cavalry Raids of the Civil War
Ghost, Thunderbolt, and Wizard
Pickett's Charge
Witness to Gettysburg

WORLD WAR I
Doughboy War

WORLD WAR II
After D-Day
Airborne Combat
Armor Battles of the
    Waffen-SS, 1943–45
Armoured Guardsmen
Army of the West
Arnhem 1944
Australian Commandos
The B-24 in China
Backwater War
The Battle of Sicily
Battle of the Bulge, Vol. 1
Battle of the Bulge, Vol. 2
Beyond the Beachhead
Beyond Stalingrad
Blitzkrieg Unleashed
Blossoming Silk against the
    Rising Sun
Bodenplatte
The Brandenburger Commandos
The Brigade
Bringing the Thunder
The Canadian Army and the
    Normandy Campaign
Coast Watching in World War II
Colossal Cracks
Condor
A Dangerous Assignment
D-Day Bombers
D-Day Deception
D-Day to Berlin
Destination Normandy
Dive Bomber!
A Drop Too Many
Eagles of the Third Reich
The Early Battles of Eighth Army
Eastern Front Combat
Europe in Flames
Exit Rommel
Fist from the Sky
Flying American Combat
    Aircraft of World War II
For Europe
Forging the Thunderbolt
For the Homeland

Fortress France
The German Defeat in the East,
    1944–45
German Order of Battle, Vol. 1
German Order of Battle, Vol. 2
German Order of Battle, Vol. 3
The Germans in Normandy
Germany's Panzer Arm in
    World War II
GI Ingenuity
Goodwood
The Great Ships
Grenadiers
Hitler's Nemesis
Infantry Aces
In the Fire of the Eastern Front
Iron Arm
Iron Knights
Kampfgruppe Peiper at the
    Battle of the Bulge
The Key to the Bulge
Knight's Cross Panzers
Kursk
Luftwaffe Aces
Luftwaffe Fighter Ace
Luftwaffe Fighter-Bombers
    over Britain
Luftwaffe Fighters and Bombers
Massacre at Tobruk
Mechanized Juggernaut or
    Military Anachronism?
Messerschmitts over Sicily
Michael Wittmann, Vol. 1
Michael Wittmann, Vol. 2
Mountain Warriors
The Nazi Rocketeers
Night Flyer / Mosquito
    Pathfinder
No Holding Back
On the Canal
Operation Mercury
Packs On!
Panzer Aces
Panzer Aces II
Panzer Aces III
Panzer Commanders of the
    Western Front
Panzergrenadier Aces
Panzer Gunner
The Panzer Legions
Panzers in Normandy
Panzers in Winter
The Path to Blitzkrieg
Penalty Strike
Poland Betrayed
Red Road from Stalingrad

Red Star under the Baltic
Retreat to the Reich
Rommel's Desert Commanders
Rommel's Desert War
Rommel's Lieutenants
The Savage Sky
Ship-Busters
Siege of Küstrin, 1945
The Siegfried Line
A Soldier in the Cockpit
Soviet Blitzkrieg
Stalin's Keys to Victory
Surviving Bataan and Beyond
T-34 in Action
Tank Tactics
Tigers in the Mud
Triumphant Fox
The 12th SS, Vol. 1
The 12th SS, Vol. 2
Twilight of the Gods
Typhoon Attack
The War against Rommel's
    Supply Lines
War in the Aegean
Wolfpack Warriors
Zhukov at the Oder

THE COLD WAR / VIETNAM
Cyclops in the Jungle
Expendable Warriors
Fighting in Vietnam
Flying American Combat
    Aircraft: The Cold War
Here There Are Tigers
Land with No Sun
MiGs over North Vietnam
Phantom Reflections
Street without Joy
Through the Valley

WARS OF AFRICA AND THE MIDDLE EAST
Never-Ending Conflict
The Rhodesian War

GENERAL MILITARY HISTORY
Carriers in Combat
Cavalry from Hoof to Track
Desert Battles
Guerrilla Warfare
Ranger Dawn
Sieges

AIRBORNE COMBAT

The Glider War/Fighting Gliders of World War II

James E. Mrazek

STACKPOLE
BOOKS

Published in 2011 by
STACKPOLE BOOKS
5067 Ritter Road
Mechanicsburg, PA 17055
www.stackpolebooks.com

Cover design by Tracy Patterson

Printed in the United States of America

10 9 8 7 6 5 4 3 2 1

Library of Congress Cataloging-in-Publication Data

Mrazek, James E.
    [Glider war]
    Airborne combat : The glider war, [and], Fighting gliders of World War II / James E. Mrazek.
        p. cm.
    First work originally published: New York : St. Martin's Press, 1975; 2nd work originally published: New York : St. Martin's Press, 1977.
    Includes index.
    ISBN 978-0-8117-0808-1
    1. World War, 1939–1945—Aerial operations. 2. Gliders (Aeronautics) I. Mrazek, James E. Fighting gliders of World War II. II. Title. III. Title: Fighting gliders of World War II.
    D785.M7 2011
    940.54'1—dc22
                                    2010052710

Contents

Chapter 6 Gliders of the Soviet Union 421

Chapter 7 Some Lesser-known Developments. 437

Appendix A Loading, Flight and Landing Plans of the U.S. 82nd
            Airborne Division for Operation "Market Garden" . . 457

Appendix B Glider Data 465

Appendix C Powered Gliders 468

Appendix D CG-4A Production Data to October 31, 1944 469

Appendix E Performance Data 470

            Select Bibliography 471

            Acknowledgments 473

            Index. 481

Introduction

This is the story of the fighting glider and of the stirring and valorous deeds of the gallant soldiers and glider pilots from many nations who flew into combat in this stealthy weapon. They made their hazardous flights in these fabric-covered, motorless and unprotected craft, while buffeted by gusting winds and their tow-plane's propeller blast; flew so slowly that they became sitting ducks for enemy antiaircraft weaponry; and finished their one-way ride skidding or crashing into enemy strongholds. Americans appropriately called them the "towed-target" infantry.

Their story has few antecedents and fewer residues. It is contained in a five-year span of history. The glider had no wartime predecessor, in contrast to many weapons used during World War II. The crawling British tanks that surprised the Germans at Cambrai in World War I were the forerunners of the fast-moving, powerful Sherman, Churchill, Tiger, and Stalin tanks of World War II. Modifications made to the famous French 75-mm artillery piece used in the first war enabled armies to use it during the second war. The dog-fighting Spads, Fokkers, and de Havilland aircraft of the first conflict evolved into the sophisticated fighters and bombers of the second one.

But the story of the glider is different. No one had ever flown a glider into combat before World War II. The first glider used in combat was a novel by-product of the fragile, translucent, sports sailplane; and only two nations, Germany and Russia, had dreamed of the possibilities of transforming the sailplane into a weapon of war. Suddenly, early on 10 May 1940, the world was rudely awakened to the startling news that a German force using some unheard-of weapon had landed stealthily on the top of the key Belgian fort of Eben Emael. That weapon was the glider.

No less to American officers than to the beleaguered Allies striving desperately to stem the onrush of the *Wehrmacht,* the German Armed Forces, the glider was an ominous, strange weapon. American and British generals had some experience with paratroopers, and some jelled ideas about them; but gliders, none—absolutely none.

Eben Emael proved that the glider could be used with devastating tactical surprise. Its potential, once studies were undertaken by U.S. military leaders, appeared awesome. Gliders might change the character of war. Rivers were no longer formidable barriers to armies, nor would they run red with the blood of troops hit while they ran unprotected across foot bridges or tried crossings in defenseless assault boats. Gliders could form air bridges over the rivers. Gliders could simplify the supply of ground operations because, loaded with supplies, they could be towed to units in critical need of supplies and released. Visionaries said that gliders could be built to transport tanks into combat, a job that no aircraft then in existence could do.

Little did our generals realize that they were laggards in their estimate of the value of the glider. Long before the Germans were defeated—in fact, by 1942—their glider effort had reached a pinnacle of technical achievement that the United States, with its tremendous resources, could not attain in a five-year intensive glider-production effort. The United States did outproduce the Germans by 10 to 1, a not unexpected accomplishment, in view of America's greater industrial resources. Nevertheless, America neither produced a glider that was nearly as large as the German Gigant, nor attained the excellence in design and technical innovations that was reached by the Germans.

In no comparable effort did America bumble so horribly from the beginning to the end of a program. The Americans were "Johnnies come lately." They were conservative. They were not daring in the development and procurement of the glider, and in its strategic and tactical application in combat, the Americans fell far short of what might have been expected. A huge U.S. glider arsenal lay largely untested and unused during the war. Tied to American operations, the British could do little better.

On 7 December 1941, neither Britain nor the United States had combat gliders. There were no qualified combat glider pilots, no glider infantry regiments, and no trucks, tanks or artillery pieces suitable for transport in gliders. Moreover, neither had doctrine for the operational employment of gliders, and few people had any idea of how, when, and where gliders could be used.

BOOK ONE

The Glider War

To Randy Clarke,
my Canadian grandson

CHAPTER 1

The Capture of Eben Emael

At 0505 hours on 10 May 1940, a mile east of Fort Eben Emael in Belgium, sturdy *Luftwaffe* gliders, heavy with Hitler's glidermen, guns and secret explosives, cut away from the towropes of the straining Ju 52 tow planes, one by one. Majestically, like an enormous hawk, each glider soared upward momentarily then banked, while its pilot quickly searched for and found the fortress walls below. From every direction, they swooped in shrieking dives and quickly leveled off as the ground raced up. One by one, they skidded silently onto the very roof of the "impregnable" fort, virtually into the mouths of its huge casemates.

Led by *Oberleutnant*[1] Rudolf Witzig, 78 Germans in ten gliders dared to attack a concrete and steel monster manned by 780 Belgians. Hardly in the history of warfare had such a small force faced such incredible odds. To crack Eben Emael's defenses, the gliders carried machine guns, grenades, assorted ammunition and explosives and, most importantly, twenty-eight of the new hollow charges, totaling five tons of explosives. The highly secret hollow charge, a fiendish invention never before used in war, was a 100-pound hemisphere of dynamite with a small part scooped from the flat undersurface. When exploded, great pressures focused in this hollow. The hollow charge was the forerunner of the design that made the atom bomb function.

In their eagerness to attack the huge Belgian casemates, the glidermen catapulted out of the doors and burst through the fabric sides of their gliders. Two squads found that the craft that had carried them now rested in a mat of barbed wire that had snagged the gliders to a sudden halt. Belgian machine gunners, quickly recovering from their stupor, started firing at the Germans as they struggled towards their assigned casemates with the heavy hollow charges in tow. The Germans frantically clipped the wire and picked their way through, as bullets twanged and ricocheted.

Getting to the tops of the casemates, they centered their hollow charges on the thick steel observation and gun turrets, triggered the fuses and fled to safety. Across the enormous surface of the fort, the charges began exploding in miniature blasts, marked by telltale mushroom-like clouds.

1. Lieutenant.

5

The DFS 230, the German glider used to attack Fort Eben Emael.

Gliders on the ground after the assault on the fort. The cupola in the foreground has been damaged by a hollow charge.

So violent was the shock, so unsuspecting were the Germans themselves of how strong the force would be, that it blew many to the ground while they were still racing away. It burst the eardrums of Heine Lange, one of the glider pilots who had placed a charge on a steel gun turret, the largest in the fort, making him virtually deaf for life.

The steel atomized under the fiery heat. Extreme pressure jetted it into the bowels of the casemates, incinerating men, blowing guns from their stanchions and creating indescribable havoc and confusion in the depths of the fort. In a matter of twenty minutes, the Germans had almost sealed the Belgians in the fort's maze of tunnels.

Meanwhile, thirty more gliders were descending out of the grey morning mists along the Meuse River onto the surprised defenders of three bridges that Hitler had also ordered to be seized. *Hauptmann* Koch, leading a glider element carrying 4 officers and 129 men, landed close to the bridge at Vroenhoven. A platoon led by *Leutnant* Schacht moved off to take the bridge, while Koch and his staff set up a headquarters and made radio contact with glider forces at the fort and at the two other bridges marked for capture. The Germans hit the defenders of the Vroenhoven bridge with such ferocity and speed that they overwhelmed the Belgians and disarmed the explosives set to destroy the bridge before the Belgians could set them off. Less than thirty minutes later, the bridge was open to German tanks and within three hours all significant Belgian resistance in the area was liquidated. Despite strong Belgian efforts to dislodge the glidermen, the Germans held firm. However, Schacht's platoon paid a heavy price, losing 7 killed and 18 wounded.

At the Canne bridge, the story was different. Belgian Sergeant Pirenne, in charge of destroying the bridge, set off the fuses to the charges inserted into the bridge just as the gliders were landing. Before the Germans could get out of their gliders and to the bridge, the charges exploded and the bridge folded into the Canne Canal.

In a short time, *Hauptmann* Koch's radio operator had the reassuring signal from the Germans at Fort Eben Emael that all was going well. Koch intermittently got word that Witzig's force was maintaining control. However, Koch had no word from *Leutnant* Schächter at the Canne bridge. About noon, he sent a patrol to find out what was up. Two hours passed. The patrol returned. Its commander reported that the bridge was demolished and Schächter's team had taken a beating. The patrol had found four glidermen dead and six severely wounded. Disappointed at not having captured the bridge, Schächter's glidermen nevertheless captured 49 officers and 250 men and left 150 Belgians dead, before they were relieved on 11 May.

At the third bridge, Veldwezelt, the German success was comparable with that at Vroenhoven. Several Belgian officers, hearing the alert signaled by

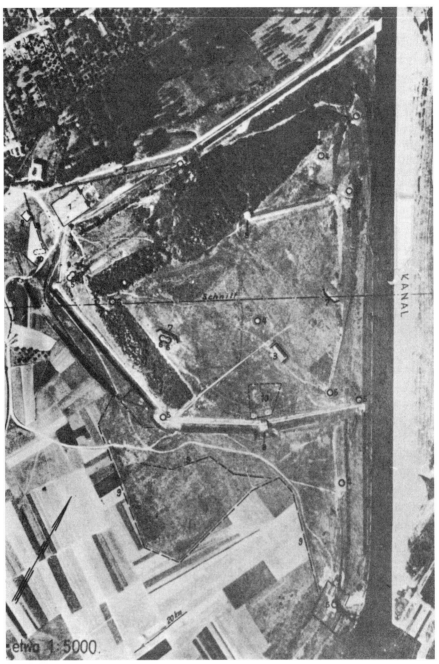

An aerial photograph of Fort Eben Emael taken by a German reconnaissance aircraft before the attack.

the fort's guns, pleaded for permission to blow the bridge immediately. A wavering senior officer advised that it was necessary to get formal orders first. Several minutes later, gliders appeared and virtually hypnotized the gawking Belgian soldiers into inaction. None could venture a guess as to what the mysterious silent machines could be, for none had ever seen aircraft without engines. The order to blow the bridge never came, and the German glider force, commanded by *Oberleutnant* Altmann, descended into the midst of the Belgian defenders and skidded to a stop right on target. Using a hollow charge against the casemate protecting the bridge, while aggressively attacking the Belgians entrenched close by, Altmann's platoon seized the bridge ten minutes later and disarmed the charges set to blow it up. In the brief but violent struggle and during the combat that ensued for the remainder of the day, the Germans lost 8 dead and 21 wounded.

Back at Eben Emael, the fort's commander, Major Jean Fritz Lucien Jottrand, ordered several counterattacking sallies from the fort. Backed by dive-bombing Stukas, the glidermen repulsed the Belgians each time. By the next morning, with his men choking from the acrid smoke filling the tunnels, no help forthcoming "and the situation utterly hopeless," Jottrand raised the white flag. *Granit* ("Granite"), the German code name for the operation, became history only hours after it had begun.

At Eben Emael, ten gliders and 78 men started a new phase of German conquest at the cost of 6 killed and 20 wounded. The lives of an estimated 6,000 German ground troops were saved—the force the German High Command calculated it would have had to sacrifice to take Fort Eben Emael by conventional attack. The Germans had also estimated that it would take six months of hard fighting.

The idea for this utterly sensational attack on Eben Emael was Hitler's and his alone. It was not just a hare-brained gimmick dreamed up to boost German morale. It was a brilliant stratagem, the most crucial strike by any element of the German military machine during that opening day of the attack against France, Belgium and Holland.

If Eben Emael had held off the glider attack force successfully, the *Wehrmacht* would have had to grind the fort into submission by a methodical, time-consuming and costly air and ground attack. Worse for Hitler's timetable of world conquest, had he been unable to seize Eben Emael (and the bridges that the fort protected) with glider forces, his armored forces would have had to make their way through the tangled Ardennes. That would have been a grueling contest. The German generals had pledged that they could win it, but there was great danger that the attack might have come perilously close to bogging down into World War I–style trench warfare, a method of fighting they had no taste for.

Hitler had to have speed, and he sought to achieve it by a total surprise. He had to have speed to overwhelm France and the Low Countries before the British armies could come to the aid of a beleaguered France, as had happened during World War I when the Kaiser's forces were about to destroy the French armies.

The glider was Hitler's surprise weapon. Never before used in waging war, gliders were potent weapons. They could disgorge tens of men and tons of violence on the heads of an unwary foe. They could be released from tow planes many miles from an unsuspecting enemy and, in utter silence, stealthily land on and around his fortifications, as Eben Emael proved. Because they were quiet and could get low quickly and skim the treetops, they could easily sneak through or avoid antiaircraft fire.

After the Germans moved into Denmark and Norway, but subsequent to the capture of Eben Emael, they began to fly gliders to Oslo, with the plan of using them in the airborne operation to seize Narvik. When *Fallschirmjäger*— parachute forces—took off from Oslo for Trondheim, a staging point for Narvik, gliders accompanied them. Narvik at that time had no airfields usable for making air landings with Ju 52's to bring in artillery and other heavy equipment to support the parachute infantry.

Glider pilots, and those who were to fly to Narvik, grew beards, and the gliders carried boxes containing a change of civilian clothes for each man. Orders were to change into civilian clothes after the operation, cross over into neutral Sweden, and return to Germany.

Because Britain controlled the sea and access by land was difficult, Narvik had to be captured by airborne assault. However, when the airborne forces took off, several of the air staff decided the weather conditions were unsuitable for gliders. Thus, gliders were never used, although their use had been planned. According to *Leutnant* Walter Fulda and *Leutnant* Heiner Lange, glider pilots who were to participate, the judgment that the weather was unsuitable was bad. Gliders, they are convinced, could have made the trip to Narvik without any problems.

The speed at which the Germans liquidated Eben Emael jarred and baffled generals, who were immersed in the lessons learned from World War I, and politicians alike. For sheer breathtaking swiftness and shock power, nothing like it had ever occurred in any war.

Hitler had kept the forthcoming attack on Eben Emael a closely guarded secret, limiting those who knew of it to the handful directly involved in planning and carrying out the operation. Pleased with his gliders, he clamped even tighter security over them after the fort was taken. German newsreels featured the capture and had shots of the action, but showed no gliders or hollow charges, leaving the impression in Germany that it was a conventional

military operation carried out by dauntless German soldiers. The German
and other Axis-country press carried accounts of the capture, but nothing
about gliders. Abroad, legends grew; the world guessed wildly. The Germans
had used nerve gas; some said sabotage. *Life* magazine published an "endive-
tunnel-treachery" fairy tale, beggaring the imagination, yet published as fact:
German workers, married to Belgian women during the construction of
Eben Emael in the years before 1940, had, under the guise of endive farmers,
planted explosives as well as endives in the tunnels scraped under the fort.

The fall of Eben Emael had a great deal to do with building an image
of German military strength, if not invincibility, in the minds of many Allied
leaders. Until the end of the war, most of Germany's highest-ranking officers
never really knew the true facts, so closely was the secret kept. In fact, it would
be years after the war before the true role of the "secret weapon," Hitler's
gliders, would be generally known.

Eben Emael was the culmination of German far-sightedness. In 1922,
Hermann Göring—years later to become *Reichsmarschall* and head of Hitler's
Luftwaffe—outlined Germany's glider program to Eddie Rickenbacker as
follows:

> Our whole future is in the air. And it is by air power that we are
> going to recapture the German empire. To accomplish this, we will
> do three things: First, we will teach gliding as a sport to all our young
> men. Then we will build up commercial aviation. Finally, we will cre-
> ate the skeleton of a military air force. When the time comes, we will
> put all three together and the German empire will be reborn.

Towards this end, the German government subsidized glider research in
the postwar period and, although there was a certain interest in gliding in other
countries, it was in Germany that the sport had its most extensive and advanced
development. There was little opportunity for the Germans to channel their
enthusiasm for flying except in this sport, owing to a condition imposed by
the Treaty of Versailles. (When Hitler later re-armed Germany, it was done
secretly initially and then in open defiance of the treaty regulations.) So the
energies of a nation that would normally have been devoted to powered and
unpowered flight were expended on gliding, with interesting consequences.

The government, strongly influenced by Göring's viewpoint, encouraged
all young Germans to fly. The *National-Sozialistisches Flieger-Korps* (National
Socialist Flying Corps, or NSFK) supplied facilities for those who, for financial
reasons, would not otherwise have been able to take up glider flying. It kept
the records of all pupils, gave tests and issued proficiency certificates. From
the beginning, it kept a detailed log, countersigned by instructors, of each

student's progress. This was the authority for the issue of various glider certificates.

The NSFK also encouraged independent organizations, especially those with means such as college-preparatory schools and universities, to establish glider clubs at their own expense. These clubs came under the supervision of the Reich Air Ministry, which issued the necessary records and certificates.

At ten years of age, a boy became eligible for the flight arm of the *Hitlerjugend* (Hitler Youth). The leaders encouraged him to build model aircraft and gave him frequent opportunities to exhibit his workmanship and fly his models. The principles of elementary aerodynamics were gradually instilled. When he reached the age of fourteen, a boy became qualified to join the flying branch of the HJ. He then started primary flying instruction on straight flight and lateral control, using the Zegling glider, an open cockpit single seater. The youth then advanced to a closed-cockpit single seater, such as the Baby Grunau, and learned to make turns. Coupled with flying instruction, the instructors showed films depicting the flight of birds. He was also taught something about radio communications, aircraft recognition and navigation.

Work with the flight arm of the *Hitlerjugend*, the NSFK or the university gliding clubs qualified youths for an elementary gliding "A"-level certificate, awarding a badge with one white seagull in flight. The "B"-level had two seagulls and the "C" three. The youngsters had to have soared once for the duration of at least 30 seconds, 60 seconds, or 120 seconds, in that order, to obtain these awards.

Advanced civilian flying qualified the budding glider pilot for one of three certificates. Certificate I called for two hours of flying time calculated from the pilot's log book in flights of at least 60 seconds duration, made over an unrestricted period of time. In addition, he had to be released, fly on his own at least once, and fly turns and circles. Certificate II called for 20 hours of flying, including a minimum of 20 flights of not less than one minute each, in a two-seater glider, while Certificate III required 20 towed starts in a glider with three or more seats.

The prerequisite glider training for aspirants to the *Luftwaffe* was to hold a Class II certificate. (During the war, civilian clubs lacked three-seater gliders, with the Class III certificate no longer being issued.) Many young Germans were trained up to this standard in the various gliding clubs, with the result that the *Luftwaffe* had a wide choice of ready-trained personnel, obviating the need for glider-training facilities.

Much of the early soaring and gliding centered in the high rolling hills around the Wasserkuppe in the Rhön Mountains. The enthusiasts at the time were not interested in getting ready for another war; they wanted to fly, and it is there that soaring and glider sailing matured. And it was volunteers from their ranks—Bräutigam, Ziller, Raschke, Brendenbeck, Stapper, Lange, Scheidhauer, Distelmeier, Schulz, Kraft and Pilz—who were to be in the attack on Eben Emael.

In the late 1920s, Öltschner, Klemperer, Hirth and a host of other Germans captured virtually every national and international glider prize. By 1929, Robert Kronfeld, an Austrian Jew (later to escape to Britain), using a variometer in his *Rhön Geist* ("Spirit of the Rhoen") sailplane, was the first to exceed a flight of 100 miles. From the heights of the Wasserkuppe, he was soon making equally long flights in the *Wien* ("Vienna"). Through those flights, he gained mastery over ridge and storm-front flying. However, it was left to another German, Wolf Hirth, while on an exhibition trip in the United States, to make the first use of thermals in order to soar.

The seed that was to grow into the military glider germinated during the period from 1930 to 1933, when technical knowledge of civilian soaring aircraft used for sport was applied to the development of a "flying observatory" glider—"Obs" as it was called—by Dr. Alexander Lippisch of the *Rhön-Rositten-Gesellschaft*, a flying club.

Dr. Lippisch brought together the best knowledge available from the sports glider and aircraft industries in Germany. By 1933, he had produced a totally new aircraft, much larger, but similar in appearance to some sports gliders. Although retaining their grace and taper, its gull wings were proportionally much thicker and somewhat wider than those of the soaring glider, to enable it to carry meteorological equipment and several scientists. In keeping the features of the sailplane, it was to differ radically from the true combat glider of which it was the progenitor. The new craft had to be towed by a powered aircraft from takeoff to within gliding range of its landing area and then released for a gradual glide to earth. As a general rule, it could not sustain its altitude by riding the air currents as could a sports glider. Its loaded weight and its design committed it to a descending glide, with little or no option for soaring. However, when the glider was lightly loaded, many pilots found it handled so much like a sports glider that they could, on occasion, take advantage of prevailing air currents to enjoy a few minutes of soaring.

For meteorological readings at high altitudes, the glider was ideal. When in free flight, it was noiseless, vibrationless, and free from the electrical emanations usually found in aircraft that are likely to disturb sensitive instruments. The flying observatory was first towed in tests by the diminutive woman test pilot, Hanna Reitsch.

General Ernst Udet, when inspecting the flying meteorological laboratory on one occasion, saw possible military applications in its design and performance. He felt it might be used to supply encircled elements or, perhaps, serve as a kind of modern Trojan Horse, by landing soldiers unnoticed behind an enemy's front lines.

German imagination also visualized that the total cargo lift capacity of an aircraft could be almost doubled through the use of a transport glider in tow. A large number of skilled sailplane pilots existed, who could be drawn upon to fly the new gliders. The glider also offered the advantages of low-cost production, ease of manufacture and expendability.

Along with *General* Udet, some of the more visionary members of the *Luftwaffe*—*Oberst* Jeschonnek in particular—began to press for a combat model. They got one. The design and development of the project was given a "secret" classification right at the start. It was turned over to the *Deutsche Forschungsanstalt für Segelflug* (German Research Institute for Sail Flight, or DFS), an affiliate of the *Rhön-Rositten-Gesellschaft.* An aircraft engineer, Hans Jacobs, assisted by glider pilots on the staff of the company, masterminded the project. The glider that grew out of this effort was designated the DFS 230.

The project got under way despite serious disagreements between the technical staff and the airborne proponents. The controversy was caused, in part, by the varying viewpoints on the tactical doctrine for glider operations.

The German military forces had experimented extensively with parachuting and had developed combat tactics for parachute airborne operations. On the other hand, no one had yet seen a combat glider, much less experimented with it. One thing the Germans realized was that landing men by glider had certain advantages over dropping them by parachute. The glider could carry a unit of men—perhaps a squad of seven to nine—and land it together ready to fight. In contrast, parachuting scattered the men into patterns 150 to 200 yards long and, for this reason, they had difficulty in getting assembled, losing much time in the process. If they were under fire while reassembling, there might be heavy losses. The gliders landed quickly in small areas, and the men were ready to fight upon landing, without having to cope with the problem of getting out of a parachute harness.

Another feature that helped to sell the advantages of the glider was its silence. It could be released miles from its target and probably land without detection. Rarely could a parachute operation have the surprise of a glider landing. But because there was no agreement on just what the objectives of the program should be, controversy raged for some months before Jacobs's team received a clear directive to go ahead.

Jacobs was to design a glider that could carry nine fully armed soldiers, glide and dive noiselessly and land on short, unimproved fields. The Germans aimed at keeping the cost at 7,500 *Reichsmark.* That figure was based on the expense of dropping ten men by parachute. In other words, the price was equivalent to the cost of manufacturing ten parachutes.

In early 1939, the strange new craft was finished. It looked very much like a large light aircraft, but without an engine. The fuselage was made of a steel tube framework covered with canvas. The wings were set high and braced. The wheels, once the glider was aloft, could be jettisoned, and the glider landed on a central ski-like plywood skid. It weighed 1,800 pounds and carried 2,800 pounds of cargo. A bench for passengers ran down the center. Hanna Reitsch, the test pilot, was soon test-flying it near Munich.

A number of high-ranking generals including Ernst Udet, the World War I fighter ace, von Greim, Albert Kesselring, Walter Model and Erhard Milch observed an experimental flight of the DFS 230 and were enthusiastic about its possibilities. Contracts were soon negotiated with the Gothaer Waggonfabrik, a manufacturer of railroad cars in the city of Gotha.

Despite the enthusiasm of a few high-level people, however, the glider's failure to win broad acceptance in German military circles worried some of the more enterprising members of the High Command. What was needed was someone to inject leadership and imagination into the project.

Oberst Hans Jeschonnek, at the time chief of operations for the *Luftwaffe* (later to become chief of the General Staff), asked *General* Student to his office. The two were long-time friends and military associates. After some preliminaries, in which he described what was being done in the glider development program, Jeschonnek, uncertain of Student's sympathy with the idea of building a transport glider, almost apologetically said, "Nobody gives a damn for the new glider. The best that could happen is that you should take it under your personal wing. Otherwise, the whole damn thing will lie dormant."

This surprising disclosure was the first intimation to Student that anything like a glider transport program was in progress. He was excited by the challenge and willingly agreed. He took over the project and personally test-flew the glider many times. In his opinion, the glider was of excellent construction, with a good ratio between empty and loaded weight. Moreover, it had outstanding flying characteristics. From the start, he planned to use this glider not only as a medium of transport but, owing to its noiselessness, as a weapon of attack. It went into production soon thereafter with his strong endorsement, and he personally named it the DFS 230 "attack glider."

The usefulness of the glider from a military point of view continued to be seriously debated, however. The chief objection came from the parachute enthusiasts, who saw in it a source of unwelcome competition. As a consequence, wide differences developed in military circles.

A Focke-Wulf FW 56 with a DFS glider.

The Gotha Go 242A in flight.

A second demonstration was held, this time for the Army General Staff. Ten Ju 52's transporting paratroopers and ten gliders carrying glidermen (towed behind ten other Ju 52's) flew to the airfield at Stendal. The gliders were cast off there, and the paratroopers jumped in. The gliders dived steeply and came to rest in close formation, discharging glidermen in units ready to fight. The parachutists, on the other hand, who had the ill luck to encounter a stiff breeze—from which the gliders had actually benefited—landed widely dispersed. In some cases, they were a considerable distance from their ammunition, which had been dropped by parachute. Though this experiment did not obscure the importance of paratroopers in a future war, of course, it at least proved conclusively that the troop-carrying glider could become a weapon of great value.

Initial models of the DFS 230 showed the need for some alterations. Loading doors had to be modified to accommodate a greater variety of loads, including bicycles and antitank guns, without the need to disassemble them beforehand. It was also desirable to change flight characteristics to enable the DFS 230 to be towed at higher speeds, thus enabling its use with several models of tow plane. A drogue parachute was added. If the pilot needed additional braking when landing, he released it to billow out behind and slow down the glider.

Soon, large-scale production was launched under the supervision of the Gotha works. Many different companies participated in the manufacture of the DFS 230; one of them was the Hartwig Toy Factory in Sonnenberg (Thuringia). By the time the war broke out, a large number of DFS 230's were ready for combat. By 1942, manufacturers had delivered 1,477 to the *Luftwaffe.*

In 1937, when *General* Jeschonnek saw that the DFS 230 was going to be produced in quantity, he ordered the *Luftwaffe* to establish transport glider schools. The government equipped each glider school with DFS 230 gliders. The schools used many different tow planes, the Ju 52, the Ju 68 and the Ju 87, as well as the Me 110 and the He 111. Even some Gloucester Gladiators that had come into German hands via Finland—which had received the aircraft from the British government—found their way into the program.

During 1940, while Churchill valiantly worked to bolster British morale, badly battered by the debacle at Dunkirk and the defeat on the continent, the Germans began the first phase of *Unternehmen Seelöwe* (Operation "Sea Lion"), the invasion of England, a hope that had long tantalized Hitler. According to *Generalmajor* Fritz Morzik, head of the German Air Transport

Command, some consideration had already been given to this operation as early as January. The German staff drew up no formal plan, however, since the lower echelons of the staff were busily engaged in working out details for other urgent military operations. The invasion plan got a further setback on 10 January 1940, when the Belgians captured *Major* Helmuth Reinberger, an officer carrying highly secret plans for the invasion of the West. It is believed that this incident delayed further planning for the invasion of England until the summer of 1940.

When France capitulated, Hitler determined to invade England via the southern counties, with gliders playing a major role. According to the initial plans, gliders were to land in the Folkestone-Hastings area and isolate and secure it for the main invading (seaborne) force, by blocking the movement of the British defense forces towards the beaches until the seaborne forces had obtained a secure foothold in England. Glidermen, followed by parachutists, were to secure a landing area. Infantry in gliders and in transport aircraft were to follow as soon as the landing area had been reasonably secured. To keep the momentum going, gliders and aircraft were then to start shuttling back for more troops and supplies until German forces had secured the "airhead." Diversionary airborne forces were to land near Oxford to draw British reserves away from the southern beaches, where the German seaborne forces would land.

One of the foremost needs was to support the airborne invasion with heavy artillery and tanks, without which it was doomed to failure. Although 500[2] DFS 230's were to carry troops and the lighter equipment, they did not have the cargo capacity necessary to carry tanks or heavy artillery. To fly the heavy equipment over, the Germans conceived an enormous glider, the Messerschmitt (Me) 321, which was to become known as the Gigant ("Giant"). The Gigant would carry 24 tons or 200 fully equipped men. This is four times as much as the largest British glider ever developed and five times as much as the largest U.S. glider ever developed. It had the cargo lift capacity of a modern Boeing 707-320B jet. The Gigant's wing was twice the length of the British Hamilcar's, 35 feet longer than the 707 jet's, and has been exceeded since only by the 450-passenger Boeing 747.

The German Air Ministry did not wait for production models to be built. It began to shift forces in the direction of the Channel and set September as the month for the invasion.

---

2. Although this is the number most often given by interrogation reports and other military sources, *Oberst* Walter Hornung, a former member of the *Luftwaffe's* Air Transport Command, considers the figure "optimistic" and estimates that only 150 gliders were then available and somewhat fewer qualified glider pilots.

The plan called for tow planes to haul gliders to a position above the western coast of France, where the glider pilots would release at 11,000 feet altitude. This height would give glider pilots enough range, it was calculated, to glide from above the coast of France to landing areas in England. Moreover, the scheme had the advantage that tow planes would not be fired at by British antiaircraft guns and would be less likely to be attacked by British fighter aircraft.

German planners were convinced that the comparative silence of gliders, along with the fact that British radar would have difficulty in detecting them because of their low metal content, gave a strong possibility that the glider assault would take the British by surprise.

More than 1,000 parachute and infantry units assembled at Goslar and nearby camps in Germany in mid-September 1940. Tension heightened when they got final orders and advance parties departed for St. Quentin, close to the air bases designated for the operation. All was in readiness.

Meanwhile, sensing peril, the British hastily began to construct anti-airborne defenses. German reconnaissance aircraft, photographing British progress on a daily basis, showed it to be rapid.

Suddenly, Hitler cancelled *Seelöwe*. The German invasion threat to England vanished for the duration of the World War II.

General Kurt Student contended that the German failure to carry out an invasion of England resulted directly from the lack of a concrete plan prior to the fall of France. He considered it one of the greatest mistakes of the war to allow England to prepare her defenses during the summer of 1940, while the German staffs were completing their invasion plans. He believed that an airborne invasion of England should have been launched at the very moment the British forces were being evacuated from Dunkirk. He felt that he could have captured London in a short time.

The cancellation of plans for the invasion of Great Britain did not stop the Germans from producing new and better models of gliders. After the phenomenal results with the DFS 230 at Eben Emael, a new kind of twin-boom, rear-loading glider, the Gotha (Go) 242, went into production at the Gothaer Waggonfabrik. An outgrowth of military demand, it could carry light trucks, guns and critical cargo for long distances.

The Air Ministry went on with the development of the Gigant, despite loud outcries from many industrialists and from the military forces involved with other war production. Messerschmitt quickly produced the first developmental model. Because the pressure to get the glider into production was so great, much testing had to be improvised, often with tragic consequences. Except for the Ju 290—incidentally, powered by American engines—the *Luftwaffe* had no aircraft that could tow the Gigant into flight on its own. As a result, test engineers resorted to an ingenious arrangement whereby three Me 110's were hitched like three horses to a chariot by tow ropes to the nose of a Me 321. This arrangement became known to the Germans as the *troika* tow, after the Russian word for a team of three horses abreast.

The Me 110, a fighter-bomber, was not designed for towing. It took great dexterity on the part of the pilots to attempt the delicate task of towing the Gigant into the air, which needed 4,000 feet of runway. For some reason, the most frequent problem was with the towing aircraft on the left, particularly at take-off, which was made at the excessively low speed of 120 miles per hour maximum. The Me 110 on the left frequently had to release prematurely, leaving a task too great for the remaining two and frequently forcing these pilots to also release early; the Me 321 was then at too low an altitude to land safely. Power differences between the tow aircraft set up tow-cable tension variations, adding to flight problems. This matter was never successfully resolved. Finally, multi-towing proved most sensitive to winds and turbulence.

It was pure luck when any of the early experimental flights overcame all these problems. Most of them ended with the aborting of the mission and the loss of one or all the test craft involved.

Because take-off speeds were proving too slow to get the *troika* combinations airborne and it was thus proving extremely dangerous, designers and test engineers began to use a rocket attached to each wing of the Me 321 to give the thrust needed to get the glider up to acceptable speeds. This worked, with rocket thrust then habitually used to get the craft off the ground. Thus, the Me 321 became one of the first aircraft to use jet-assisted take-off (JATO) as standard propulsion.

Even though procedures were evolved to make the *troika* tow safer, it was still costly in terms of tow aircraft needed. Every Me 110 in the *troika* was one less available for aerial combat. Moreover, the *troika* tow was inefficient at best and was very tiring to pilots, who constantly had to fight to maintain wingtip distance and flight speed in suitable balance and to communicate under precarious circumstances.

Searching for a better solution, designers hit upon an idea even more novel, if not more daring, than the *troika* tow. This was to join two He 111's together. Within three months of getting the contract, Heinkel designed and built a five-engine glider tug by fusing two He 111's at wingtip and placing a fifth engine at the wing junction. They built twelve of these distinctly odd-looking aircraft. The pilot sat in the port fuselage. Because it was such an unusual-looking plane, its mission remained a mystery to Allied intelligence for a long time. Unfortunately, this powerful variant of the long-serving He 111—referred to as the *Zwilling* ("twin")—was a cumbersome craft and Allied fighters found it easy prey.

Although Messerschmitt ultimately manufactured 200 Me 321's, early tests and later operational experience led *Luftwaffe* generals to the conclusion that these enormous craft were proving too difficult to operate. In addition, they were too difficult to maintain, especially against the ravages of weather in climates found in several of the theaters of war. For these reasons, production was terminated, as were plans for a sixty- to seventy-ton adaptation of the Me 321. The Germans converted all existing Me 321's into the six-engined Me 323.

Another giant glider produced by the Germans was the Junkers (Ju) 322, called the *Mammut* ("mammoth"), sometimes incorrectly referred to as the *Merseburg*. The *Mammut* was an enormous wooden all-wing glider, with a 207-foot wingspan and a cargo compartment in the center of the wing. It never flew well and the Air Ministry decided to put an end to its production when there was an adequate supply of Me 321's.

To tow the giant Me 321, two He 111 aircraft were joined at the wing tips and an additional engine added. This became the He 111Z.

Go 242A's towed in formation.

CHAPTER 2

Blood, Sweat and Tears

Prewar Great Britain, like its future ally, the United States, had not considered using transport gliders as military weapons, although the Soviet use of gliders for this purpose had long been reported. As early as July 1934, the London magazine *Flight* carried a photograph and an account of the GN-4, a five-passenger glider built by the Moscow Glider Works.

On the other hand, the British had developed a rich background of experience with sports gliders in the prewar years. During the early 1920s, soaring had taken hold in England, and a gliding association had been formed by 1929. Three years later, there were enough enthusiasts flying gliders for the association to sponsor a national championship. By 1937, British gliding techniques and glider construction had progressed enough to earn respect in international circles and to draw a group of young German glider enthusiasts to England, ostensibly to obtain instruction from British experts. Actually, it is likely these *Hitlerjugend* had a better reason for being in England: to collect information on the terrain and on military objectives, especially in southern England. Most of them soon reported for flying training with the *Luftwaffe*, where this knowledge could prove invaluable in any future conflict.

Whether the British learned anything about German military gliders is not known. In fact, it is not known whether information leaked out of Nazi Germany about the closely kept secret of that country's military glider program at any time during the 1930s. That such activities could have escaped the observation of the highly efficient British intelligence service is extremely doubtful. Regardless, the British military leadership was apparently unmoved by the potential of the glider as a military weapon. The serious prospect of a possible cross-channel glider invasion by an enemy based on the continent apparently never crossed military minds.

There was understandable complacency, as a result of British history and the belief that the Royal Navy would keep any invasion from British shores. To the British, an invasion of England by sea would be utter madness for an enemy to contemplate. A mood prevailed leading to the conclusion that if fight they must, there would be a drenching bombing from the air in the haphazard style of World War I. Certainly the nation would again show the guts to withstand such an annoyance until victory came again. Nor could they imagine for their islands an invasion such as Hitler later unleashed on Crete. Finally, innovation in the form of a massive glider counterattack, in retaliation against an enemy preparing to attack from France, was not in the style of the British naval-oriented, sea-immersed mind.

Much to his credit, however, Prime Minister Winston Churchill sent a brief instruction to his chief of staff in June 1940. It called for the creation of a 5,000-man parachute force—with a proportionate glider element—by the spring of 1941. It was a bold demand, considering that remnants of the British Expeditionary Force in France were still being evacuated from Dunkirk. His wish might have been contested by his staff, who were involved in more urgent matters, had he not adamantly signed it "P.M.W." (Prime Minister's Wish)—in other words, no arguing! What made the task even more formidable was that the British had to start from scratch in developing their airborne arm, accomplishing in little more than a year what the Germans had taken six years to do.

With traditional British vigor, the airborne program got under way. To their credit, once at the task, they seemed to do better at it than either the Germans or, a bit later, the Americans. This was true of the way the British converted their industrial effort to the task, the manner in which they organized and trained glider pilots, and generally the way they went into combat operations.

Within two days of Churchill's "wish" having been expressed, the War Office summoned Major J. F. Rock, Royal Engineers, and ordered him to organize the British airborne forces. How he was to do so, how the forces were to be organized, what arms they were to carry, what method was to be used to train them and to transport them to war—those points were not explained. "It was impossible," Rock recorded in his diary, "to get any information as to policy or task." Rock was a regular soldier; his acquaintance with aircraft was no more intimate than that of a frequent passenger. He knew nothing of parachutes or gliders beyond what he had read or was soon to read concerning their use by the enemy in the attacks delivered against Holland and Belgium six weeks before.

In short order, Rock, promoted to lieutenant colonel, formed the Central Landing Establishment (CLE) at a private airfield that was soon to be taken over by the RAF. At first, the CLE was conspicuous mainly for an almost total lack of the equipment necessary to train parachute soldiers, glider pilots, and air-landing troops. Information was equally scanty. A damaged parachute and jumping helmet captured from the Germans were the only models available. For aircraft, he had four Whitley Mark II's, which were seldom simultaneously operational.

The first glider exercise was a modest one. On an autumn day—26 October 1940—two single-seater sailplanes moved slowly behind two Avro 504 tugs. That was the glider exercise. It was the only operational equipment that Rock had to put into the air. Those who witnessed it must have required no little imagination to picture the huge fleets of large gliders which only four years later were seen by the battered and triumphant inhabitants of Britain on the wing for the Netherlands and the Rhine.

On 26 April 1941, six months later, Lieutenant Colonel Rock's forces staged an exercise for Prime Minister Churchill, although it was again no more than a demonstration. A formation of six Whitley's dropped their full complement of parachute soldiers and five sailplanes landed in formation. One Hotspur glider was towed past the prime minister. By then it had been realized that to train 5,000 airborne soldiers was a task requiring a great deal of time. Soon after this demonstration, Rock organized a Glider Exercise Unit, and experimenting with it, Rock and Wing Commander P. B. N. Davis gradually developed usable tactics and techniques for gliders. Expansion continued, and the number of glider-training elements increased considerably, until they occupied several bases of the RAF.

Although Churchill had been quite definite about the number of paratroopers he wanted in the force, he was vague about what the War Office was to do with glider forces. It is possible that the development and production of gliders—and the recruiting and organization of glider pilots and airborne forces—would have been relatively neglected had not circumstances dictated otherwise. Gliders came into their own somewhat by default. Although Churchill had directed the equipping of a 5,000-man parachute force, it was discovered that due to lack of aircraft, only 800 men could be lifted for a parachute mission. Looking around for a solution, planners turned their attention to the glider as a means of increasing the number of soldiers that could be airlifted, while minimizing the drain on the already heavily committed powered aircraft available to the nation. They saw that gliders could fill the void. Gliders would supplement the meager number of powered aircraft available to the airborne establishment and help to get the 5,000 men "off the ground" as per the prime minister's wishes. This led to the production of the eight-passenger Hotspur, the thirty-passenger Horsa and the Hamilcar, a first-rate competitor to the Gigant. They also developed the fifteen-seat Hengist as insurance against the Horsa not proving satisfactory.

The size of the first glider to come off the production line was to a great extent dictated by a number of the exigencies of the time. The British had no transport aircraft in military or commercial use in large numbers that could be converted to tow gliders, such as the Germans had in the Ju 52. For the time being, glider-towing aircraft were going to have to be bombers, then in

A Short Stirling taking off with a Horsa glider.

Troops emplaning into a Hotspur glider, November 1942.

short supply, or old biplane fighters, of which the Hart was one. The largest glider it could tow, according to calculations, was about an eight-seater with a wing span of somewhere between 50 to 60 feet.

The Air Ministry dispensed with the usual design and development procedures and other red tape and, in June 1940, it ordered the eight-place Hotspur glider into production, even though the glider had not yet left the drawing board at General Aircraft—so keen was the need. General Aircraft miraculously delivered Britain's first glider four months later.

The Hotspur proved ideal for the circumstances. Being made of wood, Hotspurs could be built in furniture factories, and their manufacture would not create an added burden on the aircraft industry, which was heavily committed to war production. Its most important asset was that it could be quickly mass-produced and was immediately ready to fly into combat.

The Hotspur I, first to come off the line, looked much like an oversized sailplane. It had a streamlined fuselage and a tapered sixty-two-foot wing. Pilots sat in tandem, and troops squeezed in behind.

General Aircraft constructed several other models of the Hotspur.

The Hotspur II had a shorter wingspan and a larger fuselage than the first model. The Hotspur III served widely as a trainer. General Aircraft also built a twin Hotspur, in an attempt to speed up the availability of a glider that could carry at least fifteen troops. For the "Twin," engineers joined two Hotspurs by means of a special center wing section, the pilot and co-pilot flying the aircraft from the port fuselage. Because of its unpopularity with pilots, however, the RAF did not order quantity production.

Ideal for training, Hotspurs I and II were not large enough to transport the heavy equipment that airborne forces would need to enable them to hit hard once landed. In time, the idea of using the Hotspur for operations was discarded as the Horsa began to make its appearance. No Hotspurs were ever used in combat.

The former Airspeed Aviation Company designed and built the Horsa at its Portsmouth Works. Typical of the whole aircraft industry, Airspeed was involved in other RAF projects and was pressed by its unending demands for bombers and fighters. Production of the sorely needed Horsas dragged, and it was not until well into 1942 that the first glider came off the production line.

This aircraft was the ugly duckling of the war, with its excellent flight characteristics disguised by an ungainly appearance. Of all-wood construction, it had a high unibraced eighty-eight-foot wing, jettisonable wheels and a central landing skid. It was sixty-eight feet long, and it stood almost twenty feet high at the top of the large fin. Loaded, it weighed more than seven tons, carrying almost its own weight in troops or cargo. Its interior has been described as not unlike a section of the London Underground in miniature. Homely as it was, it admittedly impressed with its stern, determined dignity.

It was not until 27 March 1942 that the British were able to test-fly the tank-carrying Hamilcar. Seeing this glider for the first time, Colonel Frederick Dent, the American officer in charge of glider production in the United States, remarked, "It was the biggest hunk of airplane I have ever seen put together." Tip to tip, its wing measured 110 feet. By the time several Hamilcars had been produced, the British had also turned out a light fast tank called the Tetrarch, designed to fit snugly into the Hamilcar. A sophisticated aircraft, it was far ahead of its day.

Now that the British had their Tetrarch and Hamilcar, the need for a powerful towing aircraft arose, reminiscent of the German experience with the Gigant. Fully loaded, the Hamilcar weighed more than sixteen tons, even more than a fully loaded Whitley bomber, the best available tow plane at the time.

The Halifax Mark III, a yeoman craft with new four-bladed propellers and the most powerful engines in service, first towed the Hamilcar. Later, the still more powerful Halifax Mark V took over the towing task, but even then, it was a great strain for the machine to tow the British giant, for in wing span and wing area the Hamilcar overwhelmed the Halifax.

By November 1941, the initial period of experimentation and the training of Britain's first airborne forces had been completed and a fine base laid for its forthcoming expansion. In that month, Major General F. A. M. Browning, C.B.E., D.S.O., M.C., was appointed General Officer Commanding Airborne Forces and provided with a skeleton staff. From that time on, despite a multitude of difficulties and disappointments, there was no looking back. Airborne forces were now an integral part of the British Army. They wore a maroon-colored beret, soon to become famous, and shoulder patches depicting Bellerophon astride winged Pegasus.

In January 1942, the War Office formed the 1st Airborne Division and appointed General Browning its commander. The division consisted of an airlanding brigade that would be transported and landed in combat by gliders or aircraft, a parachute brigade and a number of divisional support units. According to this type of organization and the requirement for military operations visualized by the War Office, it became obvious that more than half of Browning's division would go into combat in gliders.

Concurrently with the formation of the division, the War Office also ordered the formation of a glider pilot regiment in the army. By this step and doctrinal policies developed through their training and combat operations, the British took off on a path widely at variance with that of the Germans or the Americans.

The division and the Glider Pilot Regiment were billeted on Salisbury Plain near the Netheravon Aerodrome, with the Glider Pilot Regiment being stationed at Shrewton. The 38th RAF Wing, which was to support the 1st Airborne Division and tow its elements in gliders, was also stationed at Netheravon. This concentration of elements, all to be involved in airborne operations, enabled them to collaborate effectively.

Not only the airborne division but also the Glider Pilot Regiment introduced a new concept of war for which many agencies engaged in the war effort were not prepared, especially when it came to providing new and lighter equipment, different uniform items and helmets of a new design.

When Colonel Rock went to a flight training school with forty army officers and other ranks in order to learn the business of flying gliders, Major George Chatterton, D.S.O., got the task of raising the regiment, a task he found to be no easy matter. Fortunately, there were a large number of enthusiastic volunteers, but what they were to be trained to do beyond flying a glider had not been fully determined.

Chatterton made it his goal that glider pilots should reach the high standard as soldiers that he required of them as pilots. Not only must they be able to fly with the utmost skill and resolution, they must also be equally at home manning a Bren gun after landing, driving a jeep, or firing a rifle, an antitank gun or a mortar. Out of the many thousands of volunteers interviewed for the purpose of choosing glider pilots, very few were accepted. From these, many were unable to pass the stiff flight tests on their way through pilot training and dropped from the chosen ranks. It was only a select band who were judged worthy to follow this arduous and gallant calling.

In the end, Britain had quality pilots and a workable organization in her Glider Pilot Regiment such as American airborne commanders wanted but never got. The wisdom of the British, compared to the shortsightedness and disorganization of the Americans, was to come into stark relief in the test of combat.

Colonel Rock was killed in a flying accident late in 1942 and Chatterton, promoted to lieutenant colonel, took acting command of the Glider Pilot Regiment. Chatterton then began to put his stamp on the organization, constantly insisting upon loyalty and discipline.

Soon the 1st Airborne Division was ordered to North Africa to prepare for the invasion of Sicily. Several hundred glider pilots from the regiment accompanied the division, thus splitting the regiment. Pilots went to Africa with training incomplete and no night-flying experience, although it was the opinion of many that when they made the flight from Africa to Sicily to begin the Allied invasion, it would be a night operation. Few had experienced formation flying over long distances, especially over water.

The interior of a Hotspur, with glidermen in position for the flight.

Situations had evolved over which Chatterton had no control. He felt that glider pilots had been superbly trained by the RAF but that, except for brief periods, they were out of touch once the RAF had finished training them. Chatterton objected to the fact that many of his glider pilots had not been around an airfield for months. "After all, a horseman must live with and in the atmosphere of horses. Is it not the same for pilots? Whatever their employment or the type of aircraft they fly, they must live with and around aircraft," he said.

While he wanted closer association with the RAF, at the same time he shied away from the camaraderie and relaxed outlook of the air force. He felt that such an environment was special to their needs and good for them, but not especially good for the Glider Pilot Regiment, which was a formation of the British Army. Since glider pilots would have to fight as infantry once gliders were landed, he felt they had to have the high and unique standard of infantry discipline for which there was no substitute on the battlefield, where "once committed, there is no going back." He thus sought a compromise.

Chatterton had major obstacles to overcome to sell his point, however. In the months after the regiment was first organized, it had been handled rather haphazardly, and there were many in the higher echelons who had their own ideas as to how they wanted the regiment to work. Some of the brigadiers commanding airborne forces would have liked to have the glider pilots serving under their direct control in all matters. Chatterton felt the regiment and its men must be completely independent of any command except his, and he determined he would not bend on this point. He got his way after taking on the single-handed struggle to convince the RAF and the War Office of the logic of his viewpoint. Soon orders made Chatterton commander of the Glider Pilot Regiment. It then started to take on more of an RAF character.

Battalions became squadrons; companies became flights. A flight had 4 officers and 40 other ranks, all glider pilots. Among them, they carried four pistols, two submachine guns, two light machine guns and thirty-two rifles. An expansible organization, his squadron could have as many as five flights. When concentrated after landing, its 200 men, backed by their arsenal of weapons, could add up to an infantry battalion in combat power. The regiment became unique as a fighting force not only in the British Army but also in history. While the new elements of the regiment might work with and support the operations of the RAF groups with which they were to fly, they would at all times remain independent.

At the same time that the War Ministry was organizing glider forces, the RAF had to decide which aircraft could do the job of towing, choosing from among the Hector, Master, Albemarle, Halifax, Stirling or Dakota airframes. For a long time, Hectors and Masters towed the lighter Hotspur, but they were quite unable to deal with the larger Horsa. In June 1942, the RAF decided to use the Albemarle, a fairly fast medium bomber, as a troop carrier or a glider tug. They carried out considerable experimental work using this aircraft for towing, at a time when nothing else was suitable or available. During the operations over Sicily, they did use Albemarles, but these were succeeded in other operations by Dakotas, Halifaxes and Stirlings.

During early training, the Albemarle and glider pilots had to learn to fly in combination in an unremitting effort to learn the demanding flight skills needed for combat operations. Through weary months of training, they learned that the tug and the glider must be not only a physical, but a mental and moral combination. In other words, only the closest feeling of comradeship between the aircraft crew and the glider pilots could achieve the high standard of efficiency required.

That this lesson took some time to learn was due not so much to the pilots themselves, but to the fact that for many months they were located at fields some distance apart. By the autumn of 1942, hundreds of glider pilots had been trained and awaited action in army camps on Salisbury Plain. An adequate supply of gliders and tugs was not available, however, to keep them in training, and the pilots' skills grew stale. Moreover, they were having no contact with the crews of the tugs. Colonel Chatterton remedied the situation by gradually obtaining quarters for the glider pilots at the main airfield, but this took time to achieve.

Meanwhile, glider pilots gradually built up their flying hours. Soon Hamilcars carried tankers and their tanks on familiarization flights. One led to an extraordinary crash. The Hamilcar touched down at between 90 and 100 miles an hour at one of the fields. It careened wildly across the airfield, demolished two Nissen huts, and stopped in the wreckage. Colonel Chatterton rushed to the site. He found that the tank had shot forward right through the glider and the buildings and had come to rest, unscathed, 50 yards farther on. Rushing towards it, Chatterton met the tank driver crawling out. The driver uttered some coolly casual remarks, considering the fact that he had just been zipping along at 80 miles an hour, a speed unsurpassed by any tank in history.

On 19 November 1942, the British initiated their glider operations with "Freshman," a mission to destroy the Norsk Hydro Plant at Vermork, eighty miles inland and sixty miles from Oslo. This was a heavy water plant reportedly connected with German research on the atomic bomb. Two Halifaxes, each towing a Horsa, took off from Skiffen in Scotland. Each glider carried fifteen sappers (army engineers)—all volunteers—with Lieutenant G. M. Methuen in command. Two of the pilots, Staff Sergeant M. F. C. Strathdee and Sergeant P. Doig, came from the Glider Pilot Regiment. The other glider pilots were

Australian: Pilot Officer Davies and Sergeant Fraser, RAAF. Squadron Leader Wilkinson of the RAF piloted the first tow plane and was accompanied by Group Captain Cooper. A Canadian, Flight Lieutenant Parkinson, piloted the second aircraft.

The small force faced many difficulties. The worst of them was the fact that the Halifax crews had little experience in towing gliders. The Halifaxes were modified for the mission, but their performance was marginal for the job they had to accomplish. The cooling system was inadequate to keep the engines from overheating, as they worked harder than normal while towing gliders. No one was certain that the straining engines could pull the load the 400 miles across the North Sea. The flight over water almost all the way called for pinpoint navigation, so that the two combinations could cross the Norwegian shore almost on target. Plans dictated that once Methuen's men had destroyed the "heavy water" and the plant, he then had to lead his men through snow-covered mountains to Sweden. The Norwegian underground stood ready with guides for the long and arduous trek.

At 2341 hours, monitors at Skiffen got a faint voice by radio, believed to be Parkinson's, asking for a course to bring him back to Skiffen. The monitors worked frantically trying to plot his location. By intersection of radio beams, they located Parkinson over the North Sea. Fourteen minutes later, monitors heard a voice grimly stating: "Glider released in sea." But could it be? A quick calculation on a signal received from Wilkinson showed him to be above the mountains in southern Norway. The mission was in trouble—that much was certain.

The full story did not become known until some years after the war.

Trouble plagued the mission from the start. Weather was thick, although meteorologists promised a clear sky and a moon over the target. Before take-off, one tug's wingtip light and both towrope telephones failed. Because the use of radio was frowned upon, a simple code of light signals had to be improvised. By the time they had accommodated to these faults, darkness had fallen. What was worse, a night take-off with full load had not been practiced before. Given the "option to postpone the operation until the next day," the pilots chose to take off at night and get on with the job. By 1750 hours, Wilkinson's combination had taken wing into a darkening sky; twenty minutes later, the second followed. Wilkinson chose to fly high, picking his way through broken cloud and reaching Norway at 10,000 feet altitude. Then, just as he needed his Rebecca radio beam system to tie into the Norwegian agents' Eureka system to direct the airplane to the target, he found the Rebecca did not work. Cooper, doing the navigation, could only rely on maps, but a heavy layer of snow disguised all landmarks.

Wilkinson passed over what might have been the release point. Lacking clear identification, however, he made another circle to find the target. The Norwegian agents in the landing zone had heard the aircraft flying almost directly over them on its first attempt, but they could make no contact since the Rebecca radio beam had failed. By then, he had been flying for five and a half hours and still had 400 miles to go to get back to Skiffen. He flew into thick cloud about 40 miles northwest of Rjukan and could not climb out of it. By this time, there was barely sufficient petrol to get the tug and glider home. Ice began forming on the aircraft and, worse still, on the tow rope. Both tug and glider lost height rapidly. They sank into unbroken cloud and, somewhere in the void above Stavanger, the rope parted. Staff Sergeant Strathee started a descent in zero visibility. Dense cloud turned into swirling snow. It was at this point that the wireless operator had sent out his signal. The aircraft, unable to do any more, just succeeded in returning before its fuel ran out. The glider crash-landed at Fylesdalen, on top of the snow-covered mountains overlooking Lysefjord, killing Methuen, Strathee, Doig and five others and injuring four more severely.

Meanwhile, Parkinson flew low above the sea, trying to keep beneath the clouds until just short of the Norwegian coast. He hoped to encounter the promised clear weather there. Parkinson crossed the coast near Egersund and was heading towards Rjukan when his plane hit a mountain beyond Helleland. Somehow, the tow rope snapped as the plane crashed, but the glider, with little chance for maneuver left, made a heavy landing close by, killing three. German personnel soon captured all survivors. The *Gestapo* then took over. They poisoned the four injured in the first glider crash while they were in a hospital recovering. On Hitler's standing orders, the *Gestapo* then shot the ninteen uninjured men as saboteurs.

Was this grim tragedy to prove an omen for British glider combat experiences of the future? This was soon to be tested on the barren soil of Sicily.

CHAPTER 3

America Hops on the Bandwagon

We're going to build 350 gliders a month.

GENERAL B. E. MEYERS

This program started in confusion and will undoubtedly end that way.

JOHN C. WARREN

By 1930, gliding was still primarily a sport.[1] When a glider enthusiast invited the U.S. Army Air Corps to participate in a national glider meet at Elmira, New York, the assistant secretary of war replied that "there exists no appropriation whereby an officer on the active list could be dispatched to a duty such as you mention." The following year, the secretary of war said: "It is considered that the military value of glider flying is negligible and that the expenditure of time and funds required to teach the art is not warranted."

As early as 1922, Glenn Curtiss designed a glider that he thought might be useful as a target drone. Curtiss believed the glider might be towed by a motorboat, then released and fired upon. During the next two years, thirteen target gliders were actually built at McCook Field and distributed throughout the service for use instead of the conventional tow targets. The Army Air Corps showed no other interest, however. While acknowledging the "considerable enthusiasm" for gliding in the United States and abroad, McCook Field reported that it was adhering to Army Air Corps policy not to undertake any "large scale" investigations.

As late as 1938, the War Department was not convinced that the glider had any real value as a military weapon. Harry Malcolm, of Lombard, Illinois, suggested in August 1938 that gliders might be used to carry bombs or personnel or they might be built as aerial torpedoes. Military officials dismissed the idea by pointing out that an equivalent load could be carried more efficiently by the towing aircraft. Malcolm was informed that "the plan of your suggested method of towing gliders as practical weapons is not of sufficient military value to warrant further consideration and development."

---

1. John C. Warren's *Airborne Operations in the World War II European Theater* (USAF Historical Study 97) has been consulted for this chapter.

The Horsa was adopted by U.S. airborne troops in Britain, hence the American markings on this British glider.

Men of the 101st Airborne Division unloading a jeep from the mid-section of a Horsa.

In 1940, Military Intelligence of the War Department General Staff quoted reliable evidence indicating that the Germans had used gliders in the capture of Fort Eben Emael in Belgium, that glider practice was being carried out at many German airfields and that the Germans had already built gliders "in some numbers" and were "prepared to use them for troop and possibly tank transport."

The American military attaché at Bern reported that glider trials were carried out at Brunswick and Naunheim in March and April 1941 and related that a "General Kitzinger" (probably a cover name) told Swiss staff officers that the German General Staff attached much importance to the trials of transportation of forces by means of gliders. Twelve days after the submission of the report from Bern, thousands of gliderborne German forces began the spectacular invasion of Crete. It was the final proof that gliding was more than a Sunday pastime.

Even after the initial German successes with gliders in the war had aroused a new interest in gliding in the United States, the Army Air Corps was not in a position to accede to the more vehement proposals of soaring zealots because of the urgent military demands for powered aircraft and aircraft pilots.

As the evidence on German use of military gliders accumulated, the Army Air Corps began to develop a positive glider policy. On 25 February 1941, General Henry H. Arnold, chief of the Army Air Corps, decided that in "view of certain information received from abroad, a study should be initiated on developing a glider that could be towed by aircraft." He directed that the study be completed by 1 April. To gear up for production, his staff soon issued two classified technical instructions to its procurement offices, one for glider design studies and the other for the procurement of "2, 8 and 15-place gliders and associated equipment."

Almost before the ink was dry on the technical instructions, Army Air Corps technical officials sent preliminary engineering requirements for fifteen-place gliders to eleven companies on 8 March 1941. By May, they ordered experimental models of two-place training gliders, and static- and flight-test models of eight- and fifteen-place transport gliders. The stage was now set for a program that was soon to blossom into a monumental effort. It remained unheralded, plagued with vicissitudes, shunned and neglected and yet it was a production miracle.

In October 1941, General Arnold appointed Lewin B. Barringer, well-known in civilian soaring, as coordinator of the glider program. Barringer served until January 1943, when a plane in which he was flying disappeared over the Caribbean. Although his was largely an advisory job until his death, Barringer played a vital part in the glider program, swinging a big stick merely by virtue of being Arnold's man.

In reviewing the role of the glider program after Barringer's death, General Arnold decided to give it the staff prestige it needed by establishing an office of "Special Assistant for the Glider Program." It carried the same power as the several assistant chiefs of air staff in matters relating purely to the glider program. A day later, Arnold appointed Richard C. DuPont to this position. Richard DuPont was a soaring enthusiast, an important reason for the appointment. Equally important, however, was his family background as scion of the DuPont family. Arnold hoped through the association to bring the enormous DuPont enterprises into active support of the glider program as a way to draw industrial backing. Within five months, Richard was killed in a glider crash. Arnold immediately appointed Major Felix DuPont, Richard's brother, to the office.

Arnold's attitude toward the glider program and his relationship with Barringer are indicated in the following comments made by General Frederick P. Dent, Jr., then a colonel in charge of glider development at the Aircraft Laboratory at Wright Field in Dayton, Ohio. General Dent made these comments in an interview with the author held at his residence near Eglin Air Force Base, Florida, in January 1969.

> I would like to talk a little bit about a part of the program that is a little touchy. I think General Arnold was one of the finest leaders we ever had. He was dynamic, and he certainly did one hell of a good job during the war, not only to produce airplanes and gliders, but also to fulfill the military requirements of two different theaters. There was certainly an awful lot of pressure on him to go one way or the other.
>
> General Arnold did, however, have one very serious weakness. He did not understand engineering, and he did not understand Wright Field, although he had commanded it at one time. As a result, anything concerned with development and production was a burden to him, and he was not interested in it. As a matter of fact, from about 1938 to 1943, a period of five years, I think the records show that General Arnold visited Wright Field only once. The only time he saw a glider was when it was a completed product.
>
> General Arnold had another weakness, which was that any civilian knew more than anyone in uniform. This attitude was reflected not only in the progress of the glider program but also in different parts of the Pentagon itself. As an example, at about this time we realized that we had to set up an office in Washington as a central place for

coordinating the glider program. In addition to production and development of gliders, there was also a very active glider training program in progress. My office had stepped out of the training business at the conclusion of the training of the first class of pilots. General Arnold picked a chap by the name of Lou Barringer, a real fine individual and one of the nicest people I ever met, to head the Washington office. Lou Barringer had spent quite a bit of time as a soaring pilot, but he knew absolutely nothing about the military. He did not speak the language. He had no idea what the military requirements were and, in heading the office, he really did not give us much help. As a matter of fact, he got interested in several other developments, and these other interests hampered our program. Lou Barringer was ordered overseas to take a look again at what the British were doing when he was killed. General Arnold then had to look around for someone to take his place, and he found Richard DuPont—again, a very fine man who had had several successes in international flying meets. Again, he knew nothing about military requirements and did not speak our language.

The effort of experimenting with and developing tactical gliders taxed the ingenuity of the engineers of the Army Air Corps' Experimental Engineering Section at Wright Field and those in civilian industry. In the absence of previous American experience with transport gliders, originality and design skill became essential in the glider program.

Of the eleven companies which received the preliminary engineering requirements in March, only the Frankfort Sailplane Company, the Waco Aircraft Company, Bowlus Sailplanes, Inc., and the St. Louis Aircraft Corporation sent favorable replies. The other firms said that they had previous manufacturing commitments, which they did not prefer to alter, or that the proposed glider was too large for their facilities.

Thus, early in its development work, the Materiel Command at Wright Field, which was saddled with the job of procuring the gliders, ran into one of the major obstacles of the entire program. This was the inexperience and limited capacity of the companies that might be willing and able to manufacture gliders. Most of the established aircraft companies in the United States were expanding to produce urgently needed fighters and bombers for the European war. The Army Air Corps regarded the need for powered aircraft as paramount, and instructed the Materiel Command to place glider orders with companies not already engaged in the manufacture of powered combat aircraft. This policy severely hampered the glider effort.

Eager to begin work at once with available facilities, Wright Field officials negotiated at once with the four companies interested in the preliminary proposals.

It finally placed an order with the Frankfort Sailplane Company on 7 May 1941, for the XCG-1 and XCG-2 (X for experimental, C for cargo and G for glider) experimental transport gliders. Unfortunately, Frankfort's first glider did not meet specifications or pass structural tests. At that time, Frankfort were achieving recognition for the construction of the Frankfurt utility gliders for the Army Air Corps' glider pilot training program and gave evidence of being better suited for producing training gliders than for developing and manufacturing transport gliders. Since this was the situation, the Army Air Corps felt it better to cancel the transport contract and did so towards the end of the year.

Another contract signed with the Waco Aircraft Company of Troy, Ohio, called for one static-test and one flight-test model of an eight-place XCG-3 glider and one static-test and two flight-test models of a fifteen-place XCG-4 glider. Although Waco was a small company, it had been a pioneer in manufacturing commercial aircraft and was better prepared to handle a development contract than were most of the corporations to whom Wright Field turned in the early days of the glider program. Waco completed one XCG-3 wind-tunnel model within a few weeks.

It delivered a structural static-test model to Wright Field laboratories on 26 December 1941 and a flight-test model on 31 January 1942. After flight tests conducted early in February, the Army Air Corps found the XCG-3 satisfactory. It was accepted in April, whereupon quantity production was ordered. However, numbers were later substantially reduced in favor of the XCG-4, which, from the standpoint of cargo capacity, came nearer to meeting forecast needs.

Waco delivered the static-test model of the XCG-4 on 28 April 1942, and the first flight-test model arrived at Wright Field on 14 May. In a significant test conducted shortly afterwards, the XCG-4, carrying fifteen passengers, successfully flew in tow from Wright Field to Chanute Field, Illinois, and back—a distance of 220 air miles.

Designed by the engineers at Waco and the Materiel Section at Wright Field along the same general lines as the XCG-3, the XCG-4 differed primarily in size. It was bigger, had a gross weight of 6,800 pounds, and carried a 3,750-pound cargo—substantially more than its own unloaded weight.

In this glider, the Army Air Corps found the solution to the urgent need for a reliable, easily manufactured, durable combat craft. The glider enthusiasts had now established the basis for a production effort of remarkable proportions, achieved despite many problems and disappointments along the way.

Before Waco was able to deliver the static-test XCG-4, the Army Air Corps was forced to conclude that other contractors for experimental tactical gliders could probably not supply an acceptable fifteen-place glider. As a consequence, Wright Field gave production contracts for the Waco gliders before other companies had completed their experimental models. In fact, before the first flyable XCG-4 was delivered on 11 May, the need for the standard-production model, the CG-4A, had become so pressing that Wright Field went ahead and contracted with eleven companies for a total of 640 CG-4's.

Those contractors and those to be involved in the design and development of other models brought in many subcontractors to provide wings, steel cable, steel tubing and fittings, finally swelling the total to more than 115 companies. These companies included the H. J. Heinz Pickle Company, which manufactured wings, the Steinway Piano Company, which also produced wings, Anheuser-Busch, Inc., the Brunswicke-Balke-Collender Company and a canoe manufacturer.

The Army Air Corps continued to investigate many other glider models of comparable size to the CG-4A to determine if they had more desirable characteristics. For various reasons—primarily the need to settle on one model and get it into mass production—only one prototype was built of most other gliders, for it soon became clear the CG-4A—christened the Waco—was the favored fifteen-place glider.

During the next few months, contractors were plagued with conflicting directives about the production future of the combat glider. Although Army Air Corps officials had reason to complain about contractor performance, contractors could legitimately complain about the plague of conflicting directives issued by the military.

In March and April 1943, the Wright Field officials resolutely pressed Washington to get a firm decision on the models and quantities of gliders required. There was a note of desperation in the testimony of one Wright Field executive who, lamenting the absence of a clearly defined policy with regard to future glider procurement, summarized his view of the glider effort by observing: "This program started in confusion and will undoubtedly end that way."

General Arnold unsettled all those involved in the endeavor by saying that the glider they were producing "was not built to meet the purpose for which it was intended." In his opinion, the CG-4A involved too much engineering, cost too much, and took too much time to build: "It should be cheapened and be good for only one flight." Further, he believed it should be made entirely of wood.

Waco CG-4A landing in Lubbock, Texas.

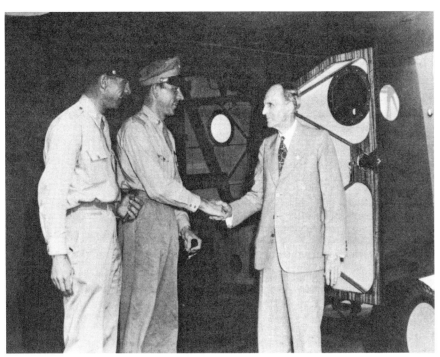
Henry Ford (right) celebrates, with Colonel Dent and Lieutenant Colonel Price, the first glider to come off the Ford production line in October 1942.

General Meyers did even more to upset designers when he expressed the belief that glider fuselage should be telescopic, its parts nesting together so that shipping space could be saved.

General Lee felt that the problem of shipping space could be solved by resorting to British producers. He announced that British production in 1943 was 1,340 Horsa gliders, and programmed in 1944 to be approximately 1,400. Revised schedules showed that British production could be considerably in excess of requirements. They were therefore planning to curtail the production of gliders at two plants and convert to aircraft construction. General Lee stated that as a result of several conferences with British authorities, an agreement had been reached: If the American government would immediately consider placing orders for gliders within the British Isles (with these two plants), then the British production of gliders would continue unabated until a decision could be reached about American requirements.

A full discussion took place at this time about the number of gliders that might be required for American operations in the British Isles. The conference agreed that 600 should be ordered to be constructed in Britain during 1943 and an additional 900 in 1944, with the entire 1,500 to be delivered on or before 1 July 1944. This discussion proceeded to the point where it was decided that orders definitely would be placed, but they never were.

From 14 to 17 April 1943, a series of meetings took place in Washington to unscramble the mess. On 15 April, Brigadier General O. A. Anderson reported that the War Department General Staff had not completed its requirements for gliders but expected to have them ready soon. General Anderson expressed doubt that gliders could be used in a major operation, stating facetiously that "haste should be made slowly in the whole matter."

In April 1943, General Meyers had submitted data on the glider manufacturers to Lieutenant General William S. Knudsen, director of war production, and requested Knudsen to come to a decision about marginal or high-cost contractors. General Knudsen recommended that the contract with Robertson and three other companies be cancelled. However, on 1 May, Undersecretary of War Robert P. Patterson notified General Meyers that he believed it would be cheaper to continue all CG-4A contracts than to cancel those of the poor producers. The Army Air Corps allowed Robertson to continue the production of CG-4A's. By August, the company had delivered sixty-three gliders.

A major tragedy finally drew public attention to the glider program and broke the spell of apathy surrounding it. On 1 August 1943, the sixty-fifth CG-4A manufactured by the Robertson Corporation of St. Louis, Missouri, carried out a demonstration flight with the corporate president, Mayor Charles L. Cunningham, other executives of the St. Louis area and military officials. High over the field, a wing suddenly disintegrated, and the glider plummeted to earth, killing all its passengers.

The Army Air Corps rushed investigators to the scene of the crash. The complex system of subcontracting, involving several stages of subassembly at various factories, and a complicated logistics chain among contractors and subcontractors made the problem of establishing responsibility for the tragedy exceedingly difficult. The investigation finally revealed that an over-machined, weakened inner-wing fitting—manufactured, ironically, by the Gardner Metal Products Company in St. Louis, a former manufacturer of caskets—had snapped.

The investigating board reported that inspection personnel at Robertson were inexperienced and had inadequate inspection equipment. Furthermore, the Army Air Corps Inspector General, Colonel L. M. Johnson, reported that his investigation of the Robertson crash left him "firmly convinced that the conditions which were in existence at St. Louis prior to this accident are prevalent throughout the country. There is little that the Materiel Command can do to correct conditions."

Poor workmanship, improper methods of manufacture and general inefficiency by contractors at the plants were all unfortunate aspects of the glider program.

On 16 March 1942, five representatives of the Ford Motor Company had conferred with representatives of the Army Air Corps Aircraft Laboratory to discuss the possibility of Ford's participation. Subsequent negotiations resulted in the award of a contract, approved on 30 June 1942, for 1,000 CG-4A's. In view of the resources, facilities, and experience of the Ford Motor Company, it is interesting to note that Ford delivered only six gliders by February 1943. While this performance was not by any means unsatisfactory for a company that had not been brought into the program until some three months after the majority of companies had been given contracts, it indicates that the problems of getting into full production were not resolved in a matter of a few weeks.

In fact, serious delays in beginning production were common to all the glider manufacturers with the exception of Cessna, which received extensive government aid not given to other contractors. The experience of the Ford Company, viewed in relation to the performance of other contractors, suggests that the agencies responsible for glider procurement should have allowed for at least a six-month period between the award of a contract and the start of quantity production. Without a well-organized program for preparing tools and equipment and ready access to materials, this preparatory organizational period should have been much longer.

If Ford's performance demonstrated the need for an unavoidable six months to prepare for production, it also soon proved the advantage of placing orders with experienced, financially sound concerns that were familiar with quantity production. The Ford glider plant at Iron Mountain, Michigan, produced more than twice as many gliders as any other company from 1942 to 1944 (inclusive). It is true, of course, that Ford was not handicapped by concomitant work on experimental glider projects. Initial delays in no way detracted from this contractor's contribution to the glider program, which was sizeable from the standpoint of numbers manufactured.

In March 1944, Wright Field procured an additional 1,200 CG-4A's from Ford. In September, the contract was further increased by 725 gliders. As part of the October 1944 procurement for an extended CG-4A program, Ford was awarded a letter contract for an additional 2,000, making a total procurement of 4,925 Wacos from this contractor. By 31 October 1944, Ford had delivered 2,418 CG-4A's and 26 CG-13A's—or 23 percent of the tactical gliders supplied for the entire glider program. Ford's unit cost of approximately $15,400 on these gliders proved the economy of efficient, experienced mass production. Most other companies did not produce a glider for less than $25,000.

While the CG-4A program was being carried out, the Materiel Command went ahead with the development of larger gliders. In June 1942, Major DuPont's office foresaw a requirement for thirty-place gliders. This was soon approved.

In April 1943, the Air Force contracted with the Laister-Kauffman Aircraft Corporation for three XCG-10 thirty-place troop-cargo gliders of wooden construction.

By the fall of 1942, the CG-4A was in production and Waco, the designer of the glider, in a position to undertake a new development project. The Air Force desired to apply Waco's experience with fifteen-place gliders to the problem of developing gliders of larger capacity. A contract was awarded to that company to develop a thirty-place troop-carrier glider, the XCG-13, having a towing speed of 174 miles per hour, a gross weight of 15,000 pounds, and a rated capacity of 8,000 pounds.

XCG-10 production lagged, and the first flight-test and static-test models were not delivered until October 1943. In the meantime, the Waco Aircraft Company had completed its XCG-13 thirty-place glider. When the XCG-13 was approved for production in the fall of 1943, work on the XCG-10 was stopped and the Laister-Kauffman contract was changed to call for the XCG-10A, a forty-two-place glider of wooden construction. Laister-Kauffman delivered the glider to the Clinton County Army Air Field, Ohio, on 30 April 1944. In August, the Army Air Corps declared the glider suitable for production.

The first flight model of the XCG-13 was delivered to Wright Field on 10 March 1943. The XCG-13 was the first of the large gliders to meet military requirements, and the Army Air Corps quickly ordered service-test and production models.

Numerous suggestions came from the front, as America gained combat experience with gliders. These ideas led to landings on packed snow and on water. Therefore, it was suggested that gliders could be used for the routine supply and logistical needs of fixed and mobile ground and air force elements of all types. It was pointed out that this kind of supply operation would be especially useful for armored forces. Another suggestion was that an airborne repair depot might be dropped wherever mechanized ground force equipment and ordnance material needed repair. Gliders might move airborne field hospitals from one location to another, and they might evacuate wounded from combat areas. They might also be used as carriers for raiding parties and in rescuing ground-force elements that had become isolated.

Many of these suggestions, which at first might have been thought far beyond the scope of gliders, were made feasible by the improvement of a pick-up device that enabled a flying tow-plane to whisk away a loaded glider from a field. It became known as the "snatch" technique. The Army Air Corps used this method extensively to recover thousands of gliders that had landed in combat. Medical units used the system to evacuate litter-patients in gliders.

During 1944, the Army Air Corps conducted studies to determine whether the Hamilcar, or any other glider, could be carried in a piggyback fashion as the Germans had done with some of their gliders. The effort was concentrated on using the P-38 attached to the top of the Hamilcar, although consideration was given to the P-38 and XCG-10 combination as well. This arrangement of aircraft had some decided advantages, but no actual flight tests were ever made.

Beginning in December 1941, the Materiel Command procured several experimental tow-target and bomb-loaded gliders. The Bristol Aeronautical Corporation of New Haven, Connecticut, built Twenty-one C-1 tow-target gliders. In May 1942, the Fletcher Aviation Corporation of Pasadena, California, delivered ten XBG-1 radio-controlled bomber gliders. Another project undertaken in 1943 was the development of the XFG-1 fuel glider, an unconventional tailless glider with swept-forward wings that would fuel a powered aircraft in flight.

On 1 April 1942, General Arnold directed the Materiel Command to make a study and perform tests to determine the suitability of combat and transport aircraft to tow gliders. Wright Field conducted extensive tests of tow aircraft, beginning in the summer of 1942. By October 1944, the Army Air Corps listed the A-25, B-25, C-46, C-47, C-54, C-60, P-38 and all four-engine bombers and transport aircraft as suitable for towing the fifteen-place CG-4A and CG-15A gliders. The thirty-place CG-13A could be towed by either a C-46, C-54, B-17 or B-24. By the end of November 1944, however, tactical considerations as well as the performance and availability made the C-47 the primary tow aircraft.

For the development of suitable tactical gliders, the Materiel Command awarded twenty-two contracts to sixteen companies between April 1941 and 31 October 1944. In addition, the Aircraft Laboratory modified a C-47 transport and evaluated foreign gliders. Four production-model tactical gliders were developed: the CG-3A, CG-4A, CG-13A and CG-I5A. The XPGC-2 was also approved for production, but no procurement of it was authorized. The converted C-47 (XCG-17) was tested and considered to have tactical utility.

The production program was plagued by discord, a mixture of misdirection and lack of direction, absence of firm goals and bad management at several levels. That this condition was permitted to exist in the production of such a sensitive piece of Army Air Corps equipment was criminal negligence on the part of many involved in the program from the War Department down and their dereliction was not long in showing.

The development of tactical gliders was one of the most difficult tasks undertaken by the Army Air Corps. Working with few precedents to guide them and handicapped by provisions that excluded the larger aircraft companies from participating, Army Air Corps engineers were nonetheless asked to develop acceptable gliders in the shortest possible time.

Key leaders vacillated to such an extent in advancing the program that they plainly lacked a good understanding of the potential of the glider. Or, having this understanding, either they were still uncertain of the glider's potential, or lacked the courage and strength to push the program. It probably survived mostly through the conviction and dedication of a few subordinates in the Army Air Corps, who had been saddled with the working-level responsibility and whose foresight gave them a basis for continuing despite the obstacles.

Meanwhile, defective gliders were coming off the line. They were to be flown by glider pilots and filled with personnel, all blissfully unaware of the danger inherent in the defective product they were using, both in training and in combat.

CHAPTER 4

Crete: Gliders Lose Hitler's Favor

In two different attacks, Greece was to feel the glider's sting. On 23 April 1941, General Alexander Papagos, commander in chief of the Greek Army, surrendered. Forces consisting of Australians, New Zealanders and men from the United Kingdom, as well as miscellaneous Greek formations, were in deep trouble. An evacuation from Greece was the only alternative to annihilation.

The Germans had sensed another Dunkirk in the making and were doing everything in their power to trap the British. In hard-driving pursuit, they rapidly converged on the ports of Porto Rafti and Rafina east of Athens, through which any evacuation had to take place. Lieutenant General Henry Wilson, leading a mixed corps of New Zealanders, Australians and British, began withdrawing towards the ports, fending off the probing German elements and determined to set a trap for them.

Wilson also realized, however, that the Germans might soon capture the ports. If they fell, he would then be forced to evacuate from the small ports of Nauplia, Kalamata and Monemvasia, a hundred miles to the south and nestled within the fingers of the Peloponnese. They were connected to the mainland by the sandy narrow Isthmus of Corinth.

The Corinth Bridge spanned the gorge-like Corinth Canal that sliced the isthmus. It carried the main artery towards the ports, vital to the operational effectiveness, if not the survival, of Allied forces in Greece. Some antiaircraft guns, several artillery pieces manned by Greek forces—all wearied by days of combat and harassment by dive-bombing Stukas—defended the bridge. Several companies of equally harried troops had been dropped off from elements crossing the bridge on the night of 23 April to bolster the strength of the defenders. They had barely dug in. A handful of engineers had managed to mine the abutments and girders and stood ready to detonate and topple the bridge eighty feet into the bed of the canal.

General Student, who was in Plovdiv, Bulgaria, along with selected elements of his *7. Flieger-Division*—the deception designation for his airborne forces—watched and waited, his attention focused on the Corinth Canal and the sensitive bridge whose capture would cut Allied forces in two and prevent their withdrawal. By capturing it, the German forces could also speed into

48

the Peloponnesus to destroy Allied resistance there. He ordered *Oberst* Alfred Sturm, commanding the division's second regiment, to take the bridge in a parachute attack.

Months before, the Germans had studied ways to take the bridge. Most of the top military commanders and staffs involved in the planning for such an operation felt that the bridge could be seized only by parachutists. Apparently, they held the view that regardless of the stunning victory at Eben Emael, military gliders were no longer a secret and their surprise value as a weapon had been lost; thus, they could not be thought of as having any value for an operation similar to Eben Emael again in history.

Most of the experienced glider pilots held an opposing view. If the "establishment" view were valid, then it followed that one could not expect infantry to make a surprise attack either, since surprise by infantry attack had been forever lost after the first infantry attack in history, whenever that had been. That was the contention of Wilhelm Fulda, who had piloted one of the gliders in the attack against the bridges near Eben Emael.[1] The majority of glider pilots felt the establishment viewpoint was very narrow, shortsighted and stupid. They worked hard to change it, but with no success in the quarters that counted. They refused to let the matter rest and felt their best opportunity to prove their point would be in pressing for a chance to make another successful Eben Emael–like raid.

Few higher-ranking sympathizers dared to voice their support of the glider pilots' views, with one surprising exception.

One day in March 1941, Fulda, then a *Leutnant* and glider instructor at Fassburg, near Hanover, got a telephone call to report to *Oberst* Stein in Hildesheim. Stein was in charge of ground operations there and had been a student of Fulda's before the war, when Fulda was an instructor in Germany's glider training program. Stein held Fulda in high esteem, respected his ideas, and agreed with his view that the glider could be used again for surprise raids.

Stein astonished Fulda. He said there was a possibility that gliders would be used in a raid under study and said: "Maybe there is a chance for a raid. I don't know. We must do what we are told now and wait and see." He told Fulda to select twelve glider pilots: "The best!" Fulda was to take charge of

---

1. Before giving his account to the author in Hamburg on 13 February 1973, Fulda, who finished the war as a *Hauptmann* flying the Me-163 rocket fighter, had never given a public statement of what transpired prior to and during the raid.

the operation, including the shipping of twelve to fifteen gliders to Plovdiv in Bulgaria. Stein warned that the mission was top secret.

By 13 March, Fulda had his small force assembled at Count Ignatiev Airfield outside of Plovdiv. There he waited for orders. Days turned into weeks without a word from anyone.

Finally, things began to bustle at the field. German parachute elements set up camp nearby, but the action seemed to bypass Fulda. Finally, one day, *Oberst* Stein flew in. He seemed depressed and paid little heed to Fulda. Fulda finally insisted on a meeting. It was very unsatisfactory, and Fulda got the impression that the possibilities of a raid had evaporated, which apparently they had. Fulda had never been so frustrated in his life. He sensed some great event was about to break and wanted to participate.

He got a motorcycle with a sidecar and driver and instructed the driver to take him from one troop element to the next. At 2200 hours, tired and cold, he drove into a parachute artillery camp, where he met an equally frustrated *Leutnant* von Sooden. Von Sooden's outfit could not become a part of *General* Süßmann's battle group that was preparing to go on an operation, because there was no way to air-land them by Ju 52's in the area where the jump was to take place.

Fulda said: "I can do it for you. I have gliders!"

The *Leutnant* had to be told what Fulda meant. Von Sooden didn't know that a military glider existed. Words stumbled pell-mell from Fulda as he hurriedly explained he had done just such an operation at Eben Emael. Von Sooden was soon convinced.

They raced to Plovdiv to see *Major Graf* (Count) Uxkull, the operations officer for the raid. He at first ridiculed the idea. Fulda and von Sooden pleaded. He relented; he would think it over. They left.

Uxkull called the next morning: "I have thought over your idea. It is good. We will use your gliders. Tell Stein."

Fulda objected to going to Stein because he did not want Stein to know he had gone over his head. Soon Stein called Fulda to his tent: "The raid is on!" They went off to a staff meeting, where they had to again convince those present, but once given the details all were enthusiastic about using gliders to seize the bridge at Corinth.

Fulda was given command and was to have six gliders and some thirty-six parachutists, including engineers, to take the bridge. He was to land first and, ten minutes later Ju 52's would drop parachutists on high ground nearby to assist him.

That afternoon Fulda, *Leutnant* Franz Phenn, Walter Lassen, Raschke, Mende and Brendenbeck took off for Larissa piloting DFS 230's towed by Ju 52's commanded by *Leutnant* Schweizer. Schweizer had led Ju 52's that had towed gliders to Eben Emael. They got to Larissa late in the afternoon of 25 April 1941. There were no German support personnel there to help them: no food, little water, no advice. They were on their own. Worst of all, there were no soldiers for them to fly to Corinth. Had the mission been scrubbed? No one could hazard a guess.

It was a miserable night, bone cold and bleak. Everyone was hungry.

At midnight, an element of German troops appeared, led by an engineer *Leutnant*. He had a mistaken idea he was to parachute onto the bridge. When he and his men found they were to land in gliders, they became more and more terrified as Fulda explained what was involved. This took another selling job by Fulda. Soon he had the parachutists calmed down and confident of the operation. Under the wing of a glider, they made their plans, organized men into glider groups, stowed the guns, demolitions and ammunition in the gliders and got set for an early morning take off.

At 0430 hours, they were on their way. Forty aircraft filled with paratroopers were taking off from other fields.

At 0658 hours, German aircraft began bombing and strafing the Allied forces defending the bridge. Their attack was barely completed when Fulda's glider released at 6,500 feet altitude and began the descent on the bridge. As Fulda had so often reassuringly told doubters, the defenders, thinking the approaching gliders to be another flight of bombers, ducked into their emplacements until the bombing was finished. It never came.

At 0740 hours, the gliders swooped down on the bridge. Fulda, Brendenbeck and Mende brought theirs down on the north side. Fulda's force caught the Australian and New Zealand defenders completely by surprise. In a few minutes, the force took eighty prisoners. *Leutnant* Phenn's glider, carrying the engineer officer in charge of operations on the south side of the bridge, rammed the abutment of the bridge. One man was seriously injured but, miraculously, the others were unhurt.

In a few minutes, the Germans on the south had taken the six Bofors guns and disconnected the wires leading to the charges on the bridge.

At that point, Fulda wanted to get the charges removed from the bridge structure. The engineer *Leutnant* adamantly refused. He had orders to disconnect the wires, but he was not to touch the charges. Apparently, the plan was to blow the bridge if the enemy became too aggressive. Fulda argued with the engineer officer. The charges stayed put. Almost a half hour later, wave after wave of Ju 52's appeared and parachutists started dropping.

The bridge at Corinth just after it had been blown by the British. Against it lies the wreckage of a German glider.

Commonwealth prisioners detailed to move a glider used in the Corinth attack.

Then what Fulda had feared happened. From a position about 250 yards away—a position from which no enemy fire had previously been taken—Fulda heard rounds start to hit the bridge. They must have been coming from a Bofors. The rounds contained tracers, and they were getting closer to the charges on the bridge with each round. He ordered those who could be freed from guarding the prisoners to start firing with machine guns at the Bofors. Too late!

A well-placed round hit the charge. *Leutnant* Phenn was on the bridge, along with a German cameraman. The bridge rose into the air, hung there uncannily, then, in a crackling, splintering roar, toppled into the canal. Phenn was killed in the explosion. The Germans had seized the isthmus at 0625 hours. They had lost the bridge by 0655 hours.

Despite the loss of the bridge, the Germans were elated by the results of the operation—gliders had again won the day. *General* Süßmann landed at the bridge that afternoon in a Fieseler *Storch* utility aircraft and congratulated Fulda. Several weeks later, Fulda was awarded the Knight's Cross, primarily in recognition of his foresight and determination in seeing a glider raid on Corinth through to a successful conclusion. With the award, he became one of only three glider pilots to receive this decoration.

Unknown to Fulda, *Leutnant* von Sooden's parachute artillery had started out not far behind his own flight. Four of the gliders were too heavily loaded and did not reach sufficient altitude. They had to be released before crash-landing into the mountains of southern Bulgaria. Two were high enough and got to Larissa. The other four were flown out from the place where they had made emergency landings in Bulgaria, took more time to gain altitude and then headed for Larissa. From there, the six took off again and, by 1500 hours, had landed at Corinth.

On 27 April, *Leutnant* Heiner Lange landed at Corinth in a Ju 52 charged with the job of getting the gliders back to the airfields, where they were to be used for the assault on Crete. He got twenty "Tommies," as he called his detail of Australian and New Zealand prisoners, and marched them to the bridge. There, the prisoners helped to dismantle the gliders too damaged to fly and moved the others to take-off positions.

Everyone was hungry. Lange and several "Tommies" dropped grenades into the canal with satisfying results and soon all were feasting heartily on fish fillets. The prisoners did their part by brewing tea in a petrol can from which the top was removed to make a pot. Later that day, Lange accompanied the detail while they dug a grave and buried one of the Australians who had died earlier that day. When he stood at the graveside and saluted the fallen soldier, Lange heard one of the prisoners remark, "That's very nice of him." Using the shovel with which the grave had been dug, Lange removed a daisy plant nearby, dug a hole and placed the plant in it.

Earlier that day, Lange had found a copy of *Gone with the Wind* in the debris of a British camp. After the detail had completed the work on the gliders, Lange went alone to the grave of his good friend Phenn, which had been marked by the tip of his glider's wing, placed upright over the grave. He turned up a few handfuls of earth, laid the book in the depression, and covered it over. So had gone one of his best friends.

With the mainland of Greece under German domination, Crete became not only the last foothold for the king and government of Greece, but also a collecting point for many scattered Greek, British, and Commonwealth elements driven from the mainland. Although the Germans had air superiority in the Balkans and over the Aegean Sea and the enemy forces on Crete posed no threat to the Germans in the foreseeable future, the nation that held that island could control the eastern end of the Mediterranean by having air bases from which fighters and bombers could interdict shipping routes. The idea of taking Crete gained greater favor with both Hitler and the German High Command as *General* Erwin Rommel sped along the African coast in the direction of Alexandria. Crete could become a stepping stone for other German forces on the move south over the Mediterranean towards the strategic Suez Canal. Moreover, German airpower on Crete would help to protect the German shipping that moved men and supplies to Rommel's divisions.

On 25 April 1941, Hitler ordered Operation *Merkur,* the code name for the operation against Crete, named after Mercury, the winged god of Greek mythology. It was to become the first full-scale airborne invasion in history.

Hitler placed Student in command of the operation and gave him two formations for the task, one being Student's own *7. Flieger-Division,* elements of which had taken Fort Eben Emael and the bridges of the Meuse by glider forays. The other was the newly formed *Luftlande-Lastenseglergeschwader I* (*LLG I*), the 1st Airborne Glider Wing. Student soon found himself in a tight time squeeze.

Five days after Hitler ordered the invasion of Crete, he directed his armed forces to invade the Soviet Union and gave 22 June as the launch date for the attack. Crete had to be securely in German hands by that time, since Student's forces had to be available for employment in the east by then.

By the end of April, *Oberst* Walter Hornung, Commander of *LLG I* had concentrated seventy-four DFS 230's at Hildesheim and prepared them for rail shipment. By 2 May, all had been loaded on three trains of flat cars. By nightfall, the first train departed for Salonika in Greece.

In two days, Hornung's Ju 52's took off from Hildesheim and nearby airfields for Salonika. Meanwhile, many trainloads of parachutists and air-landing forces were also heading towards assembly areas in Bulgaria.

More than usual security precautions were taken, for the trip was long and Student had no desire to awaken suspicion of what might be afoot as his forces moved through many countries towards marshalling areas in Greece. The men wore no unit insignia, and none could carry private papers. Identification cards bore men's names but not their unit's. The trains wended their way through German and Bohemian towns and villages and a silent, hostile Prague. They crossed Hungary—one glider pilot noting that the Danube was in flood—and then, amid increasingly friendly and enthusiastic people, entered Bulgaria, where the troops detrained and went into bivouac for about a week.

By 12 May, the trains with the gliders had arrived at Salonika. Mechanics of *LLG I*, who had arrived in the Ju 52's a few days earlier, reassembled the gliders in the days that followed. As they were assembled and checked out, Ju 52's immediately shuttled them to fields at the ancient Greek city of Tanagra and to Eleusis just outside Athens. By 15 May, the glider build-up at each airstrip was complete.

On 15 May, the troops started arriving from Bulgaria and moved into tents near the airfields. Two days later, after lunch, glider pilots formed up silently on the airstrip at Tanagra in front of a row of gliders parked along the edge. At 1400 hours, a staff car drove up. *General* Student stepped out. There was little formality. He walked slowly along the ranks, stopped at each pilot, asked where he was from and details of his experience. Occasionally, he would ask about the pilot's family. Student inspected the troops in a leisurely, relaxed way, closing each chat with a handshake. It was at this ceremony that Student made it known that the objective was Crete. Pilots then got clear-cut orders: The squadron that would tow them, the flight and their position in the flight.

On 18 May, glider and aircraft pilots got together with the leaders of the ground forces they were to carry. Details were worked out on the distribution of the ground units, down to each glider. Pilots got their courses and glider pilots their precise targets in Crete. As one pilot remarked, "With a little luck, the operation will be 100 percent successful."

That afternoon, glider personnel loaded their aircraft with mortars, ammunition, explosives and equipment for the attack. On returning to the camp, supply sergeants issued each soldier a full basic load of ammunition for his personal weapon. No detail was overlooked. Company commanders saw to it that each man carried his standard issue of contraceptives, as well as a short glossary of German-English phrases, spelled phonetically.

On 19 May, the pilot quoted previously noted "extreme and feverish preparations" in his diary and, in the afternoon, "there was discussion about the attack once more." That evening, the soldiers marched to the gliders and loaded their weapons, packs and gear. "I am quite calm," the glider pilot reassured himself and finished his entry for the day: "0715 hours Tuesday is to be the time of landing on the island of Crete."

At 0300 hours, the shrill warble of the whistles of company first sergeants aroused them all. The first glider at Eleusis took off at 0503 hours. Confusion delayed takeoffs at one field until 0525 hours. The previously quoted glider pilot reported that on his "first attempt, a truck ran into my tow rope; on the second, the towing aircraft fell out of formation, but I managed to get away." Headed for Maleme, 400 aircraft carrying paratroopers followed the 48-glider echelon from Tanagra, some to drop parachutists following the glider landings, others to chance hazardous landings on Maleme and other airfields in Crete, bringing in air-landing forces, artillery ammunition and supplies. Other aircraft, 26 DFS's in tow, took off from Eleusis and Megara.

The flight was a grueling ordeal for the glider pilots. Several gliders became separated from their tow aircraft and had to land in the sea. Another crashed on the island of Aegina, killing *Generalleutnant* Wilhelm Süßmann, commander of the 7. *Flieger-Division*. His death was unfortunate and can be judged as an unnecessary, avoidable tragedy. The glider tow over water to Crete, under the best of conditions for the most qualified glider pilot, was a delicate, hazardous task. When asked by *Oberst* Wilke, the overall commander of the air transport part of the operation, who would fly the division commander, Heiner Lange, who recommended the glider pilots for the operation, said it should be Lassen. Lassen, a certified engineer in civil life, was not even a noncommissioned officer, but was a superb glider pilot and in Lange's estimation the best person for the task. When informed of Lassen's rank, Wilke disapproved and asked for another name. This time Lange suggested Eugen Moser, a noncommissioned officer. Again Wilke refused. Was there an officer glider pilot? Lange stated that he had no man that had both superb ability and rank. Finally, Lange suggested *Leutnant* Doge, an able pilot. Doge, however, was at Tanagra.

Within a few hours, the five glider pilots designated to fly *General* Süßmann and his headquarters were called to report to Süßmann. Doge was not there. A hurried call to Tanagra got him on the way. *Leutnant* Gruppe would represent Doge at the meeting and inform Doge of what transpired.

In the walk to Süßmann's headquarters, Gruppe walked separately with the senior officer, taking the five pilots to meet the general. He was in an animated discussion all the way to the headquarters. Doge had not arrived. To the surprise of the other four pilots, the senior officer said, "Doge is not here. Gruppe will take his place."

They went into *General* Süßmann's offices. The senior officer introduced each pilot to the general. As he introduced Gruppe, he said to the general, "This is your pilot." The general then told the pilots to go about whatever preparations were necessary with his staff and left. The senior officer never did tell the general of the changes.

As the pilots were leaving the headquarters, Doge showed up. He ran to them. Gruppe told him he was too late and what had happened. Doge objected to his superiors, but it was too late.

General Süßmann and other members of his staff boarded the glider next morning. It had a complete load, enough for the long flight. An eyewitness stated that a vehicle drove up shortly before takeoff. Several typewriters and bulky packages were taken to the door and placed to the rear of it. The eyewitness realized that any additional load in Süßmann's glider, placed where he had seen it placed, would move the center of gravity towards the rear, dangerously farther back than it should be. Gruppe, as pilot, should have insisted that this additional cargo should not be placed where it had been. If the glider was fully loaded and the additional cargo added too much weight, he should not have allowed it in the glider at all.

Gruppe's glider led his element of five. Right at the take-off, his glider climbed too fast. It got and stayed well above the usual tow position as the flight took formation. Glider pilots to the rear were puzzled as to why Gruppe did not descend to normal tow position. The answer is now thought to be that he could not. The weight was causing the tail to come down and forcing the nose up, and he must have been desperately fighting at the controls to keep the glider in level flight.

Twenty minutes out, an aircraft appeared from the east. It momentarily took the eye of *Unteroffizier* Busse, the glider pilot of the right glider, from his intent gaze at his own job. Then he saw Gruppe's glider moving up and down, diving steeply and climbing precipitously.

Gruppe apparently did not have the experience to know how to stop the motion. *Unteroffizier* Moser in the left-hand glider across from Busse's also saw the aircraft come into view. Almost simultaneously, an explosion and a cloud of debris appeared where Gruppe's glider carrying *General* Süßmann had been. The tug plane and Moser's glider passed perilously close to the rubble, but were not touched by any of it. Gruppe's tow plane, the tow rope dragging behind, turned back. The others continued.

So as not to alarm his passengers, *Unteroffizier* Moser flew on as if nothing had transpired. He said nothing. There was a good chance that no one in his glider was aware that one of Germany's most promising military leaders and a key figure to this operation had just been killed. After several minutes of silence, *Major* Uxkull, who was seated just behind *Unteroffizier* Moser, asked in a low tense voice: "Does this happen often?" Moser did not answer.

What had happened to Gruppe's glider? In technical terms, excessive turbulence developed above wing surfaces. It suddenly lost lift and started to dive. Gruppe pulled it out of the dive, but the rope again pulled the nose down at the top of the climb. The wings finally twisted and exploded from internal pressures. Some accounts claim the crash was due to the excessive turbulence caused by the Heinkel bomber.

In the meantime, Gruppe's tug pilot flew towards the main land. He did not release the tow rope. He landed at Eleusis and asked several officers to come to his aircraft to see that the tow rope was still attached. He wanted no one to think he had released Gruppe. Whatever happened, he wanted to be certain everyone understood it was not his fault. Apparently reassured, he returned to his plane, took off, caught up with his formation and again took the lead.

For an hour, the *Luftwaffe* bombed the positions around the Maleme airfield, working over the Allied defenders' antiaircraft guns so savagely that few guns remained in action. Although accustomed to enemy bombings, the men sensed that something was in the wind, because of the intensity of the attack. They were right. Suddenly, the bombing ceased. Shortly thereafter, the Allied defenders saw a new sight that was quickly understood. Gliders, silent as ghosts after the deafening bombing—huge, grey and menacing— came sweeping in.

At 0704 hours, Heiner Lange saw the tow-ship wings waggling, the signal to release. He hit the release knob. He had been in tow just a minute over two hours. For the next eleven minutes, or some ten miles, he glided towards Maleme, touching ground at 0715 hours.

Student's *XI. Flieger-Korps*, formed for the attack on Crete, comprised three attack echelons. *Gruppe West* had the mission to capture Maleme airport; *Gruppe Mitte*, Canne and Retimo; and *Gruppe Ost*, Heraklion. The Retimo and Heraklion landings were to occur on the afternoon of D-Day. The elite Assault Regiment, specially trained for glider and parachute operations, had

Gruppe West's mission. General Eugen Meindl, its commander, had orders to seize Maleme and keep it free of the enemy to enable aircraft to land. He was also to reconnoiter west to Kastelli, and also to the south and east, and to keep in contact with *Gruppe Mitte.* Because the glider troops would get into action after they landed faster than parachutists, Meindl assigned special missions near the airport to glider parties, which was the key target of the invasion. The parachutists would land a mile or two farther away, where it was hoped the enemy was not too strong. There they would muster and collect themselves and their weapons for a concerted attack.

After shaking off their astonishment at the awesome sight of the gliders, the defenders cleared their wits and opened a torrential fire on these aircraft that had little defense except speed. Drilled with rifle and machine-gun bullets, the gliders began to crumple. Some of them moved relentlessly above the sea, their pilots determined to attack, seemingly oblivious to the sheet of fire. One, in landing, crashed against a huge rock. Another, speeding at seventy-five miles an hour, smashed full tilt against the ironwork of the bridge; then, in some way, its tail swung down and its nose became hitched to the ironwork. It was a grotesque sight.

In some of the gliders that had stayed on course through the hail of death and had landed without damage, only silence prevailed—all were dead in their seats. Some, hitting trees with a wing-tip, spun like tops, ripping apart among the trees and rocks. Many of the gliders lay in the midst of a tumble of bodies. Almost every glider landing ended at best in a jarring shock, splintering wood, ammunition boxes, equipment, and men catapulting towards the obstacle that had been hit. Seven dead Germans lay outside the skeleton of one aircraft. In five gliders that crash-landed in a field in rapid succession, every man was killed, either by the impact of landing or by bullets. Ian McD. G. Stewart, in his *Struggle for Crete*, wrote: "Often they came to rest under the very muzzles of enemy weapons. Aircraftsman Comeau stood transfixed beside his tent as a glider burst at him out of the bushes, one wing slithering above his head to wedge itself against the hillside. He emptied his rifle into the open doorway, blocking it with dead and wounded, before making his escape up the bank."

Gliders carrying eighty men, part of the skeleton staff of a regiment commanded by *Major* Braun, had to land on the dried bed of the lower Tavronitis River, capture the Tavronitis Bridge and prevent its destruction. Another group, commanded by *Major* Koch had a headquarters staff of the glider battalion and two companies of 108 men each. One of the companies, under the command of *Leutnant* Plessen, was to land at the mouth of the river and destroy antiaircraft guns there to ease the way for aircraft coming in to land at Maleme. This was the most practical course on which to approach the airport from the mainland. Koch and the battalion staff were to land on Hill

Gliders coming in to land on Crete.

One glider that made a safe landing.

107, the highest point in the area, an objective that had to be taken to prevent the British from using it for either artillery observation posts or defensive infantry positions. Either use of the hill would have caused fire to be placed on German aircraft landing on the Maleme airport.

The selection of the dry bed of the Tavronitis proved that the staffs that planned the invasion had done their homework well. Much of the bed could not be fired into by the British soldiers in trenches on the slopes above the river bed. As was soon to be found, this enabled glider soldiers to form up quickly, head aggressively toward their objectives and take positions on the high ground.

Plessen's company landed according to plan. With great dash, it soon overwhelmed the enemy antiaircraft crews. Successful there, Plessen changed direction, after leaving a handful of men to consolidate the German hold around the antiaircraft positions. He went after the defenders round the airfield, where he met a withering fire and was soon killed.

Major Koch had less success. His force landed along the southeast and southwest slopes of the key hill. Because of this, the two elements of the force, split by the hill, had trouble in helping each other. British and Anzac forces, stubbornly defending and looking right down on the Germans, soon began to kill and wound many of the invaders. Koch was severely wounded, but the remnants of his force finally made their way to the area of the bridge.

Braun's nine gliders landed on target. The British were ready, peppering the gliders as they swept in, and rifling and machine gunning the occupants as they struggled from the gliders. Braun soon fell, mortally wounded. But notwithstanding their bloody punishment, Braun's men seized the bridge and overran machine-gun positions on the east bank of the Tavronitis after hand-to-hand combat. *General* Meindl was quick to seize the advantage of the stronghold Braun's force had captured. He established this area as a base for continued attacks against the airfield. Later that day, Meindl was severely wounded.

Parachutists began their descent through the wicked fire almost concurrently with the last of the glider landings. The crescendo of the battle grew throughout that day and the next, until 14,000 Germans had landed on Crete.

By 27 May, Major General B. C. Freyberg, commanding the British and Anzac forces, made the decision to evacuate Crete. A force of 14,000 Germans, at an agonizing cost in wounded and dead and with the loss of aircraft and

other critical military equipment that would have served Hitler well in Russia, had cleared the island of 42,500 British, Anzac and Greek forces.

The German concept of the large-scale use of gliders came to fruition at Crete. Student felt that the greater employment of gliders would have materially reduced the number of Ju 52's lost from crash landings. Gliders were available in Germany, but time and crews were not available to ferry them to bases in Greece. Of the seventy-two gliders used at Crete, six did not reach the island, five landed too far from their objectives and the remainder landed with accuracy varying from fair to perfect, although many crashed. Overall, the glider phase of the operation achieved 80 percent accuracy and only 40 percent effective accomplishment of tasks assigned. At Maleme, the glider missions were 75 percent accurate and influenced the German gains there on the first day. At Akrotiri, the glider sorties were a complete failure because of the poor selection of landing areas and the absence of air support.

Soured against airborne operations by the huge losses suffered in Crete, Hitler and Göring paid no serious attention afterwards. They believed that the Allies had learned their lesson and that gliders in any airborne operation could no longer be used with surprise. This brought to an end the General Staff's hopes of an airborne operation to take Suez and, along with it, hopes of a projected operation to take Cyprus by an airborne attack and to use that island as another stepping stone towards Suez. In Student's words, "Crete was the grave of the German parachutists." Conversely, it was the savior of Suez.

Strong evidence suggests that although Hitler harbored some doubts about ever going through as distasteful a venture as Crete again, where the target was sufficiently lucrative, he and his generals would have given gliders and airborne forces another chance. For the time being, however, another factor had cropped up that made German leaders shelve any thought of airborne operations on a large scale. Expanding German operations in the Soviet Union and commitments in the West to ward off the anticipated Allied invasion in France sucked the German military forces into ground operations. Parachutists were being thrown in as ground forces. Transport planes were hauling supplies. The staff had no time to plan for new frills in the art of war, such as Eben Emael and Crete. The glider effort would have to wait and perhaps take other directions.

In the summer of 1941, after its employment in Crete, the *Luftwaffe* activated the three remaining groups of *LLG I* to bring its total strength to 212 DFS gliders and 52 tow-planes. In an experimental program, the 1st Group of the wing was equipped with Go 242's to test their adaptability as assault gliders. Despite its excellent characteristics, the Go 242 did not have the dexterity of the lighter and more easily handled DFS 230, so necessary for highly specialized assault missions. It was felt that the Go 242 would be more suitable as a cargo glider, and thus the DFS 230's again replaced the Go 242's.

By 1942, it became clear that any extensive use of assault gliders, in the "assault" terms of the Eben Emael and Crete experiences, was no longer a possibility in view of Hitler's position on the value of future massive airborne operations, a lack of airborne troops and general disinterest in such operations on the part of field commanders. The High Command in Berlin, faced with enormous supply problems on the Russian front, and anxious to keep Rommel's forces on the move, gradually began to turn glider units into cargo transport organizations. The transition did not come about easily, nor did it seem that there was consensus as to what their ultimate organization and equipment should be. To its credit, the *Luftwaffe* made notable efforts to adapt all glider models to move freight over the many thousands of miles that separated air supply bases from front line tanks that were spread thinly over the bleak Soviet landscape. For a time, the 1st Group of *LLG I* became a test group, equipped with the Me 321 and flew tanks, men, supplies and equipment into the Soviet Union. Instead of the twelve gliders per squadron they had had when equipped with the DFS, each squadron had only six Me-321's. However, the huge gliders did not prove satisfactory, being an excessive drain on the resources of the air transport command.

In 1941, the *Luftwaffe* activated special cargo glider formations. In 1943, it redesignated them as Cargo Glider Towing Groups. Each group had three squadrons, two with twelve Go 242's and Me 110's, the third equipped with twelve DFS 230's and twelve Ju 52's or He 128's.

At the same time, the *Luftwaffe* also organized two glider pilot training groups to man the flying formations and provide a replacement pool of skilled glider pilots. The 1st Group specialized in giving transition training for the Gigant (Me 321) and occasionally dispatched cadres to the 1st Group of *LLG* I to supplement existing crews and equipment. The 2nd Group specialized in transitioning crews to the Go 242 and gave advanced operational training to DFS 230 pilots. The equipment of these two groups varied in accordance with demands placed upon them by the tactical organizations.

In general, it can be said that a few generals tried to use gliders imaginatively for the remainder of the war and, on the whole, gliders made a substantial contribution in cargo supply, espionage and sabotage missions.

CHAPTER 5

Sicily: Tragedy and Turning Point

Ladbroke
Gliders used: 144
Taking off: 137
Returned: 4
Missing: 133
British Chiefs of Staff Committee[1]

In January 1943, on the advice of their Combined Chiefs of Staff, Prime Minister Winston Churchill and President Franklin D. Roosevelt decided on the invasion of Sicily. Plans called for General Bernard Law Montgomery's Eighth Army to seize areas below Syracuse and the southeast end of Sicily, and General George S. Patton, leading his Seventh Army, to get a foothold at Gela, to the west of Montgomery. Montgomery had been allocated the British 1st Airborne Division and Patton the U.S. 82nd Airborne Division to seize key positions in Sicily by airborne assault.

The timing of the operation depended upon reconciling airborne requirements for moonlight and naval demands for darkness. The Combined Chiefs of Staff had set as the target date the favorable period of the July moon. General Eisenhower and his staff interpreted this to mean the period of the second quarter of the moon, when there would be enough moonlight early in the night for airborne forces to drop and assemble, but complete darkness after midnight, when the moon had set, would allow naval convoys to approach. Thus, D-Day was determined to be 10 July.

Montgomery decided that the 1st Airborne Division should make a glider assault near Syracuse, to which he gave the code name "Ladbroke." The force had to land around midnight and seize the Ponte Grande, a bridge over which the north-south highway from Syracuse crossed two canals, and key terrain commanding tactical approaches south of the city. Although the presence of two Allied airborne divisions and air force troop-carrier

---

1. *Airborne Missions in the Mediterranean, 1942–1945,* USAF Historical Studies, No. 74, by Dr. John Warren (Air University, USAF Historical Division Research Studies Institute, 1955) has been used as a major source for this chapter.

64

formations presupposed that Montgomery and Patton would use airborne troops to open the invasion, Montgomery's decision to use a glider force shocked experienced airborne subordinates. Glider resources in Africa could best be described as a hodge-podge of available, marginally available or non-existent. They were disparate airborne resources, unsuitable for launching any reasonably successful airborne operation. To expect it to be made by gliders at such short notice made the outcome of a glider assault in Sicily highly doubtful.

Although Montgomery approved the glider assault, he apparently acted on inadequate information and may have been unduly influenced by General G. F. Hopkinson, recently promoted, the former commander of the Airlanding Brigade of the British 1st Airborne Division. The ambitious Hopkinson had conferred with General Montgomery and had carried from the meeting Montgomery's agreement to land gliderborne forces to open the British assault on Sicily. Following his discussion with Montgomery, General Hopkinson called Colonel Chatterton to his headquarters. Chatterton had not seen Hopkinson for weeks. He sensed that Hopkinson had committed the glider force to something and, as Chatterton later said, "He most certainly had!" Cutting to the chase, Hopkinson gave Chatterton the plan. Chatterton gasped. He made quick mental calculations. He had three months until invasion night. The glider forces had no airfields, no tow aircraft and, worst of all, no gliders. He had inexperienced glider pilots spread out in several camps, who had not flown a glider for three months. None had flown gliders at night. Chatterton informed Hopkinson of the facts.

"Oh," Hopkinson replied, "we will soon put that right. The U.S. Air Forces are going to supply tugs and gliders."

"American gliders?" Chatterton asked incredulously, since his pilots had no experience with American CG-4A's.

"Yes, what difference will it make?" was the reply.

The conversation continued, ending in a situation in which Chatterton had no option except to support the frightening operation or be relieved on the spot. He grimly gritted his teeth and said no more.

Nor was Chatterton alone in his doubts. Group Captain T. B. Cooper of the RAF, an adviser for British Airborne Forces, pleaded in vain to Montgomery's staff on the folly of a glider mission flown at night on a treacherous course. The decision stood.

Chatterton later found out that "Ladbroke" was to be one of four airborne assaults. Parachutists from the U.S. 82nd Airborne Division had to jump at Gela in Operation "Husky I" on the night of "Ladbroke." "Husky II," another parachute operation of the same division set for the next night, and a British glider-parachute operation, "Fustian," was scheduled for the third night.

Some difficult problems on the teaming up of units had to be solved before training for the assault started. The U.S. Army Air Corps' 51st Troop Carrier Wing was already in North Africa. The 52nd Troop Carrier Wing arrived early in May. A rush shipment of 500 gliders was en route by convoy from the U.S. There were four CG-4A's in Africa. The British agreed to provide 36 Horsa gliders, a squadron of 30 Albemarles and a flight of 10 Halifaxes from the 38th RAF Wing to tow the Horsas.

The Horsas sat at airfields in England. Somehow they had to be transported to Africa. No one was certain how that was to be done. To add to the difficulties, it was initially decided that the 51st Troop Carrier Wing was to transport the 82nd Airborne Division and the 52nd Troop Carrier Wing was to fly the British 1st Airborne Division. In mid-May, the Allied North African Air Forces (NAAF) reversed the assignments. The new lineup seemed logical, because the 51st Troop Carrier Wing had operated with the British in North Africa, and the 52nd Troop Carrier Wing had flown the 82nd for three months of joint training and maneuvers before leaving America. It lost its logic at the end of May, however, when Montgomery decided on a glider mission. The 52nd Troop Carrier Wing had been trained in glider operations in the United States, but it was committed to the paratroop mission of the 82nd Airborne Division on Sicily. By then, it was too late to change the missions of each wing again. The 51st Troop Carrier Wing had modified its C-47's for use by British paratroops, and there were neither time nor materials to modify those of the 52nd Troop Carrier Wing. Moreover, since the techniques of dropping American and British paratroops differed, a switch in the middle of the training period would have caused dangerous confusion.

On 30 May, the NAAF's 125 Albemarles and 8 Halifaxes from the RAF's 38th Wing—a total of 133 aircraft—were earmarked to tow 125 CG-4A's and 8 Horsas on Operation Ladbroke. In the companion airborne assault of "Husky I," 227 C-47's of the 52nd Troop Carrier Wing had orders to drop parachutists of the 82nd Airborne Division in the Gela area. The NAAF decided that the glider column would fly from fields around Sousse (in Tunisia) to Malta, head for Cape Correnti just east of Patton's designated area of operations, turn offshore to follow the Sicily coast almost to Fela and then finally head inland to the landing zones.

This route, which was to be flown at night—hopefully aided by some moonlight—required three very sharp changes in course by the aircraft over the Mediterranean. Some pilots thought the flight a mad risk and fought to get some straightening of the course beyond Malta. Their protestations were to no avail. In a conference on 22 June, all the commanders agreed—many with resignation—to the routes and schedules.

In mid-May, the 51st Troop Carrier Wing started three weeks of intensive glider-towing exercises. Until then, few of the 500 gliders ordered to Africa had arrived, so little training had taken place, even though 105 glider pilots had arrived at Relizane early in March. Elements of the British Glider Pilot Regiment with the 1st Airlanding Brigade had been at Froha for weeks, but its pilots were also very short of training. A British War Office memorandum judged that each pilot needed 100 hours flying time before being fit for an operation. None had anywhere near this amount. Furthermore, all were totally ignorant of how to fly the CG-4A's, which had landing characteristics differing greatly from those of the British. They also had little experience in night flying, since British doctrine held that glider missions at night were out of the question. The American glider pilots, on the other hand, had little advanced glider training and virtually none in realistic maneuvers. The lack of gliders caused a serious delay in training.

Earlier, a small shipment of CG-4A gliders had arrived at Accra on the Africa Gold Coast, and troop-carrier pilots were dispatched on 24 March to fly them to the fields around Sousse. They found the gliders in such bad condition from neglect and deterioration caused by tropical weather, that crews did not manage until 22 April to make four of them safe enough to fly back.

On 23 April, the first consignment of the 500 gliders allotted to the force arrived at North African ports. Port units unloaded some 50 in several days, and news flashed that the long-awaited and critically needed gliders had arrived. But authorities were in for a rude shock. Each glider arrived unassembled in crates, with five crates to a glider.

Inefficient logistics routed crates haphazardly to several ports. One port had fuselages galore but not enough wings. Another had the opposite problem. Important instruments necessary for the assembly of the gliders could not be found. For instance, assembly was delayed for several days due to a lack of tensiometers.

The situation at Elida (Algeria), one of the assembly centers, proved typical. About twenty-five of the first gliders to arrive at Algiers were redirected to Elida, because no provision had been made to assemble them at the depot at Maison Blanche in Algiers. This meant that many missing parts and much equipment that had arrived at Algiers had to be taken by truck thirty miles to Elida. Their assembly at Elida was given sixth priority and entrusted to one officer and twenty enlisted men, who had never seen a glider and had no technical experience.

The assembly of gliders had a low priority elsewhere as well and despite appeals from the NAAF, Troop Carrier Command stubbornly refused to set a higher priority, claiming that it would upset depot and service-center procedures. By 5 May, only 18 out of 74 gliders delivered to the theater had

been assembled and, by 25 May, only 30 out of 240 gliders delivered were ready
to fly. It was at this time that Hopkinson made the announcement that gliders
would spearhead the British assault on Sicily. No wonder General Delmar H.
Dunton, commander of the XII Air Force Service Command, referred in late
May to an "extreme emergency" in the assembly of gliders.

Once the crisis was recognized, it was met. The Service Command ordered
that work on gliders be given priority even over that of the Army Air Corps' pet
P-38's. American troop-carrier formations lent experienced glider mechanics.
Colonel Chatterton sent fifty glider pilots. His decision to have all his pilots
trained as glider mechanics now paid off. By 13 June, enterprising men using
assembly-line techniques assembled 346 gliders—ample enough, it turned
out, for both training and operations. Meanwhile, however, irreplaceable
training time had been lost.

Gliders were not always usable after they had been assembled. On 7 May, only
six out of twenty gliders assembled were delivered to troop-carrier formations,
because British static cables were lacking. The next day, heavy winds tore up
all the gliders on the field at La Senia. Extreme temperatures and indifferent
maintenance by inexperienced personnel caused rapid deterioration. On 16
June, the NAAF, alarmed by a flood of mechanical failures, grounded most
gliders in Africa for repairs. Ten days before the invasion, so many gliders had
weaknesses in the tail wiring that NAAF had to ground them all for three days.
Glider-plane intercom kits did not arrive until the last few days, too late for
practice and almost too late for use.

Meanwhile, the British found problems in meeting the commitment
for Horsas. They had none in Africa. Any that were to be used had to come
from England, 1,300 miles away. Most authorities thought it was too great a
distance to ferry them in by a glider-tow all the way from England. However,
an enterprising squadron leader, Wilkinson, hitched a Horsa to a Halifax
equipped with extra fuel tanks and "sauntered" nonstop over England for
enough hours to pick up 1,500 air miles, more than enough to make the
1,300-mile tow from England to Africa. Operation "Beggar" was born from
that accomplishment, calling for Halifax bombers to tow thirty-six Horsas to
Sale in Morocco.

It was an incredibly courageous enterprise. Each Halifax had to fly many
hours, of which the greater number would be spent in towing. They were very
heavily loaded, extra petrol being carried in the bomb bays, which meant that
a forced landing with wheels up would almost inevitably cause the aircraft to
burst into flames. This indeed happened on the only occasion when such a
landing had to be made. German fighters sat warmed up at airfields in France,
only 100 miles from the leg of the flight that crossed the Bay of Biscay. What
is more, for technical reasons the flight had to be made in daylight. British

fighters could protect the "Beggar" flights for only the first three hours out of England, leaving another six hours for the combinations to fly unprotected. Tug and glider had to stay below 500 feet during the entire flight.

The first day, four Halifaxes attempted the trip. Two reached Sale.

Bad weather turned back one combination, and one broke its rope in a cloud. The pilot gingerly maneuvered the Horsa through the cloud, finally breaking into the clear to find himself 100 feet above a choppy sea. The nose broke away when he ditched, and the sea poured into the fuselage. The pilots worked madly, unlashing a dinghy they had on board. They slid it through the water, which was rapidly filling the Horsa, and got out of the nose minutes before it sunk below the surface.

Nor were later flights less hair-raising. One was 300 miles from its takeoff field at Portreath, in Cornwall, when a Halifax engine failed. As the lumbering craft started losing altitude, the pilot ordered the crew to lighten ship, and it began jettisoning gear. Soon the Halifax stopped losing altitude. Dangerously low, it held on to the glider and made its way to its home field.

On occasion, the tug pilots had a tougher time than the glider pilots. One towed a Horsa from Portsmouth to Sale and landed back at his base in England after a round trip taking thirty-seven hours. Within six days, he had completed another tow. On a fourth trip, his tug and glider were reported missing, believed shot down. Another pilot delivered four gliders to Morocco in the space of two weeks. On one of these missions, twelve Ju 88's attacked. After a hopeless attempt at evasion, with his glider still desperately hanging on, he called upon the glider pilot to release from the Horsa. The Halifax's tail gunner then shot down one of the German attackers and damaged two. One the aircraft landed at Sale, members of the Halifax crew counted thirty-six holes in the aircraft from enemy cannon fire. The Horsa ditched, its crew went into a dinghy, and a ship picked it up eleven days later.

In all, thirty-one Horsas left Portreath in Cornwall in Operation "Beggar." Twenty-seven arrived safely at Sale. The effort cost two Halifaxes, four Horsas and a number of crews.

The British also had to ferry more than 360 CG-4A's from the Froha airfields, where they had been assembled after arrival via Kairouan by ship from the United States. Many of the gliders had not been test flown, nor was there time to afford this luxury. Before setting course, each tug made one circuit, giving the glider pilot a few minutes in which to judge the airworthiness of his craft. Of seven that left Froha on the first day, two released and landed back. The next day, General Happy was watching. When one of ten glider pilots came back and complained of aileron trouble, Happy jumped into the glider, made a circuit, reported it fit to fly, and sent the pilot home.

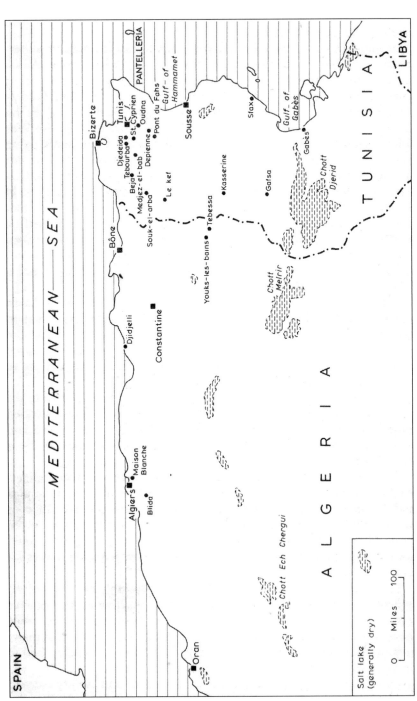

The North African–Algerian Theater

Lawrence Wright goes on to say, "There were no further complaints at Froha"[2]

The mission was gruesome. None of the glider pilots had had more than one hour of continuous flight before this. Tug and glider had to cross mountains up to 7,000 feet in elevation, flying at about 9,000 feet. A towed Horsa took about an hour and a half to reach that height. After early morning, the air was so rough that 1,000 feet or more could be lost in a single bump; one pilot reported losing 3,000 feet in ten minutes.

Wright, citing the bone-cracking nature of the flight, tells of seeking out the glider that had carried his motor bike:

> After it had been lashed into place in the glider at Froha, I had asked the Engineer Officer to make a final check. He had added further ropes and wedges that looked sufficient for a battleship in dry dock. But after that switchback ride, it was lying on one side among shreds of rope, and the fabric roof was still dripping the remains of a basket of tomatoes that I had given to the crew. It was on this trip that one Hadrian shed its tail and killed its occupants.[3]

Thus, the 51st Troop Carrier Wing was unready during the first two weeks of June for anything but limited training in the fundamentals of loading and towing gliders. By the first week in June, members of the Airlanding Brigade, under their commander, Brigadier P. H. W. Hicks, D.S.O., M.C., were having a strenuous time training to be glidermen in a part of the world composed largely of a vast plain of red clay soil, surrounded by mountainous, desolate country. It was hot and the red dust was a nuisance. The only consolation was the local wine, which the pilots discovered to be plentiful, cheap, crude and surprisingly strong.

The first practice maneuver mission with gliders and elements of the 1st Airlanding Brigade took place on 14 June, when the wing flew fifty-four CG-4A's with British pilots over a triangular seventy-mile course and released the gliders to come down on to the Froha airfield. On 20 June, glider mission "Eve" was flown in identical formations and over a similar course with the RAF's 38th Wing also participating. Although the results were good, the exercises had not been realistic. The gliders had been released by day to land on well-marked airfields.

After the second maneuver, the training period ended, and the move to the take-off fields began. According to the Troop Carrier Command, the British glider pilots logged a mere 4.5 hours in flying the CG-4A's. This

2. Lawrence Wright, *The Wooden Sword* (London, 1967 Books Ltd.), 1967, 142.

3. Ibid., 142.

included slightly more than one hour of night flying. Pilots had made about sixteen landings apiece. A British observer wrote bluntly, "Practically none of our glider pilots has sufficient training, and it is too late to rectify this omission now." Because the equally inexperienced American pilots were not scheduled to participate in D-Day operations, they had received less instruction and practice than the British. Critically, there had been no mass release of gliders either over water or at night and very little practice in landing them under simulated combat conditions. The future of the mission looked ominous.

The training ended on 20 June. Advanced echelons had begun the trek to Tunisia on 16 June, a move that was not completed until 4 July. It is perhaps as well that plans for the employment of the 52nd Troop Carrier Wing in a glider mission were never carried out. The towing of gliders loaded with men and equipment during the move to Tunisia was the only glider training the wing received in Africa. No full-scale rehearsal had been held. No time had been given to the pathfinder techniques developed at the airborne center. Above all, the wing was still insufficiently trained in formation flying, navigating and locating drop zones at night. At least one group commander later felt that the Troop Carrier Command was far too optimistic about its crews' proficiency.

On the night of 9 July, 109 C-47's of the Troop Carrier Command and 26 Albemarles and 7 Halifaxes of 38th Wing were ready to go on "Ladbroke." One hundred and thirty-six CG-4A's and 8 Horsas waited to take off. The latter, because they were big, were to be towed by the four-engine Halifaxes. Nineteen American glider pilots, who had volunteered for the mission, reinforced the British ranks. Twelve hundred men of the British Airlanding Brigade, commanded by Major General G. F. Hopkinson, stood by their gliders. The gliders also carried seven jeeps, six 6-pound guns and ten 3-inch mortars.

Their goal was the Ponte Grande Bridge, located a mile and a half southwest of Syracuse on the highway by which the British 5th Division was to approach the city. The Horsa gliders were to land between a quarter of a mile and a mile west of the bridge on Landing Zone 3, which was two small strips of land on either side of the Mammaibica Canal. The CG-4A's were to land on two zones: LZ 2, between two and three miles south of the bridge, comprised of two irregular pieces of land near the shore and having a combined area of about half a square mile, and LZ 1, about a mile west of the bridge and almost a mile inland. The latter was rectangular, about 1,200 yards long and 900 yards wide, with a small adjacent strip to the southwest. Officers later stated that all zones had been too small.

The bridge was less than a half mile west of the outer harbor of Syracuse. Nevertheless, the concentration of flak around that city had made it necessary to approach from the south and had largely determined the location of glider landing zones.

At 1842 hours, the ground crew hitched the first Halifax to its glider and the combination roared off. The tugs and gliders continued to take off in clouds of dust from six fields at intervals of less than a minute until 2020 hours. The ground crews controlled the take-offs with flags and walkie-talkies.

The 60th Troop Carrier Group of the 51st Troop Carrier Wing lined up its aircraft on the runway four abreast, each with its glider behind it. The tugs and their gliders took off alternately in pairs. Once in the air, the American planes lined up in formations of four in echelon to the right, with one-minute intervals between elements. The British flew individually, as was their custom at night.

Each transport group swept in a wide circle, assembling its aircraft. It then it headed north at 500 feet to rendezvous over the Kuriate Islands with other groups.

Trouble began before the formations had crossed the Tunisian coast. A jeep in one glider, its lashings broken by the turbulence, began to pound the glider interior to bits. The pilot hit the release lever and landed. Five other glider pilots, finding their relatively untested gliders unsound, also released. Three combinations could be seen returning at that point, their gliders in trouble. The gliders cut off near their home fields and landed. Ground crews rolled other gliders out from among reserves standing by for just such an emergency. Quick work got two glider combinations into the air and on their way to try to catch the remaining 135 combinations, then well over the island of Linosa.

From the Kuriate Islands, the 137 gliders in the main force set out toward Malta, 200 miles to the east. The C-47's flew below 250 feet at 120 miles an hour, the Albemarles at 350 feet at 125 miles an hour and the Halifaxes at 500 feet at 145 miles an hour. The straight course fell just south of Linosa, which served as a navigation checkpoint. A dying gale, blowing from the northwest, buffeted the combinations into unpredictable altitudes and directions. Ordered to fly low to avoid detection by enemy radar, some planes flew so low that ocean spray lashed against aircraft and glider.

The sun set behind them as the leading pilots sighted Malta's flashing beacon. A few fighters swept overhead in the gloom, the only escort observed during the trip. Fortunately, no enemy fighters appeared. Rounding the southeastern corner of Malta, the pilots began the seventy-mile leg north-northeast to a point five miles off Cape Passero, the southeastern tip of Sicily. Although some sighted the cape, many had to estimate their positions.

The dark mass of the cape off to the northeast loomed into the view of some of the pilots at 2220 hours, precisely the time the lead elements started

Men of the 82nd Airborne Division loading a 75-mm howitzer into a glider during invasion training in Morocco.

the scheduled eighteen-mile leg to the north. The formation began to fly over the vast seaborne invasion fleet, warships and transports that were to discharge Montgomery's ground forces over the shores of Sicily at dawn. The ships held their fire, alerted to the overflight of the airborne forces about to be launched at Syracuse.

The glider and tug combinations already seriously dispersed in the loosely formed serials got into trouble. Those that had managed to hold formation began to overrun stragglers. Tug pilots tensely peered into the murky blackness, searching for a glimpse of exhaust flashes ahead, frequently veering violently, diving or throttling back, to avoid plowing into a glider or aircraft that suddenly appeared from an unexpected direction. To avoid collision, some formations began to climb above the slower ones and briefly flew layered one above another.

In a quick radio exchange, the leading tow pilots agreed to add 300 feet to the planned 1,500-feet release altitude. This new altitude was to give two additional miles of gliding range to the "poor bastards" in tow—perhaps enough to buck the offshore winds and leave them enough altitude to find the landing zone or at least land. Except within some of the lead flights, order disappeared. A free-for-all ensued in the critical last ten minutes, while the leaders ahead started to climb to 1,800 feet and cut off.

In the dim light of the low half moon, the first seven aircraft made their run exactly on schedule, undetected and undisturbed. Then the defenders awoke. Searchlights swept the sky, and flak batteries began to fire all the way from the beaches to the city. But only two searchlights probed from near the landing area and the flak from the beaches was so light and scanty that no aircraft was seriously damaged. The wing commander later said that there was no flak within several thousand yards of the glider release point. However, the lights and flares dazzled the pilots, and the smoke of the firing, borne on the northwest wind, drifted over the shore and the release area. Confusion set in. The pilots found it increasingly difficult to judge their positions or even see the shore. Several of them found that if they turned due west, the land was silhouetted beneath the moon. Others who had to swing around and repeat their runs flew through the formations behind them. Some pilots, anxious to allow for the wind, released CG-4A's from as high as 3,000 feet so that they passed through, rather than under, the stream of traffic. Several formations had overrun each other and released simultaneously. The air was at times crowded with aircraft and gliders coming from all directions.

In this melee, teamwork between towing pilot and glider pilot proved inadequate. After all, they had never rehearsed releases under anything like combat conditions and none in near-gale winds. To add to their troubles, between 25 and 30 percent of the intercom sets, which were designed to

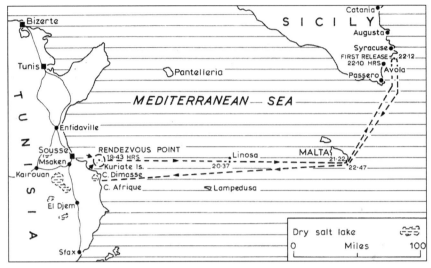

Flight paths for Operation "Ladbroke."

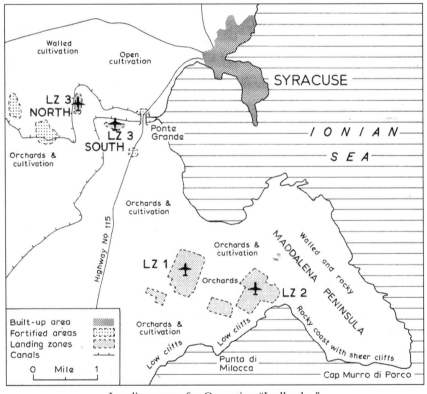

Landing zones for Operation "Ladbroke."

provide telephone connections between the tow aircraft and the glider, worked badly or not at all. The gliders were supposed to cast off on oral or visual signals from the plane. Instead, about a dozen tows released their gliders and at least half a dozen glider crews cut loose without a proper signal. Winds blew fourteen combinations of the 28th Squadron well east of its course. Two became so completely lost that they turned back. One CG-4A was accidentally released en route, and one Horsa broke loose from its tow. Two others turned back because they could not orientate themselves after reaching Sicily. Some stragglers mistook distant parts of the coast for their objective and cut away. Five landed between Cape Passero and Avola, fifteen miles south of their objective. About a half dozen more, mistakenly released in that area, came down in the water. One glider was released near Augusta, fifteen miles north of Syracuse.

Those gliders in what remained of the main serials were being released at least 3,000 yards from the shore. But either the extra 300 feet of altitude was not enough to fly the distance (because the gliders had been too heavily loaded) or, as many cursing glider pilots asserted later, the aircraft had not been 3,000 yards, but twice that, or even miles away when they were released. Even in daylight and the most ideal of circumstances, they could not have hoped to glide to shore.

Dennis E. McClendon, piloting an American C-47 towing a CG-4A with Sergeant Evans of the British Glider Regiment at the controls, was one of the four combinations in his flight element. Looking for his landing zone, McClendon headed directly at a dim shape in the water a few miles south of Cape Passero. Suddenly, the "shape" lighted up. Red lines of tracer rounds flew toward them, and then the blue-white orbs of star shells showed the outline of a merchantman. They could clearly see all the aircraft and gliders of their four-plane formation.

Captain Johnny B. Blalock, one element leader, turned into the left-echeloned element to avoid flying directly over the stacks of Allied convoys. He nearly spun out of formation and into the drink, but somehow managed to stay in number four position.

Five miles farther ahead, another ship fired at pointblank range. Again, Blalock turned and flew into the echelon to avoid the fire. This time he was just a shade too abrupt; the formation simply dissolved before him. Somehow, he passed under the other three aircraft and gliders. Since they were flying at 200 feet, McClendon knew very well that what Blalock had done was impossible. But Blalock made it.

Once released, the glider pilots had trouble in finding their way. Over half could not see the shore, and very few could recognize inland landmarks by which to get a "fix" on their landing zones. Of forty-nine gliders that landed within ten miles of their objective, only two CG-4A's landed on LZ 1. Twenty gliders landed within a mile of the zone. Only one CG-4A managed to get to LZ 2, and it hit a tree. The enemy hit a Horsa carrying a Bangalore torpedo. It was also carrying the commander of the mission, Major Ballinger. The glider blew up in mid-air.

In the case of gliders, a miss is often as bad as a mile. The CG-4A could skid to a stop within 150 yards, but any obstacle on the landing area or in the last 100 yards of the approach generally caused a crash. In such cases, the hinged cargo door in the nose of the glider usually jammed shut.

Orchards and vineyards crisscrossed the land and, especially to the east, the fields were small and bounded by the stone walls that are characteristic of southern Italy. Seven CG-4A's hit trees, and six CG-4A's and two Horsas crashed into walls. Many others had rough landings. One Horsa flew head on into the canal bank that was almost on the edge of its landing zone and only 400 yards from the bridge.

Luckily, McClendon found some unmistakable landmarks as he proceeded toward Syracuse during the next half hour. He came in forty minutes late, flew directly inland toward his assigned glider landing zone, and signaled "go" to Sergeant Evans. Evans cut loose immediately to become one of four glider pilots who landed where he was supposed to that night.

Lieutenant L. Withers, leader of the platoon riding in Galpin's glider, wasted no time awaiting the arrival of reinforcements from the gliders landing in widely outlying areas. He and five men swam the canal and made for the pillbox at the north end of the bridge. According to orders, the rest of his platoon attacked the enemy from the south. They took the bridge, removed the demolition charges and threw them in the river. Reinforcements arrived shortly from another Horsa, which had landed about a half mile to the south. By early morning, eight officers and sixty-five enlisted men were holding the bridge. They were joined at about 0730 hours by a small group, including an American glider pilot, who had fought their way northward from the vicinity of the CG-4A landing zones.

At 0800 hours, enemy counterattacks, one led by four armored cars, began. Soon heavy and deadly accurate mortar fire began hitting the British positions. Short of ammunition for all weapons, the defenders could not fire back with an adequate volume of fire to silence the enemy mortars or machine guns. A big field gun began ranging in. In finding the range, it began to shell the position heavily. The enemy pressure began to be felt as soldier after soldier fell to shrapnel and bullets.

By 1500 hours, the enemy had wiped out the small defending outposts and infiltrated the British position. At 1530 hours, only fifteen men remained unwounded, and these were cornered at the point where the canal joins the Mediterranean, in an area devoid of trees, rock outcroppings or other protection. In a matter of a few minutes, the enemy swept over the position. Half an hour later, guided to the position by several glidermen who had evaded capture when the enemy retook the bridge, a battalion of Scots Fusiliers attacked and quickly won back everything that the gallant South Staffords had originally taken.

As the seesaw battle at the bridge was taking place, survivors of the outlying gliders, too far away to come to the assistance of those at the bridge, were nevertheless writing their own histories. A Waco carrying Colonel O. L. Jones, the deputy commander of the brigade, landed near an Italian coastal battery. He saw no other gliders. Colonel Jones made a hurried reconnaissance. From the barbed wire and the number of enemy he could hear and glimpse, he assumed that an enemy battery too formidable to assault in the dark stood nearby. He therefore led his men to a nearby farmyard to await dawn.

At first light, he made another reconnaissance and, as he had thought, found a well-dug-in enemy artillery position. Colonel Jones developed a thorough plan of attack. At 1115 hours, leading a small force of staff officers, radio operators and glider pilots, he attacked. Under the protection of withering small-arms fire from others in positions behind, one wave moved forward. Drawing close, they began throwing hand grenades into the cowering defenders, who were soon overrun. Jones's party blew up five field guns and an ammunition dump.

Another element abandoned its glider, which was being rapidly swamped 250 yards offshore. With bullets and rounds of artillery churning up the waters, the men swam for shore. Major Breman, two other line officers, one medical officer, the major's orderly and a radio operator managed to reach the pebbled beach. They then had to snake through a twenty-foot belt of barbed wire, somehow avoiding any major confrontation with the enemy. Managing to do so, they started on a ten-mile march spotted with adventures. After getting by the beach defenses, they attacked and captured two pillboxes. Later, they fought several minor enemy elements. By the time they reached their parent element, they had taken twenty-one prisoners, three machine guns and an antitank gun.

A similar fate happened to so many others. Chatterton's glider, which also carried Brigadier Hicks, commander of the Airborne Brigade, released too far from shore. Chatterton realized he could not make the shore, and so steered for a black patch which loomed ahead, hoping that it was a small island. He had almost reached it when a stream of tracer bullets came from its summit. A searchlight was turned on, and he perceived he was approaching a steep cliff. He put the glider into a right-hand stalling turn and plunged seawards. At that moment, a shell hit his starboard wing and the glider, damaged, struck the waves. Its occupants began to claw their way out. Only one was injured, but they were in a sorry situation, a mile from shore, illuminated by a searchlight and under intermittent but heavy machine-gun fire.

"All is not well, Bill!" Brigadier Hicks murmured to his executive officer, as he crawled on to the undamaged wing.

The pilots and their passengers lay or crouched on the wing, watching other gliders making for the shore. Many did not reach it, but fell into the sea like their own. Soon they heard the crackle of fire on the coast, accompanied by the flash of tracer. Chatterton, Hicks and the rest decided to swim for it. Leaving the wrecked and water-logged glider, they struck out for the beach, reached it eventually and fell in with a party that had been more fortunate than themselves and was on its way to dispose of a coastal battery. After some time, they arrived at the headquarters of the airborne force.

After releasing their gliders, the troop carriers dropped their tow ropes, turned south and beat it for home at full throttle. Most of them followed orders to keep above 6,000 feet until past Malta to avoid meeting seagoing convoys. Several aircraft did encounter convoys, but because they were at high altitudes and the timing of the flight coincided with information of the airborne attack, the ships held their fire.

Malta blazed with searchlights. Beyond Malta, the troop carriers descended to 2,500 feet. Icing soon forced some to other levels. They then headed straight for Tunisia. The first aircraft of the 60th Troop Carrier Group got home at 0015 hours, and the first from the 62nd Troop Carrier Group at 0055 hours. Five pilots went astray, presumably because of erroneous information on direction from beams, with one landing as far away as Tripoli. Nevertheless, every one of the 137 aircraft that had left Africa on the "Ladbroke" mission had landed safely in friendly territory before dawn.

Despite some misgivings, the tow pilots' initial reports indicated that 95 percent of the gliders had been released at approximately the proper point. By 11 July, the staff of the 51st Troop Carrier Wing had calculated that more than seventy gliders had landed in Sicily. Even this figure seems four times more than the evidence warrants. In fact, at least sixty-nine CG-4A's came down at sea, and an average of three men in each of these gliders drowned. Seven CG-4A's and three Horsas that were missing with all on board probably shared that fate.

The mercurial General Hopkinson, originator of the attack, burst into vituperative oaths. On the morning of 9 July, he had glowingly commended the members of the 51st Troop Carrier Wing for their efficiency and cooperation. When picked up that night from his waterlogged, wrecked glider, he cursed the wing with every breath he could muster. His men did not hesitate to accuse the troop carriers of flinching from enemy flak, and the charge was later to bring about brawls between British troop-carrier and airborne men in many an English tavern.

Troop-carrier pilots accused their flight element leaders of leading them too far offshore. This is borne out by the fact that of the first seven planes that released without any disturbance by enemy action, only two gliders reached land.

Some tug pilots may have been rattled by their first exposure to flak. Others, tense and overeager, released too soon. Most misjudged their position in the darkness and confusion. Glider operations with release over water were known to be very difficult—and doubly difficult in darkness. The writers of airborne doctrine in the United States and in England would have held that a mission involving both features was unsound; it turned out to be exactly that.

Even if all the pilots had had nerves of steel and eyes like owls, many would have failed through an error in the planning. The altitudes prescribed for the gliders were not sufficient to enable them to reach their landing zones against the strong wind. The CG-4A pilots presumably did not minimize their achievements, but few of them claimed to have glided more than two and a half miles, and their average free flight seems to have been barely two miles. On that basis, if orders for the release had been followed exactly, a large percentage of the CG-4A's would not have reached the landing zones.

Of the 137 gliders that started out, only 49 CG-4A's and 5 Horsas landed in Sicily. Tow planes released all but one of these gliders at higher than 3,000 feet. About 25 of the 49 CG-4A's were reportedly released within a mile of the shore, and three others that reached land had been given added range by being released at altitudes of more than 1,000 feet greater than that prescribed; facts accounting for their being able to reach Sicily successfully. Only 9 of the 49 were released at approximately the planned altitude and distance from their LZ's.

The conclusion to be drawn from these facts was clearly seen and frankly stated by American generals Paul L. Williams and Raymond A. Dunn. The fault lay in the planning and, in particular, in the release point set for the CG-4A's. If that point had been over the shore, few pilots could have mistaken it. Also, if it had been 1,000 feet higher, the troop-carrier pilots could have adjusted their positions and the glider pilots could have compensated for the strong head wind. As it was, the glider pilots had to make the best of a bad situation.

Because so many gliders either ditched at sea or vanished with all hands, it is impossible to say exactly how many were released in the proper area. Nevertheless, it is estimated that between 109 and 119 planes, towing a force of more than 1,200 fighting men, released their gliders within what would have been in full view of the landing zones and of Syracuse itself during daylight hours. Near as they were, not more than one out of the fifteen men each glider carried was able to reach the objective area that night.

General Montgomery later stated that the taking of Ponte Grande saved him seven days. In addition, local actions around the many widely scattered gliders undoubtedly damaged enemy communications and morale. But whatever might be said to its credit, "Ladbroke" was costly and inefficient. A month later, the casualties were calculated at 605 officers and men, of whom 326 were missing, probably drowned—a total representing one half of the assault force. In return for this sacrifice, only about 5 percent of all the airborne personnel that flew from Africa had gone into action at the Ponte Grande Bridge and captured it.

On 12 July, the 51st Troop Carrier Wing began briefing for Operation "Fustian," Montgomery's bid to take the Primosole Bridge over the Simeto River, about five miles south of the city of Catania. The operation was postponed, however. The Eighth Army was slowing down and not within striking distance. Next day, however, Montgomery decided on an all-out effort to break through into the Catania Plain before the Germans could consolidate their defenses. A swift crossing of the Simeto was essential to his plan.

At 1630 hours on 13 July, the troop carriers got the alert for "Fustian." The final briefing prior to the commencement of operations took place at 1745 hours.

"Fustian" was a 135-plane mission, manned mainly by paratroopers and reinforced by glider-borne artillery. The 51st Troop Carrier Wing assigned 105 C-47's—51 each from the 60th and 62nd Groups and three from the 64th Group—to the mission. Reinforced by 11 Albemarles of the 38th Wing, these were to carry 1,856 personnel from the British 1st Parachute Brigade, with some engineer and medical personnel accompanying them. Following them would be 8 CG-4A's and 11 Horsas, transporting 77 artillerymen, 10 6-pounder guns, and 18 jeeps. Doing the towing were 12 Albemarles and 7 Halifaxes of the 38th Wing.

Paratroop aircraft began taking off from two fields at 1920 on 13 July, ten minutes ahead of schedule; others began taking off from two other fields half an hour later. It took forty-five minutes to get each serial in the air. At 2200 hours, gliders began taking off. This timing gave the paratroops about two hours to land and secure the glider-landing area before gliders arrived, a tactic in full accordance with Allied airborne doctrine.

One Halifax had to be replaced at the last minute by an Albemarle. A C-47 returned immediately with engine trouble and was replaced by a substitute.

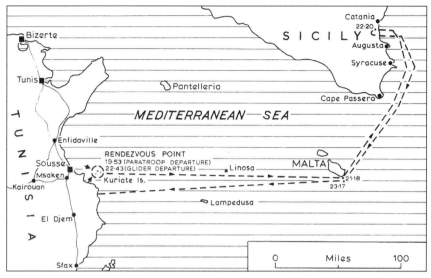

Flight paths for Operation "Fustian."

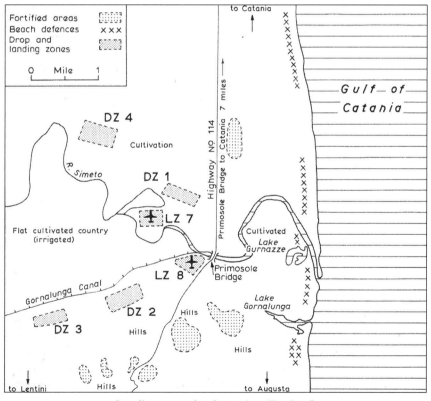

Landing zones for Operation "Fustian."

Take-off accidents and a case of faulty controls prevented two CG-4A's and a Horsa glider from leaving Africa. One C-47 and an Albemarle carrying paratroops turned back with engine trouble before they reached Malta.

The planes assembled over Tunisia at below 1,000 feet, and headed out to sea over the "Ladbroke" course. The paratroopers' C-47's flew at 140 miles an hour. The Albemarles towing the gliders cruised at 125 miles an hour and the Halifaxes at 145 miles an hour.

The weather was clear and calm, as had been forecast. The sun set before Malta was reached, but a half-moon shone brightly through a slight haze, making navigation easier than in Operation "Ladbroke." After rounding Malta, five miles to the southeast of Delimara Point, the troop carriers set out on a senselessly complex five-turn course, designed to keep them ten miles off the coast of Sicily until they were opposite the mouth of the Simeto River, yet out of the range of the guns of Allied convoys along the coast. Low-flying aircraft would be easy targets, and the airborne forces were given their course to avoid being shot at, as had happened so tragically several days earlier in parachute operation "Husky." The British naval commander had been notified of the route and the schedule for "Fustian" and had approved them. For further safety, the aircraft pilots had been briefed to fly at least six miles offshore until they approached their objective.

Somehow, however, the precautions taken to avoid convoys were not carried out. The C-47's found their complicated route passing over many ships. Pilots saw one convoy between Linosa and Malta; another, sighted north of Malta, fired on three Albemarles towing gliders.

The formations got into real trouble, however, in the forty-mile approach to Cape Passero, where the troop carrier route bordered the naval zone below. Thirty-three aircraft strafed above the ships and naval guns, alerted and tensely awaiting an air attack by the Germans, mistakenly opened fire on the friendly aircraft. Two aircraft dived into the sea. Nine others had been so shredded by fires from the ships and had so many pilots and passengers wounded, that they turned back to Africa. Two aircraft taking evasive action collided.

By the time the glider formation crossed the shore, one third had been lost. One glider released accidentally over the sea, and four were shot down. The Horsas had to reach LZ 8, a 500-yard triangle touching the bridge at one point; the CG-4A's aimed for LZ 7.

Piloting a Horsa, Staff Sergeant White could see the landing zones clearly, since enemy batteries firing below and flaming tracers and explosions ahead were "far brighter than the landing lights set out by the parachutist pathfinders." One by one, the pilots broke away from the tow planes in the intense flak. Riddled by the German fire, one landed northeast of Lentini, but only one man aboard was wounded. One crashed into the river, killing or maiming all except one airborne soldier. Another carrying the battery headquarters crashed and killed or injured everyone in it.

Sergeant White came over LZ 8 twenty minutes behind schedule. He cut off, circled downward through the fire and made a jarring landing 100 yards south of Primosole Bridge. He had no casualties, but the rough landing had shaken the jeep and gun about in the glider so that it took some time to get them out.

Lieutenant Thomas brought his Horsa down successfully, but seven miles from LZ 8, too far to give White's force any early help. Three other Horsas had landed farther away. The jeep could not be removed from one, but the personnel, along with the parties from the other two, hauled three guns through the night towards the bridge with their jeeps. There they joined up with Thomas's and White's parties. Combined with paratroopers, the force at the bridge numbered 250; they had two mortars and three antitank guns. Major R. T. H. Lonsdale was in command.

At 0630 hours, German forces, which had been rushed in by truck from Catania, attacked and drove the airborne troops from the north end of the bridge. In the seesaw fighting that ensued, the airborne forces, supported by the pounding fire of the 6-inch guns of an Allied cruiser anchored offshore, finally seized the bridge. As a result, the Royal Navy, which had so nearly wrecked "Fustian," played a part in saving it. Just before dark, Eighth Army tanks appeared in the distance, and the Germans fell back.

"Ladbroke" taught the folly of releasing gliders in the dark over water. It showed the advisability of having large landing zones and pointed up the weaknesses of the CG-4A glider: the inability to carry guns with prime movers for them and a tendency for the cargo door in the nose to jam shut during landing.

In some respects, the Allied airborne operations in Sicily bore similarities to the German airborne invasion of Crete. In each case, the attacker considered the operation a disappointment, while the defender considered the operation a more or less spectacular success. Each operation was something of a turning point for the airborne effort in the respective military establishments. For the Germans, Crete was the end of major airborne operations. For the Allies, Sicily was only the beginning of airborne operations on an even larger scale.

To a large segment of American military opinion, the Sicilian operations seemed to demonstrate the costly futility of large airborne operations. Secretary of War Stimson leaned to that view, and Lieutenant General Lesley J. McNair, commanding general of the Army Ground Forces, later wrote:

After the airborne operations in Africa and Sicily, my staff and I had become convinced of the impracticability of handling large airborne units. I was prepared to recommend to the War Department that airborne divisions be abandoned in our scheme of organization and that the airborne effort be restricted to parachute units of battalion size or smaller.

CHAPTER 6:

Sharpening the Eagle's Talons

Join the glider troops! No flight pay! No jump pay!
But never a dull moment.

The first U.S. Army air-landing unit—a troop formation that went into combat in either gliders or powered aircraft—was the 550th Infantry Airborne Battalion, activated in the Canal Zone in Panama in July 1941. Nevertheless, it was the 88th Airborne Battalion, activated in November 1942 at Fort Bragg, North Carolina, along with several parachute infantry regiments and the Airborne Command, that became the nucleus of the greatest field army to be transported by gliders and aircraft that the world has ever had. It was to grow to a force of five airborne divisions, a number of separate parachute infantry regiments and many separate support units. It was headed by a corps headquarters and, eventually, an Allied field army airborne headquarters to command combined American and British operations.

But the inauguration of the airborne effort had more than its share of indecisions. At the time of the creation of the 88th Airborne Battalion, there was no indication of its future role as a glider unit. It was organized on an experimental basis and consisted of a motorcycle company, some bicycle elements, light armor and light military guns and equipment. This basis would enable planners to experiment with it in air-transport operations, which they did on a meager scale, calling for the subordinate units to fly in any of several models of powered aircraft under various test conditions.

Experiments were conducted in loading and lashing equipment with several kinds of tie-down devices, which were later to be used in aircraft in worldwide parachute and glider operations. It was not an uncommon experience for a young lieutenant to find himself with a few men in the cargo compartment of a CG-4A glider or C-47 aircraft wrestling with a jeep that had come loose from its lashing. Such a sobering experience is reminiscent of sea stories of old, when cannon came loose to wreak havoc in the holds of ships. Nor was the experience less harrowing when live rounds of mortar or artillery ammunition broke loose and were tossed about in the cabin as the glider bounced in the turbulent air above the Carolinas, where many of these tests took place.

The first proposals for an airborne organization came from the Office of the Chief of Infantry. On 6 May 1939, it was suggested to the Operations Office (G3) of the War Department General Staff that consideration be given to organizing a small detachment of air infantry. The initiation of a study on the subject led almost at once to differences of opinion over the control of the project. The chief of engineers contended that, inasmuch as parachutists would be used primarily as demolition teams and saboteurs, the troops ought to be trained and employed by the engineers. The chief of the Army Air Corps held that logically the air infantry should be the "marines of the Air Corps." Consequently, he proposed that they be placed under the jurisdiction of the Army Air Corps and designated "air grenadiers." The chief of fnfantry maintained that parachute forces would fight on the ground as infantry and, to be effective, they would have to be trained as infantry, because "aircraft were to be regarded simply as a means of transporting them to the battlefield."

The issue was not settled quickly. In June 1940, the War Department recommended that the program be taken out of the hands of the chief of infantry and be placed directly under the G3. Shortly thereafter, that staff directorate made a new proposal: that the project be placed under the chief of the Army Air Corps, Major General Henry J. Arnold. This proposal very soon had Arnold's strong support. But it met with the vigorous objections of Brigadier General Lesley J. McNair, chief of staff of the newly organized General Headquarters (GHQ). He insisted, as had the chief of the infantry before him, that air transport was only another means of transportation, and that the primary mission of parachute forces was ground action. A later proposal was that the project be placed directly under GHQ, since the forces had elements of several branches of service in them.

The matter came to a head with a prolonged discussion on 27 August 1940 in the office of Major General William Bryden, deputy chief of the War Department General Staff. At the conclusion of the discussion, General Bryden announced that the project would continue under the supervision of the chief of infantry.

In May 1942, the War Department published *Tactics and Technique of Airborne Troops.* Although it was difficult to say that parachute forces "generally" should perform in a certain way, when no American airborne troops had as yet participated in any kind of an airborne operation, much of what the publication presented remained valid in the test of combat. Much that was in the manual was retained in later statements of policy and doctrine.

The manual did state, however, that parachute forces should seize suitable landing areas and then be reinforced by glider elements. As a result, American doctrine was exactly the reverse of German doctrine in the beginning. Its appearance at this early period lends credence to the idea that parachute-orientated leaders were already in the ascendancy. They were to prevail, despite the evidence of success that German doctrine involving the use of glider-borne forces had provided in combat.

Underlying the training program of any military element is the kind of employment planned for it. Since airborne forces had no traditional role in warfare and no top command decision had been made, a great deal of vagueness surrounded their possible employment at the time when organization began. When training commenced, the development of an airborne program was based more on the impression that the Germans had made in their airborne invasion of Crete than on any concrete notions about the probable employment of airborne divisions in some future invasion of Europe. In other words, there was simply a conviction that some airborne troops would be "handy to have around." Perhaps this is reason enough to justify a military organization, since military missions can rarely be defined in great specificity very far in advance. But until strategic planning anticipated the employment of airborne forces in specified theaters of operations, those forces could not be expected to enjoy a very high priority in training and equipment.

As early as May 1942, in its preliminary forecast for the 1943 Troop Basis, the Operations Division of the GHQ allowed for seven airborne divisions. The troop basis as approved by the War Department reduced the allowance to five divisions. But in the initial stages of the mobilization, there persisted in the minds of the GHQ staff a great deal of conflict and confusion about just when the divisions were to be combat ready, where they were to be used, what their internal structure should be and how many men within a division should be glidermen.

Glider design and production and the airborne troop mobilization program were inextricably intertwined. As a matter of fact, there was no place in the early planning for the airborne division as such. This stemmed from the philosophy of a group of hard-liners in the Army, who thought it a violation of the rule of economy of force to organize divisions solely for airborne operations. These planners assumed that specialized organizations (and their training) should be confined to parachute and special task and test units. That line of thought meant that all infantry divisions should be trained for airborne operations before their departure overseas, within the limitations of the availability of troop-carrier aircraft and gliders. This philosophy was based on the concept of airborne operations being principally the action of forces landed either by aircraft or by glider in areas previously seized by parachutists. The magnitude of this confusion was illustrated on 28 May 1942

A CG-4A glider in tow just leaving the ground.

Douglas C-47s in flight, towing gliders.

when Army Ground Forces (AGF) at Fort Monroe, Virginia, indicated that airborne divisions should not be designated as such; they should be organized as infantry divisions and then trained for airborne operations. But within a month, AGF thinking had changed in favor of a specialized organization. The previously announced policy would be discarded and specifically designated, specially organized airborne divisions should be activated.

As the people who planned the invasion of Europe in 1943 contemplated the use of an American airborne division, General William C. Lee, commander of the 101st Airborne Division, who helped guide the U.S. airborne program, was sent to Great Britain. He returned supporting the AGF viewpoint that special airborne divisions be organized and trained and gave specific recommendations on its organization. His recommendations, together with those of Major William P. Yarborough, the Army Airborne Command intelligence officer, became the basis for a new division's organization. By 19 June 1942, General McNair was prepared to accept that the division should have two glider regiments and one parachute regiment and that training and equipment should be undertaken.

The idea that the airborne division should comprise two glider regiments and one parachute regiment was another manifestation of the earlier concept that the parachutists should only be the spearhead of air-landing forces. General Lee had originally recommended two parachute regiments and one glider regiment, based on the British model. General McNair could find no valid reason for the British organization. Further inquiry suggested that it was born of necessity, rather than based on long-range plans. When intelligence information on German airborne activities was studied, no table of organization could be found that combined parachute and glider troops in one division.[1] It seemed that the Germans had organized special task forces for each operation. The parachute forces were a part of the *Luftwaffe* and the glider forces were taken from the army. In view of plans for a European invasion in less than a year, General McNair recommended that the training of standard infantry divisions continue to enable them to man planes and gliders and that two airborne divisions be formed. They were to be formed from the 82nd Motorized Division, then finishing its training. The resources of the 82nd were augmented by the necessary parachute elements to give the division the paratrooper strength it needed.

Each new division was, in effect, a miniature infantry division consisting of 504 officers and 8,321 enlisted men. It was heavy in combat troops and light in administrative, quartermaster, medical and other logistical elements. It was prepared to land in combat and strike a hard initial blow. No one

---

1. This was, of course, a mistaken viewpoint. *Fallschirmjäger* had a dual role: either to jump or ride in gliders.

expected it to fight for many days, because it simply did not have the men and equipment to do so. It had one parachute regiment, two glider infantry regiments, several battalions of divisional artillery equipped with mountain howitzers, an engineer battalion, a medical company, a signal company and a quartermaster company. It was suggested that the number of parachute and glider regiments might be altered as needed. The proposals won prompt approval in the War Department, and General Eisenhower, then commanding the European theater, expressed the hope that he might have airborne divisions in his forces by 1 April 1943.

Following this plan, the War Department activated the 82nd and the 101st Airborne Divisions at Fort Bragg, North Carolina, on 15 August 1942 under the respective commands of Generals Matthew B. Ridgway and Lee. General Headquarters initially planned to have them assigned to the Airborne Command for airborne training only, but General McNair felt that dividing training responsibility would lead to unsatisfactory results. Consequently, they were placed under the Airborne Command for both basic and airborne training.

There was no great enthusiasm amongst the new glider personnel. There is no indication that the mood ever really changed during the war, even though officers were later given $100 monthly extra in glider pay and the enlisted men $50. General Ridgway, commander of the 82nd Airborne Division, sensed that the men weren't too keen about this glider business. The paratroopers wanted no part of it, naturally. They were volunteers. But they had volunteered to jump, not to ride down to a crash landing in one of these flimsy contraptions of steel tubing and thin canvas. The others were not volunteers. They were being put into gliders arbitrarily, and most of them didn't like it.

He figured he had to do something to boost their confidence, so he asked General Hap Arnold to send a glider down, piloted by a top pilot, so that the division could see what a fine, airworthy vehicle it was. Arnold sent Mike Murphy, an old stunt flyer and a magnificent pilot with all the daring and dash in the world. They lined up the whole division for this demonstration, which was designed to convert the skeptics. Ridgway felt that the division commander should go along on this first flight, so he went out and crawled in beside Mike. As soon as he was strapped in, Murphy asked the general how he felt about doing a few loops. Ridgway told him he didn't see any sense in doing a few loops. Well, Murphy said, if the general wanted the boys to see what a glider could do, he ought "to really wring it out for them." Ridgway then said that if Murphy could stand it, the general guessed he could.

They went up to about 4,000 feet and cut loose and Murphy did everything with the CG-4A glider that a powered plane could do. It was a big ship and

Murphy did a vertical bank with it and a slow roll or two. He then he looped it three times. When they came out of the last one, the ground looked awfully close. Murphy then landed, pulling up about three feet short of the man he had positioned on the runway, just to demonstrate how well the glider could be controlled. That demonstration convinced a lot of doubters that the glider was not the death trap they had heard it was.

The airborne program continued to be buffeted by varying exigencies and unforeseen changes in plans—unforeseen at any rate to the Army Air Corps and headquarters elements that were directly responsible for running the program. The glider segment continued to be hardest hit by these changes.

Then early in 1943, the glider proponents received their first serious blow. It came from an unexpected quarter. When the time came to plan for the overseas shipment of an airborne division, the War Department General Staff surprisingly swung around to the position that the ratio of parachute to glider regiments should be changed so that there would be two parachute regiments and one glider regiment in the division. The reason for this modification stemmed more from the problem of shipping gliders on freighters than from a change in the tactical employment of airborne divisions. No one had foreseen earlier what was to occur. One crated CG-4A weighed 20,000 pounds. Even more distressing was the size of the crate used to ship the gliders. It came close to holding the record as the largest shipping container of World War II. The size and weight of gliders crated for overseas shipment was therefore a dominant factor in causing the War Department to cut down on glider shipments to overseas theaters. The reduction in the number of glider regiments was the outcome.

The 82nd Airborne Division, in the throes of getting ready for shipment to Europe, was reorganized. The 326th Glider Infantry Regiment was reassigned from the division to become, for the time being, a part of the 1st Airborne Brigade, a "catch-all" airborne formation at Alliance, Nebraska, and a glider engineer company in the division was converted to a parachute company. A parachute infantry regiment replaced the 326th Glider Infantry Regiment.

Constant conflicts between the Army Air Corps and the Army in matters having to do with the stateside training and operations of the airborne elements made the whole program drag. They became a major factor in determining the training and the nature of the operations that the airborne elements could perform and, ultimately, the success of the whole airborne effort during World War II.

The stateside performance was considerably less successful than desired. Experience to that point only forecast more of the same. Was that to be the case? Would overseas collaboration and performance be any better?

There had always been differences in pay between parachute and glider personnel, and these could only have resulted from overlooking the obvious implications for morale and esprit de corps. The low priority of the Troop Carrier Command in the Army Air Corps led to discrimination against it in the assignment of pilots and communications personnel and in the withholding of such equipment as self-sealing gasoline tanks for troop-carrier aircraft. To fly heavily armed and armored bombers at 300 miles an hour to drop bombs from an altitude of 20,000 feet—that was combat. But to fly an unarmed and unarmored transport through heavy flak at 110 miles an hour, dropping men into a battle zone from an altitude of 500 feet—that was not combat. Further morale problems for troop-carrier units arose from the idleness of glider pilots caught in training bottlenecks or shipped to the Pacific with no glider missions to fly.

Memory is usually kind in dimming some of the most unpleasant recollections of experience, and unattractive accompaniments of war have a way of fading, with the benefit of time and distance, into obscurity. Airborne war thus becomes only the sheer beauty of gliders flying stealthily through the thin clouds of a still moonlit night or the glamour of hundreds of silken canopies drifting earthward from sunny, blue skies. But in the mind of a veteran trooper, the sound of roaring engines, the order to "stand up and hook up," the cry of "Geronimo!" or "Bill Lee!" or the feel of prop blast would set racing through his consciousness deep-seated fears of jumping into the unknown, of facing heavy flak and of the depressing confusion of scattered drops in strange and hostile country. And he would know that plans for the future would have to recall the fears and shortcomings as well as the spectacle and the achievement.

A considerable part of the misfortunes of airborne operations in North Africa, Sicily and Normandy can be attributed to faulty training. In some cases, training in the United States may have been adequate, but its effects were lost when the troop-carrier formations were assigned to cargo-hauling missions for long periods of time. In other cases, the shortage of aircraft and the lack of coordination in the United States had left the training still unsatisfactory when forces were sent overseas. General McNair was interested in seeing airborne divisions trained well for ground combat rather than in perfecting certain techniques peculiar to airborne operations. He had noted a tendency of "trick outfits to overemphasize their tricks."

CHAPTER 7

Orde Wingate's Glider Legacy

General Wingate had told me in Burma that without the gliders and the skill and courage of their pilots, he could not have carried on that operation. From our experiences, we learned a lot of lessons, which I took to England for use in the invasion of France.

MAJOR WILLIAM H. TAYLOR,
COMMANDER, GLIDER PILOTS

In February 1943, General Orde Charles Wingate led a brigade of Chindits on a long-range penetration into Japanese-controlled territory in Burma. Wingate, a student and protégé of T. E. Lawrence—the famed "Lawrence of Arabia"—operated in the jungle until June. Under cover of the tangle of forests and, at times, in the valley of the Irrawaddy, his brigade blew up bridges, tore apart railway tracks and blasted mountains to cause landslides that covered the roads. A force of five C-47's, two old Hudson bombers and some light aircraft sustained the operation by dropping more than 300 tons of food and other supplies in 178 sorties to his several widely separated columns.

Although the operation served only to harass the Japanese, the experience proved invaluable to Wingate and his men. Leaders and troops got "jungle-wise." Wingate spotted and made mental notes of clearings in the jungle that could be converted to make landing strips with some work. Most of all, he gained confidence that he could repeat the performance on a larger scale. The air-ground coordination on this expedition was an Allied pioneering effort in the supply of ground troops from the air.

Summoned to the Quebec conference to advise Allied leaders on the Burma situation, Wingate managed to sell Winston Churchill on the idea of more extensive air-support operations as a way to break the stalemate in the China-Burma-India theater. He proposed a grand scheme to strike with air-landing forces in areas not held by the Japanese, establish landing fields and then move to cut Japanese lines of communication to the north. Churchill—a great one for a daring plan—and President Roosevelt gave their support to the operation, particularly since it was the only offensive action that held some hope of giving the Allies sorely needed success in that theater.

General Arnold carried Churchill's and Roosevelt's decision to Washington and summoned two fighter pilots, Colonels Philip G. Cochran and John R. Alison. Arnold named Cochran to command Project 9, the unorthodox commando-support project that was to carry out the mission. Alison became Cochran's deputy. Seymour Johnson Air Base in Goldsboro, North Carolina, became the project's headquarters. Close friends, Cochran and Alison had only a few months to collect aircraft, crate and ship them, train pilots, mechanics and crews and transfer the whole outfit to Burma, where Wingate and Lord Louis Mountbatten anxiously awaited their arrival.

Given top priority and supported by Arnold's "to hell with administration and paperwork, go out and fight" attitude, Cochran and Alison dived into their work. They called for volunteers from air-transport units stationed at Seymour Johnson and nearby bases. From an overwhelming number of volunteers, they selected 75 glider pilots, a sizeable number of light aircraft pilots—chosen largely for their additional skill as mechanics—and a number of enlisted men. By October, the first of the force of 523 officers and men were flying to India, where they landed in November 1943 and set up a base. Project 9 became the 5318th Provisional Air Unit, soon to go into action as the 1st Air Commando Force. Its airborne assault aircraft consisted of 150 aircraft: CG-4A gliders, an air-ground coordination force of L-1's and L-5's, a transport section of C-47's and C-64's and a fighter and fighter-bomber fleet of P-47's and B-25's. It also had 75 TG-5 training gliders.

The glider elements moved to Barrackpore and used RAF fields at Hailakandi and Lalaghat in Assam. Life was primitive, grimy and beardy. After the force assembled from the States, Cochran set to the task of welding his heterogeneous group and training it for the missions ahead.

Mules imported from the States were playing an important part in hauling supplies through the jungle. It was foreseen that they would speed Wingate's operation considerably if they could be flown into forward areas, where they would haul logs from across jungle paths or airstrips or carry guns and ammunition packs. To solve the especially knotty problem of flying mules into operational areas, Cochran set up a series of experiments. Since mules had a reputation for cantankerousness, Cochran's men decided to restrain the mules so that the gliders, pilots and mule handlers might survive flashing hoofs and gnashing teeth. Crews reinforced cargo floors and constructed three stalls of bamboo covered with coconut matting. For the first test flight, crews constructed special platforms to which the mules could be tied and thus immobilized. Apprehensive veterinarians stood by to administer knockout shots. Before these ideas were put into practice, an apologetic private, who

CG-4As of the 1st Air Commando Force ready for action at Lalaghat in India.

General Wingate and Colonel Cochran briefing British and American officers at Haile-kandi.

had civilian muleskinner experience, plausibly suggested that perhaps the mules could just be led into stalls and that the animals might readily comply.

This farmyard idea was tried while the nervous brass stood by. To their astonishment, three mules calmly took their places in the stalls. Surprisingly, mules became the most tranquil and adaptable glider riders in Burma. Colonel Cochran recalls that mules were naturals for the air age, leaning as a glider banked and taking turbulence and landing shock in their stride. They created no rumpus in flight, and it never became necessary for mule handlers, standing at the ready with a rifle in hand, to pacify an animal with a lethal shot.

Wingate's mission—to cut Japanese communications in central Burma and to force the Japanese to withdraw from all areas north of the 24th parallel—was part of a broad strategy to synchronize General Joseph Stilwell's forces and Colonel Merrill's Marauders and to cut Japanese supply lines conclusively. Relying on air support and on the deep-penetration principle, Wingate's strategy was to land forces by air in two open patches in the jungle between Chowringhee and Myirkyina—dubbed Broadway and Piccadilly—which he had come across in his 1943 operations.

Brigadier Carter's 77th Indian Infantry Brigade moved to Hailekandi and Lalaghat airfield and began preparations for a glider assault, the most enterprising part of Wingate's strategy.

Brigadier Walter D. A. Lentaigne, leading the 111th Indian Infantry Brigade, moved elements of his brigade to two fields, Lalaghat and Tulehal in the Imphal Plain. He then prepared for a move by either gliders or transport aircraft to Aberdeen, another opening slashed out of the jungle.

On 5 February 1944, a month before the planned airborne operation, Brigadier Bernard Fergusson, leading the British 16th Infantry Brigade, marched south on foot from Shingbwiyang, to be joined later by the airborne forces. His brigade left the road at Hamtung to break a way across some of the most difficult land imaginable, carving out each step into the hills with pick and shovel for men and animals to set foot. After they reached Hkalak Go, they set out towards Kanglai.

Here their route came close to Minsin, a Japanese radio communication center which could flash warnings of the brigade's moves. Deciding to destroy the station, Fergusson called on the commandos. On 28 February, a CG-4A took off from Lalaghat. It landed on a sandbank of the Chindwin, carrying seventeen heavily laden personnel. In the process, the glider lost its landing gear and a wing and three men were injured. Alerted by the crash landing, the Japanese attacked, but the Chindits held them off long enough for the pilots to evaporate into the jungle and start a 130-mile trek toward their base with the wounded, which they finally completed. Once the party with the wounded was on its way, the Chindits attacked and destroyed the station.

A day later, two gliders carrying patrols took off to land on a sand bar located just south of where the 16th Infantry Brigade's march would meet the Chindwin River. Their mission was to boobytrap trails the Japanese might take leading to the river and to set up roadblocks on key terrain to stop Japanese thrusts towards the brigade's crossing-points.

By 29 February, the 16th Infantry Brigade had reached the Chindwin. Fergusson selected a crossing site near Singkalind Hkamti, where the Japanese would not be likely to discover his presence. Wingate, who had landed on a sandbar in an American UC-64 aircraft, joined Fergusson there. Fergusson requested boats and equipment to cross the river, and Wingate passed the request on to Colonel Alison's commandos. Two gliders carrying two technicians, twelve collapsed watercraft, outboard motors and gasoline took off at dusk. Plowing through the sand when landing, one glider lost its wheels. As soon as the crews could unload the two gliders, the tow planes swept by and snatched the one flyable glider from the bar. It carried a litter case from the brigade to a hospital, making it the first glider medical evacuation flight for the Allies.

Undetected by the Japanese, the 16th Infantry Brigade crossed the Chindwin on 5 March, using powered pneumatic boats to push bamboo rafts loaded with men, mules and equipment.

Late in the afternoon on the same day, at Lalaghat and Hailekandi, eighty CG-4 gliders parked in two parallel rows and waited for tugs to taxi into position. Some men stood outside, smoking; others nervously entered the gliders and gave a final test pull at the lashings on jeeps, bulldozers and ammunition. It was forty minutes before the gliders were to take off for Piccadilly and Broadway.

By chance, a fighter pilot seeking directions to Lalaghat landed at Hailekandi. He was pressed into service as a courier. He flew on to Lalaghat, taking a vital photograph to Colonel Cochran, standing with General Wingate at the head of the column of gliders.

Colonel Cochran unrolled the photograph with General Wingate looking on. Taken two hours earlier by a B-25, it vividly showed Piccadilly, with white parallel lines showing obliquely across the clearing. The conclusion: the Japanese had logged the clearing to create an anti-airlanding barrier, sure death to the gliders now set to take off and land there. Only two days earlier, photos showed no trace of such obstacles. The Piccadilly landings had to be scrapped, and Wingate was then faced with developing a new course of action. He decided to start his campaign using Broadway alone. The matter settled,

A glider in tow at 8,000 feet over the China Hills.

Mules inside a glider, protected by padded bamboo poles and straw matting. They proved to be excellent passengers.

some shifting of troops took place among the gliders to adjust the forces to the single-field landing.

At 1812 hours, the lead tow plane roared down the runway, thirty minutes behind schedule. One glider, then the other, followed in double tow. The aircraft struggled heroically at full throttle over the runway. The gliders were finally raised off the turf, the aircraft having had to use almost the whole field in the straining effort. Gliders built to carry no more than 3,750 pounds were carrying 4,500 pounds—between 25 and 30 percent overweight and far beyond established safety limits—a factor that was soon to produce tragic results.

It so happened that Wingate's supply officers had no interest in the technical limitations of gliders. Their goal was to deliver supplies, and they were not versed in the temperament of the glider. Area capacity in a glider, not weight, seemed to be their criterion.

In an attempt to meet the requirements of General Wingate's officers for greater loads than prescribed, Major William H. Taylor, the glider pilot commander, had initially agreed to accept 4,000-pound loads—250 pounds in excess of prescribed limits. The Wingate supply officers argued that they required more.

Major Taylor finally approved a 4,500-pound load maximum. But then load trouble came from an unexpected quarter. Gurkha and British forces, not aware of the danger that would be caused to a glider and its passengers by taking non-regulation articles, sneaked extra ammunition and food on board. Cumulatively, all weight added up to critical overloads. Yet, despite these technical violations, gliders were going into the mission in double tow at night.[1]

Three more aircraft, each towing two gliders, followed in rapid succession. The combinations circled the field, sluggishly and monotonously climbing slowly to get at least 8,000 feet altitude to clear the 7,000-foot range to the east. The four combinations carried Colonel Alison, a pathfinding team and a protective force of the King's Regiment commanded by Colonel W. P. Scott.

Half an hour later, the main echelon, carrying Brigadier Calvert and the forward headquarters of the 77th Indian Infantry Brigade, took off. Traffic control had been well organized beforehand, and hook-ups and take-offs went like clockwork.

At the moment of take-off, all appeared to be going well. With the objective two-and-a-half hours distant, it would be at least another four to five hours

---

1. Apparently, such practices were much too frequent. One pilot complained, after another operation, that he had carried 6,400 pounds: a bulldozer, six heavy camouflage nets and many cans of gas. It took two hours to reach 4,000 feet of altitude in double tow.

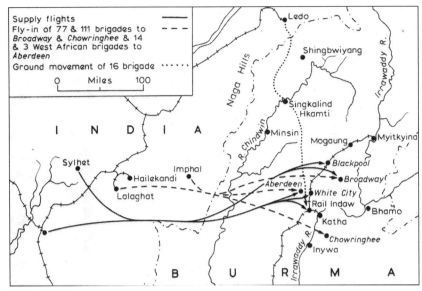

Airborne assault operations in Burma.

before Lalaghat air base had positive news of how things were going. Except for a few necessary lights, the field was dark. Some thirty gliders stood parked along the strip, awaiting returning aircraft to tow them to Broadway.

It was perhaps fifteen minutes before word reached Colonel Cochran at the field that two gliders had broken loose before crossing the mountains. One landed somewhere beyond the field. Soon an aircraft came in, far ahead of schedule. Its gliders had been lost halfway. Then more pilots returned, all with dismal reports of having lost their gliders. Tow ropes, apparently deteriorated by months of rain and hot sun, had broken. Some gliders loads were seriously off center and caused pilot fatigue or fear, making them release their gliders prematurely. Turbulence forced others to break away.

Cochran and Wingate stood helplessly by, only able to await developments and completely uncertain of how many, if any, gliders had reached Broadway. Tension broke when a faint "Soyalink" crackled through the ether. It meant "send no more gliders." General Wingate abided by the request, although Cochran urged crowding a glider rescue force into the restricted Broadway field, come hell or high water.

Colonel Alison and the leading gliders had an almost uneventful flight until the landing. Major Taylor came in first, touched ground, neatly "leapt" an elephant watering hole, lost a wheel when he hit the ground on the other side again and stopped fifty yards from the place where he had been designated to land. Several gliders carrying Chindits came in and ground to a halt. The soldiers scrambled into the darkness and evaporated into the further blackness on their way to defend the strip.

The glider with Colonel Oley Olsen, who was to command at Broadway, did not appear. Nor did the one carrying the regular lighting equipment. After a sixteen-hour struggle to get through the jungle, a rescue crew got to the glider carrying the lighting equipment, which had crashed not far from Broadway. All on board were dead.

Aerial photographs had not revealed how poor a field Broadway was for landing. Some old teak logs lay hidden in the tall grass. Deep scars from logs hauled over the area rutted the field. Six of the eight advance-party gliders had made the harrowing landings, but all suffered minor to serious damage. The radio was inoperable.

When the main flight started to land, Alison had no way of warning the incoming gliders of the perils in their path. He and his men tried shouting, but to no avail. Gliders piled into, onto, skipped over and crashed headlong into other gliders. Alison desperately wanted to tell Cochran at Lalaghat "no more gliders!" He could not.

Yet gliders kept piling in. The glider carrying the only bulldozer whistled by. All heard a terrifying crash. Everyone thought they knew then that they would never be able to hold Broadway; their only means of converting it into a landing strip was gone. Men ran over to count the dead. They found the glider fuselage among tall trees, its nose in the air, the wings ripped away. Miraculously, the bulldozer sat in front of the glider almost undamaged. Thrust forward by the impact, the bulldozer had pulled the pilot and co-pilot up into the nose, safely out of its way, as it plunged out of the glider.

At 0227 hours, the radio finally operated long enough for Alison to signal "Soyalink." Eight gliders of the second wave on their way were recalled, a ninth carrying another bulldozer continued. Cochran had sent these gliders up in single tow after determining the double tow was too dangerous. No more accidental or other releases in flight occurred.

Major Taylor's after-action report showed that fifty-four gliders carrying 839 men, forty-one tons of equipment and six mules had taken off to Broadway. In addition to the three that had broken loose near Lalaghat, a tug plane having fuel trouble cut off two. Another having electrical problems cut off two. Eight gliders landed east of the Chindwin River. The personnel from two of these got back to friendly bases along the Chindwin; those of another kept on through the jungle to Broadway. Those of another two fell into Japanese hands, and two gliders and their personnel were never found. Among premature releases over Broadway, two gliders crashed, killing all but two soldiers. Checking the gliders after the landing, Taylor found only three still flyable.

Tow-ropes laid out ready to be hooked to gliders and planes for the take-off from Lalaghat.

Last-minute reconnaissance photo of "Picadilly" showing that the Japanese had covered the airstrip with logs to prevent gliders from landing.

Suspicious of the cause, and remembering his own unexplainably rapid landing speed, Major Taylor checked his load the morning after. He found he had 6,000 pounds, almost twice as much as the glider was meant to carry. No wonder the cost in gliders was so high!

Brigadier Calvert did what he could to create some order and organization out of the chaos. He had 478 men left. Three mules arrived safely. Fortunately, no Japanese attacked, and Calvert's patrols discovered none the next day, probing as far as five miles into the jungle. Wingate got what he wanted, a landing unmolested by the Japanese. Thank God!

By evening, engineers had cleared wreckage and built a 5,000-foot runway. The field was secure. Four RAF squadrons, with some assistance from the U.S. 27th and 315th Troop Carrier Squadrons and the 1st Air Commando Group—some sixty aircraft in all—flew the remainder of the 77th and 111th Indian Infantry Brigades and supplies into Broadway from Lalaghat and Imphal, using the improvised strip without difficulty.

The fly-in continued at full speed through the night of 10 March. To complete the movement, four more flights landed at Broadway the next night.

On the same night that the first troop transports landed at Broadway, twelve gliders landed at Chowringhee, fifty miles to the south. Soaring over the mountains, the gliders swayed and dipped like flying surfboards when caught in sudden up and down drafts. Japanese antiaircraft guns opened up on them when they passed over the Chindwin River, but all got through. Flight Officer Jackie Coogan, former Hollywood child actor, piloted the first glider. Major William T. Cherry, Jr., piloted his tow plane.

Coogan cut his glider loose at 1,000 feet, did a 360-degree turn and landed at 120 miles an hour on the unlighted field, which was covered with four-foot-high grass. He immediately started laying out smudge pots to guide in the other gliders. Meanwhile, his load of Gurkha troops fanned out to defend the field.

In another glider on the same mission, pilot Charles Turner, flying over the mountains at 7,000 feet, turned around to see a Gurkha lurching to the rear of the glider, unsteady in the turbulent air. The uncomfortable Gurkha was heeding nature's call. Invasion gliders have no facilities for such human frailties. That didn't deter the Gurkha. He simply stepped onto the frail fabric covering the tubing, the only flooring in that section of the glider, and made his own facilities. Turner almost fainted when he saw the Gurkha standing unconcerned on the fabric which ordinarily supported no more than a five-pound weight. How it held his hobnailed boots is still a major mystery. But the pilot showed Major Taylor the Gurkha's footprints to prove it.

All but one glider landed safely. One overshot the field and crashed, killing the pilot and two engineers and destroying the tractor it carried. Without a tractor, the engineers from the other gliders could make little progress in building an airstrip the first night. Next day, everybody kept out of sight so as not to arouse Japanese curiosity or risk an attack.

The troops holding Chowringhee radioed their plight to Broadway. They got no response the next day. In order to make a landing field of sorts, the Gurkhas went to work at sundown slashing at the four-foot grass with their kukri knives. They proceeded to clear twelve acres of land. At 2100 hours, all heard the sound of aircraft engines. Coogan and others had already set out working beacons. A glider piloted by Flight Officer William Mohr, carrying a bulldozer and its operator, Corporal Walter Hybarger, arrived from Broadway. Four more gliders came in from Lalaghat about fifteen minutes later with more equipment. By the next morning, enough of a strip had been prepared for C-47's to start landing.

Chowringhee was abandoned after receiving a total of 125 landings through the night of 9 March. Of the seventeen gliders landed at Chowringhee, the commandos recovered fifteen by snatch take-offs.

This field was much more exposed than Broadway. Troops landing there had to cross the Irrawaddy River from east to west before they could unite with the main body of Chindits. By the night of 9 March, it was evident that Broadway could accommodate the flights remaining to be flown. Japanese aircraft attacked Chowringhee, shortly after two crippled C-47's had been flown out, and just after the last ground troops had left the area.

From the night of 5 March through to the end of Operation "Thursday," the Air Commandos flew seventy-four glider sorties.

For the Broadway operation, the enemy had no warning of Wingate's plans nor had Wingate planned deception missions, but the forced landing of nine gliders near enemy positions provided "an impromptu deception." Two of these came down in the immediate vicinity of a Japanese divisional headquarters, and three near a regimental headquarters. The enemy concluded that an assault on some installations was under way and alerted his landing fields to that effect. Perhaps the deception was more effective because of the long-planned counter-air activity of the Air Commandos—attacks by P-52's and B-25's on nearby airfields. In any event, enemy ignorance of Wingate's airborne operation afforded him time to establish his forces.

By 9 March, the leading elements of the 16th Infantry Brigade reached the Irrawaddy River near Inywa. Brigadier Fergusson again called upon the commandos for pneumatic boats and outboard motors. Four gliders took off on the afternoon of the eleventh, loaded down with the equipment. They got over the sand bar in the river just as it turned dark. John Masters, in *The Road Past Mandalay*, vividly describes the landings:

> Fires built by RAF liaison officers with the brigade vaguely outlined the area. The first glider whooshed in, overshot the runway, and disappeared. Liaison officers tried to redirect the others by frantically radioing a warning to the tow-plane pilots to correct their courses to avoid a similar incident. Apparently, the word never reached the glider pilots. The three came down still too high to come into the area outlined, overshot it, and landed 1,000 yards down the sandbar from the fires. There were no trees in the way and plenty of sand stretching down the river. All came in safely.
>
> Unloading parties dashed after the gliders. Men and mules dragged the boats, lifejackets, motors and fuel to the crossing area nearby, as glider pilots got together and shifted the gliders into position for the night snatch take-off. Pilots inserted two tall poles topped by blue lights into the ground, fifty feet apart. Atop the poles spread the looped end of the tow rope, to be caught by the suspended hook of the tow planes. At 0200 hours, tow planes could be heard and, shortly after, were seen overhead, their red recognition lights flashing.
>
> The word went up by radio that all was ready for the first snatch.
>
> The first C-47 came in, flaps down, propellers at full pitch, skimming the bar. A deft maneuver to accomplish even in daytime under ideal conditions, the C-47 pilot misjudged his course and missed the "clothes line" on the first pass. He made it on the third and, in a few seconds, the first glider, soon to be followed by two others, flew into the night. The fourth, which was the first to land, had been so badly damaged it could not be flown out. Accounts of this operation vary, but either five Jap[anese] prisoners, four Burmese traitors, or two ill Gurkhas were snatched up in one of the gliders.

On 18 March, Wingate sent a five-glider mission, code-named "Bladet," twetny-five miles south of Katha. The gliders carried a task force of sixty-five officers and men and three mules to haul the three tons of weapons, food and ammunition necessary to supply them. This was a special mission to drive towards Mandalay, cutting railway lines, blowing bridges and doing what it could to disrupt Japanese communications throughout the Kawlin Wuntho area. It could then direct the 1st Commando bombers to targets.

Again, RAF liaison officers reconnoitered for a suitable glider-landing area. They found one on dry rice paddies near Shwemaunggan, along the Meza

At the Chowringhee airstrip, gliders were moved to the edge of the field and screened under trees.

Men recently landed at Broadway behind the Japanese lines, wait beside their glider for further orders.

River, with no Japanese reported nearby. They set to leveling the low earth banks that rimmed the paddies and built fires to mark the landing area.

Describing the incident, Masters reported that the first glider made a beautiful approach and touchdown, but exactly ninety degrees in the wrong direction. It stopped with a rending crash. Another came in, landing right on the center of the strip in the right direction, but racing at such speed that it ended in the thicket rimming the paddies and virtually vanished in the tangle of bamboo and vines. A third hit a giant clump of bamboo that caught it and held it hanging, nose down.

The RAF liaison officers, with the assistance of the task force that gradually came to their assistance, recovered most of the weapons, ammunition and equipment and dragged out two of the three mules from the bush. The remaining three gliders fared little better. Major Blain, the task force commander, sent out patrols over the next few days. A number of men were wounded in sporadic encounters with the Japanese. Burdened by those injured at landing and the wounded, the force could not effectively undertake the eleven-day mission. Within seven days, light liaison aircraft started to evacuate it.

On 21 and 22 March, six gliders towed to Mahnton on the Meza River delivered twenty-one glider and airborne aviation engineers, plus ten tons of equipment. With the aid of 100 native personnel, they cleared the Aberdeen landing strip in twenty-four hours. Aircraft loaded with supplies for the 77th Indian Infantry Brigade, fending off Japanese forces at Heno, soon started landing.

On 25 March, the shocking news seeped out that Wingate had been killed in an air crash in the Naga Hills while en route from Broadway to Imphal. Shortly before the crash, Wingate was airing his greatest dream, a massive glider operation to take the Japanese stronghold at Indaw. Reaction was mixed, and many were those who drew sighs of combined relief and sorrow at his death. With his death, glider warfare as a new method in war had lost its staunchest senior advocate in the Allied ranks. General Lentaign, a staunch supporter of Wingate's tactics and strategy, succeeded him as the campaign was drawing to a close.

Glider operations did not cease completely. The Japanese were pressing the 77th Indian Infantry Brigade hard around Henu. Japanese tanks attacked on 26 March and made serious penetrations into the brigade's positions. The brigade had no antitank guns. Quickly grasping the seriousness of the situation, Lentaign ordered the commandos to fly in antitank guns. Two gliders arrived on 27 March carrying guns, which soon drove back the Japanese armor.

About 30 March, two gliders landed near a roadblock at Henu delivering four men and four tons of weapons, chiefly bazookas and ammunition. Enemy fire prevented recovery of the gliders.

On 3 April, five gliders delivered sixteen men, ammunition and eight tons of equipment to Henu to build a landing strip later known as White City, a new forward airbase. The Japanese attacked, captured and destroyed the craft, but the men escaped with the equipment. Later, the glider pilots joined the British, and the force retook the strip. Early in May, three gliders landed at Mohnyin, delivering six men and six tons of equipment, chiefly scout cars. Later in the month, five gliders delivered sixteen men and eight tons of equipment to Pinbaw to build a landing strip. Two glider pilots were killed by ground fire. The fate of their gliders was never determined.

Early in the morning of 9 May, four gliders carrying bulldozers began descents over rough ground in Burma. It was part of Operation "Blackpool." The first tug and glider appeared just as dawn was breaking. The Japanese spotted the combination, and the stutter of guns began. The glider pilot cut off, banked easily and started his descent. He leveled out and appeared to be coming in for a perfect landing, when the glider suddenly went into a vertical dive just short of the field, disintegrating in what Masters describes as "a throaty rumble." The RAF ground-control team radioed instructions to the aircraft pilots to pass on to the glider pilots, correcting the course. The next three glider pilots heard and heeded, each landing safely. Unscathed, two bulldozers moved out from as many gliders and started work on the strip. Ground control took over one glider as a control tower. The next day, five Dakotas landed. "Blackpool" became the eleventh glider operation for what had been Wingate's forces.

As April 1944 drew to an end, forces under General Stilwell, operating to the north, held the initiative in North Burma. Thanks to air supply, the Allies had cleared the Hukawng Valley, and it was evident that in due time Kamaing and Mogaung must fall, opening the way toward Myitkyina. Only the greatly weakened Japanese 18th Infantry Division stood in the way; other Japanese forces were busy in Manipur, on the Salween, in the Arakan, and around a roadblock established by the second Wingate expedition at Mawlu. Some elements of the Japanese division were engaged north of Myitkyina, fighting British-led Kachins and Gurkhas, who were advancing south from Sumprabum, which they had captured earlier.

Despite these advantages, the success of Stilwell's Burma effort was in serious jeopardy. The entire campaign had been directed toward the capture of Myitkyina and, by late April, it was evident that the monsoon would arrive before Kamaing and Mogaung could be cleared. The coming of the rains would make the long march to Myitkyina impossible if the Japanese offered significant resistance. Furthermore, the Chinese elements already in Burma would have their hands full completing the Mogaung operation. Merrill's

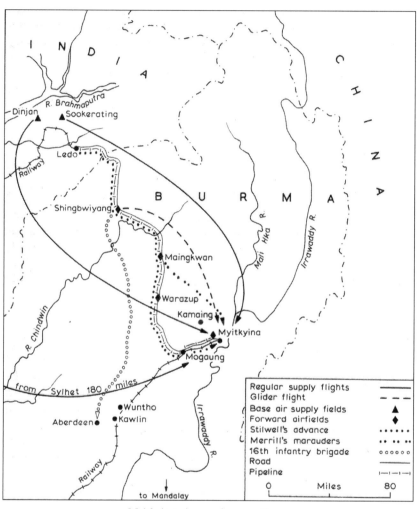

Myitkyina air supply operations.

Marauders had been so exhausted and depleted by their long marches and hard fighting that their combat effectiveness had been greatly reduced.

In these circumstances, it was evident that a quick stroke was required to attain the campaign's objective, and Stilwell had little choice but to ask one more effort of the tired Marauders. Reinforced with Chinese troops and a detachment of Kachin guerrillas, Merrill's command was divided into three combat teams and sent on a long flanking movement across the 6,000-foot Kumon Range. The Marauders traversed the mountains over almost-forgotten Kachin trails, so perilous that a score of mules lost their footing and plunged down precipices to destruction. After a seven-day march, the Marauders emerged into the Irrawaddy Valley near Ritpong, a village some forty miles north of Myitkyina.

One of Merrill's combat teams marched south straight toward Myitkyina. This group encountered only scattered enemy patrols and, on the night of 16 May, the Marauder team bivouacked south of the Mandalay-Myitkyina Railroad, only four miles from Myitkyina South Airfield, which is actually about three miles west of the town. At 1000 hours on the morning of 17 May, the Marauders swept over the field, attaining complete tactical surprise. A message had already been sent alerting headquarters to have reinforcements ready. As soon as the field was taken, a prearranged signal was transmitted to announce that the field was ready for the reception of reinforcements.

Taking the airfield was the culmination of the still-progressing drive down the Hukawng-Mogaung Valleys. It opened the way to Bhamo and a junction with the Burma Road. More important, Allied possession of the airfield made possible a more southerly air route to China. Transports could fly at a lower altitude, and lower altitudes permitted them to carry less fuel and greater payloads. In addition, possession of the airfield made possible rapid reinforcement of the small body of forces, which had effected its capture.

Plans for the fly-in of troops and equipment were completed on 1 May 1944. The crews that were to take part were briefed, and ten gliders, loaded with engineering equipment for repairing the runway, were made ready to be lifted from Shingbwiyand.

When the message that the airfield had been taken was broadcast, several C-47's of the 2nd Troop Carrier Squadron had arrived in the Myitkyina area to drop supplies to the Marauders. Four of these aircraft landed on the strip at about 1600 hours, despite Japanese fire which knocked out the hydraulic system of the first one to land. The next aircraft to arrive was an L-5 from Shaduzup, carrying panels for visual direction of glider pilots and an SCR-284 radio for control of aircraft. Before the panels could be laid out, the gliders appeared overhead and began landing.

The first glider landed safely, but the pilot failed to carry out his instructions to act as a "T" for the guidance of following pilots. The remaining gliders came into the field from all points of the compass, with no ground control whatsoever. Four pilots deliberately landed at right angles to the runway, taking very seriously a warning given at the flight briefing that the strip might be mined. Eight of the ten gliders were wrecked, but there were only three casualties to personnel aboard and most of the engineering equipment remained operable. One of the tow planes landed and evacuated the casualties. The engineers immediately began work on improving the runway.

Air transport operations into Myitkyina continued from 17 May 1944 to the end of the war, but the operations of the first three days, 17–19 May, during which gliders flew in critically needed heavy equipment, may be considered as the fly-in phase, because it was during this period that the forces necessary to hold the airfield and the equipment necessary for the emergency repair of it were landed.

In all, the Air Commandos flew seventy-four glider sorties for Wingate's forces and a total of ninety-six by the end of the Myitkyina operation. This is not a significant number when compared to those flown later in Europe, but the sorties were certainly first rate for daring and accomplishment, as was Wingate's campaign plan itself. Fifty-four gliders were lost in the operations, but the many sorties had delivered 1,059 men to their objectives. Some indication of the magnitude of the accomplishment was given by a Burma correspondent of the London *News Chronicle*, writing in 1944:

Flying over mountains 6,000 feet high, American glider pilots are evacuating British wounded from a strip cut out of jungle swamp.

In five days, they have taken out 298 severely wounded and sick men, many of whom would have almost certainly died, if they had been driven by road to the nearest base hospital.

The journey by glider takes one hour and ten minutes. By road, it takes 11 days or more by elephant, mule or [truck] with broken springs.

Wingate had used gliders with great imagination for reconnaissance, for spearheading an invasion and for bringing in supplies and equipment to his marching columns. The Commandos gave him willing and dedicated support and, in so doing, developed the glider into a weapon of war. After Burma, there could no longer be any doubt that the glider had earned its way into the ranks of qualified war materiel. The question remained, however: Would the lessons learned through harsh experience in Burma, under the tutelage of a great soldier, be taken seriously for the remainder of the war?

As the glider forays grew in number, and as Alison and Cochran gained further confidence and experience, their thoughts turned to future operations in which gliders would play a major role. They dreamed of a massive glider invasion of China to drive the Japanese northward or cut them off from Japan. According to their concept of operations, airborne armadas, consisting principally of glider echelons, were to make a series of 500-mile hops along the China coast, not unlike the jungle-hopping tactics they had tried and proved and not unlike the Marines' idea of island hopping to close in on Japan from the Pacific side. General Stratemeyer was for the idea, but it would have taken huge resources, which the theater did not have, and months of build-up. Perhaps this was the reason the plan never matured. More likely, it died because Wingate, one of the greatest advocates of glider operations, had died.

Soon thereafter, Colonel Alison received a message. When he opened it, he found it had come from General Arnold. General Eisenhower had heard of General Wingate's use of gliders, and he wanted someone from "that outfit" to come over and give him and his staff some pointers. The message ordered him to proceed immediately to Europe. Later, many of his experts and technicians left to give a hand in the Normandy invasion. Wingate had given them the opportunity, and gliders had earned their way into the ranks of Allied weapons of war. It was now up to the Allies to use what Wingate had left as a legacy.

CHAPTER 8

U.S. Glider Pilots: The Bastards No One Wanted

A division lift requires 800 glider pilots. Based on testimony, the training of glider pilots has been far below that of power pilots. . . . Obviously corrective action must be taken to assure the successful use of this vehicle to contribute its proper share to airborne operations.

THE AIRBORNE BOARD

In terms of numbers to be trained and the speed at which they were to be trained, the glider pilot training program was more ambitious than even the fighter or bomber pilot training programs. The Army Air Corps program demanded 12,000 pilots for the first year (one short-lived planner's fantasy had this figure at more than 36,000). The figure was unquestionably unrealistic and irresponsible. At the time this figure was being bandied around by heady men, the U.S. did not yet have one fully developed and flying military combat glider and only had a few two-place training gliders.

Moreover, the timing was hardly auspicious. Before long, events were to confront the originators of this plan with hard facts and lead to drastic modifications. But before this took place, severe damage to morale was wrought in the ranks of the commissioned, noncommissioned and student pilots—the men who would shortly issue from this paranoiac planning to perform one of the most distasteful combat missions in the air corps: piloting a motorless, defenseless aircraft through flak-laden skies to an unknown destiny.

The formal initiation of the glider program occurred in February 1941, when Major General Arnold, deputy chief of staff for air, directed Major General Brett, acting chief of the Army Air Corps, to implement the development of the glider. Based on proposals already received, the Army Air Corps negotiated two contracts for the training at airborne flying schools of twelve officers in courses of approximately three weeks' duration at a cost of less than $400 a student.

Students at the Advanced Glider Flying School at Stuttgart, Arkansas.

Sailplanes used in glider training at Seven Palms, California.

In June 1941, the first experimental training of Army Air Corps officers in glider piloting took place at the Elmira Gliding Area Soaring Corporation at Harris Hill in Elmira, New York, and at the Lewis School of Aeronautics at Lockport, Illinois. The training was similar to the course these institutions had been giving to their civilian students. Initial instruction was given in single-place Franklin Utility gliders, towed by an automobile. The glider was towed across the field at fifty miles per hour, and the pilot required to keep it on the ground, although he had sufficient speed to fly. Successive series of tows permitted the pilot to fly an increasing distance off the ground, and then, after releasing the tow rope, the pilot could practice approaches and spot landings.

After approximately eight hours, this instruction was shifted to two-seater Schweizer sailplanes, continuing with winch, automobile and aircraft tows. When possible, the student would "slope soar" or seek thermal activity to prolong his flight. After demonstrating proficiency, students flew these sailplanes solo from the front cockpit. Each student completed eight hours of dual tow work, that is, a tow in which a plane towed two gliders. The last part of the instruction program consisted of a cross-country tow flight. All students made at least one cross-country flight that terminated at an airport at least forty miles away.[1]

Early in July, arrangements were made for a second class of officers to receive glider pilot training at Elmira. Arrangements at first indicated that ten officers were to take this course, but it appears to have been given to twelve instructors from the training centers who, it was contemplated, would later be used as instructors or supervisors upon the further expansion of glider-pilot training. The training, conducted in two classes of six students each, was completed on September 20.

At this time, the Office of the Chief of the Army Air Corps prepared the first program of instruction for glider pilots. This program was naturally tentative and subject to change as the techniques of military glider flying were developed. The duration of the course was not to exceed four weeks, and its objective was to qualify the officer pilot at the degree of proficiency necessary for an instructor or supervisor of glider-flying training. The program encompassed glider flying, to include winch, auto and aircraft tow; thermal soaring, with particular emphasis on spot landing proficiency; and dual aircraft towing practice. In addition, there were the duties of a ground supervisor, to include use and care of equipment, and the duties of an air instructor and the duties of the pilot of the tow plane. Actual flying instruction was to last twenty-five to thirty hours, with one hour of familiarization; nine hours of winch and

---

1. For additional information about how such training is done, see James Mrazek, *Sailplanes and Soaring* (Harrisburg, PA: Stackpole, 1973).

auto tow; two and a half hours of single aircraft tow and five of double; one two-hour cross-country flight of at least thirty miles; and five and a half to fifteen and a half hours of ridge and thermal soaring.

The ground school course, which was to be "given in the classroom or on the flying field in conjunction with daily flying activities," was to include aerodynamics pertaining to sailplanes and gliders, descriptions of types of gliders and sailplanes with emphasis on efficiency, take-off technique methods, landing techniques, soaring meteorology, instruments and their uses, slope soaring and thermal soaring.

However, in spite of the training activity up to this time, no definite doctrine had been formulated on the military employment of gliders, the flying units to be formed, the size of these units and the number of men to be transported by the glider echelon. It was therefore impossible for the Army Air Corps to determine the overall number of glider pilots to be trained. Nonetheless, on 21 August 1941, the chief of the Air Staff directed the chief of the Army Air Corps to make the necessary plans for the instruction of 150 officer pilots in glider flying.

Twenty-Nine Palms Air Academy at the town of the same name in California was next selected as a major glider training center. An advanced school was not considered necessary at the time, but sites were being investigated.

Instruction was similar to that at Elmira and included thirty hours of flying. The curriculum for glider training was still in the experimental stage, since the procurement of military gliders was only just getting under way and no one really knew what a military transport glider looked like. The men familiar with the technique of glider flying were the civilian soaring enthusiasts, who had been developing the art of thermal soaring over the past ten years. Consequently, at Twenty-Nine Palms, where many civilians taught and which only had sailplanes, the instruction was principally in soaring, a flying skill that later proved of little value in military glider piloting.

One of the reasons for the early confusion and indecision that characterized the glider program was the fact that gliders and the training of glider pilots was entirely foreign to Army Air Corps personnel. There also seems to have existed then—and throughout the entire program—a disinclination on the part of various Air Corps agencies to take proper responsibility for getting the training done. The cause of this can probably be found in the ever-present antipathy of the power pilot for any other aircraft. Another difficulty was perhaps that the glider program was a borderline project, a case of divided responsibility between the ground and air arms.

This early confusion was alleviated considerably in October 1941 when General Arnold personally summoned Lewin B. Barringer to Washington to act in a civilian capacity as coordinator of the glider program. Barringer was one of the outstanding authorities on the art of gliding and soaring in the United States. He was commissioned a major in May 1942 and assigned to the Office of the Director of Air Support, where he was in full charge of all matters pertaining to gliders. Barringer continued in this position until January 1943, when the aircraft in which he was flying was lost over the Caribbean. Much of the credit for the achievement of a new and tremendous project must go to him. Not only did he play a large part in the development of the glider production and training programs, but he also "made possible the practical application of a device [that] enabled an [aircraft] in flight to pick up a tow glider on the ground."

In rapid succession, and without serious forethought, the Army Air Corps started three different and overlapping glider-pilot training programs, causing untold confusion and problems of morale.

The 1,000-pilot program of 20 December 1941 was predicated in the belief that sufficient transport aircraft would be available as tow planes for testing, pilot training and operational training. The program called for the training of qualified aircraft pilots only, preferably graduates of Army Air Corps flying schools. It was clearly apparent at that time—but conveniently overlooked later—that a large amount of skill was believed necessary to pilot a glider.

The primary course of training, which was to last four weeks, was similar to that given at Elmira to the first trainees. Graduates were to receive the rating of Glider Pilot. An advanced course called for night flying and the actual carrying of personnel under simulated combat conditions using large gliders. Training was to include a preliminary course of approximately thirty hours in two-place training gliders at Twenty-Nine Palms, California, and a further course in transport gliders at an advanced school yet to be selected. The minimum requirements for this training were that applicants should be power-aircraft pilots, who had taken the Civilian Aviation Administration's (CAA) primary or secondary course, or civilian glider pilots "who had at least fifty hours gliding time." This was later changed to thirty hours gliding time or 200 flights. The physical requirements were to be the same as those for aircrew training. The trainees were to start as enlisted men. Upon graduation, they would be promoted to staff sergeant.

While the first of the 150 officer pilots had hardly matriculated at Twenty-Nine Palms, General Arnold initiated a study to triple the pilot program in March 1942. Not only was the objective greatly increased, but the time allotted to its achievement was decreased.

In order that this mammoth training effort could be put in operation as soon as possible, a directive dated 1 April 1942 ordered the Flying Training Command to train 4,200 glider pilots by 1 July 1943. Two thousand of them were to have been graduated by 1 January 1943. This entailed an increase of

3,200 over the previous program, as the 1,000 formerly directed were included in this figure. In conflict with the procurement policy of the 1,000-pilot program, as many as possible of these trainees were to be graduates of the twin-engine advanced-pilot course and commissioned officers.

Two days later, however, the indecision that characterized this period again caused a change in policy. All glider trainees were now to be enlisted graduates of Army Air Corps advanced flying schools. Advanced pilot graduates were considered essential for the following reasons: fifteen-place troop gliders being procured were roughly equivalent in size to a B-18 aircraft. Thirty-place gliders with wing spans longer than the B-17 were under development. Formation and night and instrument flying requirements were to be commensurate to those required for powered aircraft pilots. It was also planned that glider pilots at all stations be prepared to fly as tug pilots; therefore, glider pilots with the dual background could be used in this capacity.

It was soon realized, however, that the transfer of 4,200 enlisted pilots to the program would seriously impair established pilot priorities for fighter and bomber aircraft. On 11 April, therefore, the minimum requirements for glider-pilot training were again revised. Candidates were to be between the ages of eighteen and thirty-two and graduates of a secondary pilot training course. Alternately, they were to hold or have held a private airman certificate or higher, with power pilot ratings, or be glider pilots having thirty hours or 200 flights. The program of instruction for enlisted personnel went into effect on 15 April 1942.

On 8 May, exactly thirty-eight days after the initiation of the 4,200 program, the chief of Air Staff directed that 3,000 pilots must be trained by 1 September and a total of 6,000 by 31 December 1942. An entirely new program ensued. In the course of six weeks, trainees would get thirty hours in cub aircraft, eight in two-place gliders and eight in nine and fifteen-place gliders. Qualifications were changed so that a trainee had to be either a command pilot training graduate, a holder of a CAA certificate or a former CAA pilot, whose license had not been invalidated for more than two years, and must be between eighteen and thirty-five years of age. Eighteen gliding schools sprang into existence around the country, each geared to train 80 to 212 student pilots.

Up to this time, the glider-pilot training program may be said to have been in its first formative stage. With the 6,000-pilot program under way, the first definition of the glider-pilot's role as a member of the combat team was transmitted to the training centers. It provided that primary attention would be given to their training as pilots. The pilot would receive the majority of his ground combat training in conjunction with the unit training of airborne troops in gliders, which was to come after his assignment to a transport unit. Ground combat training during glider-pilot training would not interfere with his training as a pilot. In combat, the glider pilot understood his job to be to land his glider safely, get his passengers and cargo out quickly and secure his glider. He understood he would fight after landing only in exceptional circumstances.

The Army Air Corps called upon the Army for assistance in giving infantry training to glider pilots. Actually, the action did not grow out of a desire to ensure that the glider pilots would be able to play an effective role in ground combat after landing. Its more direct origin lay in the search for a solution to the rapidly deteriorating morale among idle glider pilots who, having completed glider training, were awaiting assignment to advanced training schools. In December 1942, 2,754 such candidates were awaiting assignment to four schools in Texas and Arkansas, whose joint capacity was 600 students a month. This meant that, even if no more students completed basic training, some of those in the pool would have to wait as long as five months to pass that bottleneck. The director of glider training hoped that an active ground-training program would alleviate the state of low morale and discontent, the natural consequence of such a stalemate.

Willing to see what could be done, the Army directed the Airborne Command to furnish the necessary instructors and to work out the details with the Flying Training Command. General Chapman sent Lieutenant Colonel M. A. Quinto of the 88th Glider Infantry Regiment to the Flying Training Command headquarters to get further information. His report was that obstacles were practically insurmountable. The program would require an estimated 30 officers and 150 enlisted men as instructors. More daunting, they would have no training aids with which to work: no ranges, no bayonet or grenade courses, not even infantry weapons. The Airborne Command felt it could not do the job and that such training in fact might well fall within the province of the Army Replacement and School Commands. Moreover, then-current doctrine did not contemplate the active employment of glider pilots with airborne forces in tactical operations following landings in hostile territory.

As a result, there was an impasse. Many glider pilots went overseas with the transport groups to which they were assigned having little or no knowledge of how to fire infantry weapons and, worse, usually even less information on how to fight as infantrymen. At some overseas stations, there was time to correct this deficiency. On the whole, the American glider pilots were deplorably deficient in the combat knowledge and training that would have enabled them to fight on the ground and also to protect themselves adequately once a glider had landed.

CHAPTER 9:

Gliders Assault Normandy: U.S. Phase

In the darkness, early on 6 June 1944, three roaring streams of an airborne armada began releasing gliders and discharging paratroopers—the vanguard of Operation "Overlord," the largest combined airborne and seaborne invasion in history. By 0400 hours, elements of the U.S. 82nd and 101st Airborne Divisions and the British 6th Airborne Divisions had pierced the northern walls of Hitler's vaunted European fortress. Operation "Neptune," the airborne spear of General Dwight D. Eisenhower's field armies, had been launched.

American airborne divisions had orders to protect the west flank of the Allied forces. The British 6th Airborne Division was to seize two important bridges, the terrain east of Caen, and protect the eastern flank from what intelligence had predicted would be the main German counterthrust. If "Neptune" succeeded, Eisenhower's assault across the beaches would be less costly to the Allies, Generals Montgomery and Bradley would be able to consolidate their gains and organize their forces with less harassment from the Germans and the expanding of an Allied foothold on the continent would be speeded. That success would attend the airborne onslaught was anything but certain during the first hours of dawn.

"Neptune" called for six glider missions and a number of parachute drops from the 82nd and the 101st Airborne Divisions. The 82nd Airborne Division was to descend on Landing Zone West (LZW) in pre-dawn darkness on D-Day. This mission was dubbed Operation "Detroit." Operation "Elmira," scheduled for sunset that day, was to reinforce the division, and two more such missions—"Galveston" and "Hackensack"—were scheduled for D-Day+1. In Operation "Chicago," the 101st Airborne Division was to hit Landing Zone East (LZE), also during the pre-dawn hours on D-Day. Operation "Keokuk," scheduled for pre-sunset on D-Day, carried the division's ordnance company and other tactical support elements.

Late in May, the time that "Detroit" and "Chicago" were to take place was changed from twilight to before daybreak to give the glidermen greater safety from ground fire. Release time for "Chicago" was to be at 0400 hours. "Detroit" was scheduled for 0407 hours. Both the troop carrier and airborne commanders protested in vain that they were once more being committed to night landings and that such landings on the small fields of the Cotentin Peninsula might cost half the force in crashes alone. Fear of the accuracy of German guns during daylight flights outweighed their objections, however, and the decision stood. As a concession, the IX Troop Transport Command was authorized to use Waco gliders exclusively in those two missions in place of the heavier, less maneuverable and less familiar Horsas about two days before D-Day. The change entailed a hasty revision of loading plans and a substantial reduction in the amount carried. Since the two serials were to approach under cover of darkness, they could safely follow the same routes as the paratroops. All glider operations in the Normandy invasion were carried out at single tow.

The first tow plane in "Chicago" roared down the runway at 0119 hours. It was piloted by Colonel William B. Whitacre. Lieutenant Colonel Michael "Mike" Murphy piloted the glider christened *Fighting Falcon*. Murphy, a devil-may-care barnstormer of pre-war days, had gained fame in the United States with all who participated in the wartime glider program. He was noted for stunting a CG-4A gracefully and dexterously in the fashion of a sailplane. In charge of glider training at Stout Field in Indianapolis, Indiana, and in England ostensibly only to observe glider operations with no obligation to participate in combat, he had wangled his way into the mission to get a first hand look at how gliders operated in combat. General Donald Pratt, assistant division commander of the 101st Airborne Division, occupied the co-pilot's seat.

Strung out behind was a procession of fifty-two gliders in formations of four, each towed by a Dakota. A big Roman numeral I was painted high on the nose of Pratt's glider. A huge screaming eagle, the insignia of the 101st Airborne Division, and a United States flag adorned the canvas on either side of the pilot's compartment. In the same formation, Surgical Technician Emile Natalle looked down on shell bursts and burning vehicles below and saw a "wall of fire coming up to greet us." Still hitched to their planes, the gliders lurched from side to side, scudding through "flak thick enough to land on."[1]

Unlike the paratroopers' aircraft, the gliders came in from the Channel and approached the peninsula from the east. They were only seconds past the coast when they saw the lights of the landing zone at Hiesville, four miles from Sainte-Mere-Eglise. One by one, the 300-yard-long nylon tow ropes parted and the gliders came sloughing down. Natalle's glider overshot the zone and

1. Cornelius Ryan, *The Longest Day* (New York: Simon and Schuster, 1956), 138.

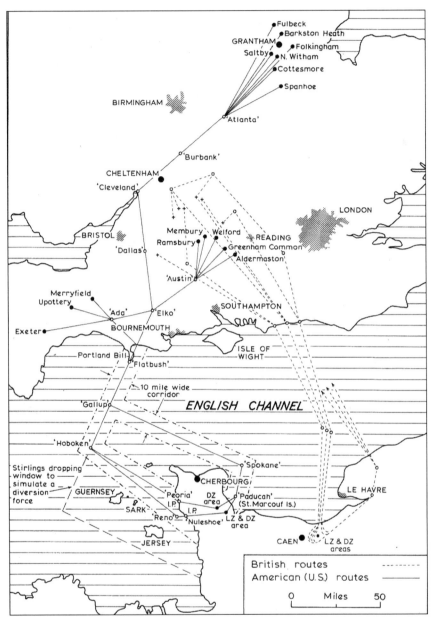

The Cross-Channel Airborne Assault: The Approach.

crashed into a field studded with "Rommel's asparagus," lines of heavy posts embedded in the ground as anti-glider obstacles. Sitting in a jeep inside the glider, Natalle gazed out through one of the small windows and watched with horrified fascination as the wings sheared off and the posts whizzed past. Then there was a ripping sound and the glider broke in two directly behind the jeep in which Natalle was sitting. "It made it very easy to get out," he recalled.

Close by, Natalle came upon Murphy's glider, a total shambles. Its brakes were unable to halt its mad 100-mile-an-hour run, and it smashed head-on into a hedgerow. Natalle found Murphy thrown from the cockpit with both legs mangled, lying in the brush of the hedgerow. The crumpling of the steel tubing around the cockpit crushed and killed Pratt, the first general officer on either side to be killed on D-Day. Ironically, his being in the mission was the result of a hurried change, since he was originally assigned to command the troops of the 101st Airborne Division that came across the channel by boat.

Brigadier General Pratt was one of two American airborne generals to land in combat by glider. A superb officer, he had no taste for such an adventure but, being a good soldier, he stoically did as he was ordered. Someone of general-officer rank had to make a show in a glider operation, and he was the one "selected," much against his wishes. As a concession to him and to allay his concerns, his co-pilot's seat in the glider had armor plate under it. To his great relief, Mike Murphy, the most experienced pilot in the organization, was assigned to fly him into Normandy. Although Murphy has claimed the contrary, there is a possibility that the extra weight caused by the armor plating in the nose of the glider changed the center of gravity and altered the flight characteristics of the glider sufficiently to challenge the skill even of Mike Murphy. This may have been responsible for the excessive landing speed. There is also one report that had there been no armor, the general might have survived. The armor caused the seat to buckle, and the general's head was fractured by the steel framework overhead.

Several others in the glider had also been killed. Somehow, Murphy managed to reach American paratroops, who had been dropped the night before, and he was soon evacuated across the channel by boat to a hospital in England. He became one of the first officers to arrive in the United States as a result of wounds received on D-Day.

Batteries A and B of the 82nd Airborne Division's antiaircraft battalion occupied forty-four of the other gliders. Medical personnel, engineers, signals personnel and a few staff personnel occupied seven of the other gliders. In all, the serial carried 155 glidermen, sixteen 57-mm antitank guns, twenty-five jeeps, a small bulldozer for the engineers, two-and-a-half tons of ammunition and eleven tons of miscellaneous equipment.

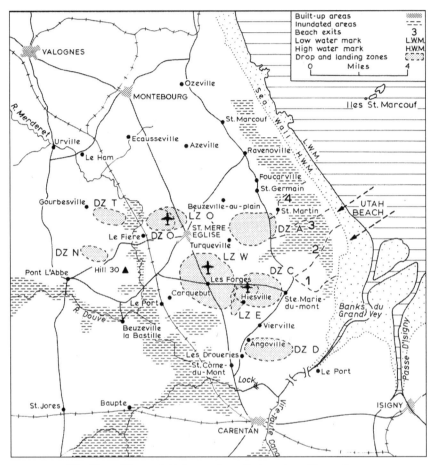

The Cross-Channel Airborne Assault: American Operations.

Like the rest of that region, LZE was flat and divided into a checkerboard of pastureland. Most fields were between 300 and 400 yards long in the St. Marie-du-Mont, Les Forges and Hiesville area. Outside the zone, the average field was considerably shorter, many being only 200 yards in length. Intelligence reports cautioned that trees averaging 40 feet in height bordered the fields. These trees had not shown up well on reconnaissance photographs and unwary glider pilots had not been told about them in briefings. They assumed that only hedges bordered the fields.

With its gliders in tow, the 434th Troop Carrier Group took off like clockwork from Aldermaston. With bright moonlight to assist it, it readily assembled into columns of four in echelon to the right. Soon after takeoff, a glider broke loose and landed four miles from the base. As luck would have it, it carried the SCR-499 radio for the division, which was to send vital messages to headquarters telling the much needed news of the division's progress and of enemy resistance. The equipment was retrieved and sent that evening to "Keokuk," but this accident prevented the division from communicating with invasion headquarters in the critical hours of dawn.

The rest of the serial of C-47 tugs and gliders reached the Normandy beaches without incident, but they encountered sporadic rifle and machine-gun fire while crossing the peninsula. The enemy shot down one aircraft and glider near Pont l'Abbe and inflicted minor damage on seven other aircraft. Gliders also took slight damage. The weather over the Cotentin Peninsula was cloudy, but the planes were able to maintain formation except for one pilot who straggled. The straggler released his glider south of Carentan, about eight miles from the landing zone. For the last twenty miles, a Eureka radio beacon system set up by pathfinders guided pilots toward flashing green lights placed in the form of a T in the landing zone. After releasing their gliders, C-47 pilots headed out over the St. Marcouf Islands, just off the east coast of Normandy, to arrive at Aldermaston in Berkshire, soon after 0530 hours. The C-47 pilots had done their job well.

But the glider pilots, groping in the black sky after release, ran into difficulties. Most of them swept in the prescribed 270-degree left turn. Somehow, in the process, many apparently lost sight of the T on the ground. Without it, most could not recognize their landing zone in the dim light of a setting moon and with broken clouds that prevented what moonlight illumination that was available.

Soon the dark forms of high trees began flashing underneath and by windows and wings, seriously unnerving the glider pilots as they tensely peered ahead into the blackness and sped into landings. The fields, rimmed by poplars, some 70 feet tall, became death traps. The trees began to sever wings, bringing gliders into awkward crashes. Farmhouse roofs abruptly

Preparations for invasion: in the foreground, crated gliders; in the center, fuselages; at the top, assembled gliders.

Tow planes alongside Horsa gliders ready for take-off to Normandy.

became small landing fields, and hedgerows braked gliders to rending halts from which no person stirred. Only a few gliders came out whole from the carnage of those minutes of terror.

It was determined later that the T that was to guide the gliders was not at the location set up in the original plans. This was one of the reasons why most pilots landed in the wrong fields. Only six landed on the zone. Fifteen landed within about half a mile of it; ten were neatly concentrated near Les Forges, one mile west of LZE. The other eighteen were scattered east and southeast of the zone, all but one landing within two miles of it.

Despite these misfortunes, the glider operation succeeded. Fortunately, it was so dark during the descent that the enemy had trouble sighting on the gliders, so there were no crashes caused by enemy fire. All but a handful of glider pilots managed to stop without harming the passengers and contents, even though the gliders ended crumpled, torn and worthless.

Besides mortally wounding General Pratt, crashes killed 4 glidermen and injured 17. Seven were missing. With occasional interruptions by rifle fire or mortar shells, it took time in the unfamiliar terrain to pry equipment out of smashed gliders and more time for the glidermen to find and assemble their platoons and companies. The 101st Airborne Division sent out a detachment at dawn to meet the troops from the glider mission at the landing zone and guide them to Hiesville. It did not return until noon, however. When it came back, it brought with it 3 jeeps, 6 antitank guns, 115 glidermen and 35 prisoners. Because of the bad drop of the 377th Parachute Field Artillery Battalion that had preceded the "Chicago" glider mission, the division had only one 75-mm pack howitzer on the northern perimeter near Foucarville and one captured German gun at the headquarters of the 506th Parachute Infantry Regiment at Culoville. The gliderborne antitank guns were therefore particularly welcomed. On D-Day+1 and D-Day+2, these guns lent their fire to an attack led by Colonel Robert F. Sink, which thrust southward against the Germans at St. Come-du-Mont. Although badly shaken in the landing, the "Chicago" mission had succeeded.

The first of the glider elements of the 82nd Airborne Division, consisting of 52 CG-4A gliders, took off on the "Detroit" mission from Ramsbury. They were towed by 52 C-47's of the 437th Troop Carrier Group. They departed ten minutes after the "Chicago" serial of the 101st Airborne Division. The same Eureka beacon and T-shaped green lights that had guided the paratroopers to the "Detroit" zone were to be used by the glider pilots. The gliders carried Batteries A and B of the 82nd Airborne Anti-Aircraft Battalion, part of the divisional staff and a signal detachment—220 personnel in all. Twenty-two jeeps, 5 trailers, 16 57-mm antitank guns and 10 tons of other equipment jammed the gliders.

The first plane of the 437th Troop Carrier Group with a CG-4A in tow lifted off the runway, and the last of the fifty-two teams left twenty-four minutes later. In other words, two teams left the airfield every minute. One glider broke its tow close to the take-off field. The aircraft's pilot swung around, returned for a substitute and delivered it to the landing zone only half an hour late.

The channel weather was good, with ten miles visibility at most points. The 437th Troop Carrier Group found smooth going until, almost without forewarning, the lead element of its sky train came upon a cloud bank which extended from 800 to 1,400 feet altitude.

On their own, the leader and many others climbed to 1,500 feet, flew over the clouds and, in two or three minutes, were able to descend through breaks in the overcast. They emerged somewhat scattered and slightly north of course. These were the most fortunate of the serial. The other pilots plunged into clouds so dense that the glider pilots completely lost sight of their tow planes. In desperation, they had to rely on dimly-lit instruments. Inevitably, that part of the formation broke, and all pilots flew virtually by "the seat of their pants." Most of them remained close to the designated course, however.

In the cloud bank, seven gliders broke away, released either by nervous C-47 pilots or by dubious glider pilots. Some had their tow ropes severed by enemy fire. Two were later located in western Normandy. Five were still unaccounted for a month later.[2]

Farther inland, the clouds became thinner and more broken, but visibility was still bad enough to cause the premature release of seven more gliders on the west side of the Merderet River. It appears that one or two pilots, catching a glimpse of the flooded valley ahead, mistook it for the sea and hastily gave the signal for release. Others behind them saw the gliders descending, assumed that the zone had been reached and likewise released their gliders.

German rifle and machine-gun fire sprayed the C-47's mercilessly once they were out of the clouds, and one crashed. The fire so tore up thirteen C-47's that when they finally limped back to England, they had to be extensively repaired. Twenty-five others carried a spattering of bullets and shrapnel scars. The gliders also took hits while still in the air. Many glidermen were wounded before the gliders landed.

About thirty-seven pilots of the original fifty-two surmounted all difficulties and reached the vicinity of LZW between 0401 hours and 0410 hours. The Eureka, which was established by pathfinder paratroopers who landed at LZO—the major glider landing area—early in the night and which was intended to guide parachute and glider echelons, was functioning and had been picked up by the leaders of what remained of the serial at a distance

---

2. After diligent search through archives, the author was not able to find information disclosing what happened to these gliders.

Gliders and tow planes circle over the Cherbourg Peninsula. Some craft have already landed.

D-Day. Waco and Horsa gliders lying in the French fields where they landed.

of fifteen miles. The T was not in operation and certain glider pilots who reported seeing a green T south of Sainte-Mere-Eglise had probably sighted the one on LZE.

Loose and disorganized though it was, part of the serial made a concerted release in two columns, with the lefthand column some 200 yards north of the landing zone and the righthand one heading over the center of the zone, at altitudes between 400 and 500 feet. Most of the stragglers that came in at odd intervals thereafter released in that general area and at roughly the same altitude. When free, the C-47's dived hurriedly to 100 feet to give the enemy less opportunity to observe them through the trees and brush. They skimmed out over the coast through a spatter of small-arms fire and headed home. The first C-47 reached the runway at Ramsbury at 0522 hours, three hours after the last of the serial left England en route for Normandy. The last straggler was back by 0610 hours.

While the descent of the gliders in "Detroit" was marked by no such confusion as had marred the British glider assault in Sicily, things did not go well there, either. Instead of circling smoothly into their appointed fields, gliders came down by ones and by twos, with each pilot following the pattern that seemed best to him. Several were under fire on their way down, and one glider pilot claimed to have been attacked by an enemy fighter (probably another glider). The main difficulty was the inability of glider pilots to identify their proper fields or, in some cases, to orientate themselves at all. The railway and town of Sainte-Mere-Eglise seem to have been the only landmarks that most could recognize in the dim light. Nevertheless, between seventeen and twenty-three managed to land on or near LZO.

Five pilots of the 84th Troop Carrier Squadron landed their Wacos in adjoining fields at the western end of the landing zone, making the greatest concentration there. Nine gliders, including two that crash-landed in Sainte-Mere-Eglise, were within two miles of the zone. Three, which came down near Hiesville, may have followed directional aids set out on LZE for "Chicago." In all, this was a pretty dismal performance.

As in "Chicago," most of the gliders got a severe battering on landing. Twenty-two of the mission's fifty-two gliders were destroyed, and all but about a dozen were badly battered. Once again, the principal cause of crashes was that the fields were too short for the gliders to land on and had high trees around them. Marshland and other hazards, such as rows of "Rommel's asparagus," accounted for nearly half the crack-ups. One glider collided with a frantic herd of cattle. The rough landings produced fewer casualties than might have been expected, however. Crashes killed three and injured twenty-three. Several jeeps broke loose during the landings, making a shambles of the interiors. Eleven of the twenty-two jeeps flown in were inoperable on arrival. The howitzers proved more durable. The American paratroops, many of whom had landed nearby earlier, raced to the gliders coming in pell-mell about them to give their buddies whatever help they could. It was not entirely a humanitarian gesture, however, since they needed artillery. They were of great assistance in unloading the howitzers. Paratroops blasted an ancient wall to get one gun out of an orchard close to Sainte-Mere-Eglise and struggled furiously with another gun snared in a CG-4A that was wrapped grotesquely around a tree. By noon, glider artillerymen at La Fiere and two or three crews with the newly arrived guns on the outskirts of Sainte-Mere-Eglise were blasting away at the Germans. The artillery was giving the airborne troops some badly needed firepower at that point. The significant fact was that US gliderborne artillery was in position miles inland from the Allied forces struggling to capture the Channel beaches, where no American artillery was yet in action.

From dawn to early evening on D-Day, the U.S. Army Air Corps flew no more airborne missions. About 2100 hours, two hours before sunset, the next great airborne action started, and soon "Keokuk" and "Elmira" forces arrived over Normandy. Allied fighters lent a hand giving cover and diving in to strafe enemy positions. Exposure to flak was reduced when the course flown by the serials was changed to enable them to approach their objectives from the east coast over the Utah beachhead.

"Keokuk" (101st Airborne Division) took off from Aldermaston in Berkshire with thirty-two aircraft of the 434th Troop Carrier Group, each towing a Horsa. The big gliders carried 157 signals, medical and staff personnel, 40 vehicles, 6 guns and 19 tons of other equipment. The gliders were to be released at 2100 hours over LZE. At 1830 hours, take-off began on what proved to be an incredibly easy mission, as far as the aircraft crews were concerned. With good weather and daylight all the way, everyone kept on course and in formation. No enemy fighters showed up, and virtually no ground fire was encountered. Battle damage consisted of a few nicks from flak in one aircraft. A detachment of glider pilots from earlier landings busily cleared LZE, cutting down trees, and the pathfinders marked it with yellow panels shaped to form a T and green smoke.

The serial arrived ahead of schedule, and the gliders started cutting off at 2053 hours. The glider pilots had a harder time than the aircraft crews, however. Many German combat elements were still around Turqueville, two miles north of LZE, and St. Come, two miles south of the zone, and other German groups located between the forces were troublesome. After holding fire as the aircraft passed over, they concentrated it on the slowly circling and descending gliders. Fortunately for the Americans, the range was too great, and the German weapons did not do much harm. Since it was daylight and visibility was excellent, most of the glider pilots landed the Horsas with no more than moderate damage, a fact worth noting in view of what happened later to the "Elmira" mission at sunset. However, bullets and accidents combined to kill fourteen men and cause thirty casualties. Ten glidermen were missing. They had landed in two gliders that landed within the German lines near Les Droueries.

The distribution of the landings indicates that most of the serial had released its gliders at least a mile short of the proper point. Fourteen gliders were concentrated in a few fields about two and a half miles northeast of LZE; five were at points several hundred yards farther east; eight were scattered southeast of the zone at distances up to two miles from it; and only five landed on the landing zone itself.

"Keokuk" was helpful rather than essential to the operations of the 101st Airborne Division. However, it was important, being the Allies' first tactical glider operation in daylight. It demonstrated that gliders could be landed in daytime without excessive losses when not exposed to fire at close range.

"Elmira" carried reinforcements for the 82nd Airborne Division. In order to limit the glider columns so that they could be protected by fighters and to reduce congestion during the glider landings, staff planners split the mission in two. One, towing 76 gliders, was to be ten minutes behind "Keokuk." The other sortie, towing 100 gliders, would leave England two hours later.

LZW was the goal, an oval about 2,800 yards long from north to south and more than 2,000 yards wide on terrain much like that of LZE. The northern tip of the oval was about a mile south of Sainte-Mere-Eglise, and the highway from that town to Carentan ran through the middle of the zone. About 1,000 yards inside the southern end of the landing zone, the highway was intersected at Les Forges by the east-west road from Sainte-Marie-du-Mont.

The first echelon contained two serials, one of twenty-six aircraft of the 437th Troop Carrier Group (towing eight Wacos and eighteen Horsas), and a second of fifty from the 438th Troop Carrier Group (fourteen Wacos and thirty-six Horsas). The Wacos were segregated in each flight to reduce the problem of flying two types of glider with different towing speeds in one formation. Within the gliders of the first echelon were Battery C of the 80th Airborne Antiaircraft Battalion, contingents of medical, signals, and divisional headquarters personnel, a reconnaissance platoon and an air support party—437 men in all. The cargo comprised sixty-four vehicles, mostly jeeps, thirteen 57-mm antitank guns, and twenty-four tons of equipment. Air transports took off from Greenham Common, Membury and Welford.

The 437th Troop Carrier Group took off from Ramsbury between 1907 and 1921 hours, and the 438th Troop Carrier Group from Greenham Common between 1848 and 1916 hours. Climbing with the heavily laden Horsas was a slow business, but all aircraft succeeded in assembling and setting out in formation. Over England, squally weather made the gliders hard to handle; they veered and pitched on their long ropes. From then on, the weather was excellent, with unlimited visibility and scattered clouds overhead at 3,000 feet. At Portland Bill, the fighter escort appeared. The sky seemed full of protective P-47's, P-51's and P-38's, a truly impressive array. Besides "delousing" patrols ahead of the column, fighters flew close cover on both sides and high cover at between 3,000 and 5,000 feet. No German challengers appeared, and the columns flew in serenely and into a deceptive enemy silence over Utah Beach.

Suddenly, at the release point, a stream of enemy bullets streaked up. The crescendo increased, riddling planes and gliders. Fortunately, the column flew through the worst quickly. Because the weapons employed were small arms and machine guns with a few 2-cm flak, casualties were not high. Nevertheless, enemy troops were close to the line of flight, and the mission had neither surprise nor darkness to protect it; two aircraft were shot down after releasing their gliders. One of the aircraft—its engines dead—dived between two trees. Both wings were stripped off, but it skidded safely to rest. Some thirty-seven aircraft returned to England with slight to moderate damage. Two had dead engines; one was decorated with sixty-five bullet holes, and one limped in with the crew chief holding its shattered feed lines together. Three men had been slightly wounded.

LZW, a short six miles from the coast, should have been easy to locate. The terrain was still plainly visible, and some pilots saw a panel T and green smoke, near which a Eureka beacon was sending out signals clearly received on the Rebecca sets in the planes. However, because of a still-unknown emergency, the T, the smoke and the radar were all not on LZW but two miles northwest of it. The potential source of confusion was that the T and green smoke had been set up for the "Keokuk" mission in the vicinity of LZE, two miles east of Les Forges.

Guided by Gee[3] and by visual identification of the terrain, the leader of the 437th Troop Carrier Group headed straight for LZW and released his glider there at 2104 hours, followed by almost all his serial. Ten minutes later, aircraft of the 438th Troop Carrier Group appeared over the zone and made their release, but part of the serial had erroneously released its gliders over LZE. Release altitudes were generally between 500 and 750 feet. From those heights, a Waco could glide more than two miles and a Horsa less than a mile. After releasing their gliders, the troop carrier pilots swung their planes into a 180-degree left turn, thereby exposing themselves to fire from the Germans around Saint-Come-du-Mont. They scooted over Utah Beach to England.

---

3. A ground-pulsing beacon.

No one who knew the situation on LZW at that moment would have recommended landing gliders on it. The wedge of the German resistance between Turqueville and Carquebut extended across the northern part of the zone and isolated it from the terrain taken by the 505th Parachute Infantry Regiment. The paratroops around Sainte-Mere-Eglise could not get through the belt of German forces to reconnoiter LZW, let alone to set up beacons there. Until late in the day, General Ridgway had every reason to believe that the entire zone was in German hands. This was why he had decided to place the beacons and markers in the vicinity of LZO. He had attempted to get word of the situation to IX Troop Carrier Command—first by radio and later by panels laid out for a reconnaissance aircraft—but the message was not received and the panels were not observed.

During the afternoon of 6 June, two battalions of the U.S. 8th Infantry Regiment had landed on the invasion beaches, driving the enemy from the southern portion of LZW. Small seaborne elements of the 82nd Airborne Division under Colonel Edson D. Raff made two unsuccessful attempts later to push the Germans from the rest of the zone. However, when the gliders arrived, the Germans still held most of the northern quarter. From their lines south—almost to Les Forges—the sector was a no-man's-land. It was full of snipers, traversed by German patrols and under observed fire from mortars and an 88-mm gun on high ground near Fauville. Raff's men did their best to steer the gliders to safety by waving yellow flags and making an F of orange smoke, but the glider pilots either did not see them or did not know what to make of the unexpected signals.

Raff described the alarming situation to which he was a helpless by-stander:

At approximately 1,500 feet, headed directly for LZW, was a serial of approximately 60 C-47's towing Horsas with CG-4A's following. The troop carriers released their gliders directly over what proved to be an enemy position in the woods. As soon as the troop carriers approached, the whole hill on the opposite side opened up with small arms, Schmeissers, and even antitank guns firing at the C-47's and gliders. Despite this fact, the gliders were released right over the landing zone, and many of them landed there, although others obviously realized that something was wrong and landed between our forward tank line and Le Port. Almost all the gliders were forced to make crash landings, and here it was noted that the Horsa glider seemed to break into many pieces, while the CG-4A's framework was more or less intact. The difference between the two upon impact was visible to me as an eyewitness. The Horsa seemed to fall apart. One or two gliders, not making their turn, landed on the hill occupied by the enemy. One of them landed beside what we believed was a pillbox. At least one glider landed beside our still burning tanks, and after its passengers had fled, it burned on the spot. The C-47's then proceeded east and came back low over the landing zone, although some of them scattered and flew back behind our own positions.

I ordered Major Ingersoll to gather up and assemble all officers and men of the division, including the glider pilots, near the crossroads, with the hope and intention of collecting enough men to make the breakthrough to Sainte-Mere-Eglise. By next morning, I had perhaps in excess of 200 men, but not more than about 150 of them were trained infantry soldiers. The medical detachment, which evidently had come in on some of the gliders, established an aid station at the crossroads at Le Port, where many of the gliders were assembled. We saw other gliders come in later, and this time I noted that the Germans held their fire until the gliders got in very low and very close.

As a final hazard, landings had to be made in the face of obstacles greater than those on the other zones. Not only were there "postage stamp" fields 200 yards long, bordered by fifty-foot trees, but some of the designated fields turned out to be flooded. Others were studded with poles more than five inches thick and ten feet or more in height. Trip-wires for mines had been attached to many of the poles but, fortunately, the mines themselves had not been installed.

A Horsa, carrying Captain William W. Bates of the 53rd Troop Carrier Wing, made a fairly typical landing. Unable to reach a large field, the pilot picked a small one, lowered his flaps and landed at about seventy miles an hour. The glider bounced twice. When about ten feet off the ground on its second bounce, it crashed through a row of trees, which stripped it of its wings and landing gear. The craft scraped to a stop ten yards behind Raff's forward positions. There were plenty of bullet holes in the tail, but the only casualty was a soldier who suffered a broken leg as a result of leaving his safety belt unbuckled during the landing. The cargo, an ammunition trailer, was intact, and was unloaded in twenty minutes.

All things considered, the glider pilots did fairly well under difficult circumstances. Only two gliders in the first serial landed on LZW, but twelve came within a mile. All but one or two were within two miles of it. In the second serial, all but one of the fourteen Wacos flown by the 88th Troop Carrier Squadron landed on or very near the zone; nine Horsas hit the zone and six came within a mile of it. On the other hand, a dozen Horsas in that serial landed near LZE, and four missed the zone by about three miles. Few, if any, followed the pathfinder aids to LZO, and the 82nd Airborne Division therefore considered the release inaccurate.

Thanks to greater durability and longer gliding range, the Wacos established a much better safety record than the Horsas. More than half of them landed intact, while only about 20 percent of the Horsas were undamaged. Three Wacos and twenty-one Horsas were destroyed, a large number by enemy fire.

Glidermen altered their tactics against enemy anti-airborne defenses as gliders continued to pour into Normandy. In the case of landings north of Les Forges, glidermen jumped out of gliders and into the nearest ditch before the Germans could range in with artillery, mortars or machine guns. Unloading waited until night or until it was clear the glider was not a target. In spite of any delays, most of the men and material that had landed in friendly territory on or near the landing zone had filtered through to Colonel Raff's command post on the north side of Les Forges in just a few hours. Five glider pilots were killed, four missing and seventeen wounded or injured; five glidermen were killed and eighteen injured or wounded, but none were missing.

The second echelon of "Elmira" contained one fifty-aircraft serial from the 436th Troop Carrier Group at Membury (two Wacos and forty-eight Horsas), and another from the 435th Troop Carrier Group at Welford (twelve Wacos and thirty-eight Horsas). With them went a paratroop aircraft of the 435th which had failed to drop its troops the night before. The greater capacity of the Horsas enabled these serials to carry much more than those in the morning missions. The first serial carried the 319th Glider Field Artillery Battalion and a few other artillerymen, medical elements and engineers, a total of 418 airborne soldiers. It lifted thirty-one jeeps, twelve 75-mm howitzers, twenty-six tons of ammunition and twenty-five tons of other equipment. The second serial was occupied exclusively by the 320th Field Artillery Battalion with 319 glider artillerymen, twelve 105-mm howitzers, twenty-eight jeeps, thirty-three tons of ammunition and twenty-three tons of supplies.

The troop carriers set out unaware that the 82nd Airborne Division was marking LZO instead of LZW. They did receive a last-minute telephone call from the 53rd Troop Carrier Wing, directing them to make a 180-degree right turn after releasing their gliders instead of the left turn prescribed in their orders. Presumably, it had been learned that the Germans still held the St. Come area in strength.

The lead aircraft of the 436th Troop Carrier Group took off at 2037 hours and that of the 435th Troop Carrier Group about 2040 hours. As the 435th Troop Carrier Group circled upward to form its column of fours, one Horsa broke loose and one aircraft turned back, its generators burned out. (Both loads joined the 437th Troop Carrier Group on the "Galveston" mission.)

Good weather and swarms of Allied fighters made for an uneventful flight but, presumably because of the impending darkness, the fighters turned back at the St. Marcouf Islands.

The sun set a few minutes before the serials reached Utah Beach and, as they passed over Normandy, the terrain lay in deepening shadow. The pathfinder forces on LZE had long since ceased operations. Undistracted by landmarks or rival beacons, the second installment of "Elmira" headed for the Eureka and the visual aids set up by the 82nd Airborne Division in the vicinity of LZO.

To their surprise, the serials ran into fire bad enough to make earlier flights seem like a milk run about three miles inland. Long sloping streams of deadly flak looped towards the armada, brilliantly lighting the darkness. The fire grew hotter as the gliders started releasing. It poured at them as aircraft made a 180-degree turn to the right. Some aircraft caught enemy fire all the way back to the coast. German marksmanship was aided by the white-hot flame dampeners on the C-47's glowing brightly in the semi-darkness.

Flight Officer Fowler peeled away from the formation on release and somehow made a safe landing. He joined the troops from his glider, and they fought it out with the Germans for several days. He killed nine of them before he and several others were captured. American fighters then strafed the German captors and their prisoners, and he barely missed being hit. During the attack, he managed to escape, after killing an *Oberst* (Colonel) and several German soldiers. He finally made his way back to the 435th Troop Transport Group wearing the dead officer's binoculars.

Fortunately, the enemy barrage took a less deadly toll on aircraft and gliders than first feared. The damage it caused aboard the aircraft was proportionately about the same as to the previous echelon. In the first serial, the Germans hit thirty-three aircraft, and two troop-carrier men were wounded. In the other serial, three C-47s ditched in the English Channel because enemy hits caused engine and fuel-system failures. Naval vessels rescued the crews. Two aircraft had to make emergency landings in England; twenty more were damaged, but their crews repaired them in a few days. One member of the 435th Troop Carrier Group was killed and one wounded. Aircraft of both transport groups had scattered and returned in driblets, some landing as late as 0300 hours the next morning.

The initial glider release in this part of "Elmira" occurred at 2255 hours, five minutes ahead of schedule. The second serial released its first glider at 2305 hours. Most of the lead serial released its gliders more than a mile short of LZO, and six gliders were released at least five miles east of the zone. The main body of the second serial was quite accurate, but five of its pilots flew to LZW by mistake. Undoubtedly, they failed to use the Rebecca directional beacon.

Once again, small fields and enemy fire played havoc with the glider landings. The fire in some places was intense and killed or wounded many glider troops in the one or two minutes immediately before the gliders landed. Despite strict orders to land at a slow speed, some pilots brought their Horsas in at 100 miles an hour. Since the fields were short—some only 100 yards long—and since the twilight made a precise approach over the hedgerows increasingly difficult, even the most careful pilots were lucky to escape a crash.

Counting some damage done by enemy fire after landing, only thirteen out if eighty-four Horsas were left intact, and fifty-six were totally destroyed. Despite widespread feeling among the glider pilots that the Wacos—with their gentler glide and tougher frames—would have done better than the Horsas in this particular landing operation, none of the fourteen Wacos on the mission survived intact and eight were destroyed. Of 196 glider pilots, 10 were killed, 29 or more were wounded or injured and 7 were still missing at the end of the month. Twenty-eight glidermen died, and 106 were wounded or injured. All those missing turned up within two days.

Once again, glidermen scrambled from the gliders and streaked for cover to get out of enemy artillery fire. Unloading was postponed until after dark. The cargoes had come through surprisingly well. The 435th Troop Carrier Group estimated that thirty-nine of its forty-eight glider loads were usable, and this is confirmed by estimates from glider units that forty-two out of fifty-nine jeeps, twenty-eight out of thirty-nine trailers and fifteen out of twenty-four howitzers were serviceable. However, because of enemy fire, the material could not be collected or used immediately.

The focal point for the landing of gliders in the first serial was almost two miles northeast of LZO. This put them near and, in some cases, within the German positions. A member of the divisional artillery staff, who had come with the serial, gathered about 200 men of the 319th Glider Field Artillery Battalion and led them during the night into the lines of the U.S. 4th Infantry Division east of Sainte-Mere-Eglise. Other groups made their way back with more or less difficulty, and at 1715 hours on 8 June, the glider field artillery battalion went into action near Chef-du-Pont with almost all its men and six howitzers.

All except five gliders of the second serial, carrying the 320th Glider Field Artillery Battalion, released near LZW. One or two released a few seconds too soon northeast of Sainte-Mere-Eglise, landing within a mile of LZO. Major Robert M. Silvey of the battalion, who had landed during the "Detroit" mission that morning, waited beside the pathfinders on the zone and had soon gathered about half the battalion and two howitzers. These began firing at 0930 hours on 7 June from positions 400 yards west of Sainte-Mere-Eglise. Patrols then guided party after party of glider troopers with equipment from gliders in outlying areas. By the evening of 8 June, the battalion had eight of its howitzers in action, including two landed in the vicinity of LZW. It had also gathered practically all of its personnel.

Reports of the hazards and confusion that plagued "Elmira" prompted the 53rd Troop Carrier Wing to make certain changes in its "Galveston" mission. This was the first glider mission scheduled for D-Day+1 and carried artillery, jeeps and glider infantry for General Ridgway's 82nd Airborne Division. Landfall was to be made four miles south of Utah Beach on the north side of the Douve Estuary. Instead of using LZW, the pilots were to release their gliders in the vicinity of LZE, about a mile west of Ste-Marie-duMont, and their homeward turn after release would be made to the left instead of the right. These changes would keep the serials out of range of the enemy north of Sainte-Mere-Eglise and in the Tourqueville enclave.

Fifty C-47's of the 437th Troop Carrier Group took off from Ramsbury for "Galveston," towing thirty-two Wacos and eighteen Horsas. The 1st Battalion of the 325th Glider Infantry Regiment and part of an engineering company—a total of 717 personnel with seventeen vehicles, nine pieces of artillery and twenty tons of equipment—rode the gliders. A second serial, the 434th Troop Carrier Group from Aldermaston, had fifty aircraft and fifty Wacos transporting the headquarters of the 325th Glider Infantry regiment, the Reconnaissance Platoon of the 82nd Airborne Division and sundry engineers and artillerymen, in all, 251 men. In addition, it carried twenty-four vehicles, eleven guns, five tons of ammunition and one-and-a-half tons of other material. Joining the mission were two aircraft of the 435th Troop Carrier Group towing Horsas that had aborted the "Elmira" mission.

More than half an hour before dawn, the aircraft lifted off from the two fields starting at 0439 and 0432 hours. Visibility was poor, it was raining and there was a gusty wind. The aircraft towing one Horsa of the 437th Troop Carrier Group, overloaded by 1,000 pounds, could not get the glider moving fast enough for the combination to get off the ground and had to release the glider. The pilot brought it to a stop on the end of the strip. Another was accidentally released during assembly of the sky train and landed near Portland Bill.

One glider combination after another roared down the field. Lieutenant Rendelman had his turn. The rope of his glider tightened. As it did so, the glider nose pulled downward. Rendelman pulled back on the controls and, a fraction of a second later, the glider was on its way down the runway with roller-coaster sound and speed. Sergeant Edward H. Shimko and his mortar squad sat tensely in the fuselage behind with twenty-two boxes of antitank rifle grenades, an 81-mm mortar and thirty-six rounds of mortar ammunition lashed tightly to the floor.

No more than seventy-five feet into the take-off, when tension on the tow system was greatest, all heard an explosion to the back of Lieutenant

Rendelman. No one knew what happened. Rendelman took little notice, with his eyes glued ahead in those critical moments of take-off.

In a few moments, as he went faster, wind started to blow in behind him. He turned around and saw runway pavement speeding by underneath. Then he realized that the nose latch had broken under the pull. He was airborne. The glider nose had opened at the base, looking like a tremendous whale taking a gulp of air.

Wind shrieked into the opening. Sergeant Shimko threw off his seat belt and jumped forward. He grabbed the steel framework of the nose, struggling to pull it closed. By then, several of his men had joined the effort, and Rendelman cut loose. The glidermen managed to get some rope around the nose tubing. Using some of the lashing rings on the floor of the glider, they pulled at the nose until it closed and tied it.

Rendelman landed the glider back at Ramsbury. He found an empty glider there, and Shimko transferred the load and got ready to go. Rendelman was at a loss, because he was not certain where his designated landing zone was. Colonel Donald French, the deputy group commander, told Rendelman he would tow the glider with a spare aircraft that was available, but he could not tell them exactly where to cut off, since the main column was far ahead at that point. Shimko, not one to be left behind, assured Rendelman he knew where the glider should cut off and would give him the signal. Soon they were again on their way.

Meanwhile, as the flight continued far ahead, pilots found the Channel and Normandy weather better. The rain had given way to thin, high and broken clouds and the visibility became excellent. Since the sun was up and the Normandy coast plainly visible, navigation was not difficult. The serials passed over or near many Allied ships. Since it was daylight, the glider formations with their identifying strips were universally recognized. Some of the gliders, sluggish because of overloads, were hard to manage, and some formations became scrambled. One glider pilot got understandably squeamish seeing C-47's directly above and beneath him.

Between the coast and the landing zone, both serials flew into rifle and machine-gun fire from Germans who had been pushed south from the Utah Beach area on the previous day and had not yet been mopped up. The 437th Troop Carrier Group also got caught in flak fire after a turn which probably brought them over the German salient around St. Come.

The group arrived at 0655 hours, five minutes ahead of schedule. Its serial came in low and released most of its gliders between 200 and 600 feet, and a few of them even lower. Release at such altitudes meant that the gliders could not glide much more than half a mile or stay in the air over half a minute. It decreased exposure to enemy fire, but it increased the chance of accidents. All but five or six of the gliders were released too soon and landed between the two southern causeways and LZE, the greatest concentration being a mile northeast of Sainte Marie-du-Mont.

The gliders landing east of LZE had only an occasional sniper or mortar round to harass them, but they suffered many accidents. Of the eighteen that started, ten Horsas were destroyed and seven damaged, with seventeen personnel killed and sixty-three injured. Nine Wacos were destroyed and fifteen damaged, but only twenty-two of their passengers were injured. None were killed. The glider pilots apparently had no deaths and few injuries. The lone combination carrying Shimko found the going rough. It came in over the coast of France from north to south at an air speed of about 160 miles per hour, skimming the treetops. German fire concentrated on the single glider all the way from the coast to the landing area.

It landed at 0718 hours in a mined field three miles north of Caen. Fortunately, no mines were set off. The glider cut through some barbed wire on landing, ripping the fuselage and wings.

Shimko and his men scattered immediately and stayed still for a few minutes to see what would happen. After that, they made a reconnaissance of the immediate vicinity and found no Germans; they had left when the glider came in. There were trenches all around, about six or eight feet deep, and underground living quarters about every 500 yards. Having found no Germans in the immediate vicinity, they unloaded the glider, put the equipment and ammunition in hedgerows in the area and took up a defensive position. After a brief encounter with retreating Germans, Shimko and his men tried to relocate their position. Deciding to march westward, they encountered British troops and finally located their unit one week later. Rendelman, who had remained near the glider, was captured and sent to Buchenwald. Fortunately, he survived.

The 434th Troop Carrier Group, flying second in "Galveston," reached its release area at 0701 hours, nine minutes ahead of time. Unlike the first serial, it appears to have released over LZW and, despite the lack of beacons and markers, to have done so very accurately. The 82nd Airborne Division credited it with twenty gliders landed on the zone, nineteen within a mile of it and eight within two miles. One was two and a half miles off, and one four and a half miles away. Accidents destroyed sixteen Wacos and damaged twenty-six but killed no troops and injured only thirteen. Moreover, at least nineteen jeeps, six trailers and seven guns came through satisfactorily. The enemy forces around Turqueville still kept LZW under fire, but the gliders were unloaded in fairly good time in spite of them, and the glider troops assembled near Les Forge. Eight of the 437th Troop Carrier Group's aircraft returned damaged from enemy shellfire, and eighteen of the 434th Troop Carrier Group's aircraft were also damaged.

The last glider mission in Operation "Neptune" was "Hackensack," which was flown to LZW two hours after "Galveston." Its lead serial, fifty aircraft towing thirty Horsas and twenty Wacos, was provided by the 439th Troop Carrier Group at Upottery. This carried the 2nd Battalion of the 325th Glider Infantry Regiment and most of the 2nd Battalion of the 401st Glider Infantry Regiment, which was attached to the 325th and acted as its third battalion. These numbered 968 personnel, of whom Horsas carried more than 800. The cargo included five vehicles, eleven tons of ammunition and ten tons of other supplies. The other serial consisted of fifty aircraft and fifty Wacos of the 441st Troop Carrier Group from Merryfield. It carried 363 soldiers, mostly service personnel of the two aforementioned battalions, and eighteen tons of equipment, including thirteen 81-mm mortars, twenty jeeps, nine trailers and six tons of ammunition. A pathfinder aircraft, piloted by Colonel Julian M. Chappell, commander of the 50th Troop Carrier Wing, and Lieutenant Colonel Kershaw of the 441st Troop Carrier Group, accompanied the serial to guide it to the zone.

Take-off from static hook-up began at 0647 hours from Upottery, and about 0717 hours from Merryfield. Some of the troop carriers complained that the airborne troops had seriously overloaded their gliders, making them difficult for pilots to handle. The sky was leaden and the air so rough that spectators on the ground could easily see the gliders pitching. After the gliders left England, conditions improved. The ceiling rose from 2,000 to 8,000 feet, and the clouds thinned out. Over France, clouds were scattered at more than 3,000 feet and visibility was excellent. Like the daylight missions of the day before, "Hackensack" had many fighters to protect it from the English coast onward, thus reassuring all in the sky trains. They approached LZW via the east coast over the St. Marcouf Islands and Utah Beach. No enemy fighters appeared, and enemy ground fire was negligible until the landing zone was reached. There, gliders became the primary targets. The lead serial began releasing gliders at 0851 hours, nine minutes ahead of schedule, and the other released its first gliders at 0859 hours, eleven minutes early. Serials then banked to the right and went home as they had come. Meager small-arms fire during and after the homeward turn scored some hits. Three aircraft in the 439th, and eight in the 441st were damaged, but none was lost. Between about 1000 and 1038 hours, all pilots arrived at their bases, except one who landed at Warmwell; his detour had been caused by one dead engine.

Glider release had been made from about 600 feet. The 439th Troop Carrier Group seems to have released by squadron, and since there was no marking on the zone to guide them, the glider pilots headed wherever they saw a promising spot. A dozen gliders from one squadron came down near the northern end of the zone under intense fire, killing several of the glider troops. Most of the gliders in another squadron landed about a mile west of the zone, while several landed about two and a half miles east of it from a third squadron. The last squadron's gliders were released over the southwest side of LZW, with the result that some came down in the flooded area which at that point extended very close to the zone, if not actually into it. Of twenty-nine Horsas accounted for, twelve landed within a mile of the zone, seven more within two miles of it, nine from two to four miles away and one nine miles off. Of the Wacos, seven were within a mile, six more within two miles and six between two and four miles away.

Small fields, high trees, flooded marshland, poles and wires set up by the Germans, debris from previous glider landings and enemy fire caused numerous accidents. No fewer than sixteen Horsas were destroyed and ten damaged in landing; fifteen of the soldiers aboard them were killed and fifty-nine injured. Of the Wacos, only four were destroyed and ten damaged, apparently without casualties. Two glider pilots in the serial were killed, and ten, possibly eleven, injured.

For no obvious reason, the comparatively inexperienced 441st Troop Carrier Group did vastly better than the three preceding serials. It made a concerted release over the northern part of LZW, and its gliders started down in the approved spiral pattern. The hazards and obstacles already described forced many glider pilots to zigzag about, looking for a safe landing place, but by daylight, in Wacos released above 600 feet, they could pick and choose in an area of several square miles. At least twenty-five gliders in this serial hit the zone, another ninteen were within about a mile of it and the remaining six were probably not far off. Although eight Wacos were destroyed and twenty-eight damaged, only one of the airborne occupants was killed and fifteen injured. Eighteen out of twenty jeeps and eight out of nine trailers came through unscathed. One glider pilot was killed and five injured. Highly accurate, with few casualties and with cargoes almost intact, this one serial reached the standard that glider enthusiasts had dreamed of.

By about 1015 hours, all battalions of the 325th Glider Infantry Regiment had reported in. A glider battalion instantly struck westward to Carquebut to eliminate Germans, who had held out stubbornly there on the previous night against the 8th Infantry Regiment (which had come in by sea). The battalion arrived at its objective early in the afternoon only to find that the Germans had withdrawn. It then followed the rest of the 325th Glider Infantry Regiment to Chef-du-Pont, where the regiment was to report for duty as the 82nd Airborne Division reserve. That evening, the 1st Battalion reported 545 officers and men fit for duty; the 2nd Battalion, 624; and the 3rd, 550. Only 57 glidermen were missing from the regiment, all but one of them being from the 1st Battalion. Despite the death or injury of 7.5 percent of its men from flak or crashes and the fact many had been severely shaken and bruised, about 90 percent of the glider regiment was ready to fight.

In all, U.S. glider landings and troop and equipment readiness satisfied the invasion planners. To some, the results vastly exceeded expectations. The pre-dawn missions had demonstrated that gliders could deliver artillery to difficult terrain in bad weather and in semidarkness, and put 40 to 50 percent of it in usable condition within two miles of a given point. The missions on D-Day+1 had shown that infantry elements could be landed within artillery range of an enemy by day and have 90 percent of their men assembled and ready for action within a couple of hours. While some felt that the "Chicago" and "Detroit" missions proved the feasibility of flying glider missions at night, the general consensus was that landing in daytime—or at least about sun-up— had proven to be much more accurate and much less subject to accidents and that the vulnerability of gliders to ground fire had been overrated.

American experience in Normandy indicated that the Waco was easier to fly, much easier to land and much more durable than the Horsa. Such a conclusion was not entirely warranted, since the American pilots were not as familiar with that glider. In addition, the low release altitudes of the American missions and the use of fields of minimum size for landings had combined to show the Horsas in an unfavorable light. In Normandy and in later operations, the British got good results with the big gliders.

General James Gavin rued the fact that glidermen did not have at least some rudimentary skill in piloting a glider. As he pointed out, some glidermen found themselves seated beside a wounded glider pilot, suddenly faced with getting the hurtling, heavily loaded glider safely to the ground. Fortunately, as he stated, the CG-4A was not too hard to fly, "but having to do it for the first time in combat was a chastening experience; it really gave a man religion."

In the hope of recovering a substantial proportion of the gliders used in "Neptune," 108 sets of glider pick-up equipment had been sent to England. Although IX Troop Carrier Command had put half its pick-up sets in storage—with a further 20 sets being damaged—and had only a limited number of crews qualified for pick-up operations, its resources proved to be more than sufficient. The American Horsas in Normandy were practically incapable of being flown. All but about forty of the Wacos were also found to be unserviceable or inaccessible to pick-up aircraft. Many of the remainder were damaged by vandals before they could be picked up. Some gliders in marginal condition might have been repaired on the spot or after a short flight to some base in Normandy. However, the troop carriers did not and could not have guards, bases or repair elements in Normandy for many weeks after "Neptune." The ground forces, hard put to sustain their fighting men, opposed the landing of any nonessential personnel, and the few bases in the beachhead were jammed to capacity with fighters. Bad weather and the combat situation combined to delay recovery operations until 23 June. After that, fifteen gliders were picked up and flown back to England. The technique worked well. However, 97 percent of the gliders used by American forces in Normandy were no longer combat-worthy and were left to rot in the narrow pastures in which they landed.

The status of the glider pilots after landing was anomalous. They were Army Air Corps troop-carrier personnel and, while they had been given some training in infantry tactics, it had been short and relatively sketchy. On the other hand, they constituted 20 percent of approximately 5,000 men brought into the battle area by glider. Plans called for them to assist in the unloading of the gliders and the clearing of the landing area, to assemble under the senior glider pilot in their vicinity and to report to the headquarters of the airborne division for such duties as might be required of them. It was contemplated that they would guard command posts and prisoners until a firm link-up with the amphibious forces was made and then be evacuated as soon as possible.

A majority of the glider pilots followed this pattern and, on the whole, did very well. About 300 gathered at Raff's headquarters near Les Forges, and 270 of them were evacuated to the beaches on the afternoon of 7 June. About 170 others, who had been guarding the headquarters and prisoners of the 82nd Airborne Division west of Sainte-Mere-Eglise, departed for the beaches with 362 prisoners at noon on 8 June after General Ridgway had addressed them in a speech, later embodied in a commendation, which thanked them warmly for their good service in Normandy. Most of the rest were collected and evacuated within three days after they landed.

While many glider pilots, particularly those landed in outlying areas, fought alongside the soldiers from the airborne units for a day or two, combat was limited to a short period during unloading and assembly by the great majority. There are few cases in which glider pilots were killed or wounded after leaving the vicinity of their gliders.

Out of 1,030 American glider pilots reaching Normandy, all but 197 had been accounted for by 13 June. What had happened to most of those missing at that time is indicated by a rise in known casualties from 28 on 13 June to 147 on 23 July. Of the latter total, 25 were dead, 31 wounded and 91 injured. An additional 33 who were still missing were probably prisoners.

The discipline and ground combat training of the glider pilots was criticized by the airborne personnel and by some of their own members. However, the policy of quick evacuation had worked well in Normandy and had won general acceptance. As long as it was assumed that glider pilots could and should be quickly evacuated, there was no justification for giving them extensive infantry training. It seemed much more important to improve their proficiency in tactical landings.

The 82nd Airborne Division's after-action report stated that the chance of becoming a casualty in a Horsa was 16 percent in darkness and 11 percent in daylight or 50 percent more than CG-4A rates.

Colonel Harry L. Lewis, commander of the 325th Glider Infantry Regiment, reported that thirty-five of his men flying in Horsas had been killed and one in the CG-4A's. Thirty-one men in Horsas had been wounded, twelve in CG-4A's. His regiment flew in 48 Horsas and 148 CG-4A's.

Operation "Neptune" proved that gliders could do their part in an airborne operation. They had carried 95 howitzers and antitank guns, 290 vehicles, and 238 tons of other cargo, in addition to 4,021 men. Two-hundred twenty-two Horsas and 295 Wacos had taken off from airfields in England. Somewhere en route, four of each had aborted their missions. Among the landing casualties, 123 came from among the troops who flew in the CG-4A's and 340 from those in Horsas, representing some 11 percent of the whole glider force. It was a substantial cost for an invasion foothold, but a cost that might have been tripled if the same number of forces had had to come over the beaches from landing craft and then struggle overland to objectives taken in minutes by glidermen coming in by air.

Perhaps a better solution than "Neptune" would have been one Generals Marshall and Arnold endorsed. Arnold complained bitterly in his book *Global Missions*:

It was obvious that General Eisenhower's staff had no intention of using airborne troops except for tactical missions directly in [the] rear of the enemy lines. The Air Force wanted to use these troops strategically, i.e., take a mass—four or five divisions—drop them down in a specially selected transportation center, for example, an area where there were several aviation fields, a locality that would be astride the German lines of communication, a position, the holding of which would make it impossible for the German troops to advance reinforcements and supplies, but definitely an area some distance behind the actual battlefield and beyond the area in which reserves were normally located.

For instance, the spot we had selected in connection with the Battle of Normandy was an area somewhere around Paris, where we believed the dropping of four, five or six airborne divisions would make it impossible for the Germans to hold out for any length of time against our troops, which were then on the beachheads. And the site we had tentatively selected for strategic paratroop operations when our troops reached a position approximately along the Rhine was an area far to the rear of the German lines, about halfway between the Rhine and Berlin—a zone far removed from any German reserves, which contained airdromes that we could use for supply, reinforcements, and such operations as were deemed necessary.

We presented these ideas to General Marshall, and he in turn asked us to send our planning team to Europe to sell the proposal to General Eisenhower and his staff. We sent them, but we didn't sell the idea to the SHAEF staff. We felt one of the advantages of these operations would be that the troops would drop in localities where there was no assembly of enemy reserves. We knew that every time we dropped airborne troops directly in the rear of the German lines, the paratroopers came down right in the midst of the reserve German divisions, and the landings of our airborne and glider troops following them in had to be made under the most difficult conditions. The Germans, anticipating this close-in drop, usually set up stakes and wires in the open fields.

General Marshall stated in his letter to General Eisenhower of 10 February 1944 that if he (Marshall) were in command of Operation "Overlord," this was exactly the sort of thing (dropping near Paris) he would do. The minds of General Eisenhower and his staff, however, were fixed on the necessity of obtaining the port of Cherbourg as quickly as possible; moreover, airborne commanders were apprehensive about an armored counterattack against an airhead. To the first objection, it could be replied that a port would have been less necessary if supplies were going in by air.

82ND AIRBORNE DIVISION GLIDER MOVEMENT TABLE

Serial	Airborne Unit	Carrier Unit	No. C-47s	CG 4A	Hor-sa	Takeoff Airfield	LZ	LZ Time
	Mission 'Detroit' (D-Day)							
28	Btys A & B 80 Abn AA Bn	437 Gp	52	42		Ramsbury	0	0400
	Hq 82 Abn Div (–)			6				
	ASP (Glider)			1				
	82 Abn Div Arty			1				
	82 Abn Sig Co			2				
	Mission 'Elmira' (D-Day)							
30	Bty C 80 Abn AA Bn	437 Gp	26		13	Ramsbury	W	2110
	Hq 82 Abn Div				4			
	Cmd Veh, Div Hq			3				
	82 Abn Sig Co			1				
	ASP (Glider)			1				
	82 Abn Div Arty			1	1			
	Hq 80 Abn AA Bn			2				
31	307 Abn Med Co	438 Gp	50		18	Greenham Common	W	2120
	82 Ron Plat			11				
	82 Abn Sig Co			1	9			
	Hq 82 Abn Div				9			
	ASP Vehicles (Prcht)			2				

Serial	Airborne Unit	Carrier Unit	No. C-47s	CG 4A	Hor-sa	Takeoff Airfield	LZ	LZ Time
32	319 Gli FA Bn	436 Gp	50		40	Membury	W	2300
	320 Gli FA Bn				4			
	82 Abn Div Arty			1	2			
	307 Abn Med Co			1	1			
	Co A 307 Abn Engr Bn (–)				1			
33	320 Gli FA Bn	435 Gp	50	12	38	Welford	W	2310

Mission 'Galveston' (D-Plus-One)

34	1 Bn 325 Gli Inf	437 Gp	50	28	15	Ramsbury	W	0700
	Co A 307 Abn Engr Bn			4	3			
35	Hq & Hq Co 325 Gli Inf	434 Gp	50	40		Aldermaston	W	0710
	82 Abn Div Arty			5				
	Co A 307 Abn Engr Bn			2				
	82 Abn Ron Plat			2				
	Cmd Veh 508 Prcht Inf			1				

Mission 'Hackensack' (D-Plus-One)

56	2 Bn 325 Gli Inf	439 Gp	50	10	15	Uppottery	W	0900
	2 Bn 401 Gli Inf			10	15			
37	2 Bn 325 Gli Inf Sply	441 Gp	50	18				0910
	2 Bn 401 Gli Inf Sply			18				
	Serv Co 325 Gli Inf			3				
	Cmd Veh 505, 507, 508 Prcht Infs			11				
	Totals		428	240	188			

Equipment Damaged in Landings

Daylight

	Jeeps			Trailers			Guns		
	No.	%	No. carried	No.	%	No. carried	No.	%	No. carried
Horsas	5	12·1	41	3	9·3	32	2	25	8
CG-4A	14	20	70	5	20	25	2	22·2	9

Darkness

| Horsas | 19 | 31·6 | 60 | 11 | 28 | 39 | 7 | 58 | 12 |
| CG-4A | 11 | 47·8 | 23 | 1 | 20 | 5 | 7 | 25 | 28 |

CHAPTER 10

Gliders Assault Normandy: British Phase

At about 2200 hours on 6 June 1944, three Horsas towed by Albemarles lifted off the Tarrant-Rushton Airfield in Dorset, one after another. Their mission was to destroy a major German coastal gun battery at Merville, sited to sweep the Normandy beaches and sea with deadly fire. The four 6-inch guns protruded from under a six-foot-thick concrete roof. Mines and barbed wire ringed the monster emplacement. If the glider force failed in its mission, fire from the Merville guns could later reach ships at sea carrying the British 3rd Infantry Division and also rake troops as they landed and crossed the beaches.

Major General R. N. Gale, commander of the British 6th Airborne Division, ordered the fifty-eight-man force of volunteers to crash land in the heart of the German position, relying on the concrete emplacement to tear off glider wings, and to arrest the progress of the fuselages.

A parachute battalion went ahead to be dropped in advance. It would assemble, breach the battery's defenses from the outside and assist the glider force. A five-glider support force was also en route carrying antitank guns, jeeps loaded with ammunition and scaling ladders for the paratroopers.

Right at the start, the combinations hit rough weather. Barely away from the airfield, one rope broke. To the chagrin of its passengers and crew, they had to land. The other combinations forged into the murk, finally climbing above it. But they then found dense cloud masses ahead. The Albemarle pilots wove around clouds when they could and ploughed through many others. Glider pilots gamely kept on, although buffeted severely.

Halfway over the Channel, the passengers and crew in the glider piloted by Staff Sergeant S. G. Bone felt a sudden heart-stopping deceleration. The arrester parachute, deployed to brake the glider when landing, had unaccountably broken open. The combination quickly began losing altitude. Bone realized what had happened and jettisoned the parachute seconds later, but the damage was done.

A Horsa being loaded by men of the 6th Airborne Division with a 6-pounder antitank gun.

A Jeep being pushed up the loading ramp into a Horsa.

Fortunately, the glider was still in one piece, but the tremendous jerk had severely strained the rear of its fuselage at the tail junction. How this would affect the landing was yet to be seen.

Things had hardly been sorted out, when tracers started reaching for the glider and tow plane. They were over the French coast, not more than 1,000 feet up, with heavy cloud directly above. Pilot Officer Garnett at the controls of the Albemarle did not flinch. He pushed through increasing flak to just above where he believed the objective was. But he was not sure, and he began to circle. The Germans had the combination in their sights and kept firing, while Garnett circled the area four times. In agreement with Garnett that the objective was close, Bone cut away from the Albemarle so as not to risk being shot down. He realized he was running out of time. He started towards what he thought was the battery. At 500 feet, he realized his mistake. It was the town he saw. He turned away, but he had to get landing attitude. He leveled off and brought the glider into a safe landing, but more than a half mile from the battery.

The remaining glider, piloted by Staff Sergeant L. D. F. Kerr, had better luck getting to the French coast, but then it started taking flak. In short order, two men were hit. Kerr circled the objective area four times, but not before two more men were shot. He released, saw what he thought to be the battery, aimed for it, streamed his parachute, heard the slap of orchard tree tops against the fuselage and mushroomed headlong into them, making a rending stop fifty yards from the battery. Outside, the glider was a torn shambles, but the fuselage, though scarred by rocks and trees, was intact. Inside, all was a jumble of groaning wounded, whole but dazed survivors and equipment. The first man had barely left the glider when he spotted a German platoon advancing on it.

The glidermen quickly opened fire, felling the foremost of the Germans, who, it was then realized, were reinforcements trying to get through to the battery. The glidermen drove the Germans back and then took up defensive positions among the trees and held off German assaults for five hours. No Germans broke through the British line.

Although they had not landed where planned, their efforts were proving invaluable. Lieutenant Colonel T. B. H. Otway, leading the 150 paratroopers—all he could collect of his badly scattered 600-man battalion—attacked the battery while the glidermen held off the German reserves. Paratroopers crawled forward and managed to push Bangalore torpedoes under the wire. They blew two gaps, and parachutists streamed through. Sweating, grimy paratroopers threw themselves at the Germans in dugouts and trenches rimming the emplacement, fighting hand to hand. The Germans fought back with determination until one, seeing the paratroopers' badges somehow

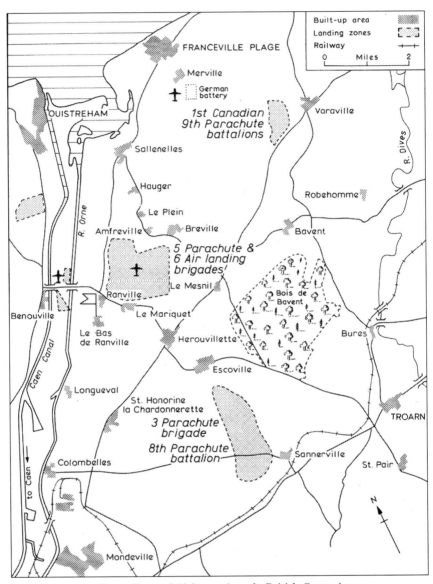

The Cross-Channel Airborne Assault: British Operations.

through the dark, screamed "*Fallschirmjäger!*" and the remaining Germans—some twenty-two in number—surrendered. Otway's men threw explosives down the tubes of the guns, found to be of 75-mm caliber. Otway had lost five officers and sixty-five men.

Meanwhile, another force in six gliders was on the way to capture two vital bridges. One was a swing bridge across the Caen Canal connecting Caen and the English Channel. The other crossed the Orne River, a few hundred yards away, running parallel to the canal. Three gliders had orders to land within 50 yards of the east end of the canal bridge, the other three 50 yards west of the river bridge. According to the plan, the 7th Parachute Battalion, landing some 1,000 yards east of the Orne Bridge, would reach the glider forces by capturing the bridge within half an hour of the glider landings. D-Day was nine minutes old when the first six combinations of Horsas and Halifax bombers crossed above the French coast, followed closely by four others.

At 5,000 feet and just above the outline of the French coast, glider pilots cut away from their tow planes far enough from the bridges for their towing aircraft to turn back unheard by the Germans; the gliders could sneak in like thieves in the night. It was so quiet and normal after crossing the coast that it seemed like just another airborne exercise to some.

For the men in one glider, their chief worry was whether the obstruction poles they had seen in reconnaissance photographs would wreck the glider when it came in to land. They were ready to face this risk, but knew that it was serious. To guard against it as far as possible, they all linked arms in the glider and braced themselves. Their most vivid memory is of the long time that elapsed between the moment of release and the moment of landing, even though it was only seven minutes. In fact, what they had thought to be poles proved to be holes dug by the Germans a few days previously. They had not had time to set up the wooden uprights.

The glider piloted by Staff Sergeants J. H. Wallwork and J. Ainsworth landed heavily, but safely. There was a loud crash as the wheels came off and sparks flashed past. They thought they had "bought" it, because the sparks looked like tracer bullets. In fact, they were caused by striking a wire fence. They had thrust up the exit door during the glide, and as soon as they came to rest, Ainsworth dove out and landed on his head. On getting to his feet, his first impulse was to feel his limbs to see that they were all there. His glider had landed precisely on target. Two more came in close behind, not far from the quaint Norman inn owned by *Monsieur* Georges Gondree.

Madame Gondree, who did not sleep well during the war, heard unusual rustling in the air outside the open bedroom window. She rushed to her husband's bedroom and shook him. At the time, they slept in separate rooms, not because they wanted to, but because that was the best way of preventing

German troops from being billeted in their house. She said, "Get up! Don't you hear what's happening? Open the window." Gondree was sleepy, and it took him some time to grasp what she meant. She repeated, "Get up! Listen! It sounds like wood breaking." He opened the window and looked out.

The window that Gondree opened was on the first floor of a cafe on the outskirts of Benouville. It is situated a few yards from the western end of the steel swing bridge that crosses the Caen Canal. By decree of the French government, it is now known as "Pegasus Bridge" (the design on the shoulder patch of the British 6th Airborne Division). It was moonlight, but he could see nothing, although he did hear snapping and crunching sounds. A German sentry stood at the bridgehead a few yards away, and Gondree, whose wife was an Alsatian and spoke excellent German, suggested that she should ask him what was happening. She leaned out of the window and did so, while her husband observed his face, clearly visible in the moonlight. His features were working, his eyes wide with fear. For a moment he did not speak. They then saw that he was literally struck dumb by terror. At last he stammered out one word: "*Fallschirmjäger!*"

"What a pity," *Madame* Gondree said to her husband, "those English boys will be captured." They both thought at that moment that what the sentry had seen was the crew of a bomber bailing out. Almost immediately, firing broke out and tracers began to flash across the night sky. Having two small children, the Gondrees took refuge in the cellar, where they remained for some time listening to the spasmodic sounds of battle outside. Then there was a knock on the front door, and a voice called on them in German to leave the cafe and walk in front of German troops. They remained where they were until *Madame* Gondree, clad only in her nightdress and shivering with cold, urged her husband to go up and see what was happening. Gondree did so. "I am not a brave man," he said later, "and I did not want to be shot, so I went upstairs on all fours and crawled to the first-floor window. I heard talk outside, but could not distinguish the words, so I pushed open the window and peeped out cautiously . . . in front of the café, I saw two soldiers sitting near my fuel pump with a corpse between them."

Somewhat unnerved by this sight, Gondree could not clearly understand the reply of the soldiers to his greeting in French, but he thought one of them said, "*Armee de l'air*," and the other, "*Englische Flieger*." He still thought that they belonged to the crew of a crashed bomber, but he was worried by the uniforms they had on and also by the fact that they seemed to be wearing black masks. This was scarcely reassuring, but the innkeeper, mindful of the danger in which he and his family appeared to stand, determined to continue his investigations.

He went to another window, this one looking on to the canal bank, which ran at right angles to the road crossing the bridge. Peering out, he saw two more soldiers who lifted their weapons and pointed them at him. By then there were a number of flares burning in the sky, so that he could see quite plainly. One of the soldiers said to him, "*Vous civile?*"

He replied, "*Oui, oui,*" adding something else that he does not remember.

The soldier repeated, "*Vous civile?*"

After a moment, the innkeeper realized that these were the only words of French the soldier knew. Gondree had been a bank clerk in Lloyds Bank in Paris for twelve years and therefore spoke good English. But he did not wish to let that fact be known at that moment, for he was not sure who they were. One of the soldiers then put his finger to his lips and gestured with his hands to indicate that Gondree should close the shutter. This he did, returning to the cellar.

Nothing more happened for some time until the Gondrees heard the sounds of digging in their vegetable garden outside. They looked through a hole in the cellar, and "there was the wonderful air of dawn coming up over the land." Shapeless figures moved about. They seemed peaceful enough and, to Gondree's astonishment, he could hear no guttural orders, which he always associated with a German working party. He turned to his wife and said, "*Ils ne guelent pas comme d'habitude.*" The light grew stronger, and he began to have serious doubts as to whether the people he could see were in fact the crew of a bomber; their behavior seemed to him to be very strange. Gondree told his wife to go to the hole in the cellar, listen and tell him if they were speaking German. She did so and presently said that she could not understand what they were saying. Then he in turn listened, and his heart began to beat quicker, for he thought he heard the words "all right."

Then there were the sounds of knocking. This time, Gondree opened the door to be confronted by two men with coal-black faces. He then realized that it was face paint, not masks, that they were wearing. They inquired in French whether there were any Germans in the house. He answered "no" and brought them in to the bar. With some reluctance on their part, which he overcame by smiles and gestures, he took them to the cellar. Arriving there, he pointed to his wife and two children. For a moment, there was silence. Then, one soldier turned to the other and said: "It's all right, chum." At last he knew that they were English, and he burst into tears.

Madame Gondree and her children kissed the soldiers at once and, as a result, they were immediately covered with black camouflage paint. *Monsieur* and *Madame* Gondree were, in all probability, the first French civilians to see

The landing zone for the main force of the 6th Airborne Division.

British airborne forces when they landed by parachute and from gliders on the morning of the Allied invasion of Europe.

Whatever resistance the Germans made came mostly from a few noncommissioned officers, deserted by their men who had fled into the night. Major R. J. Howard, in charge of the support gliders, ordered the glider pilots to unload the heavy weapons and to do so as quickly as possible. The enemy was expected to counterattack from Benouville at any moment.

"That's a funny sort of make-up. You look like a Red Indian," Howard said to Sergeant Wallwork, the first pilot of his glider. Then he realized it was blood, for Wallwork had been badly cut by splinters of Plexiglas and wood. The sergeant went on unloading the glider and then took his place in the defense. Howard rushed forward a Piat, a hand-held antitank weapon, to cover the approaches to the bridge, and he placed it in position near Gondree's land. It opened fire and destroyed the first of three old French tanks sent in by the Germans as the vanguard of their expected counterattack. Its ammunition continued to explode for more than an hour, giving the impression that a great battle was raging at the bridge.

Later, *Monsieur* Gondree opened his small cafe, tending the wounded and adding a more convivial sound to the noise of battle. He uncorked ninety-seven bottles of champagne, carefully hidden for just such a day as this. The German occupying forces had been kept happy with a concoction made by his wife from rotting melons and half-fermented sugar, which the Germans bought at twenty-five francs a glass and drank with gusto.

After a brush with a German patrol, the sound of grinding gears in the darkness seemed to indicate the presence of a tank. However, it proved to be a German staff car with a motorcyclist behind it. The first burst of fire checked but did not stop the car, and it roared over the bridge, only to be met by another and more accurate burst, which sent it reeling into the ditch. The German officer in charge of the bridge's defenses was removed from the vehicle, along with two empty wine bottles, a number of dirty plates and a quantity of rouge and face powder. Declaring that he had lost his honor by his failure to maintain the defenses of the bridge, the officer asked for death.

In the meantime, two gliders had landed to seize the Caen River Bridge. One came in close, the other 400 yards away. The forces in the closest glider, led by Lieutenant D. B. Fox, quickly attacked. They were supported by men under Lieutenant T. J. Sweeney from the second glider. They fought their way across the bridge.

Having crossed it, Sweeney found a small house on the other side occupied by a tiny old lady and her husband. In his best French, he explained that he and his men had arrived "*pour la liberation de la France.*" The old couple was frightened. Initially, they thought he was a German carrying out an exercise for the purpose of deceiving the French inhabitants, who might thus be induced to give themselves away and provide new victims for the Gestapo. Such German ruses were greatly feared throughout the invasion area and go far to explain the apparent indifference or covert hostility with which Allied troops were at first greeted. When dawn came, the little old lady, realizing that this was not some ruse, kissed Lieutenant Sweeney and made ready to rejoice. Like Major Howard at the bridge over the canal, he had been busy developing defenses to hold his bridge. Glider engineers soon discovered that for some unaccountable reason, the Germans had placed no explosives to blow up the bridges to prevent them from falling to the Allied forces intact.

Soon the long column carrying the main glider force was on its way from England to France. Lieutenant Colonel Iain Murray could see the outline of the immense armada. His glider carried Brigadier Hugh Kindersley, the commander of the 6th Air Landing Brigade, some of his staff, and Chester Wilmot, the writer, who was making a running commentary into a recording machine.

Turning in from the coast, the visibility became very poor. A combination of cloud, smoke, and dust caused by bombing obscured the ground completely. This may have been a godsend, for it made the considerable flak inaccurate. Nearing their objective, the glider pilots found the visibility improved, and they could soon see the flares put out by the Independent Parachute Company. The gliders cast off from their tugs. As aerial photos had shown, the Germans had antiglider "Rommel's asparagus" in the glider landing areas. In the last few yards, one post tore a wingtip and one collapsed when hit head-on by the cockpit. Murray thought this one must have been loosely placed by some patriotic Frenchman employed by the Germans.

Soon after landing, he found that Chester Wilmot's recorder had been smashed by a piece of flak shrapnel, which was most unfortunate. However, Wilmot had a good picture in his mind, and the description he later gave in his book *Struggle for Europe* gave a very clear account of events up to the time of landing.

Apart from occasional rifle and machine-gun fire, there was no great opposition, and they soon gathered at the rendezvous to await the dawn. As soon as daylight came, they went down to the Pegasus Bridge to find that one glider had landed within 100 feet of it. This was a remarkable feat on the part of the glider pilot. It had enabled the troops he carried to rush the bridge and capture it before it could be blown. This was a very vital task, for the use of the bridge was of great assistance to the commandos and the main body of troops in crossing the river.

General Gale waited at midday on this bridge to hand over control to Lord Lovat and his commandos, having bet Lord Lovat a case of champagne that he would not be there at the appointed time. As the hour approached, there was no sign of him, but as the clock struck noon, a piper seemed to appear from nowhere, leading Lord Lovat and his commandos to relieve General Gale and win his bet.

Eleven Horsas came in to the parachute landing zone carrying engineers, antitank guns for the paratroopers and two bulldozers. Pilots found landing-control lights difficult to see through the dust and smoke.

One glider pilot said goodbye to his tug pilot, heard a "good luck" come back, followed by the familiar jerk. The noise of the wind gradually receded to the background and the speed dropped back to a more modest eighty miles per hour. Paddy, his co-pilot, had handed over the controls and was intently watching a battery of flak on the right, whose tracer seemed to be a bit too near. Paddy motioned to it and, almost at once, as the pilot put on half flap, the flak turned and seemed to find another target. They saw the target, another Horsa, well below. It was flying towards the flak. Just a second later, the Horsa switched on its emergency lights and illuminated a small row of trees between the pilot's glider and the T along which the second Horsa was flying. It crashed.

Fortunately, Paddy's glider was coming in just right. There came a little bump, and then another, something like a ditch. Then a wheel seemed to stick and started to swing the glider round. With a deft touch on the opposite rudder and brake, it straightened out and stopped. Paddy and his pilot heaved a sigh and then immediately shot out of their seats: They were on the first light of the T and not in their correct position on the extreme left of the T. Having been forewarned by a training mishap that this might happen, they arranged that Paddy should jump out and wave his torch to show the rear of the glider. At the same time, the pilot jumped out, grabbing personal items and rifles with feverish haste, and they took up positions on either side of the glider.

All got ready to beat a hasty retreat if another glider started coming in on top of them, but there was not a sign of anything in the sky. It was like being at an appointed place at the right time, waiting for someone to arrive, and then being "stood up." Everyone felt like that at first. Then a feeling of being abandoned took hold. Even the Germans did not greet them. Where were the pathfinders who had put the T out? Not a soul, not a noise, nothing. Paddy stared towards the pilot in the blackness and said, "Let's get the tail off."

They went inside the glider and began to undo the nuts holding the tail. They had them off within a quarter of an hour, but the tail would not budge. They called the two drivers over. An odd tug of war ensued: one Horsa Mark I versus four tired and sweating airborne types. The glider won. While the men sat back exhausted for a moment, it sat there quite contentedly, for all

Tank-carrying Hamilcars gliding into Normandy.

The scene after the landings. One glider has crashed in flames.

the world as if it were back in England. They thought of blowing the tail off, but the noise it would make and the type of equipment inside ruled that out. Then, just as they had picked up the hand saw, they heard the sound of approaching aircraft. Right above them, the air blossomed with billowing parachutes. It was a wonderful sight, and they did not feel lonely any larger. For the next five minutes, they busily dodged kit bags dangling from the feet of heavily loaded paratroopers. One even landed on the Horsa's tail, but nothing happened. When the paratrooper was then asked for help to get the tail off, he simply grinned and vanished. An Albemarle on the left lit up in flames and brought them all back to earth with a jolt.

Gliders crossed other gliders' approach paths unknowingly. Gliders whizzed past from opposite directions, seeing each other go by only when the distance closed to thirty feet or so. But with the Horsa's ability to absorb punishment, few men were hurt. One bulldozer broke through the floor as its Horsa careened over the earth, but it stayed with the glider until it stopped. Seventy-nine Horsas were landing, their pilots having great difficulty because of the appalling conditions.

Staff Sergeant Leslie Foster saw a flaming British aircraft dive towards the ground. He kept looking for the church tower and other landmarks that marked turning and landing points. There was the tower. He spoke into the intercom, thanking the tow pilot for the ride and got an "OK, 'Matchbox,' best of luck."

Foster reached for and pulled the release. The glider slowed and flew alone over the fields of France. He put down half-flap and turned slowly to port, a full 180 degrees. The landing field stretched out in front of them. He increased to full flap and put the nose down. Everything seemed to be going extremely well when a warning shout came from his co-pilot: "Leskite coming in from . . ." It was too late to do anything but pull back hard on the stick as the other glider soared up under and across him. There was a terrible tearing, crashing sound, and he saw the other cabin hang for a split second under him and then fall away. The speed dropped alarmingly as they hovered with the nose up. He quickly brought up the flaps and pushed hard on the stick to try to get up some speed. It was obvious that the undercarriage must have gone in the crash, and he realized that it would have to be a "belly landing"—if they were fortunate enough to reach the ground in one piece.

There was no sound from the men inside, but the roaring of the air increased as the needle moved faster and faster. It was no use letting up. He would have no brakes, and his safest bet was to hit the ground as soon as possible and pray that the hard French soil would halt them before they hit the trees at the far end of the field. Ninety . . . ninety-five . . . the screaming of the air past the fuselage. One hundred . . . one-hundred ten . . . full flap on . . . up with the nose . . . and they were tearing through the high French corn, the red earth pouring through the broken floor. Nothing but the long straight parting of the corn. Then, suddenly, the open patch before the trees. Hard kick on the right rudder. Would it work? They slewed round in a great half-circle, the soil shooting high in the air. As they stopped, almost touching the trees, there was a tearing sound, and a very tired port wing fell to the ground. When they had extricated themselves from the remains, they found that one of their Thermos flasks was miraculously unbroken, and they examined themselves as they sat sipping the hot tea. A few scratches on the co-pilot. A few on Foster. No passenger casualties.

Others were not so fortunate. Many of their gliders landed far from the zone, others snapped off wings on the poles, or on the heavy cable which the Germans had strung between the poles, connecting them to fused artillery shells. These went off when shocked by a glider's impact.

Staff Sergeant A. Proctor was the last of a flight of Horsas to arrive over the landing zone and, as a result, came in at the end of a long line of gliders on the approach. For that reason, he presented perhaps the best target, and the German gunners gave him their undivided attention. Evasive action became essential. As there was no room in the approach area, he dived away into the wind with the intention of pulling out at the last moment and making a crosswind landing. The plan worked well until he pulled up to about 100 feet from the ground and turned crosswind. The area he had chosen to land in was heavily studded with anti-invasion poles, but there was no alternative but to land there. In a rapid survey of the ground, he made an interesting discovery: the methodical Germans had erected the poles in a distinct pattern, and it was this that saved him. He maneuvered the glider until they were flying a few feet over the poles, then ordered full-flap, and as the next gap appeared he thrust the stick forward. Both wings struck poles simultaneously. With a great rending of wood, he landed heavily, but still on a straight course, coming to a halt before reaching the next alternating row of poles. Five trembling artillerymen emerged from the cockpit and assured him that they had never doubted his ability. At the time, it seemed kinder to believe them.

The second pilot, Sergeant Wright, took charge of the unloading. While that was being done, Proctor thought it might be prudent to see what was going on outside. It was then that he heard the whine of bullets uncomfortably close, and he realized with some alarm that they were probably being directed at him. He went to ground with speed and observed that the fire was coming from a church tower about 500 yards away. He shouted a message to this effect to the glider, to which Sergeant Wright replied, "Come inside then, you silly . . . " Saving his rude remarks until later, Proctor asked for the Bren gun. Worming his way around the glider, he sited the gun and opened fire on the church tower. This silenced the enemy fire. Unloading was then completed, farewells exchanged, and the Royal Artillery left at high speed.

Sergeant Proctor and Sergeant Wright took a compass bearing and set off in a direct line for their own rendezvous, coming upon another Horsa that had struck a pole head on while landing in the same area, killing both pilots in a horrible fashion.

Meanwhile, the glider engineers, with their two bulldozers, hurriedly began to get landing strips ready for the arrival of the largest serial of the British portion of Operation "Neptune," consisting of sixty-eight Horsas and four Hamilcars. Both machines were at work on preparing landing strips within an hour of landing. In eight hours, well within the margin of time allotted, they had cleared the four strips of glider debris and filled in the antiglider postholes that had been dug by the enemy. The engineers worked without pause or intermission, all the time under sniper, mortar and shellfire. By the time the leading glider carrying General Gale appeared, the sappers had cleared two 1,000-foot airstrips and lighted them with flares. Although the airstrips provided much landing space, it was far from adequate for the forty-nine remaining enormous birds that had made it to their objective. A vicious crosswind made matters worse. The pilots crowded their Horsas into the strips where they could, but some could not avoid the poles fringing the strips that the engineers had not had time to remove. Some piled into other gliders.

When he cast off, Staff Sergeant T. W. Pearce found the air crowded with gliders, parachutes and discarded towropes. Without warning, his glider got a rending jolt. He had just collided with another glider. He was 600 feet up. He struggled to get control and just barely managed to land sideways, coming to a juddering halt in tall corn. His first pilot turned to him and said: "Time for a cup of tea, Tom!" (They had two flasks strapped above their heads. One was still intact. The "pin-ups" that had also accompanied them were also still taped in place.) Chopping their way out of the wreckage, they dashed over to the other glider or, perhaps better said, to what was left of it. In the mid-air crash, the tail unit had been destroyed, and it had dived vertically from 600 feet. Pearce had lost two of his own flight, but everyone in the other glider had perished.

Hugh Wheldon, later on a famed newscaster of the BBC, came in on one of the gliders, escorted by a cloud of fighters. But nothing, absolutely nothing, about D-Day was turning out as expected. There was no fierce fighter opposition . . . no signs of flak . . . no wrecked gliders in the fields below.

In his glider, some of the "Red Devils" about to penetrate the Atlantic Wall were sucking jujubes. Or they looked like jujubes . . . looking again, Wheldon saw that they had taken the barley sugar from the special airborne rations that were supposed to last for three days.

"Put them away," he said sharply, before they devoured the compound cakes of porridge. "Want to live on grass?"

"But, sir," one Irish rifleman said, "they're very good, them sweets."

They were not gliding in the accepted sense of the word. As always, it was as if they were "in a very old railway carriage being yanked across the sky." As always, they had rehearsed for this for weeks and months: landing on fields and roads and hills. Once, they even turned over in the air. Sitting upside down, strapped into his seat, the platoon sergeant, famed for his ferocity, had recited the Lord's Prayer seven times without pause or punctuation.

From the moment they crossed the French coastline, sweat began to run down the back of the glider pilot's neck. There were two little runnels of it, "like bacon fat." He was working overtime.

"We're casting off," he said, and Wheldon turned round to strap himself into his seat. At first he could not believe it, but Mullins, the company runner, was asleep. Mullins was a magnificent character, later to become a sergeant. He had been very good company all the way and had now apparently decided to have a quiet nap just before the tow plane discarded them.

"Come on, Mullins," Wheldon said, "we're invading Europe." Groaning, Mullins rubbed at his eyes and, looking bored, began to buckle up.

The glider came down with all the grace "of an empty can," as Wheldon recounted. It made a perfectly smooth landing on a soft field on a glorious summer's night. Other gliders, quite undamaged, did the same. But it was pretty difficult to believe it. They had been warned and trained, trained and warned, that the dangerous time was the moment immediately after landing, when they would be disorganized and defenseless, relaxing in the relief of being down.

Like everybody else, Wheldon had to leap out of that cardboard aircraft and become part of an organized unit, oriented around the Bren gun. He leapt out, and the grass smelled fine and sweet. There seemed to be action everywhere and machine guns were hiccupping, but nobody seemed to be firing at them.

After two hours in the glider, he wanted to relieve himself first, certain that the others would gather around the machine gun. When he looked around to make sure that they had adopted an all-round defense, he saw that all of them were following his example. Despite the rifles and the ammunition, despite the camouflaged smocks and parachute helmets, despite the blackened faces, they looked like small boys on a Sunday school treat. The absurdity of it dawned on them all, and they dove down behind the Bren gun as if their lives depended on it.

Their next job was to leave the landing zone, which was not an area conducive to good health, and rendezvous with the rest of C Company, the

1st Battalion of the Royal Ulster Rifles, in a patch of woods. C Company as a whole would then go to the battalion, waiting to attack. When they reached the patch of woods, one of the riflemen from another element was waiting.

As they crouched to talk, Wheldon noticed that the man was feeling like the rest. He had this dreamy, slightly mystified, let's-try-to-take-it-seriously look.

"Sir," he whispered, "it's a miracle. Not a casualty. Not a single Anglo-Saxon man. Every Anglo-Saxon man arrived unharmed. The whole Anglo-Saxon company's here. It's an Anglo-Saxon miracle." While they were cowering there, McCutcheon came out from the wood. He was the bravest man Wheldon ever knew, the best man he ever knew.

"Sir, come to headquarters," he said.

"Let's get on," Wheldon said. "We don't have to go to company headquarters. Got to get on."

"Sir," he said, with determination in his voice, "I would like you to come to company headquarters."

They plunged into the woods through nettles and brambles. Right in the center, there was a lean-to hut and a small fire. They had been on the soil of France for fifteen minutes, and the men had been in that hut ten minutes at the most! Nodding like a chummy canteen hostess, Rifleman Rimmer handed Wheldon a cup of tea.

Once on the ground, the glider pilots began fighting as a unit and were soon in action. By evening, ninety-three pilots composing "Force John" were dug in and defending their landing zone from the southwest. One of them, Captain B. Murdoch, found himself involved in a sharp action against tanks. He was acting as loader at the time on a 6-pounder antitank gun, of which the layer had been killed. Captain Murdoch took over, and he and the other gunners miraculously succeeded in destroying four out of five enemy tanks.

Although General Gale had a substantial force available from the gliders that had started from England by then, he had them at substantial cost. In his serial, forty-nine out of the seventy-two gliders that took off landed according to plan. Five made forced landings in the United Kingdom, three in the sea and fourteen were lost.

Of the fourteen gliders that failed to reach their destination, one, piloted by Major J. F. Lyne, had been hit by flak in the tail when crossing the coast and the tow rope broke. The glider was in clouds and immediately began to descend. On coming out into clear air, it was again hit, a shell bursting in the center of the fuselage. The jeep it was carrying was damaged, but no one was hurt. Beneath the glider, blinking gunfire and arching tracers broke the blackness. To choose a suitable spot for landing was a nerve-racking task for the pilot. The glider sailed remorselessly earthward, and a pale patch loomed up at the last moment. It "seemed to be a little less dark than the rest of the countryside." It was an orchard, and Major Lyne crashed his glider into it, breaking his foot and cutting the face of his second pilot. Those were the only mishaps on his aircraft.

The party of seven set off, their object being to find someone who could tell them where they were. They soon ran into Germans, and the party hid under nominal concealment in a field until dawn to avoid detection. They then found a farmer who directed them towards the Dives River. They crossed it by swimming and joined up with some Canadian parachute forces that were isolated near Robehomme. By then, they were entirely surrounded by the enemy, and it took them three days to break out and reach Ranville. Throughout that time, the French inhabitants were of the greatest help, and their grapevine information service enabled Lyne and his men to know the exact position of the enemy at all times. During their wanderings, they met with a farm laborer and his family who produced "a portrait of Queen Victoria tastefully executed in Nottingham lace" as evidence of their love of England and provided them with a meal, a map torn from a school atlas and two pocket dictionaries.

Eventually, Major Lyne and the rest entered the Bois de Bavent and there, exhausted by forty-eight hours of stumbling through marshland, hiding in ditches, swimming streams and thrusting their way through unyielding undergrowth, reached at long last a road running in the right direction. At that moment, the enemy appeared. The weary men sprang into action. "We managed to eliminate two lorry-loads of Germans and a car with four officers in it," Major Lyne reported, "by the simple process of throwing hand grenades at them. They were all wiped out. By this time, we were all very tired." When they eventually reached the landing zone after another fight, they had marched forty-five miles from the place where the glider had landed.

Men like these and their comrades—stubbornly holding the perimeters of the landing zones—made possible the mass landing of gliders on the evening of the first day, which had been watched so thankfully by Private Owen from his slit trench on the bank of the Caen Canal. In a maneuver as technically perfect as the changing of the guard at Buckingham Palace, every Hamilcar carrying tanks and 112 out of the 114 Horsas landed and poured out the 6th Air Landing Brigade and a number of other units, including the Armoured Reconnaissance Regiment—all under intense shelling.

Hamilcars and Tetrarchs engaged in their own unique and totally surprising, if not precarious, adventures. In one Tetrarch, Major Barnett heard his Hamilcar pilot saying over the intercom, "The landing zone is in view, prepare to cast off from the tug." Seconds later, the tank crew felt the nose of the glider rise as though on the crest of a gentle wave as the rope was released. On full flaps, it nosed into a steep dive towards the north-south landing lane on LZN. The Hamilcar cut through young corn at nearly eighty miles an hour, lurching violently and sloughing away half a wing at an obstacle pole. Sensing touchdown, the tank driver started the engine. Once the Hamilcar had come to rest, the co-pilot "pulled the plug out" to drain the oil from the shock absorbers and allow the fuselage to sink wearily onto the ground. Spoiling for action, the tank driver threw off the tank's mooring ropes, and the Tetrarch nudged forward, striking the trip-wire to open the nose door.

Other Hamilcars, jostling for position in the eager dive for fields in the landing zone, found little space left. One of them slammed into a Tetrarch that had suddenly appeared forty yards ahead, and the tank was tipped over. This was the only casualty among the Tetrarchs. Even at that, it was not long out of commission; the crew was unhurt. Helped by another tank crew and its tank during the night, they righted it.

Some of the gliders were barely scratched. Even one that ripped a hedgerow would have flown again. One of the first fatal casualties was a Hamilcar pilot, Staff Sergeant C. B. Robinson, killed by mortar fire at landing. Pilots assembled in an orchard, trying unsuccessfully to dig defensive trenches with inadequate tools—a failure that thoroughly upset a platoon of tough paratroopers intending to position themselves there. It almost produced a state of civil war between the two factions.

The next day, the glider pilots proceeded to the beaches, past the crumpled Horsas and over one of the bridges that the forces they carried had captured and defended. There, a ship took them to England and a debriefing.

Rumbling out of the gliders, intent upon heading swiftly southeast through fields and hedgerows to their pre-arranged rendezvous near Breville, Tetrarchs found the ground littered with discarded parachutes that had brought troops and supplies that had been dropped earlier in the day. The nylon canopies and rigging lines, winding around the sprockets, choked and immobilized half the tanks only 300 yards from their gliders. The colored canopies of the parachutes were easy to see from a distance, and the drivers had a chance to steer around them, but the camouflaged paratrooper parachutes merged deceptively with the ground. Dusk made it doubly difficult to see them. The tanks were trapped within an unyielding nylon net of snaking lines amid the crops there. Most crews struggled desperately to get the spaghetti-like tangle unraveled. Mercifully, the enemy did not harass the disgruntled crews.

By noon on D-Day, ten antitank guns, together with the tanks brought in by the Hamilcars and the ground forces brought in by gliders, had joined in the overall effort of the British 6th Airborne Division to clear the east flank of the invasion of Germans. They had effectively silenced the German battery at Neville and were helping to drive off counterattacks.

Men of the 6th Airborne Division beside the glider in which they landed. Note the writing in chalk on the side of the Horsa.

A Horsa which crashed into a wall near Sainte Mere Eglise, killing two of its passengers.

CHAPTER 11

Abandon Glider!

I said, "I've heard a lot of wild reports in my life, but that's the wildest I ever heard! The Japs can't possibly tow gliders here from their nearest base, and certainly, they're not going to waste their precious carrier decks on any such nonsense. My God!"

ADMIRAL WILLIAM F. HALSEY TO ADMIRAL HUSBAND E. KIMMEL,
SEVERAL DAYS AFTER THE JAPANESE ATTACK ON PEARL HARBOR
(FROM ADMIRAL HALSEY'S STORY)

In April 1941, one year after the Germans first used gliders, Captain Marc A. Mitscher, then the assistant chief of the Bureau of Naval Aeronautics, directed the production of a personnel- and equipment-carrying Navy glider. The Navy quickly reacted to the German airborne invasion of Crete that month and, within a fortnight, decided to produce enough gliders to transport a Marine battalion. It quickly contracted to develop and build two float-wing gliders that could land upon water. One glider was to carry twelve passengers, and the other model, sporting twin hulls, twenty-four passengers.

So enthusiastic was the U.S. Marine Corps about the glider as a military weapon that it pressed the Navy's Bureau of Aeronautics for production before an experimental glider had been built. The Marines wanted 100 twelve-place and 50 twenty-four-place gliders, enough to transport two battalions. Although there was no strategic plan for the use of the amphibious gliders, the Marine Corps wanted to be prepared to use any weapon and any method of attack that could be developed, and it wanted it in its arsenal ready to go. Conservative heads decided that until experimental gliders could be tested and questions relating to the technique of towing settled, however, there should be no large-scale procurement.

In view of the German sinking of Allied shipping, glider enthusiasts argued that the demand for transport gliders would be enormous as soon as models were flying. The Germans had not only demonstrated the usefulness of these aircraft in the capture of Crete, but the Germans were also making extensive use of gliders to supply Rommel in Africa according to the latest information. This was Hitler's method of overcoming the problem of Allied control in the Mediterranean. The glider sponsors in the United States saw that U.S. military forces were faced with critical shortages of supplies because of the growing number of ships being sunk and saw a way to move critical supplies over water quickly by means of large cargo gliders. They also wanted to solve the problem of jumping from island to island in the Pacific over the head of the Japanese fleet.

In spite of the enthusiasm, success in the development of gliders was certainly less than desirable. The program was in chaos, and major delays were commonplace. The pressure to expand the program was strong, however. At this stage, the Marine Corps had raised its sights and asked for sufficient gliders to transport four battalions and enough replacement equipment for three successive operations. All too quickly, the Navy upped requirements from 150 to 1,000 gliders. By June 1942, the program looked toward 1,371 gliders, and 3,436 pilots and co-pilots flying 10,800 men, despite the evidence that gliders would be about as useful on the Pacific islands as pogo sticks. So contagious was the expansive attitude that one contractor proposed to the Navy the production of 12,000 twelve-place amphibious gliders.

Regardless of the optimism in certain quarters, delays in building test gliders continued to grow, so that it was not until October 1942 that the Navy got its first test glider, more than a year and a half after the program was first visualized. This so dimmed the outlook for the Navy's twenty-four-seat development models yet to be built that some planners recommended the British twenty-five-place Horsa glider be used as a hedge against the failure of the former program. Desperate for usable aircraft, the Navy strategists now looked to the Army's fifteen-place CG-4A to fill Marine Corps needs. The fly in the ointment was, however, that the Horsa and the CG-4A were not amphibious and were difficult to adapt to that type of warfare. Consequently, that plan was dropped. The delays in the program actually acted as a dissuading force to those who were intent on its development, and these delays served to enable the Navy and the Marine Corps to make a more thorough study of the glider as a weapon suitable to their needs in the Pacific. By September 1942, the services gradually took the viewpoint that gliders were a less efficient means of transport than powered aircraft and that they were not practicable over great distances, particularly in weather that would make it necessary for glider pilots to fly by instruments. By the middle of October 1942, it became evident that the glider program was "satisfactory in no respect," although a review board suggested the continuance of certain parts of the program. The Navy soon dropped two of the four major contractors.

The hopes of certain advocates in the Marine Corps for the extensive use of gliders in the Pacific dwindled. They realized they knew little regarding the abilities of the glider, and little experience was coming in from any other source to enable them to take a sound position. Although the Navy was seriously involved in deciding whether the Marine Corps would be able to use gliders in the Pacific, it too was making little headway in coming to a decision on the matter. Apparently, the Navy was withholding a decision until experience could be obtained, even though General Thomas Holcomb, the Commandant of the Marine Corps, recommended that the Marine Corps glider program should be abandoned in view of the number of adverse reports (April 1943).

In May 1943, one of the contractors finally delivered the first flight-test glider. The delay in delivery was ostensibly caused by difficulties in installing a retractable tricycle landing gear on the machine, but it was really due in large measure to manufacturer inexperience in building gliders.

By 1943, American fortunes in the Pacific had so remarkably improved that the need for gliders had become less urgent. By then, opinion had changed conclusively. Studies concluded that military gliders, whether amphibious or land-based, were of no value to the Marine Corps and cited a year's study and observation of production and operations in the United States and abroad. The two services also concluded that the military glider was not a proven weapon and that the Marine Corps had no use for unproven equipment. Finally, the funds and personnel involved in the program had been of such magnitude and the results so dismal that it was felt there had been an unnecessary and unjustifiable use of resources. No one wanted more of this unconscionable waste. One company charged the Navy $150,000 for each of the fifteen gliders it built—about five times the average cost of the Army's CG-4A. Another company brought costs down to $100,000 dollars for each glider, still more than three times the Army's average cost.

Undismayed, supporters of the program continued to push for its continuance, maintaining that the main trouble with the Marine Corps organization of glider troop battalions and its operational planning was that it had got going too early, far ahead of the production of gliders. The program's adherents also maintained that uninformed senior officers never divorced the fragile sailplane from the combat glider. Many people who returned from the South Pacific said that float-wing gliders would have been useful at Guadalcanal in bringing men, fuel and supplies to the beachhead. Sentiment for the glider persisted in some Navy quarters, despite growing Marine disenchantment. This segment thought the Navy should take charge of the program and "develop gliders for naval supply operations, such as carrying gasoline and high priority cargo." Even so, by the close of 1943, it appeared to everyone that the glider program would continue to have a low priority.

Exasperated with the way the program was going, Thomas Gates, Jr., the assistant secretary of the Navy for air, sent a memorandum to one of his assistants involved in the program on 4 September 1943, stating in effect that the production of one of the manufacturers "looks like a mess, and that it has followed a course some predicted. Who wants these goddamned gliders? Why not cancel the whole damned contract right now, call it a day, save man-hours and money." He tolled the death knell of the program. Whatever residues then remained in actual gliders and materials were transferred to the Naval Aircraft Factory in Philadelphia and the Naval Aircraft Modification Unit at Johnsonville, Pennsylvania, by the end of 1943, and the program ended. At its peak strength, the Marines' glider organization had 36 officers, 246 men and 21 gliders.

The glider had come over the intellectual horizon of naval leaders a bit too unexpectedly. As with Army Air Corps leaders who knew too little about this maverick aircraft, who could see no way to the stars through supporting it or flying in it, and whose time and materials were drawn to more glamorous aircraft, so it was with the admirals. Admirals sail in ships, not in "sailplanes" or anything coming close to this unknown weapon of war, which had no proven qualities.

The U.S. naval glider XLRQ-1, which also had retractable gear for landing on the ground.

CHAPTER 12

"Dragoon": The Southern Pincer

If a glider should break loose at sea, the towing aircraft will circle the glider and send out normal distress signals stating glider down at sea!

62ND TROOP CARRIER GROUP, OPERATIONS ORDER, 13 AUGUST 1944

At about 0630 hours on 15 August 1944, the first gliders of the final Allied invasion to strike Hitler's shrinking fortress in Europe began taking off from a cluster of airfields near Rome and from other airfields extending 150 miles down the Italian coast. They were to fly for some four hours behind serials of hundreds of planes loaded with paratroopers. The force was on its way to "Dragoon," a mission to drop forces in the Argens River Valley, well behind the Mediterranean coast of southern France, and to cut off German forces in the coastal area from German forces to the north.

The U.S. Seventh Army staffs began planning "Dragoon" in February 1944. A shortage of airborne forces and air transports put the staff in a quandary about who could be freed from other critical commitments for the job ahead. It was not until a month before D-Day that the situation jelled and specific airborne formations received orders forming them into the 1st Airborne Task Force, a provisional airborne division-equivalent formation commanded by Major General Robert T. Frederick. Brigadier General Paul L. Williams took command of a Provisional Troop Carrier Air Division assigned to transport Frederick's task force.

American airborne units, together with the British 2nd Parachute Brigade Group and special elements activated for the mission, had been rapidly assembled near Rome to prepare for "Dragoon." The War Department sent thirty-six officers for General Frederick's staff. Most were from the U.S. 13th Airborne Division, with a few from the Airborne Center.

The British 2nd Air Landing Brigade, the U.S. 550th Glider Infantry Battalion and an assortment of signal and other support units made up the glider troop elements, totaling some 2,700 men. Horsas and Wacos, piloted by British and Americans, respectively, were to bring in more than 220 jeeps, trailers and guns and the major portion of supplies and ammunition.

Nine pathfinder aircraft with 121 paratroopers took off at 0100 hours from Marcigliana in Italy to mark the parachute dropping zones around Le Muy, lying on the Argens River in southern France, about twenty-five miles west of Cannes. A short while later, the first aircraft carrying the main parachute forces followed. Some predictions concerning what was to arise through the morning could be made from what befell the pathfinders. They reached France exactly on schedule and approximately on course. Over the Riviera, they encountered a blanket of fog, through which they had to grope by dead reckoning supplemented by vague relief maps of the terrain. The nine-aircraft serial lost its way, circled back to the sea and made a second run. After about half an hour of circling, one aircraft dropped its chalk and went home. Two other aircraft separated soon after that, and one dropped its team about 0400 hours. The last team jumped at about 0415 hours on its sixth run.

All three teams of airborne troops landed in the same general area, a wooded and mountainous region between Frejus and Grasse ten to fifteen miles east of Drop Zone C. Some aspects of the terrain may have deluded the navigators into thinking they were over the drop zone. Two were sure they had dropped in the right place. Lost in the woods and far from their objective, none of the three teams reached the Le Muy area in time to act as pathfinders or even to take part in the fighting there.

Without the pathfinders but helped to some extent by the Eureka beacons operated by the *maquis,* most of the aircraft with the paratroopers groped blindly for clues as to where to discharge their chalks. Some of the ten serials carrying the 5,600 paratroop infantry and artillery did notably well and dropped their men and equipment right on target by means of dead reckoning. Others dropped men as far as ten miles from Le Muy. The fog and the uncertainty created led to the wide dispersal of paratroopers and had an adverse bearing on "Bluebird," the morning glider mission that was warming up at that point.

At 0518 hours, the first of thirty-five Horsa combinations, towed by C-47's of the 435th Troop Carrier Group, took off from Tarquinia, with the others following at one-minute intervals. They crossed Cape D'Uomo at 0612 hours, followed eight minutes later by the 436th Troop Carrier Group, which was towing forty CG-4A's. They were hardly off the coast when one Waco combination turned back, its C-47 engines overheating.

The last Horsa had just passed over Corsica when General Williams radioed the serial commander to turn back. His instructions were that they should land at fields in Corsica if fuel was low, although this was a slight possibility, since the planes had been in the air only slightly more than an hour. General Williams had foreseen trouble if the C-47's had to delay releasing the Horsas

Men and gliders of the 1st Airborne Task Force, recently landed at La Motte.

Posts set up at La Motte as an antiglider device.

over the target because of the reported fog. Although the maximum Horsa load was only 6,000 pounds—about its rated cargo capacity—the heavy glider made a gross load that would tax the C-47 for the long flight under the best of conditions, leaving little fuel for emergencies towards the end of the aircraft's round trip.

General Williams pondered the wisdom of his decision. He had to decide what to do about the returning Horsas. He had a hasty conference with Colonel Frank J. McNees, commander of the 435th Troop Carrier Group, and Colonel T. Beach of the Airborne Task Force staff. They decided for an afternoon mission.

Turning back somewhere near Corsica, one aircraft with engine trouble and another short of fuel released their Horsas. Both gliders landed safely on the island. The rest of the serial continued to Tarquinia, meeting a substitute C-47 en route. It was towing the glider that had turned back from the earlier take-off. Seeing the returning Horsas, the C-47 pilot, thinking the whole airborne operation had been cancelled, also turned back. His glider pilot's relief at not having to go the whole way was to be short lived, however.

Then came the CG-4A combinations. As they passed the halfway point from Corsica to the release point, one glider either blew up or disintegrated from overstress, and its debris scattered over the Mediterranean, leaving no trace. Soon, another one's towrope parted, and it peeled off from the formation, circled downward, and landed on the water. An Allied naval vessel, witnessing the glider's descent, sped to the craft and got to it some minutes after it had landed. Fortunately, the CG-4A had buoyancy to remain afloat long enough for the ship to rescue the pilots and all the drenched passengers.

The serial approached the drop area at 0820 hours to find the still impenetrable layer of fog hanging over the Argens Valley. The group leader decided to risk waiting out the fog. He began a large lazy circling maneuver over Le Muy and kept this up for an hour. At about 0926 hours, with his fuel dangerously low, the fog cleared enough for pilots to see ground features, and the leader flashed a red light, followed by a white one, and the glider pilot cut away.

Thirty-seven gliders got down, bringing in the 64th Light Artillery, some headquarters personnel for the brigade and ammunition and equipment. General Frederick, who was one of the few to have parachuted in close to the correct area during darkness, had his headquarters operating at the time of the glider landings, and he radioed the 436th Troop Carrier Group that only thirty-three gliders had made it to the LZ. Four gliders must have landed well outside the LZ.

The British paratroopers quickly occupied the village of Le Mitan on the eastern edge of their drop zone. They set up their headquarters in the village and, at 1000 hours, after staff personnel had arrived in the first glider mission, the task force also set up its headquarters there. One battalion of the brigade moved west, seizing eighty prisoners in the hamlet of Clastron, a mile and a half northwest of Le Muy, and making contact with the 517th Parachute Infantry Regiment at La Motte. Another battalion pushed south and had taken the tiny village of Les Serres on the north bank of the Nartuby, less than half a mile from Le Muy, before noon. Then it ran into difficulties. The enemy had strong positions around the bridge that spanned the Nartuby just outside Les Serres. Hampered perhaps by the absence of the artillery carried by the recalled Horsa serial, the British did not have the punch to take the bridge until late afternoon. By that time, the reinforcements carried in the afternoon missions were overhead.

Troop carrier operations on the afternoon of D-Day began at 1504 hours, when the 35 Horsa-towing aircraft made their second start. The big gliders carried 233 troops, 35 jeeps, 30 guns, and 31,378 pounds of ammunition, a total load of 248,000 pounds. The Waco-towing substitute from the 436th Troop Carrier Group, which had mistakenly returned with them in the morning, joined them in the assembly area. The 435th Troop Carrier Group had sent an aircraft to Corsica to pick up one of the Horsas released there on the first trip. Glider and tug joined the formation at the first marker boat, northwest of Corsica.

The air was calm and slightly hazy. Over the battlefield, the smoke was thickening and the maximum visibility near Le Muy was five miles. The aircraft released thirty-seven gliders over LZ O at 1746 hours. Parachute serials followed the Horsas and dropped thousands of men.

After the parachute drop came "Dove," the big glider mission. Seven serials, each forty-eight-combination strong, towed 332 Waco gliders carrying the 550th Glider Infantry Battalion, additional artillery and support troops numbering about 2,250 men. With them were 25 howitzers and 166 vehicles. Course, formation, flight procedure and navigational aids were the same as those employed in the morning glider mission. The leading aircraft of each successive serial, except the last two, was eight or nine minutes behind the leading aircraft of the serial ahead. As it turned out, this spacing was somewhat tight.

The glider pilots had been briefed at 1300 hours, and the aircraft and gliders were in position an hour before take-off time. The 442nd Troop Carrier Group began its take-off from Follonica at 1535 hours in heavy dust. At the southern end of the line, the 64th Troop Carrier Group at Ciampino, mindful of the facts that it was more than an hour's flight from the command assembly point over Elba, had put its first aircraft in the air at 1510 hours. The last group aloft was most likely the 440th Troop Carrier Group which, delayed

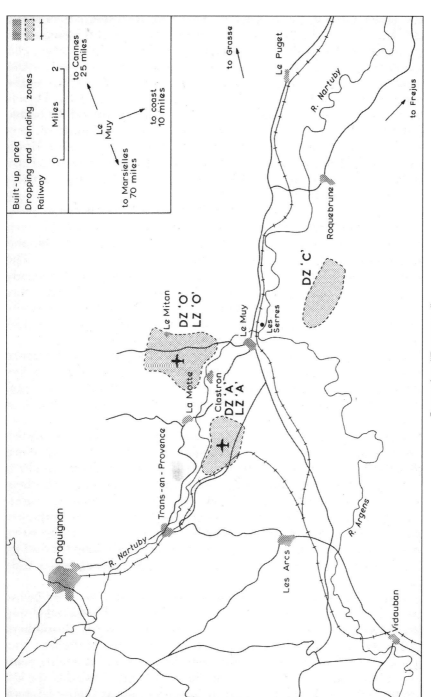

Built-up area
Dropping and landing zones
Railway

to Cannes
25 miles

Le Muy

to coast
10 miles

to Marseilles
70 miles

Miles
0   2

to Grasse

Le Puget

R. Nartuby

to Frejus

Roquebrune

DZ 'C'

Le Mitan
DZ 'O'
LZ 'O'

Le Muy

Les Serres

La Motte

Clastron
DZ 'A'
LZ 'A'

Trans-en-Provence

Draguignan

R. Nartuby

Les Arcs

R. Argens

Vidauban

Operation "Dragoon."

by dust at Ombrone, took from 1610 to 1646 hours to complete its take-off. One glider was no sooner in the air than it had to make a forced landing. Its load was trucked back to the field and loaded on a substitute, which made a successful flight two hours later. An abortive take-off in the 438th Troop Carrier Group was likewise followed by transfer of the load and dispatch of a substitute.

Trouble began as the 332nd Troop Carrier Group crossed the coast. It later claimed to have been impeded off Point Ala by the Horsa-towing aircraft. This is hard to believe, since the records show that the Horsas had passed Elba by 1610 hours, while the 442nd Troop Carrier Group was not due there until 1631 hours. The parachute serials may have caused the delay, although it seems unlikely that a parachute mission could be mistaken for one towing gliders.

After passing Corsica, the glider towed by the leading aircraft of the 442nd Troop Carrier Group had to be ditched because of weakness in the tail. This proved to be the more serious delay. The group made a full turn to avoid a possible accident and to keep in touch with its leader. All personnel aboard the glider were later rescued. Several gliders released prematurely, and three or four came down at sea off the French coast. Most of the occupants were saved.

All groups found the landing zones and saw fluorescent T's. The panels showed up well. All serials and about 95 percent of the gliders reached the landing area. Unfortunately, the serials jammed up, largely because of the delay encountered by the 442nd Troop Carrier Group, so that four serials were over the area at the same time at one point. At 1827 hours, seventeen minutes late, the 442nd Troop Carrier Group arrived and took fifteen minutes to release its gliders. The 441st Troop Carrier Group arrived simultaneously with the 442nd Troop Carrier Group. Though the 442nd was at LZ O and the 441st split between O and A, the congestion was considerable. The two zones were unusually close together, with the route to LZ A leading along the southern edge of O. The 440th Troop Carrier Group, which arrived at 1840 hours, made a 180-degree turn to avoid the congestion and the blinding western sun and approached LZ A from the west. The 436th Troop Carrier Group arrived about 1848 hours to release twenty-one gliders on O and twenty-six on A. It found aircraft of the 441st Troop Carrier Group still releasing at O, and aircraft and gliders of the latter group and the 440th Troop Carrier Group crisscrossing spectacularly over A. One minute later, the 438th Troop Carrier Group arrived at LZ O and released its gliders.

The 62nd Troop Carrier Group cut loose its gliders over LZ O between 1854 and 1900 hours, and the 64th Troop Carrier Group began its release over A at 1905 hours. Comparatively free from interference by groups ahead of them, the 62nd and 64th found that the 1,000-foot intervals between their own elements were insufficient. The rear elements climbed over the forward ones to make their release, with the result that several layers of gliders were in the air at once and that many gliders were released at excessive heights. Some in the 62nd were released at more than 2,000 feet and some in the 64th as high as 3,000 feet.

Dodging and diving with agility, the glider pilots managed to avoid colliding in mid-air. However, their first sight of the landing zones revealed something for which neither their briefing nor the available photographs had prepared them. The fields were studded with obstacles, which consisted of the so-called "Rommel's asparagus." The poles were set in rows from fifteen to forty feet apart. Wires had been stretched between them, but the paratroops had cut the wires. Mines had been set, but the Germans had not been able to get fuses for them. As a result, the glider pilots were able to set their gliders down between the rows of poles by adroit maneuvering

In the circumstances, it was natural that they should land wherever they could. Even in the lead group, the 442nd Troop Carrier Group, the pilots of the last twelve gliders found no room on their assigned fields. They coasted down south of La Motte, about two miles away. Fortunately, their loads were principally vehicles and extra ammunition, for which there was no immediate need. The glider detachments of the 62nd and 64th Troop Carrier Groups found their fields completely filled with gliders and had to crash-land at average speeds of eighty to ninety miles an hour. Though they sheared off their wings on the poles and hit all kinds of obstacles, the pilots managed to get their passengers and cargoes to earth with an astonishing degree of safety.

The gliders, however, were a total loss. The 60th Troop Carrier Wing reported two weeks later that only two gliders were serviceable and that only twenty-six could be salvaged. Indications are that the gliders in the three rear serials, which arrived after the good landing grounds were pre-empted, fared even worse. In the hectic time following the invasion, such gliders as were salvageable were left unguarded. Weather and pillage combined to destroy them. Not one was ever recovered.

In making the landings, 11 glider pilots were killed and more than 30 injured. About 100 of the glider-borne personnel were seriously hurt. Very little damage was done to the cargoes, although great difficulty was encountered in getting them out. (For example, the 62nd Troop Carrier Group reported that all its gliders crashed but only one load was damaged.)

The relatively high casualties among the pilots were caused partly by the obstacles into which they crashed and partly by heavy equipment in the gliders, which lunged forward against them at the moment of impact. Most of them felt that had the Griswold nose, a special protection for the pilot, been used, it would have greatly reduced the casualties. They also favored use of parachute arrestors (general installation of which had been considered and given up due to lack of time), heavier lashing for the loads, and safety belts for the personnel. Some pilots suggested that jeeps or tractors should have been employed to pull gliders that had landed in one wave out of the way so that the next serial could land.

After leaving the release area, the troop carriers dropped their towropes at a designated point, turned right and returned according to plan. One aircraft was hit by a burst of flak and forced to come down in the sea off the French coast. All aboard were saved. The destruction of this single C-47 was the only appreciable damage the Germans were able to inflict.

In general, flak was even slighter than it had been in the morning. At no time during the day did enemy aircraft attack the airborne missions. The fighter escort left early by prior agreement in order to reach its base before dark, but no German prowlers were on hand to attack the unprotected rear of the returning column. At 2138 hours, the last aircraft of the 62nd Troop Carrier Group hit the runway at Galera. The troop carriers had completed their mission.

The effort put forth on D-Day may be summarized as follows:

> Sorties Intended: 857
> Sorties Accomplished: 852
>> Glider Sorties, Waco: 372
>> Glider Sorties, Horsa: 36
> Paratroop Sorties: 444
> Personnel Delivered: 9,099
>> Paratroops: 6,488
>> Glider Personnel: 2,611
> Glider Troops on or near LZ: 90–95%
> Paratroops on or near DZ: 50%
> Drop Casualties: 2%
> Landing Casualties: 4%
> Artillery Pieces Delivered: 213
> Vehicles Delivered: 221
> Other Supplies and Equipment: 500 tons

In achieving this record, most aircraft and flying personnel had flown between 600 and 1,300 miles on two separate missions within a period of less than twenty hours. They had accomplished the dawn paratroop mission in the face of warnings that problems of take-off, assembly, formation flying and navigation at night might make it impracticable. They had carried out a large glider mission with a degree of success that put "Ladbroke" to shame and compared favorably with the glider missions in "Neptune."

CHAPTER 13

Arnhem: Grasp for the Rhine

On 16 August 1944, General Eisenhower created the First Allied Airborne Army to manage his airborne operations. The premise upon which he formed the field army was that airborne and troop carrier formations are theater-level forces and plans for their combined employment must be prepared by the agency having authority to direct the necessary coordinated action of all land, sea and air forces in the area involved. Sorely needed, it was a tardy response to the inadequate coordination of airborne resources in past operations and to the need for a single headquarters guided by a man of sufficient stature and rank to give direction and leadership. Eisenhower assigned Lieutenant General Lewis H. Brereton to command the field army, with General F. A. M. Browning as his deputy. Brereton created an XVIII Airborne Corps, subordinate to his headquarters, and placed it under the command of General Matthew B. Ridgway.

General Brereton had operational control over the IX Troop Carrier Command. Ridgeway's XVIII Airborne Corps consisted of four U.S. airborne divisions—the 11th, 17th, 82nd and 101st—smaller separate U.S. airborne elements, all British airborne forces and such Royal Air Force troop carrier elements as might be allocated from time to time.

General Brereton began training programs, but they were hobbled on occasion, such as when two troop-carrier wings, urgently needed for glider-tow and parachute-jump training, were sent to participate in "Dragoon," the airborne invasion of southern France. When available, troop-carrier crews practiced day and night flying, dual glider tow and glider pick-ups. They operated with the 82nd and 101st Airborne Divisions, providing aircraft and gliders for practice loading and unloading drills, simulated air landings and practice tactical glider flights.

In the forty days after the formation of the field army, General Brereton had his staff worked out plans for eighteen different operations. Most of them were scrubbed because the ground armies moved too fast, forcing troop-carrier wings to supply the ground units by air. "Transfigure" was cancelled, as were "Boxer," "Linnet" and others. Glider pilots got briefings, re-briefings and more briefings. Gliders had been packed with their combat loads—ropes hitched to noses—and parked in readiness for take-off. Glider troops usually waited nervously in barbed-wire-enclosed assembly areas, near or adjacent to airfields, and prepared to fly the one-way trip in the gliders at short notice. On more than one occasion, the land tail—the trucks, tanks and equipment not normally carried in the air—had already put to sea to cross the Channel, expecting to link up with the airborne units.

Gliders were gaining increased importance in Brereton's concept of airborne operations. "Linnet" was a prime example of this. The U.S. 82nd and 101st Airborne Divisions, the British 1st Airborne Division and the Polish 1st Parachute Brigade were to fly two major airlifts a day over two days to seize Tournai in France, to hold a bridgehead over the Escaut River and to control the roads leading northwest through Tournai, Lille and Coutrai. Such was the intensity of the operation that the first lift had 120 aircraft towing two gliders each, 350 aircraft towing one glider each, and 1,055 parachute aircraft. The total length of the flight column was more than two hours. The second lift, even more imposing in glider participation, comprised 880 tug aircraft with double glider tow, 307 aircraft with single glider tow and 126 parachute aircraft. A lift of 75 tugs with two gliders each and 114 parachute aircraft was scheduled for the morning of D-Day+1, and 436 parachute aircraft were to fly a resupply lift that afternoon. On D-Day+2, the British 52nd Division, which was capable of being lifted by air, was to begin airlanding operations. Each hour, from H-Hour to H-Hour+11, 36 aircraft were to land, unload and depart at each of three airstrips. This operation was to be completed on D-Day+3. "Linnet" was shelved for a new version—"Linnet II"—and this plan was also cancelled when overcome by events. Nonetheless, airborne muscles were now flexing for some championship encounters.

On 5 September 1944, General Eisenhower directed the airborne field army to operate in support of Montgomery's 21st Army Group until after the Rhine had been crossed and then be prepared to operate on a large scale for the advance into Germany. This was the kind of support General Brereton, his staff and commanders had been awaiting. It now appeared that some of the doubts that had been built up within the supreme headquarters were to be dispelled, and all were only awaiting the favorable opportunity. It was not long in coming.

The same evening that "Linnet II" was cancelled, Montgomery asked General Brereton to seize the Rhine bridges from Arnhem to Wesel in order to prepare for a ground advance by Montgomery's force to the north of the Ruhr. Later on, the plan, called "Comet," was narrowed to the Nijmegen-Arnhem area. The British 1st Airborne Division, with the Polish 1st Parachute Brigade, had to seize and hold bridges over the Meuse at Grave, over the Waal at Nijmegen and over the Lower Rhine at Arnhem. The U.S. 878th Airborne

Men of the 77th Parachute Field Artillery wait beside their gliders for the take-off to Arnhem.

In a field in Holland, Dutch people help the troops to clear a glider.

Engineer Battalion was to then prepare an airstrip for the airlanding of the British 52nd Division. D-Day was set for 8 September. Postponed once because of the weather and twice because of the uncertain ground battle, Montgomery cancelled "Comet" on 10 September.

Flight-readied since 2 September, British and Polish troops stood by awaiting the next operational alert. A few days later, Montgomery settled on "Market," an ambitious plan to cut off major German forces in Holland and perhaps exploit the "attractive possibility" of the British turning both the Rhine and the German Siegfried Line. It called for Brereton's forces to seize bridges that would open the way for armor of the British Second Army to drive to the Zuider Zee in the coordinated ground follow-up operation, called "Garden." The U.S. 101st Airborne Division was ordered to seize bridges and roads along the route between Eindhoven and Grave; the U.S. 82nd Airborne Division had to capture the bridge over the Meuse north of Grave and the bridge over the Waal at Nijmegen; the British 1st Airborne Division, with the Polish 1st Parachute Brigade, had to seize the bridge over the Lower Rhine at Arnhem. The British 52nd Division was to go into the Arnhem area by airlanding as soon as an airstrip could be prepared. The ground attack would be on a narrow front, running northward from the British Second Army's line along the Albert and Escaut Canals in northern Belgium. For much of the distance, only a single road would be available for the advance and supply route. Spearheading the ground attack would be the Guards Armoured Division of the XXX Corps. Its time schedule called for it to reach Eindhoven, about fifteen miles north of the Escaut Canal, within eight hours. It was to take Nijmegen, more than forty highway miles northeast of Eindhoven, by noon on D-Day+1. Arnhem, eleven miles north of Nijmegen, was to be reached by noon on the following day.

The first question was whether "Market" should follow the pattern of Sicily and Normandy in being another night operation or whether an attempt should be made to conduct a major airborne operation in daylight. Difficulties of navigation and of assembly of forces on the ground in darkness were well known, and this was to be a period of no moon. At the same time, the German night-fighter force—relatively intact with an estimated 100 operational *Nachtjäger* within range—might be more formidable than the day fighters, and it would be more difficult for escorting fighters to protect the column at night. Flak could be expected at night as well as in daylight. Moreover, the IX Troop Carrier Command had not been practicing night glider assemblies in formation for the last three months, meaning that gliders should probably be taken in during daylight regardless of when the paratroopers made their drop.

On the other hand, flak would doubtless be far more accurate in daylight, and it was primary concern for the slow, low-flying troop carriers. Overwhelming air support against flak positions and against enemy fighters seemed essential for a daylight airborne operation. General Brereton believed that sufficient air support was at hand, and he believed that the air force could knock out most flak positions in advance of the arrival of the airborne armada. Correspondingly, he decided on a daylight operation.

Another question to be decided was the routes the troop carriers should follow to the target areas. Several factors, not always compatible, had to be taken into account. Aside from following prominent terrain features, which would simplify navigation, the route should be the shortest and most direct possible; it should respect traffic control patterns of IX Troop Carrier and RAF flight elements; it should avoid barrage balloon and antiaircraft areas in Great Britain; it should avoid known and suspected flak batteries; it should avoid turns over water; it should make landfall over prominent, irregular coastline; and it should proceed the shortest possible distance over hostile territory.

Preliminary studies suggested two possible routes. The most direct lay across the North Sea from Orford Ness in Suffolk, passing over the Dutch Islands and turning northeast near Hertogenbosch. That route required a flight of some eighty miles over enemy-held territory. A more southerly route led from North Foreland in Kent to Belgium, where it turned northward near Gheel, crossed the front lines and passed over sixty-five miles of enemy-held territory.

General Williams recommended that both routes be used, with the U.S. 101st Airborne Division taking the southern route and the U.S. 82nd Airborne and the British 1st Airborne Divisions following the northern route. If only one route were used in the initial lift, the column would be so long that the enemy might be alerted in time to bring effective fire against the rear elements or the aircraft would have to fly in parallel columns so broad that some could not avoid known flak locations. Another advantage in having two routes would be that on subsequent days, the reinforcing and resupply lifts could be routed either way, if weather or enemy action ruled out one while the other remained open.

General Browning's original plan had called for the 101st Airborne Division to go into the Grave-Nijmegen area and the 82nd Airborne Division into the Eindhoven-Uden area, but the use of two routes as outlined by General Williams made it desirable to transpose the objectives of the two divisions to avoid crossing routes, based on the stationing of the forces in England. General Brereton accepted the recommendations and changed the divisions' missions accordingly.

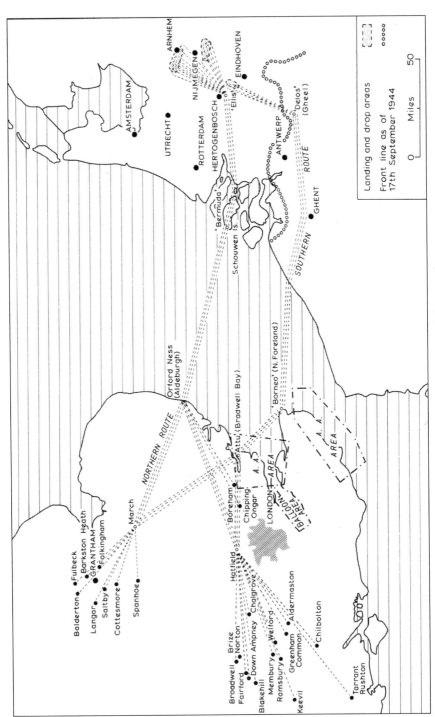

Operation "Market Garden": Approach.

No problem was more important from the point of view of airborne commanders than the selection of drop zones (DZ's) for the parachute drops and landing zones (LZ's) for the gliders. After careful examination of terrain studies and enemy defense overprints, the troop-carrier commander and the airborne commanders made the initial selections at a conference the next morning. They had to consider accessibility to assigned objectives, ground formations, avoidance of flak and enemy defenses and concentration of the airborne forces. Again, compromise was necessary. It was generally desirable for paratroops to drop directly on an objective or as close to it as possible. In this case, however, the DZ's could not be close to the bridge objectives, because flak concentrations protected those bridges. For the same reason, cities had to be generally avoided. Rivers and canals might be hazardous for parachute forces, but streams and ditches in the target area were also a great advantage: they were effective antitank obstacles.

The British 1st Airborne Division had the honor of taking the bridge at Arnhem. Its commander, Major General R. E. Urquhart, drew up the simplest plan that would meet the requirements. Even this, however, involved a minimum of two lifts. As it eventually turned out, three were required. All of the division was to be used, together with the Polish parachute brigade. One factor to be considered was the route to the objective and the arrival there. The German airfield at Deelen and the town of Arnhem itself were very well protected by flak. As the bridge was just to the south of Arnhem, the comparatively slow flying aircraft stood no chance, if they approached too near to it in daytime. It was necessary, therefore, for the dropping and landing zones to be well beyond the range of the guns at Deelen.

Since the terrain around Arnhem is woodland for the most part, the number of suitable open fields was not very great. Four were eventually chosen. The first three were immediately north of the railway running through Arnhem to Utrecht, the farthest of them being about eight miles from the bridge. The fourth zone was south of the railway and somewhat larger than the others. A fifth, close to the city itself and near the small village of Warnsborn, was chosen as the place where supplies were to be dropped after the landing.

Major General Maxwell D. Taylor, commander of the U.S. 101st Airborne Division, was dissatisfied with General Browning's original plan for the disposition of his division. That plan would have spread the division in seven separate areas along an axis some thirty miles long. General Taylor was anxious to concentrate his forces. Sharing his views, General Brereton stated: "Such dispersion destroys its tactical integrity, renders it incapable of fighting as a division and presents insurmountable problems of resupply. Each small group is susceptible of being destroyed in detail." The airborne field army commander-in-chief raised further objections from the air point of view: the difficulty of making accurate drops on the numerous small drop zones, the problem of finding suitable drop zones in each of the areas and exposure of the air lifts to hostile fire over a large area.

Finally, General Taylor received permission to discuss the problem with Lieutenant General M. C. Dempsey, commanding the British Second Army, under whose ultimate command division would operate on the ground. As a result, the proposed seven areas for the first drop were cut to two general areas.

Another factor influencing the selection of drop zones appeared when General Williams determined that it would take two hours for a regiment to assemble after landing and another three hours—a total of five—for it to reach the city. The principal concentration of the 101st Airborne Division troops would be in the area designated Landing Zone W, located between Zon and St. Oedenrode, west of the main highway. One regimental drop zone, DZ B, would be in the south part of that area, about a mile and a half northwest of Zon. Another regimental drop zone, DZ C, was chosen in the north part of the area, a mile south of St. Oedenrode. All gliders for the division were to land on LZ W. The third regimental drop zone, DZ A, was about five miles north of DZ B and located southwest of the Willems Vaart Canal near Veghel.

General Taylor also agreed to divide this regiment's drop zones so that one battalion could come down about three miles to the northwest in DZ A-1 on the opposite side of the canal and astride the small Aa River. This disposition was to facilitate quick seizure of the bridges in that area from both sides.

All drop and landing zones for the 82nd Airborne Division, with the exception of one rifle company's DZ just west of Grave, were north of the Meuse. Drop Zone O (intended for two battalions less one rifle company) was immediately north and west of Ober Asselt and about a mile and a half east of Grave; the DZ for the other battalion of that regiment was about a mile and a half east of the main DZ O. All of LZ O was for gliders. Drop and Landing Zones N were south of Groesbeek, and Drop and Landing Zones T were to its north.

Since dispositions had already been made for the "Linnet" and "Comet" operations, only minor changes in troop locations proved necessary. The 101st Airborne Division was in the south of England—the Newbury area in Berkshire—and close to IX Troop Carrier Command fields; the 82nd Airborne Division was in the Midlands near Nottingham, also close to troop carrier fields. The British 1st Airborne Division was still at fields in the Swindon-Wiltshire area, and the Polish 1st Parachute Brigade was in Lincolnshire, near

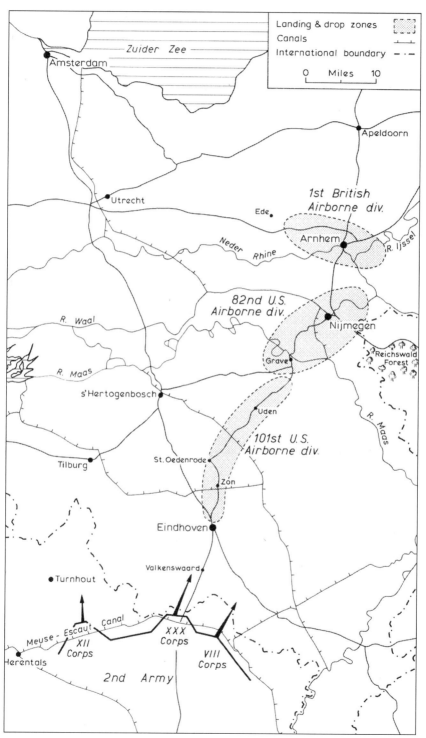

Operation "Market Garden": Divisional Landing Zones.

Grantham. Troops began moving to the take-off fields on 15 September and were sealed in at daylight the next day. The magnitude of the operations is probably better grasped in terms of the number of airfields used. "Market Garden" used twenty-four—seventeen for U.S. elements and seven for British.

Troop-carrier arrangements included rather elaborate plans for navigational aids. Even though the operation was to be conducted in daylight, they would be used to ensure identification of routes and drop zones. Eureka (radar) and compass beacon equipment were set up at wing assembly points; departure points on the English coast were marked by Eureka, compass beacons and occult (light flashing a code letter); and, midway across the North Sea, there were marker boats with Eureka and green holophane lights sending code letters. Aircraft on the southern route would pass over a white panel T and yellow smoke—5,000 yards before reaching enemy lines—after turning not far from Gheel. Pathfinders would precede the columns to each division area. A pathfinder team from the 82nd Airborne Division would mark DZ O, and two teams from the 101st Airborne Division would mark DZ's A and B. Pathfinder aircraft would carry special radar equipment by which the crews would find their way to the target areas from the boat markers. The division pathfinder teams would mark the DZ's and LZ's with Eureka, compass beacons, colored panels and colored smoke.

Troop-carrier officers gave a great deal of consideration to keeping column time and length short, in order to have the greatest protection from escorting fighters and have carriers over enemy-held territory in the shortest time possible. Formation intervals could be tighter than those used in night operations, and troop-carrier plans provided that the aircraft fly in three streams, with the right and left each separated from the center by one and a half miles.

Air formations had to allow a certain amount of maneuverability and, at the same time, ensure good concentration for massing paratroops and gliders on the ground. The C-47's were to fly in nine-ship elements in a V of V's comprising serials of up to forty-five aircraft in trail, with four-minute intervals between the leading aircraft of each serial. Glider columns would form into pairs of pairs echeloned to the right, in serials of up to forty-eight aircraft towing gliders in trail, with seven-minute intervals between heads of serials. Altitudes had to be decided with a view to avoiding small arms as well as heavy flak, to dropping troops and releasing gliders at minimum safe altitudes and to assuring clearance of incoming aircraft with those returning from the target area.

Initial plans called for the 38th and 46th RAF Groups to tow 335 Horsas and 13 Hamilcars on D-Day; 293 Horsas, 15 Hamilcars and 10 Wacos on

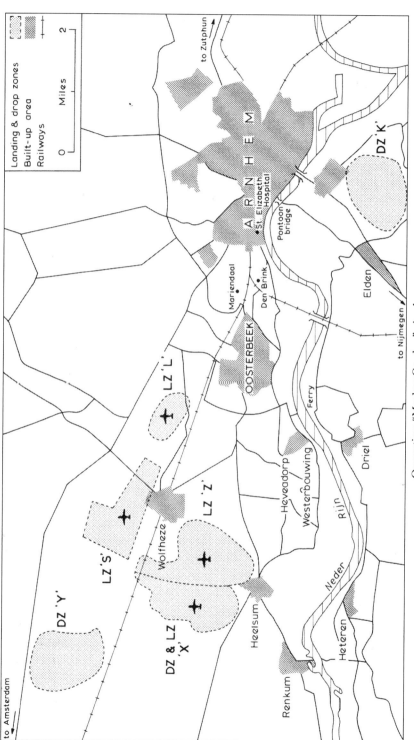

Operation "Market-Garden": Arnhem.

Legend:

Landing & drop zones
Built-up area
Railways

0   Miles   2

D-Day+1; and 16 Horsas and 10 Hamilcars on D-Day+3. The actual take-off figures differed only slightly from these.

By 0900 hours on D-Day, 17 September 1944, the weather was fit for take-offs from all bases. Gliders towed by Dakotas, Halifaxes, Stirlings and Albemarles started taking off from Brize Norton, Fairford, Harwell, Keevil, Tarrant Rushton, Broadwell, Blakehill and Down Ampney at 0945 hours. All 359 gliders scheduled for D-Day take-offs got off successfully. One combination had to turn back because of engine trouble. It took off again, but it had to return to be rescheduled for the D-Day+1 lift.

While these flights were taking off, others carrying the 82nd and 101st Airborne Divisions were taking off from other fields in England bound for landing and drop zones in the Netherlands.

The fleet of gliders was part of an even larger armada, including hundreds of aircraft carrying paratroopers. It began going through patches of cirrus cloud and, before it had crossed the English coast, heavy turbulence caused twenty-four gliders to release. One crashed on landing. Twenty-two landed satisfactorily at various fields and were recovered and scheduled into the D-Day+1 lift.

Just beyond the coast, flight serials broke out into a bright clear sky. Before long, other mishaps occurred. Two towropes parted, with the gliders landing in the water. Three tow planes developed engine trouble and cut their gliders loose. One of these landed in the water and one on Schonwen Island.

Men in one of the gliders sloshing about in the waves began to see water spouts nearby. A German coastal battery was ranging in on their glider. The firing continued for two hours, but the Germans still had not hit the glider when a British Sea Rescue service craft managed to get to the glider and remove the men, saving all hands. Similar rescues saved the men in the other three gliders.

Eight hundred and twenty-one B-17's flew ahead of the airlift and attacked known flak positions and any gun that dared to fire on the transports; 371 RAF fighter-bombers cannonaded barges, trucks and flak; 322 RAF bombers hit other targets. Three thousand tons of bombs rained down on the flak that morning. Allied fighters—550 from the U.S. Army Air Corps alone—raced through the skies, eyes peeled for German fighters. Two enemy flights near the Rhine were sighted, but they dared not challenge the Allied armada. Transport pilots, less concerned with flak than in any previous airborne mission, flew unswervingly towards glider release and parachute drop zones.

There was very little flak until Groesbeek. At that point, the gliders began to take some hits. Flak severed one towrope, but the remaining gliders all made it to within gliding range of the landing zone. They cut loose and started maneuvering for landing. A light wind caused a small percentage to overshoot the landing zone.

Gliders lying at the end of tracks thay have made in Dutch fields when landing.

Alan Wood, a war correspondent with the airborne troops, typing his despatch in a wood near Arnhem.

In *Defeat in the West* by Milton Shulman, the German war reporter, Erwin Kirchoff describes the landings:

> It was early on the Sunday afternoon of 17 September. The movie theaters in the small Dutch towns were slowly filling up, and the streets and highways along the canals and small streams were crowded with young people on bicycles. And then, out of the blue sky, roared several hundred enemy fighter-bombers. Their aim was to attack the German defensive positions and locate the flak positions. They had barely disappeared beyond the horizon when, coming from the west across the flooded coastal areas, the aircraft and gliders carrying regiments and brigades of the enemy's airborne army appeared.

The troops bailed out from a very low altitude, sometimes as low as sixty meters. Immediately after that, the several hundred gliders started to land. In those first few minutes, it looked as if the masses coming down would suffocate every single life on the ground.

Two Hamilcars touched down on ground too soft to bear them. Their wheels ploughed into the ground, and the gliders nosed over. The accident made the 17-pounder artillery pieces each carried unserviceable.

An enterprising young musician jumped from one of the first gliders and started playing the regimental march of the King's Own Scottish Borderers, "Blue Bonnets over the Border." The rest of the glider formation skidded to a stop to the tune. He continued to march and blow, oblivious of German fire and whizzing gliders, until all his regiment landed.

Thirty minutes after the last of the more than 325 gliders had landed, personnel had cleared the craft of all material they had transported.

A Dulwich schoolmaster-turned-glider-pilot landed General Richard Gale in a ploughed field. Dust and earth forced its way up into the big black Horsa. A landing wheel was whipped off in a ditch; the glider hit a post and swiveled around on its nose. "Fine work, my boy," the general said, as he stepped out. They tried to free the general's jeep from the twisted wreckage but could not do so. They got out of the field and crossed through a crop of waist high corn to the village road. Past the village was the country house that the general had picked from a map as his temporary headquarters. When they got there, a gliderman kicked open the door and lurched in with his submachine gun, his eyes peeled for Germans. Inside were two pairs of short-sighted eyes peering out from the faces of two spinster ladies in their nightdresses. They held candles up at him and said, *"Bonjour."*

Soon, they were fussing over the English general. The two old ladies insisted on serving him a breakfast of bacon and eggs.

All the primary paratroop objectives had been taken. The general ordered his Red Devils to dig in and "infest the area." Gale's enlisted aide, concerned that "his general" should have suitable transportation, spotted a chestnut mare not far from the Horsa. He soon had his general mounted in true cavalry style. The general badly needed some means of transport over the tricky farmland with its hedges and woods. The horse was "just the job."

At the dawn muster formation, the soldiers found the general walking the horse round the garden of his headquarters. He tied her up among the jeeps that had collected in the courtyard. But on her next journey out, she got hit by shrapnel.

One glider, piloted by Lieutenant A. T. Turrell and his men, was shot down between Nijmegen and Arnhem, but it succeeded in making a good landing. Thirty Dutch helped to unload the glider, among them a girl who had to abandon her search for a green parachute among those lying about. She wanted it, she said, to make a dress of that color. Under the guidance of a Dutch priest and a local official, the party set off for the division on the other side of the Rhine. On the way, they encountered six Germans, whom they disarmed and locked in the local jail, after first making them take off their uniforms and put on civilian clothes. The men eventually reached the neighborhood of Arnhem by crossing the Lower Rhine in a ferry.

"We had left in very filthy weather indeed, low cloud and rain, but after a while, it improved," Major R. Cain of the South Staffords stated later (he would go on to receive the Victoria Cross for his actions during this battle). A little while after mid-Channel, he saw the coastline of Holland in front. It was a buff, fawnlike color, with white and grey streaks. The next thing he recognized was the Rhine. Then they got flak puffs all around them and bits of tracer. Cain ordered all of his men to strap in. Geary, the glider pilot, put the aircraft into a dive approach. It seemed to be about treetop level when he pulled it out straight and shouted: "Hold tight!" They landed in a ploughed field, got out and took up all-round protective positions. All of the area was divided up into square fields with small, tree-lined unimproved roads dividing them. It was very neat and very square. The trees were elms. Cain could hear very little firing and it was a long way off. There was no other activity.

The glider pilots, having safely brought their forces to the battle, were as heavily engaged as their passengers. Those who had flown in the first lift helped to hold the landing zones and then, when the second lift came in, fought side-by-side with the King's Own Scottish Borderers and eventually formed part of the defense of the divisional headquarters established at Hartestein. With them were two soldiers of the Royal Engineers 4th Parachute Squadron. One of their officers, Captain H. F. Brown, would receive a Military Cross for the manner in which he led the sappers, who were fighting as infantry.

A landing glider crashes on its nose and turns over.

U.S. troops examine a crashed glider behind the German lines in Holland.

When General Browning, piloted by Brigadier Chatterton, took off from Harwell Airfield, his glider looked like the inside of a gypsy caravan. Bicycles, bazookas, bedding rolls, radios and an assortment of items for his command post cluttered it. The glider surged as the Stirling bomber powered down the airstrip. Browning had arrived for the "show" immaculately dressed, his Sam Browne belt and holster glistening, trouser creases knife-edged and with a swagger stick in his gloved hand. All were in high spirits.

Aloft, the fantastic sight awed him. Thousands of gliders and aircraft stretched in every direction. Spitfire and Tempest fighters whizzed by, gaining altitude to hover over and protect the plodding glider formations. Some of the combinations had to fly through clouds; turbulence there caused seven gliders to cut loose and land before reaching the coast. Two gliders ditched later over the sea. One managed to make a good water landing, while the other broke up on impact with the water. The glider convoy stretched some fifty miles among the many other aircraft carrying parachutists.

On release short of Nijmegen, Chatterton started circling down, creating a great imaginary funnel, ending his downward flight in a skid that brought him abruptly into a small cabbage garden behind several farm cottages. A few Dutch peasants wandered up and watched almost disinterestedly as General Browning and others in the glider got out and started towards a forest some distance away, where the headquarters was established for the XVIII Airborne Corps.

Chatterton's glider had flown in an American serial carrying the staffs of Operation "Market." Twenty-eight other gliders had landed in the same zone. Messerschmitts attacked the area, killing an RAF photographer. Up to then, the immense armada had mesmerized the German ground troops into inaction, but they awakened and reacted, lobbing artillery rounds into the area. A short while later, German forces assembling nearby began to fire at Chatterton. In the distance, Chatterton and his passengers heard a great roaring like a waterfall. They ran out into the open, disregarding the German fire. Coming towards them overhead, they saw a vast armada of aircraft, each towing two gliders. It was the American transport column looking like a swarm of angry bees. The sight staggered the British, as well as the Germans. They stopped firing and watched with awe.

At 0950 hours on D-Day, the first of 482 C-47's started taking off from Grantham airfield. Those not towing the 50 gliders carried parachutists. Gliders carried elements of the headquarters of the 82nd Airborne Division and the XVIII Airborne Corps. It took fifty minutes for all of them to get into the air. By the time the last of the aircraft had lifted its wheels, the lead aircraft was almost a third of the way to the landing and drop zones near

Groesbeek in Holland. By 1350 hours, 33 of the 50 gliders had landed, with 209 officers and men, 8 antitank guns, and 24 jeeps with trailers and radios. Within a half hour, the headquarters' radios were functioning in a patch of woods 1,000 yards west of Groesbeek.

At 1400 hours that same day, 53 gliders carrying headquarters elements of the 101st Airborne Division and its artillery, signals, engineer, reconnaissance and advance parties began to land two miles northwest of Zon. Seventy gliders started on the mission. Two had separated from their tow planes while over England and had landed there. Fifteen others had cut off between England and the objective, some shot down by German gunners. Three crashed on landing. Nonetheless, 252 men made it to the landing zone, and 32 of the 43 jeeps sent on the mission arrived undamaged on the LZ.

Because of fog earlier in the morning, the gliders did not start taking off until after 1000 hours on D-Day+1.

The flak over Holland was thicker than the day before. Nineteen gliders were lost before the serials reached the landing zones. Flak cut two tow ropes and knocked one Horsa from the sky. It killed the pilot in one tow plane of the 545th Squadron of the 46th Group, but the second navigator, although slightly wounded, took over the controls and, in a quick conversation over the radio with the glider pilot, decided to try to complete the mission. Flak then tore away the Horsa's ailerons, but both managed to make it to the LZ, where the Horsa released. With the first navigator assisting, the second navigator flew the aircraft to Martlesham Heath, where he successfully landed.

Meanwhile, shells impacted in the landing zones. Two truck loads of German infantry arrived only a field away from one of the zones. In the distance, there was the drone of aircraft that grew louder by the second to grow into a tremendous roar as serial after serial of tow planes passed near and over the landing zones, releasing their gliders.

Fifty Germans in nearby positions, overawed at the sight, gave themselves up. The gliders descended through heavy fire, but few gliders had any difficulty in landing. The fire was so intense, however, that it was decided to abandon two gliders without unloading them. Before they were abandoned, they were set afire so that no equipment would fall into German hands. Before the day was over, forty-nine gliders had been set afire, although it was only in the case of these two that the equipment was lost.

Hamilcars discharged their tanks, and the two truck-loads of German riflemen turned tail. One tank headed for a nearby village to deal with snipers in a church tower. With eight rounds, the snipers disappeared.

On D-Day+1, the largest glider lifts of the operation—450 each in the 82nd and 101st Airborne Divisions—took off. The 82nd took off between 1000 and 1100 hours carrying two glider field artillery battalions, one parachute field artillery battalion, part of the divisional antitank battalion and the medical company.

The Germans had attacked from the Reichswald and seized a part of the landing zone early in the day. The parachutists had made a mid-morning attack and had driven the enemy off the landing zone, but the Germans still had much of it under fire. General Gavin sent a message to England in an effort to have glider pilots notified to land on the west side of the landing zone. Heroic paratroopers, realizing that the German presence was imminently dangerous to gliders soon to be landing, fought off the encircling enemy forces. Sensing the danger, First Sergeant Leonard A. Funk rallied the Americans in the vicinity. He marched at the head of the force, shooting his way across 800 yards of open ground. Spotting four 20-mm guns, Funk, with two others, then attacked and destroyed each gun and crew. Then he turned on three flak guns close at hand and, leading a small group, he put them out of action, killing fifteen of the enemy.

Flak hit glider pilot Flight Officer Lawrence W. Kubale in the right side of his head. He blacked out momentarily. Coming to, he found the sergeant, a gliderman who was by no means a pilot, at the other controls doing his best to fly the glider—and succeeding up to that point. Blood streaming from his right temple into his eyes, shrapnel in each of his arms and in severe pain, Kubale nevertheless took over again. He skillfully managed to land right on target when released.

Other gliders that landed near the Reichswald came under intense and damaging fire. While several hundred gliders were landing on the correct landing zone, twenty-five gliders of the 319th Field Artillery Battalion continued over the zone, beyond the Reichswald, and landed about five miles inside Germany. About half the men got back to the division within a few days. The glider pilots explained that they had failed to get a green light signal from the tugs, and thought they should not release.

Four hundred and twenty-eight gliders of the 101st Airborne Division made it to the landing zone. They brought in 2,579 of the 2,656 men of the 327th Glider Infantry Regiment and parts of division support command that had taken off. Twenty-six men had been injured or wounded and fifty-one remained unaccounted for. This massive lift brought in 146 jeeps and some trailers, in addition to the sorely needed infantry,

While it was mentioned in after-action reports, a psychological phenomenon, a sort of mass compulsion, apparently took hold among glider and C-47 pilots. Pilot after pilot witnessed cut-offs going on in the flights ahead and alongside, and this caused an "if they can, why can't I" compulsion to develop, thus leading to the aborting of 45 percent of the glider mission. To an extent, this phenomenon reflected directly the standard of discipline of participating air units. It was not a high standard by anyone's measure.

On D-Day+2, the 82nd Airborne Division had no glider support mission, and the 101st Airborne Division had bad luck with its. Three hundred and eighty-five took off. The armada flew over the fields of England. The chain of aircraft stretched as far as the eye could see. Below, they could see the coastline and the Channel with its treacherous currents, followed by Belgium. Flying in close formation, the air fleet then encountered heavy fog banks. Visibility was so reduced that only the first few feet of the tow line could be seen at times. Tug ships changed their course abruptly without the glider pilot expecting it, jerking so that the gliders flopped over and had to cut loose. Then came flak and heavy machine-gun fire. Soon they could see black smoke and dirt and knew that they were nearing the landing zone. They felt naked up there, knowing that thousands of faces, both friendly and enemy, were upturned to see them pass. The fires surrounded the gliders with the spit of a thousand devils. It penetrated through the tail assembly, the floor, the very men themselves. Ships and gliders went down, but the huge formation never faltered. Eighty-two broke their tow combinations over England, 17 landed in the Channel and 16 in Germany, 31 in friendly territory and 26 remained unaccounted for. Between 209 and 213 gliders—only half the force—made it to the landing zone. The lift cost the division 29 killed and 41 injured in crashes and a total of 225 men remained unaccounted for.

Despite the above incident, the division was finding better organization and unit effectiveness than hoped for in its glider operations. Previously, the division had left newly landed glider forces to try to find their assembly areas by themselves. In an experiment, it sent five officers and twenty enlisted men as a glider reception task force in the first glider to land on D-Day. From then on, these men hovered near the glider landing areas, some in jeeps, some on foot. As gliders came in, they sped to the gliders, met the chalks, quickly orientated them and pointed out directions to their assembly areas or units. Regardless of the amount of training in orientation before missions, it had been found there was a loss of time on landing and some units became lost after leaving their gliders, especially when pilots did not bring gliders down in the expected fields. The new system proved highly effective in getting the glider units organized and ready to fight.

On D-Day+2, most of the British missions were parachute resupply drops, with the exception of a forty-four-glider operation. Many of these gliders had taken off on previous days, but because of rope breaks or other mishaps they had not completed the journey. Some were not to fare better on D-Day+2. Seven ropes broke, two of them in a cloud while over water. Each glider ditched successfully.

Take-offs had been delayed until late in the morning because of bad weather. Flak was unusually heavy. It severed one towrope. The two pilots in another glider were shot in the legs but managed to land on target. One glider was shot down, out of control. Five others were forced down in Belgium and Holland short of the landing zones. Then another towrope broke or was cut by flak.

No Allied fighters gave cover to the flight, a puzzle to the transport pilots who were finding the flak much heavier than the preceding two days. It turned out that the fighters had gone up according to schedule and had got to the rendezvous point on time. There were no transports in the sky. The fighters are reported to have assumed that the transport operation had cancelled, because the weather was so bad. They returned to their bases. The enemy positions were thus not attacked as in previous days. This may account for the heavy losses to air transport. Thirteen resupply aircraft did not get back to their bases, and many that did return had flak damage.

D-Day+2 brought British glider operations to a close in a battle that was to prove so disastrous to British forces at Arnhem. Six hundred and ninety-six gliders had taken off in the mighty effort. Six hundred and twenty-one made it to landing zones or very close to them. Of 203 gliders that released successfully for one of the landing zones on D-Day+1, 189 landed where planned, a remarkable achievement. Twelve landed very near in the adjacent landing zone.

The weather sharply curtailed air operations for four successive days, with none at all possible on D-Day+5. But on D-Day+6, the largest lift took off, carrying American personnel. The 82nd Airborne Division lost 21 gliders before the column left English shores, 43 were lost from there to the landing zone at Groesbeek and 10 were unaccounted for. The 101st Airborne Division fared better. Of its 84 gliders that took off in England, 77 got to their landing zone near Zon.

In the entire "Market" operation, 902 gliders of the 82nd Airborne Division started off from England. Seven hundred and sixty-three landed within 1,000 yards of their landing zone and 102 outside this radius. Some 37 were unaccounted for. Of the 988 gliders that carried elements of the 101st Airborne Division, 767 landed 5,000 men on or near their landing zones in the seven days of air-transport operations. Twenty-nine had been destroyed getting to the LZ's; 41 soldiers were injured and 225 remained unaccounted for.

Operation "Market" was an airborne operation of unprecedented magnitude. A total of 34,876 troops had gone into the battle by air: 13,781 by gliders, 20,190 by parachute and 905 by aircraft on a prepared landing strip. Gliders brought in 1,689 vehicles, 290 howitzers and 1,259 tons of ammunition and other supplies.

The contribution of American glider pilots, once they had landed, became a contentious problem of major proportions. More than 1,700 glider pilots made the one-way trip. Once on the ground, they represented about 5 percent of Allied strength in the drop area. This was the equivalent of a glider regiment in numbers, but they turned out to be a real detriment to the operation as a whole.

If the glider pilots available to the 82nd Airborne Division on D-Day+1 had been organized and trained to participate effectively in ground combat, they might have been assigned a defensive sector for the time, especially along the frontage facing the Reichswald. This might have released parachute forces there for an attack on the Nijmegen Bridge. Such an attack conceivably could have resulted in the earlier capture of the bridge and the relief of the British 1st Airborne Division at Arnhem. The British airborne corps considered that the British system under which glider pilots were assigned to the Army rather than the Air Force, were organized into the equivalent of battalions, companies and platoons and trained to fight as infantry, was far superior to the American.

It reported that the stand made by the 1st Airborne Division, and its subsequent withdrawal across the Lower Rhine, would have been impossible without the assistance given by the organization and training of the 1,200 glider pilots. Commanders of both the 82nd and the 101st Airborne Divisions expressed a need for better organization and control of glider pilots after landing. It was a problem that had been anticipated in maneuvers. It had appeared in operations in Sicily, Italy and Normandy. Despite repeated recommendations for improving the situation, the problem was as evident as ever in Holland. General Gavin described it in this way:

One thing in most urgent need of correction is the method of handling our glider pilots. I do not believe there is anyone in the combat area more eager and anxious to do the correct thing and yet so completely, individually and collectively incapable of doing it than our glider pilots.

Despite their individual willingness to help, I feel that they were definitely a liability to me. Many of them arrived without blankets, some without rations and water, and a few improperly armed and equipped. They lacked organization of their own because of, they stated, frequent transfer from one Troop Carrier Command unit to another. Despite the instructions that were issued to them to move via command channels to division headquarters, they frequently became involved in small-unit actions to the extent that satisfied their passing curiosity or simply left to visit nearby towns. In an airborne operation where, if properly planned, the first few hours are the quietest, this can be very harmful, since all units tend to lose control because of the many people wandering about aimlessly, improperly equipped, out of uniform and without individual or unit responsibilities. When the enemy reaction builds up and his attack increases in violence and intensity, the necessity for every man to be on the job at the right place, doing his assigned task, is imperative. At this time, glider pilots without unit assignment and improperly trained, aimlessly wandering about, cause confusion and generally get in the way and have to be taken care of.

In this division, glider pilots were used to control traffic, to recover supplies from the LZ's, to guard prisoners and, finally, were assigned a defensive role with one of the regiments at a time when they were badly needed.

I feel very keenly that the glider pilot problem at the moment is one of our greatest unsolved problems. I believe now that they should be assigned to airborne units, take training with the units and have a certain number of hours allocated periodically for flight training.

General Ridgway, commanding general of the XVIII Corps (Airborne), did not go along with the proposal to place glider pilots under the command of division commanders for full-time ground training. "British practice to the contrary notwithstanding," General Ridgway thought that glider pilots were where they belonged: in the troop-carrier squadrons. They could receive whatever ground training they needed with their associated airborne division. This apparently was no change from the policy that had created the problems of so much concern to the airborne division commanders.

The problem of resupplying the troops by air had not yet been solved satisfactorily in Operation "Market." Airborne commanders were in agreement that resupply by parachute should be regarded only as an emergency expedient. The scattered drops meant that the fighting strength of the division had to be weakened to provide recovery details, and many bundles were lost. Gliders, when they could get in, were much more reliable, of course, but the use of one-way gliders, each requiring a pilot, was an expensive method.

These gliders, used in the invasion of Holland, were collected to be repaired for use in the airborne assault on Berlin.

The most striking feature of the plan was that the whole operation was to be carried out by the light of day. The Allied air forces were supreme in the air, and attacks by fighters of the *Luftwaffe* were neither expected nor feared. The profusion of Spitfires, Thunderbolts, Mustangs, Typhoons and other fighters was so great that the protection they could give was rightly regarded as overwhelming.

There remained only the antiaircraft defenses of the enemy. As has been said, these were formidable and increased daily. The dropping and landing zones were at extreme range, and this meant that the transport and tug aircraft would have to follow the shortest possible route. The long, roaring columns had to fly over the Dutch islands where the Germans had established considerable flak resources over the preceding four years in their effort to counter the bomber streams headed for the Ruhr.

Around the objectives themselves, light flak was being concentrated in ever larger and larger quantities. Nevertheless, the planners felt confident that the losses which might be incurred from flak would not be so great as to imperil the operation. As it turned out, they were right. It was only during the latter stages, when it became necessary to drop supplies to the men on the ground, that casualties became severe.

In retrospect, the fighting on the ground as part of the overall operation shows it to have been a credit to the Allied field forces, although it seemed a dismal failure initially. The German High Command, in an effort to win time for efforts on other fronts, had hoped to establish three successive lines on which to stand and fight along the Meuse, the Waal and the Lower Rhine. They were in the full throes of preparing to do so when a blow fell with devastating suddenness from out of the skies, skies which Göring had once boasted would ever belong to the *Luftwaffe.* In the space of a few hours—not days—their concept of defense collapsed. In one bound, the British Second Army leapt nearly sixty miles towards the German frontier and became deeply ensconced in what the enemy had fondly hoped would be his front throughout the winter.

Before a week had passed, the Allies had secured all the bridges over two of the three rivers and possessed that most valuable of all assets in war, a firm base for future operations.

The enemy's reaction to the airborne attack, though immediate and violent, achieved no more than a limited success. As has been told, the Germans could claim the recapture of the most northerly of the bridges and the thrusting back of the 1st Airborne Division—with the latter taking heavy casualties—over the Lower Rhine. This is a fact which must be neither minimized nor exaggerated. The loss of many gallant and highly trained men in an operation of great daring and much hazard must be set against the gain to the general conduct of the campaign as a whole. In the end, the gain was considerable.

The resolute seizure of the bridge at Arnhem, which was under British control for three days, combined with the holding of a defensive position north of the river for nine days, forced the enemy to devote large resources, among them the remains of two SS armor divisions, to the task of ejecting the audacious Urquhart and his men. Had the Germans not been under this necessity, their counterattacks farther south against the American 82nd and 101st Airborne Divisions could have been pressed with much greater vigor and might possibly have succeeded, at least for a time. That they failed must be written largely on the credit side of the ledger when calculating the profit and loss incurred by the operation—or, to vary the metaphor, because a duelist pierces the chest but not the heart of his adversary, he has not failed in his attack. He has, after all, inflicted a grievous, perhaps mortal wound. To the British 6th Airborne and the U.S. 17th Airborne Divisions was reserved the honor of inflicting that wound on the Germans less than six months later, north of Wesel on the other side of the Rhine. Their swift and overwhelming success would scarcely have been possible if the battle of Arnhem had not been fought.

OPERATION MARKET

U.S. IX Troop Carrier Command—17–30 September, 1944

Aeroplanes		Gliders
3,989	dispatched	1,899
3,743	effective	1,618
87	destroyed or missing	
845	damaged	

	TROOPS*	
20,011		10,374
	total carried 32,519	

	GLIDER CARGO	
	Trailers	Jeeps
carried	526	830
effective	465	710
	2,856 tons	

R.A.F. 38 and 46 Groups—17–25 September, 1944

Aeroplanes		Gliders
1,341	dispatched	697
1,191	effective	621
55	destroyed/missing	
350	damaged	

	TROOPS	
186		4,215
	total carried 4,401	

	GLIDER CARGO	
	1,431 tons	1,026 vehicles

Casualties—17–30 September, 1944

AIR UNITS	Killed	Missing	Wounded or Injured	Total
IX TCC Crews	31	155	66	252
IX TCC Glider Pilots	12	65	37	114
RAF TC Crews	31	217	17	265
British Glider Pilots	59	636	35	730
2d Air Div	1	63	34	98
Total	134	1136	189	1459

GROUND TROOPS, 17–25 SEPTEMBER, 1944				
82nd Airborne Div	215	427	790	1432
101st Airborne Div	315	547	1248	2110
1st Airborne Div	286	6041	135	6462
1st Polish Parachute Brig	47	173	158	378
Hq Brit Abn Corps & Signal Pers	4	8	—	12
Total	867	7196	2331	10394
TOTAL	1001	8332	2520	11853

* Includes British troops, exclusive of those carried in British planes and gliders.

CHAPTER 14

Bastogne: Gliders Leap the Ring

When the German counteroffensive broke through the Ardennes in mid-December 1944 in the drive that was to end in the Battle of the Bulge, Eisenhower had just two divisions in his strategic reserve, the U.S. 82nd and the 101st Airborne Divisions. They were recuperating in the Rheims area after the "Market" operation. Pressed for forces to stem the Germans, Eisenhower reluctantly committed the 82nd Airborne Division into the lines near Stavelot–St. Vith, while the 101st Airborne moved to Bastogne.

By the night of 20–21 December, German armored elements had closed the ring on Bastogne and had overrun the field hospital of the 101st Airborne Division. General Anthony McAuliffe, commanding the division, began sending his wounded to the civilian hospital in the city as a temporary measure, because all his medical personnel had been captured. He requisitioned supplies from civilian food stocks, but could do nothing about rapidly diminishing ammunition. An inventory conducted on the afternoon of 22 December found that his artillery was down to fewer than ten shells per gun. Resupply by air was the only way to get the ammunition. He sent a message requesting 104 planeloads of ammunition and rations.

The Army Air Corps organized supply operation "Repulse" to fly supplies to the division and other isolated units fighting to turn Rundstedt's offensive. In the next two days, some aircraft managed to get through the heavy weather and drop parachute supplies to the beleaguered division. On Christmas Day, the weather was so foul that a 116-aircraft mission had to be scrubbed. In the meantime, German tanks hit the encircled division in a desperate effort to penetrate its defenses. The division fought back, but the artillery and antitank ammunition was perilously low and there was practically no fuel. Worst of all, the hospital could not handle the growing number of wounded—counted at 400 and growing—many of whom urgently needed of surgery. Eisenhower directed the Army Air Corps in England to make every effort to get supplies to the 101st Airborne Division. Reports predicted bad flying weather over England the next day, although it might have been possible for planes to take off from fields in France. There were not enough parachute containers in

France, however, and a parachute-packing unit, which had been alerted to move to the Continent, was also held up in England by the weather.

Anxious for his wounded, McAuliffe radioed a request that surgeons and medical supplies be flown in by glider, the only possible way any surgeons could get to his division. About the same time, perhaps on the suggestion of the division commander, McAuliffe's G4 radioed the Army Air Corps to try to get ammunition in by glider, as materiel going by glider needed no such special packaging as was necessary for a parachute drop. The Army Air Corps had retrieved gliders from the Holland operations and had hundreds sitting on French airfields. The only questions remaining at that point was how to load them and take off.

It was 26 December and still dark outside. At one base in France, Lieutenant O. B. Blessing was sleeping off the Christmas holiday. A crew chief yelled, "Hey, lieutenant, they want to brief you!" He was sleeping so soundly that he did not hear the first call. The sergeant came over, shook him and repeated the message. Blessing got to the briefing shack as fast as he could throw on his clothes, with no inkling of what was "cooking." At 1452 hours, he was in the air with a load of ammunition, the most surprised pilot alive. Everything had happened so fast, he was not yet fully about his wits.

Blessing's glider was one of eleven winging their way to Bastogne. In the mist ahead, several gliders flew with surgeons and medical personnel, jeeps fitted with litters, surgical kits, ether and other medical supplies. Those gliders landed before the Germans encircling the division caught on that gliders were coming in.

Blessing had a smooth flight up to that point and almost regained some composure, but he soon stiffened with fright when all hell broke loose below. He gave a split second's glance at Flight Officer Charles F. Sutton, his co-pilot, who looked no less frightened. Sutton, he realized, was "praying enough for both." A bit more confident as a result, Blessing once more glued his eyes ahead.

He eyed the tracers. Still in tow, he maneuvered as best he could between the obviously heavy concentrations, but just before releasing, he heard clattering among the steel tubing, and the tail shuddered. He turned and saw light coming through many holes. Miraculously, however, the tail held on, and he landed successfully.

Lieutenant Wallace F. Hammargren was coming close to releasing. As he raised his hands towards the black, pool-ball-size release-lever knob, the towrope parted a foot away from the nose of the glider, probably hit by flak.

A second or so later, the pilot flashed the white light from the tow plane's astrodome, giving Hammargren the release signal.

Another pilot, Lieutenant William Burnett, and his co-pilot, James Crowder, came in low over some treetops. Enemy 20-mm explosive-tipped rounds started fragmenting as they hit the fabric, ripping it to shreds on one side. Northwest of the landing zone, a piece of shrapnel broke the flying wires in the tail, and the glider became sluggish. Burnett barely managed to make the turn towards the field, but he landed successfully.

Most of the other gliders became targets for the last few minutes, but all came in with their loads intact, landing more than 32,900 pounds of cargo.

⊷ ⊣⊰◈⊱⊢ ⊶

But this glider effort did not begin to meet the needs of a situation rapidly growing more serious. Aircraft at bases in England, loaded with parachute-packed supplies, soon stood ready, but the weather gave no indication of improvement. The need was so great, however, that 301 aircraft took off on instruments as the mist swept across the runways and cold fog blanketed vision. Fortunately, they were able to drop 320 tons of supplies within the ring around the encircled airborne division. The weather was so thick on the return flight that it forced a number of planes to land at fields in France to wait for better weather before returning to English bases.

The next day, 27 December, fifty glider-plane combinations from the 439th Troop Carrier Group started for Bastogne from fields in France. For most of them, the flight proved uneventful until they were near the release point.

Lieutenant Charles Brema ran into intense, accurate automatic-weapons fire coming from Germans near a railroad junction at Bras and from woods half a mile east of Remagne. He released at 1230 hours, made a 270-degree left turn, and made it out of range of fire. He touched ground racing towards trees ahead, but could not brake the glider. The trees did, after a telephone pole had first clipped off part of one wing. The trees first took a whole wing and then the other, perceptibly slowing him with each impact. Sweat oozed from under his hands, tightly holding the wheel.

Nearby, men from the 101st Airborne Division rushed towards the glider and pulled open the door. Brema thought they wanted to see if he was still alive or perhaps congratulate him for making it in without getting killed. Instead, they started pulling and hacking at the lashings binding the ammunition to the glider floor and ran off with it, leaving him unceremoniously to his own devices. He took a little time to check the glider. He could not find a single bullet hole. The glider's fuselage had also not suffered any damage in landing. He felt let down.

Other gliders were on their way down. Realizing that the pilots would get little more help than he had, he ran from one glider to another as each landed to give what help he could to each pilot.

Another pilot, Lieutenant David H. Sill, with the 92nd Troop Carrier Squadron, caught flak for seven minutes; it increased to a high intensity and lasted until about four minutes before he released. Then the flak seemed to miraculously stop looking for him. When Sill cut away at 3,200 feet, he could see the smudge-pot markers below. He made a 360-degree right turn, then a 180-degree left. Gliders were all around making various patterns coming in. While still well above the ground, his glider got a jarring bang in the rear and, glancing out, he saw another glider passing a few feet above him on the left, its right wheel dangling. He landed successfully about a mile from General McAuliffe's command post.

Lieutenant Gans had an uneventful flight until he saw the red light on the top of the tow ship start flashing the signal they were ten minutes away from the landing zone. Black puffs began to pop all about their line of flight. He soon saw "white trails" from tracers off in the distance and aircraft overhead—whose aircraft was a mystery to him. The tow plane pilot flashed the white light from the astrodome, the signal to release. Machine guns began chattering. Gans cut off. He saw where to land, but let two other gliders go in ahead. He followed, hit a fence, pulled a wheel off and stopped.

As Lieutenant Mack Striplin's glider got close to the landing zone, he could see German 88's below starting to shoot at his combination. He could hear machine guns chattering. When he had cut off, he saw a strange sight during the run-in: "silvery star-shaped balls" or tinfoil-like objects floating in the air (probably a "window" dropped by high-altitude aircraft to deceive German radar). One was below him, not more than twelve feet from the glider. Striplin flew through the bizarre phenomena. The balls did not dissipate, but soon passed from sight.

Of fifty gliders that started, thirty-five landed close enough to the defenders at Bastogne to get their supplies through. Reports are singularly silent about the remaining gliders, although one mentions that four were shot down. The gliders had brought in 106,291 pounds of cargo. Some 45,000 pounds in fifteen gliders did not make it. It is entirely possible that all fifteen had been shot down—particularly if they were near the end of the air serial— since the Germans were fully alerted by that time. When the powered aircraft turned back, they suffered serious casualties. Before they had reached home, seventeen of the fifty that started that morning had crashed.

Wounded soldiers being placed aboard a cargo glider attached to a field hospital.

Heavy fog continued over the United Kingdom. Of 238 aircraft that were ready, only 188 managed to get off. They dropped 162 tons by parachute without losing an aircraft, but they too had to land at continental bases for the night. By then, supplies had also been loaded in British containers, so that the 38th and 46th RAF Groups could be used in getting supplies to Bastogne.

But that evening, all further air supply missions were called off. A ground corridor connection had been opened, and trucks were getting through to the 101st Airborne Division. More than 94 percent of the supplies sent by air—1,046 tons—landed successfully in the divisional area.

General McAuliffe paid several visits to the hospital. He found the surgeons who had come in by glider "dead on their feet" and working around the clock to tend to the wounded.

CHAPTER 15

The Soviet Union: Glider Pioneer?

While this glider transport experiment [Russian transport of infantry in gliders attached to bombers] first attracted attention and caused much comment among aviation writers and experts, the military leaders among other great powers took little heed of the glider potential, except for the war-minded Germans.

KEITH AYLING

IN *THEY FLY TO FIGHT*

Just after dark one day in the spring of 1943, gliders took off from an airfield whose name, if it had one, is now lost. Their destination was secret. The Soviet Union was fighting for its life. No one was yet convinced that her armies had conclusively stemmed the German onslaught. The gliders carried Matjus Sumauskas, president of the Supreme Soviet of the Lithuanian Soviet Socialist Republic, Henrikas Zimanas, editor-in-chief of Komunistas, and seventy others. They were all Lithuanians and members of Operative Group II, organized to launch partisan movements in German-held Lithuania.

Some 600 miles behind German lines, the gliders cut away from their tow planes. It was black below. Some came in to fairly good landings. One crashed, killing all. Zimanas's glider hit an obstacle and was virtually demolished, with the pilot killed and the passengers badly bruised or severely injured. The accident hurt Zimanas's spine and leg. Despite his injuries and the arrival of an evacuation aircraft, he remained with the mission, assisting as best he could as a radio operator while the other partisans made their way to the Kazyan Forest. Regaining strength, although limping and in severe pain, Zimanas caught up with the main force in the Kazyan Forest. He then went with it to Lithuania.

Nothing was ever known in the West during the war of these isolated but daring partisan operations behind German lines that were frequently launched with gliders. It was through those missions that the use of transport gliders was finally coming into its own in Soviet military operations, the culmination of years of preparation.

Like the Germans, the Soviets had long been avid gliding and soaring enthusiasts. The Soviet Union was one of the few countries to compete with the Germans with any degree of success in the development of gliding. The meager amount of information allowed to seep out of the Soviet Union gave no idea of the great activity centered around glider development there. Soviet progress appears to have anticipated that of Germany by perhaps as much as five years, a fact of immense historical significance.

In the Soviet Union, the state took a direct interest in soaring. Under its support, Soviet glider pilots began to gain international recognition shortly before World War II. In 1925, the Soviets held their first national glider competition in the Crimea.

While Germany originally used the glider as a subterfuge to improve its aeronautical technology and skill resources, the Soviets embarked upon a substantial glider development program for entirely different reasons. Germany's interest in the glider was rooted in those of its qualities that could serve military ends and took absolutely no notice of its commercial value. In the Soviet Union, it was the other way around. Military use became a coincidental offshoot. Soviet commercial aircraft could fly passengers and cargo into areas that had no trains and where roads were impassable in bad weather. The aircraft was solving historical communication problems that had reined in domestic development over the centuries. The aircraft was meeting a vital economic and political need at a critical point in the history of the Soviet Union. The Soviet expansion of commercial air transportation strove to keep up with the increasing demand to fly more and more passengers and cargo.

Short in technological skills and lacking the industrial capacity and production know-how to turn out the increasing number of aircraft demanded of a strained economy, the Soviets turned to the transport glider as offering a way to double air-cargo capacity, using substantially less resources in airframe materials, aircraft, engines and fuel than would be necessary to achieve the same cargo lift with powered transport aircraft.

By then, Soviet-built gliders had been towed long distances in single tow. Experiments were started in double and triple tows, with the thought that ultimately a single aircraft could tow many transport gliders carrying passengers in "glider train" formation. So rapidly did they progress, that by 1939 they had managed the art of towing as many as five single-place gliders with a single aircraft, a feat never matched elsewhere and an accomplishment not surpassed outside of the Soviet Union since.

Although Soviet interest focused chiefly on sport gliding in the 1920's, the government decided to expand Soviet gliding activities in the 1930's. In 1931, a dramatic upsurge occurred when the *Komsomol* passed a resolution calling for an unheralded expansion of the gliding movement during the

Ninth Party Congress, held in January. The *Komsomol* announced a threefold purpose in its resolution: first, it sought to build an enormous pool of glider pilots through training programs; second, it hoped to gain useful information for its aeronautical research program through research and development and the testing of new glider models; and third, it was setting out to capture as many world records as it could.

To back up the program, the government built a glider factory in Moscow in 1932. It set production goals at 900 primary trainers and 300 training gliders per year. It named Oleg K. Antonov, an aircraft engineer and designer who was to become famous for his glider designs, to head design and engineering at the plant.

Shortly after the *Komsomol* resolution was passed, eighty leading glider and light-plane designers assembled at Koktabel. They studied twenty-two glider designs and selected seven for construction and tests to be made in 1932. In retrospect, the pace at which the whole movement progressed gives some indication of the importance the government placed on the program.

In thirty-six days of tests, Soviet glider pilots flew 662 flights, averaging more than an hour each in the seven gliders to be tested. Together with testing conducted on other gliders from distant parts of the Soviet Union, they established six new Soviet records. During that year, V. A. Stepanchenok in a G-9 glider looped 115 times and flew upside down for more than one minute in a single flight. Soviet glider pilots went on to perform new and unexpected aerobatics and carried out long-distance tows and a multitude of other feats. By 1939, Olga Klepikova flew a glider 465 miles to capture the world distance record, a feat that was unbeaten for twenty-two years. On the same occasion, B. Borodin flew two passengers for more than four hours in a single flight and, with that feat, the transport glider was born. It was then up to some perceptive person to recognize the significance of the flight, and it appears that this was not long in happening.

Although Soviet authorities saw the transport glider as a solution to commercial needs for more air lift, they apparently concurrently saw that the transport glider had some military potential. Military and commercial development began simultaneously in the very early 1930's, perhaps in 1931 or 1932, and ran on closely parallel paths. The Moscow glider factory was their design and production focal point. In 1934, the Moscow glider factory produced the GN-4, a five-place glider that could transport four passengers and was designed for towed flight.

The idea for a multi-passenger towed glider, as opposed to the two-passenger soaring glider already flown, must have blossomed in 1932 or 1933, inasmuch as Groshev (designer of the transport glider GN-4), had one on the drawing board then. The GN-4 appears to have been a modest development compared with others then on the drawing board, for General I. I. Lisov, in his *Parachutists—Airborne Landing,* published in Moscow in 1968, reveals that as far back as 1932 the work plan for the Voenno Vozdushniy Sily (VVS) design bureau included the G-63 glider, a craft that could carry seventeen soldiers or a like amount of cargo. What is even more remarkable is that the bureau was daring enough to include a requirement for a fifty-man glider, the G-64, which was to be towed by a TB-1 bomber.

While there are those who would criticize such bold statements as an attempt to bolster the Soviet ego with another first or discount them as pure propaganda, there is evidence based on what was to come that the statements did not come from unrealistic fantasy. In 1935, the Soviet magazine *Samolet* (Flight) discussed the use of gliders for carrying passengers, citing an eighteen-passenger glider, and having a photograph in support. The article goes so far as to give an illustration of a transport glider train drawn by a four-engined aircraft. This would mean that the 1932 VVS design requirement was realized, in part, by 1935 or earlier, since gliders cannot be designed, built and tested overnight. On 9 October 1935, the *New York Times* reported that a 118-passenger glider with a ninety-two-foot wingspan, the G-3, had been built by the experimental institute in Leningrad and test-flown several times. It was to have been flown from Leningrad to Moscow the same month. This was undoubtedly the glider reported in *Samolet.*

In his book *Without Visible Means of Support,* Richard Miller mentions that the Soviets experimented in 1934 with a thirteen-passenger troop glider, grossing 8,000 pounds. In that same year, the Soviets could boast ten gliding schools, 230 gliding stations and 57,000 trained glider pilots.

Around 1934, a new concept took hold, fostered by Lev Pavlovich Malinovskii, head of the Scientific Technical administration of the *Grazhdanskiy Vazdushniy Flot* (Civilian Air Fleet). Malinovskii conceived the idea of using a low-powered freight glider plane, easy to produce and cheap to operate, that could solve some of Russia's long-distance fast freight needs. The fully laden glider would carry around a ton of goods and be powered by a single 100-horsepower engine. The engine would assist the tow plane during take-off. Once safely airborne, the glider would cast off and deliver its cargo to a distant terminal under its own power.

Because most of the models were underpowered, only one or two went beyond the experimental stage. Several apparently grew into sizeable ten-passenger models, and there is a strong likelihood that these models, with engines removed, became the first of the larger twenty-passenger transport gliders developed in the Soviet Union and observed during the mid-1930's.

While Soviet designers and engineers were busy at the task of creating and producing the new aircraft, military leaders went about the task of building airlanding and parachute forces to use them. By 1933, the first of these formations appeared. The Soviet Union startled the world when 1,200 soldiers landed by parachute with all weapons and equipment during maneuvers around Kiev. Later in the year, aircraft transported a complete division, together with armored vehicles, from Moscow to Vladivostok, a distance of 4,200 miles. Minister of War Kliment Voroshilov was fully justified in stating at a congress in 1935: "Parachuting is the field of aviation in which the Soviet Union has a monopoly. No nation on earth can even approximately compare with the Soviet Union in this field, far less could any nation dream of closing the existing gap by which we are leading. There can be no question at all of our being surpassed."

That gliders were used in these maneuvers is not confirmed, although they may have been. Because of the secrecy surrounding them and the fact that they were so similar to powered aircraft in appearance, their presence among the powered aircraft could have passed unnoticed. Terence Otway states, however, that "by 1935, [the Soviet Union] had gone a long way towards creating an effective airborne force, including parachute troops carried in gliders."

In the Caucasus maneuvers of 1936, the paratroopers participated publicly. From that point forward, however, all exercises and maneuvers of the arm were carried out in strict secrecy. Keith Ayling reports in *They Fly to Fight* on a large number of personnel carried in gliders, in one instance, in 1936. They were undoubtedly from the same Caucasus maneuver.

After dropping the veil of secrecy over airborne developments, the Soviets did not entirely neglect the fledgling airborne arm, contrary to foreign observer indications. By 1940, they approved an airborne brigade of 3,000 men, of which more than a third were glider troops. By mid 1941, in a doctrinal turnabout, glider troop elements disappeared from Soviet troop lists, although glider manufacture continued. Only recently has information become available that in 1941, just before the war started, the Soviet Union had already built a glider tank transport, the world's first, which was capable of transporting a light armored vehicle. Shortly after this flight, Germany invaded the Soviet Union, and no more experiments with that glider were conducted. However, the daring experiment, far ahead of those of any other nation manufacturing gliders, gives some indication of the extent of the Soviet Union's interest in, and progress with, the glider as a military tool.

To what extent German military leaders learned from Soviet transport glider developments is not certain, but those developments certainly could not have gone unnoticed, in view of a curious succession of events involving both the Soviet Union and Germany. In a much overlooked clause, the Treaty of Rapallo of 1922 enabled the German military to produce and perfect in

Russia weapons forbidden by the Treaty of Versailles. To that end, the Soviets turned over the remote, disused Lipetsk airfield, about 310 miles southeast of Moscow, in 1924, where they established a flying school and also tested aircraft.[1] Through these activities, the Red Air Force gained information about German technical developments.

In 1923, the Germans opened a "Moscow Center" liaison office in Moscow, manned by German officers who reported to the Defense Ministry in Berlin. Junkers and other German aircraft manufacturers built factories in the Soviet Union, staffed by German officers and aircraft engine experts. Many officers, such as August Plock, Hermann Plocher and Kurt Student, who were later to become generals and who occupied important posts in the *Luftwaffe*, served in the Soviet Union in the 1920's. *General* Student, who masterminded Hitler's glider attack on Eben Emael while an infantry officer, visited the Lipetsk airfield every year from 1924 to 1928.

Three factors strongly suggest that early German development and use of the transport glider followed Soviet developments by three to five years. The Soviets must have had their transport glider on the drawing board perhaps as early as 1932 to enable them to produce their five-passenger GN-4 in 1934 or earlier. The Germans produced their *Obs* (flying observatory) in 1933 or 1934, a glider that was not a true transport vehicle but closer to a scientific laboratory. Second, foreign observers saw Soviet transport gliders in flight in 1935 or 1936, carrying perhaps as many as fifteen to eighteen passengers. The nine-passenger German DFS 230 glider did not appear before 1938, and it proved to be a substantially smaller model than those seen in the Soviet Union up to that time. Third, the Russians had large airborne organizations in planning in the early 1930's and actually flew them in the large airborne drop at Kiev in 1935, while it was not until 1938 that the Germans finally organized their 7. *Flieger-Division*.

Although Soviet military leaders conducted few and only marginally useful air assaults during the war and the glider saw only limited use as a military transport to support these operations, it did play some role.

For the Dnjepr River crossing operations of 24 September 1943, the Soviets planned to use thirty-five gliders to transport heavy guns and equipment. In planning, the glider landings had been sandwiched in between the first and second massed parachute drops. Apparently, the glider phase was not

---

1.The Germans also established an armor school in the Soviet Union, which was instrumental in providing valuable experience to the fledgling *Panzertruppe*.

implemented. Apart from this, it was used extensively in partisan support operations and in many raids.

German forces found guerrillas annoying and persistent. Although guerrillas lived off the land to a great extent, the regular military force kept them supplied with weapons and ammunition by glider and, where possible, by powered aircraft. The magnitude of these operations and the importance played by the glider can be judged by the fact that in counterguerrilla operations conducted just in and around Lipel alone, the German forces overran one field that held more than 100 gliders.

Gliders transported rations, weapons, medical supplies and, at the same time, provided partisans with key personnel and important orders and information. Gliders landed by night on emergency airfields and during the winter on the ice of frozen lakes. This support enabled the partisans to carry out successful attacks on railroads, roads, airfields, bridges, convoys, columns of troops, rear area command agencies and even troop units. The Germans suffered heavy losses of personnel and materiel. The Germans flew reconnaissance missions to discover air-drop and landing fields in partisan-held areas, attacked airlift operations wherever they were identified, used deception by setting up dummy airfields and giving fake signals and eventually activated a special antipartisan wing, comprised of 100 Ar 66's. The results achieved against the guerrillas, especially in the central sector of the front, remained unsatisfactory. In the final analysis, this use of airlift by the Russian Air Force must be considered a success, since the relentless night airlift operations enabled the partisans to carry out their tasks.

After the war, Soviet interest in gliders did not immediately wane, and new models were reported, though sources of these reports are few and hard to find. As late as 1965, the Soviets had three glider regiments, which they have since deactivated.

CHAPTER 16

Some Gliders That Never Fought

While glider development went on in Great Britain, Germany, the United States, and Russia, there was little notice or knowledge by these great powers of glider development elsewhere. Yet some surprising developments took place in countries far distant from the locations of major glider production and their theaters of operational use.

These nations undertook the development and production of gliders without the benefit of experience gained by the major producers. Each did a surprisingly creditable job.

JAPAN

Japan is perhaps the first of these other countries that should be mentioned. Unknown to even her friendliest Axis partner, Germany, Japan embarked on a glider development program in 1941. She had precious little antecedent upon which to base her efforts. Until 1935, the Japanese had never taken sports gliding seriously.

In that year, Hirth, the famous German soaring pilot, arrived in Japan with his Goppinger I and III soaring gliders to show the Japanese something of the art of soaring. He performed at Tokorozawa with both of these gliders and so impressed the Japanese Air Force generals that they sought his advice about introducing glider flying into the training of pilots as a step prior to the pilots learning to fly powered aircraft.

Apparently, the Japanese Air Force thought enough of the possibilities of using the glider to order the production of several soaring models patterned on the German Goppinger. When the Japanese invaded China, Japanese military authorities turned their attention to the pressing matters of the enterprise, and glider development stopped.

In 1940, the word of the German accomplishment at Eben Emael filtered into Japan. Several months later, German generals vaunted the achievements of the daring glider operation at Eben Emael to Japanese and other Axis attachés when they took them on a tour of the shattered Allied defenses in Belgium and France. The Japanese attaché reports on the German achievements with gliders further impressed Japanese generals as to what the glider could accomplish. From this time on, the Japanese Army and Navy initiated steps that, although never vigorous, nonetheless assured continuous attention to the subject.

In 1941, the Japanese Army constructed its first troop-carrying glider of consequence, the Ku-1. The Navy followed a short while later with a contract to the Japanese Aircraft Corporation to produce the MXY-5, a thirteen-passenger glider.

The Army soon launched into the development of the Ku-8, a glider that carried twenty-two men, and one which, after several modifications, became their mass-production model. Four hundred were built. The Japanese Army also decided to produce a tank-carrying glider, the Ku-6. Not much is known of this glider, except that at least one model was built, and it flew with a tank on several occasions. The Army planned to use it to counter the American invasion of Japan. They had in mind flying the glider and light-tank combination into areas where the Allies threatened to make landings or where landings had already been made.

By 1940, the Japanese had organized both glider and parachute airborne units, starting with small experimental elements of squad size. They soon organized larger, battalion-size "raiding" formations. These were ultimately consolidated into two 6,000-men divisions that each had two glider regiments plus division troops. Each regiment had 900 men—rather small, by Allied standards, for glider requirements.

Japanese prisoners of war interrogated by the U.S. Army Air Corps reported observing Japanese gliders and glider training being conducted in Manchuria, but no Japanese combat glider operations ever took place there.

When MacArthur launched his long-vaunted campaign to carry out his promise to return to the Philippines, the Japanese moved some of their glider forces to the south. They planned to place them in a wide-ranging strategic reserve, with the ability take off in a matter of hours to repel one or more of MacArthur's possible thrusts while the amphibious forces were still struggling over the beaches.

Japanese gliders, tow planes and airborne units began the long, frequently interrupted trek, starting from Nishitsukuba. The various elements converged first on the island of Cheju Do in Korea. They then flew to Shanghai and on to Taiwan.

By November 1944, however, MacArthur had already set foot on Leyte. The Japanese ground forces there were in serious trouble, and the Japanese decided the forces en route should be launched against U.S. forces in Leyte, with the exact mission to be determined.

In the meantime, the first echelon of the ground-support elements of their glider assault force had also arrived at Taiwan by ship. The Japanese

The Australian DHA-G2 suction-wing test glider.

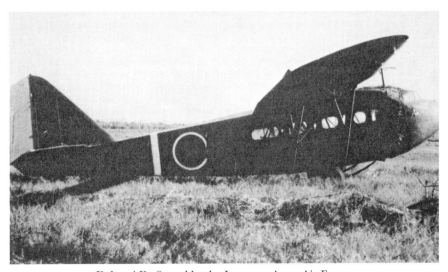

Kokusai Ku-8 used by the Japanese Army Air Force.

began a glider infiltration to Clarke field, sixty miles north of Manila. Towing with Type 97 bombers, the Japanese managed to get twelve gliders to the Philippines. About the time the last had arrived, the Japanese command at Clarke got wind that the Allies had sunk a ship carrying the second echelon of 300 men, a much-needed ground-support unit with supplies, before it had reached Taiwan. Only three men survived. The loss of this force, combined with the fact that the Japanese situation on Leyte had deteriorated, made a glider foray with what could then only be a token force foolhardy. As a result, the plan was cancelled.

By January, MacArthur was in Luzon, Manila had been captured, and the last of the Japanese about to be driven into the sea. A desperate, hopeless venture, they planned to try to hold onto the north end of Luzon, with the aim of retaining a beachhead for re-invasion. They again planned to land glider forces at Clarke field to bolster Japanese strength there. However, they called off the landings when U.S. forces landed at Lingayen Bay, 100 miles to the north of Clarke, on 9 January 1945, eliminating the last of the Japanese-held ports in the Philippines.

In last-minute desperation—all hope of winning the war lost, but anxious not to lose Okinawa for the negotiations ahead—the Japanese looked desperately for some means to bolster the Okinawa garrison, heavily pounded by the U.S. Navy and under ground attack by the Marines and the Army. They prepared an assault force of eight gliders to take off from airfields around Yokota, Japan. They scheduled the landings for 20 August 1945. In the meantime, however, atom bombs had incinerated Nagasaki and Hiroshima, and the war had ended by 15 August.

A more aggressive use of gliders by the Japanese forces did not take place for many reasons. Most important was the lack of aircraft to tow the gliders. Another and almost equally important reason lay in the lack of fighter cover for any planned glider operations. By the time the Japanese had produced a substantial glider-airborne arm, the tide of war was flowing swiftly against Japan. Militarily, Japan was exhausted, her resources were severely drained and she was unable to afford any frills. A lack of belief in or enthusiasm for the new weapon was probably another factor—the same factor that colored much of the Allies' thinking.

AUSTRALIA

Australia—geographically isolated and gravely endangered by Japanese advances in the Philippines, Malaysia, Indonesia and Burma—was interested in the possibilities that the glider held for army forces that would fend off Japanese landings on any of her isolated shores. The Australian Army planned the use of gliderborne units that could be flown quickly from key airfields across wide expanses of desert to threatened areas.

In 1942, the Royal Australian Air Force contracted with de Havilland Aircraft (DHA) to produce a six-place glider, the DHA-Gr. Several were built. A later modification, the DHA-D2 was also built. When the Japanese advance in the Far East slowed down, the Australians gradually stopped the development of transport gliders, but not before they had built an unusually versatile glider, considering their lack of technical experience in the field when they first entered it.

ITALY

It is uncertain when the Italians took an interest in the transport glider. However, by 1943, they had produced the AL-12, an especially trim and flyable glider. It carried ten men, but apparently only one glider was built.

FRANCE

The French Army, impressed with what the Germans and the Allies had done with gliders, planned the building of transport gliders immediately after France's liberation. A contract was made with the Fango works. They constructed the Castel-Mauboissin 10 or CM-10, an all-wood glider that carried a jeep, a trailer and three to six men. It was an advanced development considering that France entered the field a decidedly late comer.

However, budgeting restrictions, combined with a change of heart on the part of the military, began to have its effect. A program that had projected the building of some 100 Mauboissins was cut back and only 6 were ultimately built. Most were finished after the war ended.

When the army discontinued production of gliders, some funds were allocated to turning the existing gliders into powered aircraft. The ultimate development was a glider-turned-jet, the CM-101R.

CHAPTER 17

"Varsity": Assault across the Rhine

arly in 1945, the Allies agreed on a three-phase campaign to end the
war against Germany. It included several airborne assaults on enemy
positions across the Rhine, north of the Ruhr River between Emmerich and
Wesel. "Varsity," one of these operations, would send British and American
airborne divisions to assist the British Second Army making an amphibious
crossing of the Rhine near Wesel. The plan for this operation was ambitious.
It called for landing 17,000 glidermen and parachutists and thousands of tons
of supplies, armor and other heavy equipment in just four hours. As such, it
was the most enterprising airborne operation ever planned. In a doctrinal
turnabout, airborne drops were to follow, not precede, the beginning of the
ground assault by the British Second Army.

Dynamic General Miles Dempsey, the field army's commander-in-chief,
established the objective for the airborne troops and set the tone for the
operation. Rather than let the airborne divisions take the safer, but less
daring, alternative of dropping close to the Rhine, where they would soon
have the assistance of his ground troops (a plan suggested by some of his
more conservative staff officers), he chose otherwise.

He ordered his airborne forces, the British 6th and the American 17th
Airborne Divisions, to land near and secure the Diersforder Wald, a wooded
area four miles east of the Rhine. This meant that the airborne forces were
making a relatively deep penetration, which raised the possibility that the
Germans might cut the divisions off from the main ground assault. However,
the risk was well worth the gamble, he felt.

Although scarcely 100 feet higher than the river surface, the woods
covered the highest point near the Rhine. This meant that this excellent
observation spot had to be denied to German artillery observers and made
available for Allied use. The woods, moreover, camouflaged and protected
German artillery batteries that could rake Dempsey's men as they crossed
the river. Until airborne troops cleared the woods of the enemy, the Second
Army would find it next to impossible to bridge the Rhine because of the fire
the enemy could place on bridge sites.

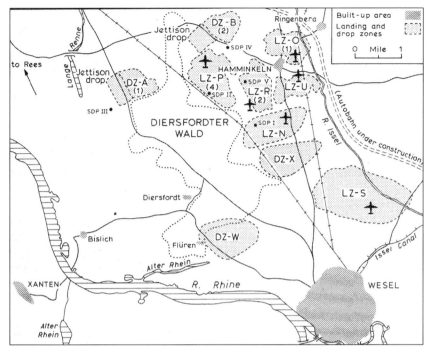

Operation "Varsity."

It would take several hours after the amphibious crossings had begun for General Dempsey's forces to capture bridging sites on the far bank and move bridging equipment up. Airborne landings to capture the woods could take place some time in the morning. The time was later set at 1000 hours.

The staff selected six glider landing zones and four paratroop drop zones. Nine zones were on or near the east side of the woods and one paratroop zone was on its west side. All ten zones were in an area less than six miles long and five miles wide—an unprecedented degree of concentration.

Firm, level fields and meadows, averaging 200 to 300 yards in length, formed a checkerboard throughout the zone. Small hedges, light fences and ditches skirted many of them. No "Rommel's asparagus" showed up on aerial photographs, nor other man-made military obstacles. (Indeed, none were found in the landing zones after the landing.) A double-track railroad cut diagonally across the area from northwest to southeast. A few hundred yards to the east of the railroad, a high-tension power line on 100-foot pylons presented a major hazard to gliders and billowing parachutes. The Issel bordered the eastern edge of the area and was a water barrier sixty feet wide, running south-southeast. Although many other minor hazards existed, it was most important to avoid depositing the airborne forces in the woods in or beyond the Issel or against the high-tension line.

Transports and gliders fill the air as the 17th Airborne Division sets off for the Rhine.

Gliders facing in all directions, as they landed, in a patchwork of German fields.

Being aware that Wesel was a logical place to cross the Rhine, the Germans had massed an estimated ten divisions within twenty miles of the assault area. These divisions had been so reduced by attrition, however, that their combat effectives were fewer than 50,000 men; their authorized strength was 150,000. Among them were two or three armored divisions with perhaps 100 tanks and self-propelled guns; these were reported to be more than ten miles from the assault area. A maximum of 12,000 troops, which included two divisions and a brigade battle group, were thought to be within a ten-mile radius of the airborne assault. If they concentrated in the Diersforder Wald to oppose the amphibious landings, the airborne attack at their rear and on their flanks would cut them off. Because it was believed that the Germans were expecting an airborne assault, it was more likely that they would keep their main strength behind the Issel, with only a holding force in the woods. In that case, the airborne troops might be encircled.

"Varsity" involved both British and American air elements. The U.S. IX Troop Carrier Command had orders to transport the airborne divisions. It assigned 226 C-47's and 72 C-46's for lifting the paratroops of the 17th Airborne Division, 243 C-47's for the 6th Airborne Division and 610 C-47's, many of them to use the double-tow technique, to tow 906 gliders carrying the 17th Airborne Division glider elements. The 38th and 46th Groups of the RAF supplied 440 aircraft to tow an equal number of gliders carrying the glider forces of the 6th Airborne Division. The flight path was not excessively long and only the last six miles of it were over enemy territory. But to deliver two divisions within two hours and thirty-seven minutes required precise timing, since the British forces would fly from England and the Americans from bases around Paris.

Brigadier Chatterton's Glider Pilot Regiment had been reinforced after its losses at Arnhem by a high proportion of pilots of the RAF, who attempted to learn to both fly a glider and to fight as soldiers in a short space of time. When that bright spring morning dawned, every pair of pilots in the 440 British gliders that took off knew how to fight.

The troop carriers based in England had orders to enter the continent at Cape Gris Nez and fly a dogleg course to Wavre, thus avoiding the radar range of German-held Dunkirk. The flights from England and France were to merge over Wavre in Belgium. This location caused the least possible detour for the transport wings stationed in France and could be reached by all wings without their interfering with each other's courses or assembly areas. From Wavre, three traffic lanes, one and a half miles apart, led northeast for ninety-two miles to Weeze, the principal assembly point, located fourteen miles west of the Rhine.

At 2000 hours on 23 March, the British began a heavy artillery barrage against the far bank of the Rhine and the drop zones and landing zones that had been selected for the airborne operation. An hour later, this artillery barrage was lifted, and the first wave of the British Second Army assault boats pushed out into the Rhine. To the south, the U.S. Ninth Army assault began at 0200 hours on 24 March. All the crossings were completely successful; there was little German resistance from the far bank of the river. By dawn, nine small bridgeheads had been secured in the Wesel-Emmerich area, some twenty miles along the river, although there was fierce fighting at some points. *Fallschirmjäger* held Rees, ten miles northwest of Wesel, throughout D-Day and kept the British 51st Division pinned close to the river. Enemy troops also held Wesel proper.

At 0710 hours, aircraft of the RAF's 38th and 46th Groups, flying Stirlings, Halifaxes and C-47's, started off from the runways of airfields in East Anglia. They towed 381 Horsas and 48 Hamilcars up into a bright clear sky, carrying the Airlanding Brigade of the 6th Airborne Division. U.S. Army Air Corps aircraft flew the parachutists of the divisions. Aircraft were taking off from eleven fields in all, the many columns marshalling in the sky over Hawkinge in Kent to form one gigantic fleet. It crossed France near Calais, then headed towards Brussels. Simultaneously, American planes began lifting the 17th Airborne Division from twelve airfields around Paris. They marshaled and headed towards Brussels to converge with those coming into view from Calais. Everything was going smoothly. A thousand fighters swept the sky above the plodding columns.

Brigadier G. K. Bourne could see the Rhine, a silver streak, and beyond it, a thick, black haze, for all the world like Manchester or Birmingham as seen from the air. For the moment, he wondered whether the bombing of Wesel, which had preceded the attack upon that town by commando elements, had been mistimed. If this were so, then all the landing zones would be obscured by clouds of dust blowing from the rubble created by the attack.

The landing zones were indeed dusty, but the dust did not prevent glider pilots from making successful landings. By 0945 hours, the formation was approaching its objectives, flying over the Rhine at an altitude of 2,500 feet. Three hours and ten minutes after take-off, the leading British gliders neared the landing zone. A *Times* aeronautical correspondent riding in a Halifax reported:

> Away at the right, a farm building was burning itself out. Nearby, a field was strewn with white, blue and red parachutes, but of their former wearers there was no trace; they had already advanced into the pall of smoke, which hung like a gigantic curtain over the

battlefield, hiding all that was going on underneath, blotting out the horizon and smudging the blue sky with dirty grey-brown fingers. In the middle of the field sprawled an up-ended glider.

As we approached the dropping zone, the danger of collision became very real. The Halifax rocked dangerously in the slipstream of machines in front, and perspiration trickled down the pilot's face as he tried to keep the tug in level flight while the glider was preparing to cast off. . . . "Two miles to go," the pilot shouted. "OK, tug," came the reply. "Can you take us a little lower?"

The nose of the Halifax dipped down slightly. Then we heard the voice of the glider pilot again. "Hello, tug, I am casting off now." "Cheerio, old man. Good luck. See you again soon." The Halifax gave a bound forward as it was relieved of the load of the glider. The Horsa started to dive steeply away to the right, and we turned upwards and to port, climbing swiftly to get out of the tangled stream of gliders and tugs. . . . We were over the battle area now and, in a few seconds, gliders and the ground were lost in a sea of smoke. All that remained were the tugs, with their towropes dangling behind them.

Occasionally, one could see the flash of a gun. . . . The contending ground forces now had the stage to themselves, for in the smoke and dust of battle, the air forces could not intervene further. As we turned for home a few puffs of flak appeared. A Halifax in front had one wheel of its undercarriage hanging down; obscured by smoke, a Hamilcar glider had force-landed in the corner of a field. Ant-like figures were busily engaged in unloading a gun and light tank.

For half an hour after we had started back, the unbroken stream of tugs, gliders and parachute-troop-transports still flowed eastwards.

It was now nearly time for Brigadier Bourne's glider to cut off. In accordance with orders, but against his will, since he wanted to see what was happening, he had strapped himself in. They began to go down in a steep glide, and he listened with strained interest to the excited exchange between the two pilots, neither of whom had been on operations before. He heard the first pilot say to the second, "I can see the railway." Bourne felt relieved. And he soon saw the terrain racing past the windows. They landed very fast, went through a couple of fences and stopped with a jerk. The men inside, all of them belonging to the Defense Platoon of divisional headquarters darted out and took cover under a low embankment, on top of which was a post and rail fence. There was a lot of firing about a mile away. They had arrived only about 600 yards from the preordained spot. After landing, the airborne elements moved off, reached two farms, where they observed docile German

A glider snagged in a tree after the Rhine crossing.

Troops of the First Allied Airborne Army leaving the glider in which they landed.

prisoners standing in lines, and went to their headquarters at the Kipenhof farm. Throughout the action, there was a lot of sniping from the eastern edge of the forest.

Sergeant J. H. Jenkins found the weather on 24 March to be fine and clear. He had an uneventful take-off and soon linked up with the main stream. What a stirring sight! Glider combinations as far as the eye could see, with an umbrella of fighter escorts that put heart into all of them.

They eventually crossed the Rhine at Rees, as planned. That's where their troubles started. Montgomery, in giving effective cover for his ground assault, had laid smokescreens, which completely obscured the ground below when coupled with thin, low cloud cover. As a result, they were in the hands of the tug crew, praying that the navigator's dead-reckoning skills would give the correct release point. Suddenly, they saw the green aldis lamp flashing from the rear gunner's turret and, with a "This is it, Skipper," the co-pilot pulled the release knob. The airspeed dropped. Selecting a quick trim, Jenkins took a hurried look at the starboard wing tip, noticed it was pointing at a slightly darker patch in the cloud, and turned sharply until they were heading for it.

They glided down, completely isolated, and only their compass reading told them they were heading in the right direction. Then the fireworks started: a series of ominous thumps from all around, and a swishing sound nearby as another glider plunged earthward, with pieces falling from its burning fuselage. The altimeter was reading a fraction under 2,000 feet and still they could not see the ground. The co-pilot stuck his head through to the rear and called for safety belts to be fastened. It was then Jenkins decided to take a chance. He would do a blind box-turn on wing tip and compass and lose 200 feet on each of the east, north and west legs. He would then turn south again on the original heading and pray that they had not drifted too far off track. He followed this plan, and they were on their 180-degree "reading" once more at 1,300 feet.

By this time, the co-pilot had discarded his safety belt and was coolly standing up in the cockpit, peering down into the murk. Suddenly, he let forth a great shout: "Church spire ahead, ten degrees starboard, Skipper!" Thank God for the RAF and that co-pilot in particular. Jenkins looked across. For the first time, he saw a miracle: the smoke and cloud was still a blanket, but just about half a mile ahead—or so it seemed—there was a small circular opening, about the size of a dinner plate, and up through this hole that beautiful church spire was pointing triumphantly to the heavens. They altered course slightly, turned over the spire at 600 feet, put on full flap and went in.

The ground suddenly appeared a few hundred feet below, with the stones in the cemetery standing out stark and white. Down and down they went, air speed now down to seventy-five and, leaving a chunk of their starboard wingtip up a tree, rumbled into a soft ploughed field. They finally came to rest about 100 yards from their planned touchdown. In seconds, the passengers were scrambling out, two being sniped as they did so. The co-pilot and Jenkins followed suit—after automatically setting the flaps to neutral—and hastily set up the Bren in one of the deep furrows alongside. As they lay there with tracers arcing overhead, the co-pilot casually remarked: "Comforting thought that most of the 'muck' is a foot above the tracer, don't you think!"

After things had quieted down sufficiently to unload, they remembered the Thermos of tea. Jenkins made a dash for this and unscrewed the cap on returning to the lea of the farmhouse wall. He found to his great mortification that a bullet had gone clean through the bottom and the contents had saturated the outer covering. "Oh well, it was probably cold anyway!" Andy Anderson, his co-pilot, said.

Some gliders landed within 200 yards and others within 50 yards of their objective. This nearness was despite an artificial haze that was caused by the bombardment and bombing of Wesel and, in places, reduced the visibility to less than 220 yards. Some landings were more, and others less, eventful. The gliders carrying the *coup-de-main* parties of the Royal Ulster Rifles and those carrying the Oxfordshire and Buckinghamshire Light Infantry were particularly successful. The former delivered a party in six gliders that landed with pinpoint accuracy at its objective on both sides of a bridge over the Issel. The latter succeeded in only landing on the west side of its bridge. This bridge was speedily captured, but it subsequently it had to be blown up, at night, to stop a German counterattack headed by a Tiger.

Despite the careful planning and execution of the operation, unforeseen circumstances were inevitable and important. They were also mostly in favor of the Allies. It happened that many men of the 513th Parachute Infantry Regiment were dropped by mistake on the divisional landing zone before the gliders arrived. They did not waste a moment in checking their whereabouts. Instead, they immediately went into action with utmost resolution against a bewildered and fiercely resisting enemy. The paratroopers took many casualties, but by the time the British gliders started swooping in, the field was safe.

The haze, smoke and dust over the combat area had not only reduced visibility but also partly shielded incoming gliders. Although many gliders were released as much as 1,000 feet higher than was planned, 90 percent of them landed on or near their zones—many within 100 yards of their objective. Six missed the landing area by more than a mile, but they came down in territory held by American airborne troops. About 10 of the 416 gliders carrying British elements were shot down, and 284 were damaged by flak, partly because they were released too high. Ground resistance was vigorous and effective, and only 88 gliders came through completely unscathed. Fires completely destroyed 37 that had landed.

The glider contingent would have had an even harder time had it not been for the presence of British paratroops on DZ's A and B and of American paratroops dropped by mistake on the landing zones near Hamminkeln. Thus, the operations were not a good precedent for glider landings on zones not previously occupied by paratroops. Nevertheless, the gliders did bring in 3,383 personnel, 271 jeeps, 275 trailers, 66 guns and a wealth of other equipment, including trucks and bulldozers.

By nightfall on D-Day, all organized German resistance in the British sector—from the western edge of the woods to the Issel—had been broken. The airborne invaders had become united with the forces moving up from the Rhine. Six bridges across the River Issel had been seized intact and more than 600 prisoners taken.

The 17th Airborne Division, which had been thrown into the lines in the Battle of the Bulge, had only recently been withdrawn from the lines and was in a rear area undergoing reconstitution. As soon as it was assigned to the "Varsity" assault, the training which had heretofore been exclusively of a ground nature was altered to include airborne training. The 194th Glider Loading and Infantry Regiment of the division initiated lashing instruction. It received enough gliders to lift one rifle company at a time. Companies conducted exercises involving tactical glider landings with emphasis on rapid orientation, assembly and combat firing on ground similar to the Wesel area.

Other preparatory activities ensued. The regimental S2 set up a war tent and fitted it with necessary sand tables, map boards and lighting equipment. Stringent security measures governed. The regimental commander instituted pertinent administrative measures, with emphasis on a series of show-down inspections, ordnance repairs and vehicle maintenance.

The regiment soon got its allocation of 345 gliders for the air movement, 41 fewer than it needed. The regimental G3 subdivided the allotted CG-4A's among the units of the regiment and prepared loading plans. In view of the fact that a total of 386 CG-4A gliders was required to fly a glider regiment, only 50 percent its jeeps and trailers were included in the air echelon.

The land tail and base echelon of the regiment were prescribed and organized in accordance with instructions from the division. The 53rd Troop Carrier Wing, to which the 435th, 436th, 437th and 439th Troop Carrier Groups were assigned, had the wing and group glider officers visit the regimental war tent, where they met the leaders of the glider elements they were to fly into Wesel. The S3 then briefed them on their respective ground missions. It was later discovered that these officers had not been previously briefed on the impending operation by their own air commands. This occasioned some misunderstandings between the regiment and 53rd Troop Carrier Wing. Liaison was also established with the three assigned regimental departure fields near Paris.

Likewise, liaison was made with the 1st Airborne Brigade of the British 6th Airborne Division. Those efforts went much more smoothly. The Commando Brigadier visited the 194th Glider Loading and Infantry Regiment at Chalons. The time and place and way the two units were to conduct their efforts at Wesel became a matter of discussion. Because it was considered likely that the initial contact would be made at night, a ready means of mutual identification was deemed essential. It was felt that the traditional beret of the Commandos would afford a most suitable silhouette; in order that the Commandos should have some similar means of identifying the airborne troops during hours of darkness, it was decided that the latter should attach their parachute first-aid kits to the front of their helmet nettings, thus providing a distinctive outline.

The three marshalling areas each had one battalion of the regiment. In general, they were more than satisfactory, with each consisting of a pyramidal tent camp enclosed by wire. Strict security measures prevailed relative to the regiment's camps, despite the fact that the more relaxed air elements themselves had not, as yet, adopted their additional operational security measures. Briefing of the platoon leaders and enlisted personnel commenced immediately upon arrival. So complete and intense was the preparation that each gliderman was given thorough instruction on every phase of the operation, from the overall theater picture down, including his own individual assignments.

The loading of gliders commenced at 0600 hours the day before D-Day. As had been so frequently the case before, problems developed with the glider pilots. Glidermen were responsible for the proper loading and lashing of equipment in the gliders. At the same time, the glider pilot was responsible for seeing that the load in his glider was a flyable load. Thus, in order to avoid any discrepancies, arrangements had been made with the Army Air Corps flight formations for their glider pilots to be present at their respective gliders during the loading phase. As it turned out, however, very few pilots were present. This was occasioned by the fact that it was not until 1300 hours D-Day that the pilots were briefed that an actual operation was on. Until then, the pilots had believed that the presence of the airborne on the field was in the nature of a "dry run."

By 1300 hours, the airfields' military police cordoned off the areas, and the pilots were briefed. Glider infantry battalion commanders attended the briefing. Immediately following this, the glider pilots marched to the airborne marshalling area where they received a five-hour briefing on their ground missions. Upon completion of this instruction, and realizing that the operation was not a "dry run," the glider pilots immediately proceeded to the runways, located their gliders and "now seriously checked their loads." This resulted in a considerable amount of confusion and readjustment of loads, which adherence to the original plan would have averted.

The loading was finally coordinated properly by mid-afternoon, and crews "stacked" gliders and tug aircraft on the runways in parade-like take-off formation commencing at 1800 hours.

At 0730 hours the next morning—following a hearty breakfast and the usual policing of the tent area to leave it neat and clean—the 194th Glider Loading and Infantry Regiment climbed into gliders and the leading gliders took off in double tow.

Only a few minutes after the lift of the American airborne elements had begun, a pathfinder aircraft took off from Chartres. Within ten minutes, the first aircraft swept over Chartres in serial formation and headed for the assembly point at Wavre. Having taken off from the other fields around Paris, six additional serials took up their positions behind the leader. Not one of the C-47's in the formations failed to take off or had to turn back.

The first four paratroop flights, made up of 181 C-47's, carried 2,479 troops of the 507th Parachute Infantry Regiment and the 464th Parachute Field Artillery Battalion to DZ W. This drop zone was located on the south side of the Diersforder Wald and 2.5 miles northwest of Wesel. When the aircraft arrived, DZ "W" was under a pall of smoke. The aviators caught glimpses of the Rhine, but the ground beyond the river was invisible except through an occasional rift in the smoke. Ground fire was slight and although twenty-nine aircraft were hit, not one was shot down. Most of the aircraft of the first serial, however, lost their way. They dropped 693 men at about 0950 hours. Although these forces landed about two miles northwest of the drop zone, they rejoined the rest of their battalion within an hour. The second and third serials placed their paratroops squarely in the drop zone. The fourth serial reached the zone about 1005 hours and dropped the 464th Parachute Field Artillery Battalion accurately, but in a somewhat dispersed pattern. By

1300 hours, however, the artillerymen had nine of their twelve howitzers in position and firing.

Within three and a half hours, the 507th Parachute Infantry Regiment had taken all its assigned objectives. At 1300 hours, it made contact with advanced elements of the 15th Division. By 1803 hours, the U.S. paratroops joined forces with the British airborne forces on the northern border of their sector and, at 0200 hours on 25 March, a patrol to the southeast reached the British forces in the Wesel area.

The last three of the seven serials carrying American paratroops lifted the 513th Parachute Infantry Regiment and the 466th Parachute Field Artillery Battalion to drop them on DZ W. This drop zone was on the east side of the Diersforder Wald, about 1.25 miles east-northeast of DZ W. The whole air echelon, which comprised 2,071 men and sixty-four tons of supplies, was flown from Achiet in seventy-two C-46's. The pilots completely missed their assigned crossing point over the Rhine, partly because of poor visibility and partly because of their lack of experience in flying their new planes in large formations. As a result, they deposited their paratroops about 1.5 to 2 miles north of DZ W in the British sector, southwest of Hamminkeln.

At 1008 hours, as the first aircraft began to drop its chalk, the serial was raked by intense and accurate flak and small-arms fire. This fire continued from positions along the Issel while the C-46's were making their right turn after the drop, and some firing followed them until they got back to the Rhine. The C-46's caught fire easily, so that the German guns destroyed nineteen planes and damaged another thirty-eight of them.

Upon landing, the 513th Parachute Infantry Regiment attacked the enemy in the vicinity of DZ W. By 1230 hours, a nucleus of the regiment had formed and begun to move toward its pre-planned position in the drop zone. By 1530 hours, most of the regiment had reached the proper area.

Among the more than 1,000 aircraft in the armada, 610 C-47's were towing 906 Wacos. Gliders of the 680th and 681st Glider Artillery Battalions and the 155th Anti-Aircraft Battalion followed close on the tails of the last of the gliders transporting the 194th Parachute Infantry Regiment. All headed towards LZ S, about two miles northwest of Wesel. In all but the last fifteen minutes in the air, all was uneventful. Much of the flight was over France and ground held by the Allies. Intelligence had done its work well, and wherever Germans dared challenge the armada, fighters and bombers took them on. The actions of the U.S. Army Air Corps and the RAF became increasingly evident as the gliders approached Wesel. Plumes of dust rose high as bombs hit enemy guns.

In his article "The Approach to Wesel," Howard Cowan of the Associated Press recounted:

The wings of the glider vibrated violently—almost shook you out of your seat, and you knew something was wrong when the pilot began maneuvering desperately to break up a "tail flutter," a malady that shakes these things to pieces in a matter of seconds. And you closed your eyes and clenched your teeth and prayed.

Then, without an instant's warning, your seat dropped from under you.

Your helmet flew off and you were on your knees on the floor. That's just the way a glider rides. The man next to you wasn't wearing a helmet and blood is streaming down his ashen face. He's a casualty even before we've been landed—his head bashed against the metal framework.

For three agonizing hours, it went on this way. You'd watched the Seine and Maas [Meuse] Rivers slide past and knew the next big stream would be the Rhine. Before you were ready, it was snaking below across the shell-pocked plain.

Things began happening fast—too fast. Above the sustained roar of wind ripping past cloth-covered ribs of the glider, you began to hear crack! pop! snap! . . .

You shook hands, wished each other luck, and glued your eyes on the pilot, waiting for him to push the lever, which would cut the glider loose from the tow plane.

The haze thickened from shells fired into the landing area by Dempsey's artillery trying to silence enemy ground fire; added to this, smoke from smoke-generators protecting the [field army's] river-crossing operation crept over the landing zone. The crescendo of antiaircraft fire seeking the glider increased mile by mile from the Rhine on. Glidermen now saw black mushroom clouds rising above the manmade haze as planes, mortally wounded, hit the earth and burned angrily in their death throes. Flying in at 600 feet altitude, planes and gliders were too low to get essential landing visibility. The OK for [aircraft] to climb came in time to get gliders to 1,000 feet, and then at 1,036, the lead glider cut away from his tow plane.

As Cowan's glider was about to release:

Bursts of rifle fire were accompanied now by the popping of machine guns and a guttural whoomph of 88-mm shells. You unconsciously lift off your seat and brace as if to meet hot metal singing through the smoke. You find yourself dodging and weaving from something you can't even see.

Then the pilot's hand goes up and forward.

"Going down!" he shouts, and the nose pitches forward steeply. The speed slackens and the roar of the wind dies down and the battle noises suddenly are magnified into a terrifying din.

"Now," says the sergeant, "is when you pray."

The right wing tilts sharply as the shadow of another glider flits past.

It almost hits us.

Smoke is thick and acrid—almost like being inside a burning house.

You can see half a dozen buildings aflame on the ground. Dozens of gliders are parked at crazy angles on every field. Everyone with a weapon has it cocked and across his lap.

Then, before you know it, the ground is racing underneath. You are in a pasture, crashing through a fence, bounding across a gully, clipping a tree with a wingtip. You've made it—landed and nobody hurt.

You relax for a moment, but realize a split second later that that was a mistake. Bullets are ripping through the glider.

"Get outta here! Get outta here!" someone shouts, and prayers give way to curses as first one and then another kicks savagely at the door.

Men spill onto the grass haphazardly and begin crawling toward a ditch just beyond a barbed-wire fence. You're getting shot at from a house at the other end of the meadow.

Hot lead whines overhead. Bullets uproot little cupfuls of moist green turf around you until you are digging your toes in and clawing the earth with your fingers to move forward. Your pack snags on the bottom strand of the barbed-wire fence, and it seems hours before you're free.

You roll into the shallow ditch. A foot of red, slimy water makes no difference. It actually feels good trickling down the open throat of your woolen shirt and filtering into the toes of your boots, and you're tempted to drink it, for your mouth is parched.

Everyone is out of the glider. You check up and find that two men are hit—both medics. One has a bullet through the top of the head—it went in and out through the top of his helmet—but he's still conscious. The other was shot through the calf of the leg.

You're fairly safe for the time being, unless another glider swooping in lands on you. It shears off the top of a nearby tree and makes a neat landing 100 yards down the field.

The firing slackens as minutes tick by and more gliders come in. Soon, you muster enough courage to crawl out of the water—it's getting cold and uncomfortable by now—and take a cautious look around.

You find the area cleared and shooting over, at least in this pasture. Someone gets a jeep to take the wounded to an aid station, and the rest of the party strikes out for the regimental command post.

Now that the enemy fire was becoming so intense, glider after glider began releasing a mile short of the set release point. The air above became dense and eerie with their shrieking dives. Pilots desperately searched for their correct fields and went in fast. Where a pilot could not find his landing area, he frantically sought for an open space somewhere. Landing areas were now crowding up with gliders piling in, with those that had landed and with those that had been torn to shreds. Pilots unable to find their right fields— or even their proper zone—had to adroitly maneuver in without slicing an incoming glider or a parked one. Gliders began colliding in the air. Despite the circumstances, pilots bravely did what they could to bring their cargo to the battle intact.

Up to the last few minutes, the flight for Flight Officer Olin P. Vossler of the 98th Squadron of the 440th Carrier Transport Group was like a training flight. Just before he released, he could hear the crack of what he later thought must be an 88, then thick machine-gun fire. Seconds after release, he heard bullets ripping the floor and hitting the frame. Suddenly, his glider shuddered and "stopped" in mid-air from a direct hit. It raced madly towards the field. To his dismay, he saw five Horsas and some CG-4's on the ground ahead and telephone poles and lines crossing his path. He hit two different poles, knocked them over, and became tangled in telephone lines that must have helped to stop him.

He yelled to the "doughs" inside to "run like hell!" and get down flat as far from the glider as possible. "It's liable to explode!" He and his co-pilot ran to a nearby foxhole. When the firing let up, he sneaked close to the glider to find a 1.5-foot hole through the right wing and holes in the nose and tires. He found his squadron glider captain, and they crawled into a foxhole for the night. Eighty-eights began pounding the gliders in the various landing fields. Glider pilots saw many paratroopers hanging from the trees, lifeless in their harnesses.

A Hamilcar glider emptied of its Bren gun carrier cargo.

Hamminkeln railway station on D-Day plus one. A glider has landed across the track.

Lieutenant Clarence J. Benkoski, pilot, and Jacob Zichterman, co-pilot, got the green light and cut off. A glider two positions ahead had a wing shot off and went straight down into the trees, ablaze.

The gliders and tow ships were catching intense flak and small-arms fire, so Benkoski steepened the bank to get away. Then their tow ship received a burst in the left wing-tip. That was immediately followed by a 20-mm burst directly behind Zichterman's seat, which tore through the jeep's front right fender and on through the top of the glider. At the same time, they were hit by small-arms fire. Zichterman saw a triangular field and suggested that they land there.

They were hit about two-thirds of the way down, hit antiglider posts in landing and approached an irrigation ditch. Benkoski pulled back on the stick and got enough lift to receive only a slight bump; he continued through another fence to stop ten feet beyond. They got out of the glider and lay low for about two minutes. The jeep driver got into the vehicle, and they all lifted the nose while he drove it out.

They made their way to the rally point, where prisoners were being marched in by droves and guarded in the woods. They then proceeded to their assigned roadblocks. Zichterman picked a spot about seventy-five feet from the crossroads in the northeast quadrant and dug in between the 57-mm antitank gun and a machine gun.

All hell broke loose after dark. At 2355 hours, they were attacked by a tank firing a machine gun, an 88-mm cannon, two 20-mm "flak wagons," an estimated seventy-five men with automatic weapons and two mortars. Bazookas drove the tank back, causing it to roll over one of the 20-mm flak vehicles. A 57-mm antitank gun close by fired one round, but it couldn't get the tank in its sights.

The tracers set fire to a glider behind them and to a house to the left. This lighted up the area, and Zichterman could distinguish German forms on the corner and dodging around the house on the southwest corner of the crossroads. He fired his carbine at them at minute intervals, a few rounds each time, but didn't see any direct effect.

Two Germans voluntarily came through a defensive roadblock to one of the glider pilots. He started to take them prisoner. The glider infantry sergeant who was in charge of the defensive positions told the pilot they were not taking prisoners. The pilot sent them down the road and shot them with his .45-caliber semi-automatic pistol.

Later, at about 0300 hours, two more Germans came up to surrender. He tried to get them to halt. They didn't. He killed them with a machine gun.

When morning came and they came out of their holes, there were thirteen dead Germans. About sixteen injured were routed out of a house. Zichterman helped round up prisoners and searched a few houses.

They were told they were going back to the Rhine. They crossed the Rhine on a "Limey" truck ferried on a barge and slept on the west bank. The next morning, they rode to the British reception post aboard a DUKW, took a truck to Helmond and, from there, a aircraft to England.

Benkoski felt that the glider pilots had been left in "a hell of a situation" to have to go on a mission that promised tough fighting without adequate weapons—merely the small arms issued to a glider pilot. He thought that he should have had a light machine gun, a bazooka, a Browning automatic rifle, grenades and some sub-machine guns. His after-action report advised, "Let's get some of these weapons in the squadron, plus two 57-mm's that fire from the shoulder."

Despite it all—due in large part to their better discipline and greater experience, coupled with personal fortitude—the glider pilots did a magnificent job. A high percentage came in right on target. By 1140 hours, the last of the 572 gliders in the first glider serials was on its way towards the ground. They had delivered 3,492 men, 202 jeeps, 94 trailers, munitions and artillery. The Germans hit 140 of some 295 planes towing gliders, and 12 C-47's crashed in and around the glider landing zone. Eighty-three gliders had landed outside the designated landing area.

CHAPTER 18

The German Effort Continues

By 1941, German ground commanders at the extremities of the many extended, far-away lines of communication were critically in need of supplies and equipment. The German Armed Forces were advancing deep into the Soviet Union. General Erwin Rommel had landed his *Deutsches Afrika Korps* in Africa, and German forces there, with their mounting successes, were being given the strongest logistical support Germany could furnish. One way of surmounting the problem of long, guerrilla-interdicted supply lines—consuming days of shipment time in the Soviet Union—was to use air supply. With the British Navy in control of the Mediterranean, the most practical way to supply Rommel and sustain his drive towards Alexandria was by air. Aircraft played a major role in delivering supplies, but gliders began to assume more and more importance as time went on.

They also played an important role in the Soviet Union, where many of the German forces became surrounded in the course of conducting maneuver warfare. The only practical means to get adequate supplies to these pockets that had no airfield and no makeshift landing strips that would support powered aircraft was by glider. In North Africa, a similar condition developed, especially after German fortunes began to turn. It was at this juncture of the campaign that gliders, especially the Go 242, came into their own.

To make the glider operations and training more effective, the Germans discarded their policy of creating a special task force for each operation and began to organize glider transport elements. This was most likely done for the Go 242 early in 1941 and undoubtedly was finished about the same time as the Me 321.

After the creation of these organizations, the gliders began to be used in diversified ways. For example, a limited number of Go 242's were fitted out as maintenance and repair shops. Thus equipped, they were towed to the front where and when needed. Once landed, they were used for the maintenance and repair of fighter aircraft. In certain instances, they supported the maintenance facilities of armored formations.

The overall command of the glider activities resided in the *XI Flieger-Korps*. Research and development were coordinated within that command.

The corps controlled the organizations structuring the glider fleets, and the headquarters of the corps provided the gliders and pilots, including those who went to the aid of encircled German forces in such places as such as Kholm, Welikije Luki and Tarnopol.

Starting on 21 January 1942, Kholm was completely encircled by Soviet forces. The stronghold was defended by a force of about 3,500 men from various elements and several arms and services and under the command of *Generalmajor* Theodor Scherer. This force defended tenaciously and successfully held its position against all Soviet attacks.

The battle area of Kholm was so limited that transport aircraft could not land. Unfortunately, the only airfield in the pocket was situated in the immediate vicinity of the main line of resistance. There, it was constantly exposed to direct fire by all enemy weapons. At the end of February 1942, an attempt was made to land on this field. This operation, ordered by the commander-in-chief of *Luftflotte 1* [1st Air Army] against the advice of the chief of Air Transportation, resulted in the loss of five out of seven Ju 52 transports and of a part of the aircrews participating in the effort. The *Luftwaffe* mounted no further ventures of this sort. All German commanders agreed that supplies could only be brought into in the Kholm area by glider and parachute.

At the rate of one ton of payload each, the DFS 230's initiated the support operation. Later, the larger Go 242, towed by He 111's of the Fifth Special Purpose Bomber Group was used for carrying very heavy items of equipment. The payload of each Go 242 was about 2.5 tons. During the first stages of the operation, nine landed on the airfield. Frequently, both gliders and cargo were lost through enemy antiaircraft fire. Even when they landed without mishap, there was no way of taking off again, and the crews remained in the pocket to participate in the defense. As the German-held pocket was reduced, only dauntless DFS 230's were able to make landings, finally landing on one street of the village. Eventually, even this grew to be impossible, when Soviet forces further reduced the perimeter.[1]

Early in 1942, *Luftwaffe* general Kesselring, the commander-in-chief of all operations in the southern theater, met Hitler and Mussolini at Berchtesgaden

---

1. The German force held out until 5 May 1942, when the encirclement was broken and it was relieved.

to map out Axis operations for the Mediterranean area for 1942. At this meeting, Kesselring suggested a combined airborne and seaborne invasion of Malta, which Hitler accepted. The next day *General* Student was called in and directed to plan and carry out the airborne phase of this operation. During April and May 1942, Student drew up his plan and conducted maneuvers with both German and Italian airborne elements in preparation for the operation. Student was to have five *Fallschirmjäger* regiments under his command—approximately 20,000–22,000 men—and the Italian *Folgore* airborne division, with about 3,000 paratroopers. (Student generally rated Italian forces as mediocre, but he considered the troopers of the *Folgore* division as elite forces.) In addition to those airborne assets, eight Italian divisions were to participate, including armored units comprising about 150 tanks and 800 specially trained engineer troops for duty at the beachhead. Included in the parachute formations were two German and one Italian engineer battalion, and it was Student's plan to utilize these forces to prepare landing areas for air-landing forces after the initial assault. Five hundred gliders were marshaled for the operation.

After about two months of planning, training and making necessary preparations—the actual invasion was set for late in August—Student was called to report at the end of June 1942. To his great surprise, at this meeting, Hitler cancelled the entire operation. Student later stated he believed that the assault on Crete and the German losses there played a small part in changing the *Führer's* mind, with the main reason for the cancellation stemming from Hitler's lack of faith in the Italian forces. Student believed this lack of faith came as a result of continuing reports by Rommel of Italian deficiencies and, more directly, to a personal report made to Hitler the previous day by the commander of the *Deutsches Afrika Korps*. While the taking of Malta was vital to the success of overall German operations in the Mediterranean, sufficient forces were not available to undertake the operation, and Hitler preferred to cancel it rather than risk heavy losses should the Italians crack. This was a great disappointment to Student, who firmly believed that the attack would have succeeded. He was banking on this to demonstrate the effectiveness of the airborne idea and to vindicate the questionable results of the airborne operation against Crete.

In October 1942, Hitler suddenly reversed his policy of rejecting airborne operations and ordered Student to employ his forces to rupture the coastal road at Alder, halfway between Tuapse and Sukhuni, thus interrupting the flow of Soviet reinforcements and supplies coming from Georgia. Once this was done, the German forces were to move southeast down the coastal road and capture Batum, an oil pipeline terminal port on the Black Sea. This plan entailed the employment of some 16,000 airborne personnel of the *7. Flieger-Division*, about 400 transport aircraft and 250 gliders. Take-off bases were selected in the Crimea. At this time, the division was in Normandy and was sped to the Crimea by rail. The troops were fully prepared and the necessary aircraft and gliders were being assembled when the Russian Caucasian Army started moving so rapidly that the operation had to be cancelled. The airborne forces already assembled were withdrawn to the vicinity of Vitebsk and put into the lines as ground forces. It was Student's opinion that if he had had a few more days, the operation could have been undertaken with some chance of success.

Earlier, at the beginning of 1941, Student had been ordered to study the possibilities of taking Gibraltar by means of an airborne assault. After some review, a negative report was submitted, declaring that the capture of Gibraltar from the air was not possible. Due to the characteristics of the fortress, there were only two possible places where a landing could be made: one at an airfield just north of the Rock and the other a small parade ground. Regardless, both of those areas were overlooked by the fortifications, and any forces attempting such a landing would have been decimated before they could attack. The only other possibility would be to bring ground forces through Spain, but nothing further was done to launch an assault on Gibraltar "in respect to the neutrality of Spain."

For the administration and inspection of all heavy air-transport elements on the Eastern Front, a special command was created in November and headquartered in Warsaw. Glider units were then shifted to Warsaw, where they came under the command and control of the *Großraum-Transport-Flieger-Führer*. In the central sector, the Russian attack rolled forward from its former base at Dnjepropetrovsk and moved northwest to Zhitomir. The Go 242 gliders of the unit were employed in carrying supplies to the forward areas and evacuating wounded on return flights; meanwhile, at Brobriusk, the glider units were doing similar sorties in the Gomel salient. More than half of the Eastern Front's strength had been concentrated in the Dnjepr bend in December. Aircraft serviceability was declining as winter set in, and the unit found itself pinned down by air superiority along the entire length of the front. Transport units had been flying transport and evacuation sorties steadily for six months, but with the launching of the Russian winter offensive in mid-December, all possibility of withdrawing any *Transportfliegergruppen* for rest or re-equipping vanished. The Germans employed gliders on a large largest scale in the aerial resupply and movement of forces. Gliders were also part of the tactical air arm. Three gliders—carrying technical supplies, maintenance personnel and/or ammunition—were assigned to each *Stuka-Geschwader*. The gliders were towed with the wing on each change of base. Workshop installations in some gliders were successfully employed. Other gliders delivered saboteurs and commandos behind enemy lines.

The first large-scale employment of military air transport for tactical evacuation was during the German retreat from the Kuban in the Soviet Union in 1943. Every aircraft and glider that could be made serviceable was used to rescue some 82,000 isolated elements and much of their equipment over a five-week period. At its peak, 6,000 to 7,000 soldiers a day were flown to safety. Initially, gliders flew in reinforcements in the Crimea, but the operation changed to evacuation in 1944. Ju-52's with floats were used in the Crimea, where flights were over much greater distances than in Kuban. Evacuation of key personnel from other pockets became a frequent mission as the Eastern Front contracted. The total number of forces evacuated was more than 500,000 in the last two years of the war. Additionally, 50,000 tons of weapons and materials were salvaged by air. It was only in Africa that tactical evacuation was insignificant. From Libya and Tunisia, wounded were evacuated by air whenever possible. Large forces, were evacuated from the islands of Sardinia, Corsica, Rhodes and Crete and from Greece and the Balkans in late 1943 through 1944. DFS and Go 42 gliders were extensively used in these evacuations.

CHAPTER 19

Mussolini's Rescue and Other Glider Operations

Tales of escape and rescue—dramatic, romantic, sometimes fantastic—are to be found in the history of every epoch of every people, but my escape from the Gran Sasso appears even today as the boldest and most romantic of all and, at the same time, the most modern in method and style.

BENITO MUSSOLINI, STORIA DI UN ANNO

On 25 July 1943, Hitler called *SS-Hauptsturmführer*[1] Otto Skorzeny, a brawny officer, to Rastenburg. He had decided that the future welfare of Germany, to some extent, involved the rescue of Mussolini, hidden away by his captors for some months. He felt that Mussolini had been betrayed by the king of Italy with the assistance of the king's friend Marshal Badoglio. As related in *Commando Extraordinary* by Charles Foley, Hitler said to Skorzeny, "I cannot and will not leave Mussolini to his fate. . . . He has got to be rescued before these traitors can surrender him to the enemy."

In quietly spoken words, he then turned to Skorzeny and told him: "You, Skorzeny, are going to save my friend. . . . You will avoid no risk. . . . You will succeed and your success will have a tremendous effect on the course of the war. This is a mission to which you will be answerable to me personally!"

With a double handclasp, Hitler sent him off. For the next seven weeks, German intelligence gave Skorzeny every assistance it could to find Mussolini's whereabouts.

For Hitler, the rescue of Mussolini promised a revival of Fascist military energy, a second wind for his deflated prestige and reassurance to all the other little Mussolini's of the satellite countries, whose loyalty to Nazi Germany might be flagging.

For the king and Badoglio, the removal of Mussolini meant the final collapse of the Fascist power. The possession of his person was a trump card

---

1. An SS rank equivalent to major.

in their deal with the Allies. Mussolini's guards had strict orders not to let him get away alive.

┉━ ⵣ◊ⵥ ━┉

Ultimately, the Germans located Mussolini and his jailers in a newly built hotel on the Gran Sasso, near Aquila, in the Abruzzi Mountains. The area was bristling with antiaircraft guns and defense cordons manned by *carabinieri*. The word was that 250 were billeted in the hotel. Their defenses were impossible to take. The Italians had overlooked nothing—nothing, that is, except an individual's determination to get through.

There was only one possibility: if an orthodox German land assault was ruled out, only the sky was left. A parachute operation was not possible. The altitude ruled it out. The air was thin and paratroopers would be dashed to pieces. Moreover, they had nowhere to land. But gliders!

Air photos showed a triangular patch by the hotel. Skorzeny thought that if it were really flat and smooth, gliders might be able to land. Aggressive glidermen might reach Mussolini before his guards could bayonet him. Skorzeny figured he had three minutes in which to reach Mussolini after landing. The landing triangle was incredibly small, and gliders had never before come down in such a rarefied atmosphere. He estimated that of a 100 men in the attack force, 20 might survive—a pitifully small number to attack a position defended by 250.

Skorzeny fought for a glider attack. He was given the green light. The gliders took off after an aircraft pilot had made a reconnaissance run over the area several days earlier with Skorzeny. Skorzeny's plan was that the first two gliders and their ten men would land and cover the landing of the third glider. A fourth glider was to follow in to the landing area.

The first three glider combinations took off. The fourth and fifth ran into bomb craters and never took off, but Skorzeny was unaware of the mishap. The combinations climbed to 12,000 feet, where they entered clouds. Emerging, Skorzeny found that the two leading gliders had vanished. One was being towed by the aircraft pilot, who was to lead the gliders to the objective, so Skorzeny was forced to lead the way.

Wedged in his seat, Skorzeny could not see where he was going. He drew his knife and hacked vents in the canvas sides. He peered through them to the granite mountains below. The Gran Sasso gradually loomed ahead. Yes! That was it . . . the hotel on its dizzy perch on the triangular ledge. He signaled to release. His glider swooped gracefully down to the hotel. To the pilot's disbelief, Skorzeny pointed to the ledge. The sloping shelf seemed built more for a ski jump than for a glider landing field. It was studded with big boulders.

The pilot gazed ahead in mesmerized disbelief that he was going to land there! Skorzeny shouted "Dive . . . crash . . . but land! As near to the hotel as you can."

They got closer, and the drag brake sucked out and billowed from the tail. Suddenly, the glider, jolting and pitching over the boulders, stopped in a shuddering crash.

Skorzeny forced his way out. He and several others dashed up the escarpment into the hotel. In an energetic search through the surprised garrison, they located Mussolini. Skorzeny entrusted the Fascist leader to his brawniest subaltern.

Soon, several other gliders landed and glidermen rushed to Skorzeny's assistance. One glider crashed to smithereens. Within a short while, a single-engined Fieseler Storch, a light utility aircraft, made it into the landing area. Skorzeny squeezed Mussolini behind the pilot and climbed in. Twelve men clung to the tail of the Storch. It revved its engine. They dug in their heels until the engine was racing madly, and then released the aircraft. The small aircraft manfully rammed the rocks in its way, slithering upward gradually, leaped a deep crevasse and Mussolini was free.

THE CROSS-ATLANTIC TOW

The feasibility of towing gliders across the Atlantic was demonstrated in April 1943. Carrying vaccines destined for the Soviet Union, along with aircraft, radio and engine parts, a CG-4A in tow behind a Dakota aircraft made history in a twenty-eight-hour leapfrogging trip along a secret route across the blustery Atlantic. Actually, the trip was conducted in easy stages, the twenty-eight hours being flying time only. Nevertheless, the flight was risky. Snow falls almost constantly along the Atlantic coast of Canada at that time of year. As the co-pilot of the glider, Royal Canadian Air Force Squadron Leader F. M. Gobiel said later, if they had not gone, then "we would have been sitting in Canada fishing until the end of the war." Gobiel thought they were adequately prepared, however, since they had tried out some experimental day and night bad-weather flying with the glider before the Atlantic flight.

The worst part was the first leg from Canada. The pilot found he had to climb into a strong wind. This made for a plodding flight speed. After three hours, they got to 9,000 feet, and ice began to form on the glider. The first leg took twice as long to fly as scheduled. The glider played "funny tricks." Contrary to Gobiel's hopes, the tow rope never seemed to be "in a gentle curve in front of your nose" as he had found in the experimental flying:

One time you may be going to one side, then the other. Then you are going away up and you sit waiting for the jerk when the rope tightens up, and the next second, if the weather is very bad, you are dropping in a beastly swing from maybe 50 to 100 feet above the tug to 25 feet below it.

Both pilots took turns at the controls, but for power pilots such as they were, it was a sobering experience to find that neither could really loosen up at the controls. There was no autopilot to take some of the strain. They had to be on the alert every minute, anticipating the tow line, the turbulence, the up and down drafts. They had to scramble through the two-foot space left between the cargo and the roof of the glider to get food in the rear of the fuselage. Neither liked the experience. But what they found most frightening was the turbulence. Frequently, it was so great they thought the glider was about to be torn to pieces. In one storm, some of the ballast tumbled violently in the glider, hitting the roof and then going "down through the floor." At other times, the snow was so thick that the sergeant had to fly on instruments only and as much of the tow rope as he could see.

This route was the worst that could have been taken, although the shortest. Many gliders might well have been ferried by the thousands of different aircraft crossing the Atlantic during the war over normal routes or via Africa, when the weather was more temperate. But this single flight was the only one ever made by glider across the Atlantic.

OPERATION "VASSIEUX"

One little-known German glider operation, erroneously recorded by most sources as exclusively a parachute operation, took place in the foothills of the Alps. The French *maquis*—partisan forces—in the vicinity of Vercors sat astride the routes of withdrawal of German forces, which were in southern France in anticipation of countering Allied landings there.

On 21 July 1944, the Germans landed ten gliders at Vassieux, some more at Weilern and others on other *maquis* communication centers, effectively removing the threat posed by the partisans in the region.

THE ATTEMPT TO CAPTURE TITO

In February 1944, Winston Churchill stated in the House of Commons that the Yugoslav guerrillas were containing a substantial amount of German military power. It has since been estimated that the Germans had to keep fourteen divisions in Yugoslavia to control the country and maintain their lines of communication. This German commitment meant fewer divisions for the Allies to fight on other fronts.

The Yugoslav resistance was led by Tito and centered at his headquarters in Drvar. In an attempt to break the back of the resistance, the Germans decided to capture Tito.

Early in the spring, they assembled ten gliders on an unprepared field in the Banta region north of Belgrade. From there, they were towed to Kraljevo, where they prepared for the operation along with 100 selected men of *SS-Fallschirmjäger-Bataillon 500*. It was a bold undertaking and the glider pilots had no taste for the operation. Once landed, they were assured that they were to be relieved by ground elements advancing on the location. On the other hand, three partisan divisions were reported in the vicinity of Drvar. The odds were not good.

The night before the operation, a severe thunderstorm hit the German assembly area. While it did little damage, it was the start of a week of foggy unflyable weather that led to one postponement after another. After seven days, the Germans called it off.

Several weeks later, the Germans scheduled another operation to start from Agram. This time, the force was larger; it was to use fifteen gliders in a combined glider-parachute operation.

The fifteen gliders carried a reinforced company of the battalion and several mountain artillery guns. They became the leading serial in the stream of aircraft carrying parachutists. From the time the last gliders took off until the first landed was an hour, even though the overland distance between the takeoff field and Drvar was not great. Assembling the formation in the air and climbing to altitude to get over the mountains lying between the two points took much of the hour.

The force landed at Drvar on 25 May 1944. Tito was initially surprised, but he managed to escape. Heavy fighting ensued, and ground elements were eventually needed to relieve the beleaguered airborne force.

TAKING THE SOVIETS TO YUGOSLAVIA

Yugoslavia was the location of a very unorthodox special glider mission described by Ronald Seth in *Lion with the Blue Wings*.[2] Three Horsa gliders were said to be at one of the airstrips near Kairouan in Tunisia, and the squadron was instructed to bring them to Comiso in Italy.

In early spring 1944, an American troop-carrier squadron flew the glider pilots to Tunisia. Landing at dusk on the desolate, abandoned airstrip, the pilots found the Horsas lonely and dejected. They were the last remnants, except for the wrecks and the litter of rusty tin cans, of the masses of men and machines that had packed these North African airstrips, roads and olive-groves, when the British 1st Airborne Division had set up its headquarters there as its base for the assault on Sicily.

The Horsas had been at the mercy of wind, rain and Arabs for six months, but there was no question of carrying out a proper inspection. Indeed, there

---

2. This entire section on the Yugoslav operation is based on this source.

was no one in the party qualified to do so. Consequently, the pilots climbed into the cockpits the next morning, tentatively tested the creaking controls, patted the woodwork for luck, and flew off on a 250-mile journey across the Mediterranean for Comiso.

There, they loaded each glider with a jeep and anything else that would make up 7,000 pounds weight. They tested the loading, since they had not been supplied with charts, by arranging the jeep and boxes in such a way that a man swinging on the tail could just lift the front wheels clear of the ground. If rough and ready, this simple method always proved satisfactory.

They flew on to Bari in Italy, a hazardous flight, with the tugs. Barely clearing the high hills, they flew through heavy snow and a northeast gale, providing an experience that was extremely unpleasant. At Bari, the reason for this activity became apparent. An unidentified organization in Cairo had asked that a Soviet military mission, headed by Generals Korneyev and Gorskov, be flown by glider to Marshal Tito's headquarters in Yugoslavia. The mission had already made one attempt by Dakota, but had been prevented from landing by heavy snow, which made gliders the only alternative method of infiltration. Given the codename of Operation "Bunghole," the tugs were to be C-47's of the U.S. 64th Troop Carrier Group, with the glider pilots and gliders British—a truly Allied effort.

On arrival at Bari, the American tug pilots insisted that the Horsas could not be lifted over the Dinaric Alps. The flight to Italy had made this self-evident. The Horsas were discarded, although they were to die honorably in a vineyard twenty miles northwest of Cannes. They were replaced by American Wacos. The squadron's training had been carried out on Wacos, so three were flown to Bari the next day and test flights with up to 4,500-pound payloads were conducted. General Korneyev insisted that his officers should take part in these flights in the positions they would occupy during the journey. Except for Staff Sergeant McCulloch's decision to execute a 360-degree turn over the town from about 300 feet on his landing approach, the tests passed without incident.

The Russians wanted to be landed in German-occupied Yugoslavia, in a valley called Mendenapolu—the honey field—about two miles north of the small town of Bosan Petrovac, midway between Zagreb and Sarajevo, in the eastern foothills of the Dinaric Alps, which had peaks up to 8,000 feet. The landing zone was 100 miles inland from the Dalmatian coast and 250 miles from Bari.

A diversionary raid was to be made on Zagreb with fifty Flying Fortresses from the U.S. 15th Air Force. They were to have a fighter umbrella of a mixed force of Mustangs, Thunderbolts and Spitfires. The take-off was timed for 1100 hours, thus making "Bunghole" the first daylight operation.

After two days of non-flying, wintry weather, the skies cleared, and the take-off went forward as planned. The C-47 tugs were under the command of U.S. Lieutenant Colonel Duden and flown by American pilots. They were navigated by an Australian, a South African and a New Zealander from their respective air forces.

The glider combinations rendezvoused with the escort fifty miles to the north and off the coast, opposite the Eighth Army's forward positions in Italy. Together, they headed northeast across the Adriatic at 8,000 feet in a cloudless sky giving unlimited visibility. It was extremely cold. Although the far-flung escort of fighters were occasionally glimpsed wheeling and banking high overhead and far below, most of the time the gliders had the sensation of being alone and defenseless in the midday sun.

The forces made landfall dead on track over the island of Zirje. Snow blanketed the Yugoslav coast. The sharp outline of the towering range of the Dinaric Alps came into view while still fifty miles away. There was no sign of civilization in the tortuous foothills, ribbed and ridged with ravines, and patched with forest under the deep white carpet below.

The air became turbulent. The turbulence steadily increased during the next half hour until the flight rocked and swayed over the last saddle with 500 feet to spare, peaks towering on either side. As the hinterland opened up, they knew that they were coming up to the target area. In a few minutes, after obtaining a "fix" on a large river, the tugs turned about and the gliders cast off about four or five miles away from their objective. As they circled to land, thin wisps of smoke came up from straw fires below them, the first welcome indication that a correct pinpoint had been made—welcome, because the tow-rope telephone-type intercom on all the gliders had been unserviceable from the very beginning.

Within seconds and a few yards from each other, the gliders touched down—perhaps flopped in the snow with a sickening jolt would be a better description—reared vertically on to their noses and settled slowly back. The "landing run" was about 20 feet, and since they were about 4,000 feet above sea level, the ground was covered with soft snow about three feet deep. This marked the first landing in Yugoslavia by Allied aircraft since the German occupation.

After being forcibly embraced by almost unbelievably dirty and bearded Yugoslav partisans, they were hurried to a hut in the forest that lined the valley. The Russians were full of *bonhomie*, laughing and shaking hands with all within reach. The generals had adopted avuncular poses, and even a colonel, who had sat throughout the flight nursing a submachine, grinned broadly for the first time.

After a quick meal, accompanied by suitable speeches in various languages that were all unintelligible to the Englishmen, who replied with equal unintelligibility, they set out for Petrovac in sleighs.

BUDAPEST

By the latter part of 1944, the Soviets had surrounded Budapest. A German relief operation launched on 3 January 1945 failed to break through to the German garrison in the city. The Germans began a massive air-supply operation, primarily by parachute drop, since no landing fields in the area held by the Germans were safe from Russian mortar fire or antiaircraft guns.

By the end of January, Budapest was a city in siege. Ring upon ring of Soviet antiaircraft guns and searchlights girded the city. Experienced German pilots claimed that of all the belligerents, the Soviets had the deadliest and most-feared antiaircraft guns.

The parachute drops were not successful to the extent hoped. A continual pall of smoke and haze hung over the athletic field in the city and other suitable drop areas close by. Parachute drift after release from the aircraft led to the loss of many containers to the enemy. Aircraft losses were severe.

In mid-January, it became evident that parachute drops were not the solution to the urgent supply problem facing the beleaguered German garrison. A hurried call went out for glider pilots from the many disbanded air-transport units. Some had to be plucked from frontline combat to join the units into which they had been drafted. Within one week, pilots were reporting to Wiener Neustadt and other airfields just south of Vienna. Gliders had to be retrieved from stores accumulated in distant depots when the air-transport units disbanded. In a matter of days, gliders had been loaded and secured to flat cars, and trains were on their way.

Glider sorties were sporadic because of many problems. After the gliders began arriving, there were not enough pilots, nor enough technicians to assemble them and get them flight-ready. Frequently, there were not enough flyable tow planes available for glider tows or fighter cover was not available. On 5 February, the Germans managed an eleven-glider operation. Six made it to the release point over Budapest, four of them were shot down in the approach to land at the athletic field.

One of the more spectacular and, at the same time, tragic missions took place on 9 February. Ju 52's, Do 17's and He 111's towed forty-eight gliders towards Budapest. Before they could get to the release point, twelve gliders had been shot down or had aborted because their tow planes had crashed. Thirty-six gliders managed to reach the field and land successfully. However, by this time, the Russian guns had the range of the tow craft and downed all but two of the remaining thirty-six. Thirteen men were killed and twenty-nine wounded, and ninety-six were missing from the mission.

On 13 February, twenty gliders took off for Budapest. None of the tow planes returned, and the fate of the gliders was never determined by the command at Wiener Neustadt. The irony of these operations is that the glider pilots had little information about the severity of the enemy antiaircraft fire they would encounter; information was purposely withheld so as not to lessen their determination to complete their mission.

MORESBY: MISSION ABORTED

At 0825 hours on 5 September 1943, the U.S. 503rd Parachute Infantry Regiment took off from Port Moresby in 84 C-47 transport aircraft. An Australian parachute artillery regiment—25-pounders—reinforced the regiment. To assist a three-pronged Australian drive for the important Japanese-held port of Lae, the paratroopers were to seize an airstrip at Nadzab, some twenty miles inland. The air formations included 302 aircraft: A-20's laid smokescreens to hide the drop zones from enemy observers; B-25's bombed and strafed the landing area; and B-17's carried a "basket" of twelve bundles of equipment in each bomb bay, a parachute on each bundle. These had been specially designed for the mission and contained ammunition, heavy machine guns and supplies. They would be dropped according to signals from the ground wherever needed. Squadrons of P-38 fighters flew cover above, and P-39's guarded the flanks; heavy bombers carried bomb loads to drop on enemy positions at the nearby Heath Plantation.

Three deaths and a number of fractures occurred in the jump, but the paratroopers found little resistance on the ground, and they quickly organized a perimeter defense. An Australian engineer battalion that had set out on foot six days earlier joined them, and work proceeded on the airstrip. The shuttling by air of the Australian 7th Infantry Division from Marilinen to Nadzab—an operation that required several weeks—began thirty-six hours later.

No gliders were used in the Nadzab operation. Eleven, loaded with Australian men and equipment, were waiting to take off at Port Moresby on 5 September, when their mission was cancelled. It was said that the use of the gliders was cancelled because the outstanding success of the parachute drop made them unnecessary, but a contributing factor was the concern for the safety of the men they would carry. All the gliders were showing signs of deterioration. On the flight from Brisbane, where they were being assembled for the operation, one glider had lost its tail-assembly in mid-air, and the crew had been killed in the resulting crash. Thirty-five pilots and thirty-five mechanics, the first glider contingent for the Southwest Pacific, had arrived in Australia in February 1943. In April, another twenty-six pilots and twenty-six mechanics had joined them. Their crated gliders—twenty-seven of them—arrived shortly afterwards. None of these gliders was ever used in tactical operations. Some of the pilots and mechanics were later assigned to various other duties among widely separated troop carrier units and others were returned to the United States.

GLIDER RESCUE MISSION

On 13 May 1945, a C-47 flying on instruments struck a ridge in the Orange Mountains in Dutch New Guinea. Of the passengers, the three survivors included a WAVE corporal, Margaret Hastings. Search planes located the wreck, but the area in the interior, called Hidden Valley, was inaccessible by trail. Men, followed by supplies, parachuted into the valley to prepare a strip suitable for glider landings and recovery by snatch technique. Two medical corps men also parachuted in and rendered aid to the survivors.

Glider crews on Wakde Island prepared for the rescue operation. On 28 June, the first glider landed successfully. They loaded the five passengers, including the survivors, and were snatched thirty minutes later. In two subsequent sorties, the parachuted men were flown out by glider. Sentani airstrip on Hollandia served as the base of operations.

LUZON: THE ONE AND ONLY PACIFIC OPERATION

Right at 0600 hours on 23 June 1945, a C-46 carrying paratroopers of the U.S. 11th Airborne Division took off from the Lipa airstrip on Luzon. Six CG-4A's and one CG-13 glider brought up the rear of scores of aircraft that followed in a V of V's on their way to Aparri in northern Luzon. Fighters hummed overhead. This was a first for gliders in the Pacific. Although hundreds were at airfields scattered throughout the Pacific islands, none had yet been tested in combat. The tactical objective of this mission was to hasten the collapse of organized enemy resistance in northern Luzon. The forces to be dropped were to make contact with American and Philippine guerrillas to the south to free the Cagayan Valley.

The parachute and glider landing zones were the same: an abandoned enemy airstrip five miles south of Aparri. They flew to the rendezvous point at Camalaniugan, 250 miles by direct route from Lipa, the staging area for the airborne forces. To avoid alerting the enemy, they approached the rendezvous point over the China Sea, adding 100 miles to the course. Glider tow planes carried neither paratroopers nor cargo. The gliders carried a total of nineteen troops, six jeeps, one trailer, machine guns, ammunition and radio and medical supplies.

At precisely 0900 hours, the aircraft reached the drop zone, which pathfinders had marked with colored smoke. Fighter-bombers laid down a smokescreen, blinding the hills to the southeast where the Japanese supposedly had artillery that could reach the drop zone. Paratroopers and gliders "unloaded" from the aircraft in a single pass over the field. Glider landings were equally accurate, although the grass on the strip was denser than appeared from photo interpretation. A wing-tip collision between two CG-4A's was the only imperfection in the glider phase.

Three days after the drop, the 511th made contact with the U.S. 37th Infantry Division, sealing off the Cagayan Valley. The captured strip was later used for supply landings and to evacuate casualties.

FINAL ALLIED OPERATIONS IN BURMA

In April 1945, C.C.F.T. transports and gliders played an important part in the final stages of the campaign in Burma, getting airfields at Pyinmana, Toungoo and Pegu into operation in time for quick support of the IV Corps advance. At Pegu, the transports carried out a familiar role, delivering reinforcements that would enable the ground forces to hold and consolidate their gains. In preparation for these activities, a reserve of 86,000 gallons of gasoline was built up at Meiktila to permit the temporary operation of C-47's from that advanced base. Gliders loaded with bulldozers, runway lighting equipment, jeeps, tractors, scrapers, gasoline, radio equipment, food and water were ferried into Meiktila until fifty-five gliders were on hand.

IV Corps bypassed Pyinmana and secured Lewe Airfield south of the city on 20 April. At 0850 hours the next morning, eight C-47's of the 4th Combat Cargo Squadron towed one glider each to Lewe, after delivering supplies to Meiktila. The gliders contained a tractor, a scraper, two bulldozers, a jeep and trailer, a power saw, gasoline, rations, water and nineteen men. The first glider was released over Lewe at 0955 hours and the last at 1015 hours. Some of the gliders were damaged in landing—one beyond repair—but none of the equipment was lost. The machinery was put to work immediately, but the gasoline was left aboard the gliders until it was needed. This was a mistake because Japanese fighters, making one of their last sweeps over Burma, came over Lewe on the morning of 22 April and set the gasoline in five of the gliders alight. This incident delayed work on the airfield for only a few minutes, however, the strip was 4,500 feet long and by noon. The first transports landed at 1600 hours that afternoon, only sixty-four hours after the ground forces had driven the Japanese away.

While Lewe Airfield was being repaired, a division overran Tennant and Kalaywa Airfields at Toungoo. A bulldozer that had accompanied the advancing column filled enough craters at Tennant to permit glider landings, but most of the equipment with the ground forces was put to work on Kalaywa. On 23 April, after delivering supplies, six C-47's of the 4th Combat Cargo Squadron lifted six gliders loaded with construction equipment from Meiktila and released them over Tennant between 1015 and 1045 hours. The Tennant Strip was in much better condition than the one at Lewe. A C-47 carrying a number of personnel and equipment landed at 1415 hours, and a 6,000-foot runway was ready by 1600 hours. Improvement of the field continued throughout 23 April, and fifty-six transports landed with supplies the next day.

Ground forces reached the well-sited strip at Zayatkwin, thirty-two miles from Rangoon, on 4 May. Although Tennant Airfield was barely serviceable, C-47's of the 1st Combat Cargo Group and 117 RAF Transport Squadron towed gliders from there to Zayatkwin on the morning of 5 May. Handicapped by weather, in addition to craters in the runway, the engineers made slow progress. When Lewe Airfield became temporarily serviceable on 8 May, eight more equipment-loaded gliders were towed to Zayatkwin. Momentarily improved weather and the added equipment enabled engineers to open the strip to C-47's before nightfall on 8 May and to C-46's the next day. Zayatkwin was the southernmost airfield opened in the IV Corps area during the drive on Rangoon.

Men of the U.S. 11th Airborne Division landing near Appari in the Cagayan Valley on Luzon.

Appari, Cagayan Valley. A jeep and equipment is unloaded fron a CG-13A glider.

A DFS 230 German glider with Vassieux in the background. In July 1944, Nazis burned every building in the town, wiping out men, women and children.

CHAPTER 20

What Might Have Been

Whether airborne troops could maintain themselves in prolonged action from an airhead independent of connections with ground troops was a question never answered in the war. After the operation in Holland, General Brereton tended to feel that airborne forces should not operate without relief by ground troops for longer than three days. Early in 1945, however, he changed his mind and became eager to prove the feasibility of an independent airhead and pushed forward planning for such an operation.

He planned to land his forces by glider, parachute and aircraft onto a strategic airhead near Kassel, Germany. The assault would be conducted in four phases. First, the U.S. 13th, 17th, 82nd and 101st Airborne Divisions and the British 1st and 6th Airborne Divisions would go in by glider and parachute to seize airfields and airstrip sites and to set up defenses. He estimated that this would take three to six days. Next, he would land four infantry divisions—the 2nd, 84th, and 103rd Infantry Divisions and one other not designated—on the airfields and strips. Then, he would launch an offensive to the northwest to seize the high ground east of Paderborn and cut lines of communication east and southeast of the Ruhr, towards which the Allied field armies to the south could advance.

Two airborne divisions with aviation engineers would go in on D-Day and on D-Day+1. Thereafter, one infantry division would go in each day until all had been inserted. All aircraft would then be devoted to resupply and evacuation. Bombers would have to fly an important share of the resupply missions.

General Eisenhower said that he "would dearly love to have one big airborne operation before the war ended" and "it would really be fun to do." Whether or not the operation would be ordered hinged on finding the divisions. On 15 March, the target date was announced as 1 May.

By this time, the Allied ground armies were advancing so quickly against a rapidly disintegrating German resistance that this vast operation was made unnecessary and planning went forward on Operation "Eclipse," the political coup of all time—the capture of Berlin by an Allied airborne assault. It called for Allied airborne forces to seize Templehof Airfield, Berlin's major air terminal, along with the Gatow, Oranienburg and Staakin airfields. They were then to take Berlin. Thousands of CG-4A's, CG-15's, CG-13's, Horsas, and Hamilcars stood ready to take part in the biggest airborne offensive ever known. It was intended to scoop the Soviet capture of the German capital.

The operation was never given the green light. On 23 April 1945, the Soviet armies began to enter Berlin. A momentous opportunity had slipped from the Allied grasp.

One German officer claims that the Soviets started marshalling an enormous number of gliders at airfields close behind Soviet lines during the months before they launched their ground offensive against Berlin. If this is correct, it is possible that the Soviets planned to beat the Allies to the punch, especially if it looked as though the Soviet ground armies would not beat "Eclipse" to Berlin. This would mean that the Soviet Union intended to have Berlin first and at all costs, regardless of Allied military or political efforts.

World War II is the only glider war the world will ever see. By the time Allied commanders learned how to use their glider forces and gained courage to do so, conventional forces had won the war in Europe and in the Pacific, but at a terrible cost in time, blood and materials.

It is impossible to measure how the effective use of glider and other airborne forces might have shortened the war and resulted in less bloodshed by capturing objectives in hours—as in the case of Eben Emael—which armored thrusts took days to reach.

Unfortunately, senior ground generals in Germany, Japan, Great Britain and the U.S. had been schooled in the use of organizations and tactics that were founded in the experience of World War I. There was not a single senior ground commander in the field anywhere in the world, with the exception of Generals Wingate and, possibly, Montgomery, who is known to have given creative forethought to how to employ airborne forces. They were simply ignorant of the potential of the glider as a military weapon. Most never came close to a glider.

General Elwood Quesada, who fought as an American fighter pilot, feels that Army Air Corps and Army senior generals considered the glider an untested weapon. Generals are known to prefer to fight with weapons tested in at least one previous war. This is a fact of history that has many precedents.

General Patton took delight in beating enemy generals to objectives. He took equal delight in "getting there" ahead of his fellow Allied generals. He felt airborne operations to be of questionable value, since he arrived at proposed airborne objectives before the airborne operations got under way on several occasions.

Yet had he had a better knowledge of gliders and their potential to airlift supplies, especially fuel, he would have been furious to be told there were thousands of gliders parked along air strips from which C-47's were taking off to carry much-needed fuel to his armored columns. These gliders—and thousands of grousing glider pilots sorely in need of something to do—could have been carrying fuel in gliders in tow behind the C-47's. It would have more than doubled the amount of fuel being flown forward. Yet it was not done.

Gliders might well have been flying gasoline stations to the lead tanks of Patton's columns, landing in fields alongside the road. This was never done. It could have been. Patton should have realized that the opportunity to use airborne troops existed and asked that they be used. He did not.

About the only example of airborne troops being used to paralyze the enemy's system of command, communication and supply to create diversions and to spread confusion and disorder deep in enemy rear areas was the glider landings in support of General Wingate's operations in Burma. In this case, the troop-carrier aircraft were mostly American, the ideas British and the personnel British and Indian. Similar objectives might have been appropriate to Europe and North Africa, but there was an important difference. Because of the jungle in Burma, it was difficult for the enemy to move reinforcements into the area where forces were landed and the threat of armored counterattack was not great. Quite the contrary was true, of course, in Europe, but that disadvantage might have been overcome through the skillful use of tactical aviation to isolate the battlefield and to provide close ground support.

Although the opportunity certainly presented itself several times in Europe, airborne forces were never used to block retreating enemy elements until the main ground forces could destroy them. It is possible, for instance, that the drop of two or three airborne divisions between Falaise and Argentan on or about 12 August 1944 could have closed the escape route of the Germans in the pocket, bringing about their complete destruction.

The Burma operations implied something of this concept on a small scale. Leaders thinking in bigger terms, however, were always disappointed. As related earlier, Generals Arnold and Marshall were both eager to try a bold, deep airborne penetration for the invasion of Normandy.

Undoubtedly, the tagging of gliders as "gliders" did much harm to their cause in the United States. Despite efforts to divorce the glider from the widely held belief that it was just an overgrown sailplane, the connotation was there, and it led to serious confusion and doubt relative to the level of performance and merit of this new weapon in the power-orientated air force. "Better," as Colonel Dent has stated, "for the whole program, had the glider been referred to as a motorless transport, which it actually was."

Nothing that occurred in airborne operations during the war ever proved that glidermen were anything but as efficient as or more efficient than paratroopers. Unlike parachutists, they landed with guns that did not have to be laboriously put together and squads did not have to be untangled from parachutes and gradually assembled. Glider units landed ready to shoot and—barring accidents—they were not dazed or disoriented as many a paratrooper is liable to be, especially if he has landed on his tail and snapped his neck a bit. Wind conditions never were a serious factor in planning a glider operation, as opposed to parachute operations.

Britain's General Frederick A. M. Browning felt that the advantage of gliderborne forces over paratroopers had been demonstrated, wherever it was possible to use the former. His viewpoint was that personnel carried by gliders landed in formed, even if small, bodies and carried with them a more liberal supply of ammunition, transport and comparatively heavy weapons than did paratroopers. Glidermen could land in most country that was suitable for paratroopers, although their range might not be so great. Gliders could be released some distance from their landing zone, thus not exposing the aircraft to as much risk of flak. Gliders released in the correct place were difficult flak targets. There was probably more risk, he considered, in parachute troops being dropped in the wrong place than there was of gliders being released incorrectly.

The German generals, Student particularly, supported the viewpoint voiced by General Browning. Not so the Americans, for many reasons and with few of them being based on the logic of Generals Browning and Student. Even up to the time of "Eclipse," that lost opportunity, American glider-supported airborne thrusts—less so the British ones—never did reach the zenith they should have simply because U.S. military leaders never had an open mind about their employment. The Army Air Corps was "gung ho" on bombers and fighters and wedded to conventional piston-propelled aircraft performing in mass formation according to tactics developed in World War I. Content at having won the struggle for independence as a service and backed by the world's most formidable industrial might geared to turning out ample quantities of aircraft to win the war conventionally, they needed no gliders and no V-bombs. Initially, they could do without jet propulsion. It was about as simple as that. The U.S. Army Air Corps left it to the Germans to do most of the basic innovation in aviation during the war.

No up-and-coming U.S. commander could afford association with the transport arm of the Army Air Corps without risking professional suicide. Air commanders became generals by flying bombers and fighters, not by flying the slow C-47, let alone a glider. At least this proved to be the case in the U.S. armed forces. By contrast, the Germans did have *General* Student and the British had Brigadier Chatterton, both glider pilots who attained high rank. Not one American glider pilot assigned to air transport units rose above the rank of major from what can be determined in existing sources. A few officers in the glider-pilot training program and in glider production became colonels.

The weight of the U.S. Army Air Corps resources was thrown into backing the "air-power through bombing" concept. Air transport received only passing recognition and support; the glider effort, initially received none. Much of the air arm's attention to air transport came as a result of the intention to drop parachutists, with little interest in towing gliders.

As long as the U.S. Army Air Corps was committed to a policy of "proving" the decisive capabilities of strategic bombing, attention to troop-carrier needs could not be more than secondary. Although General Arnold was an airborne enthusiast, he was more of a strategic bombardment enthusiast. In his study of recommendations for the postwar establishment, Colonel Julian J. Ewell, who had commanded a regiment in the U.S. 101st Airborne Division, noted in November 1945: "Troop carrier and airborne are inseparable. Each has many other commitments but in the actual combat operation they must cooperate perfectly. The relatively slow growth of America's airborne potentialities in this war has been primarily due to Air Force indifference to [its] own troop carrier needs."

Although the British did better than the Americans in producing gliders and had a better organized glider element—and when operating on their own may have been more enterprising in their use—their glider effort was tied to American thinking and action in the use of gliders for many reasons: the availability of tow planes for one and the necessity for integrated planning and operation between the U.S. and Britain.

Many British general officers rode gliders into combat. Brigadier Chatterton flew General Hopkinson, who was a qualified paratrooper, to Sicily and General Browning to Nijmegen. Lieutenant S. C. "Bill" Griffith, later to become famous in the world of cricket, flew General Gale, commander of the 6th Airborne Division, into Normandy.

Only two American general officers were flown into combat by glider. One was killed in the crash of his glider in Normandy. General Anthony McAuliffe, with his typical *élan*, realized that the glidermen of the 101st Airborne Division needed an example. Perhaps aware of how the airborne general officers had neglected this aspect of leadership, he flew into Holland in a glider. The parachute idea had taken hold among the senior American airborne commanders. It became the way to go about things, for there was no present or future glory in riding a glider into combat to compare with the awards forthcoming via the parachute route.

Is there another and possibly more important lesson to be learned from experience with the glider in World War II and with the helicopter in Vietnam?

The U.S. Army has its own helicopter, its own helicopter pilots and aviation generals. They operate under the same major command as the troops they fly into combat. There is a singleness of command purpose: they go in as a combat team, and there is no question that this will be so, or heads are chopped.

The U.S. glider story during World War II would have achieved many more successes—more efficiently—had all glider operations and personnel belonged to the U.S. Army. Glider pilots could have been better organized, trained and disciplined—and happier. Generals like Ridgway and Gavin would have seen to this and would have satisfied the glider pilot's yearning to do more than corral and guard prisoners and unavoidably get underfoot and be bothersome to airborne commanders in the heat of combat. While American glider infantrymen were being killed in Holland, and the British Glider Pilot Regiment suffered 157 killed and 469 wounded as they fought alongside British infantry, some U.S. glider pilots were camera shopping in Nijmegen, where they had drifted after the landings. They caused a serious morale problem to ground commanders, as it might well be understood. Glider pilots do not deserve criticism for such happenings. They were part of a system that was at fault.

In a manner of speaking, the same kind of basic ailments that plagued the glider program in the air forces also affected the sound development of the glider ground combat organizations of infantry and artillery. The glider trooper ended up as a most unwanted stepchild, forced to take a back seat to his more glamorous parachute-jumping airborne counterpart. Moreover, the organization and training of the glider forces—plagued by lack of doctrine, vacillation and change in higher echelons that constantly modified the glider organizations and hard pressed for high-caliber men—was further hampered by the problems that hobbled the glider promotion program. A paratrooper could get his jumps and a paratroop unit or part of it could get its airborne training if there were only a single C-47 aircraft available. To the gliderman, an aircraft parked and ready as a glider tug was of no use without a glider to haul, and there were long periods when whole airborne divisions were out of balance in their training cycles because paratroopers could undergo training but not glider troopers. There were also times when there were ample gliders, but the aircraft had been spirited off.

A glider infantryman had three strikes against him on his one-way journey into combat. First, the towing aircraft could be hit, lose power or crash and have to let loose its glider. For almost any minor reason, it could cut off the glider to leave it to its doom. Second, if the glider pilot found a good reason, he could do the same. The sweating glider trooper had no say in the decision, although his interests and the interests of his command would at least be served by his continuing, even taking into consideration the vagaries that may have caused the glider pilot to abort the mission. Many glider pilots released without reason, some certainly out of cowardice. Third, the poor glider passengers had no parachutes.

In contrast, paratroopers had more options than their glider companions, and they knew it. If the aircraft turned back, they went with it to a safe landing. If seriously damaged down, there was a good chance most could manage to get out of the plane before it cracked up and parachute to safety.

In all fairness, I did witness airborne generals riding in glider training and orientation flights given to airborne divisions stateside. This is to their credit. But there was more safety in parachuting into combat—and certainly more prestige—and every general looked for this and left the glider colonels to ride gliders into combat, especially after the death of General Pratt in the Normandy glider landings. Events have since proved their apparent wisdom, since most American "jumping generals" advanced far in their careers.

The glider still has a place in war. The question is: will military men accord it that place? The answer in most nations is probably not. Expensive, noisy, powered aircraft and helicopters are best supported by parasitic industries that support a technology from which the richest profits flow. A six-passenger helicopter is manufactured at ten times the cost of a fifteen-passenger glider. The "flying crane" helicopter can carry a tank 500 miles. The glider can carry a tank 1,500 miles at one tenth or less of the cost. The helicopter has the advantage in that it can move about freely under its own power. In addition, it is more versatile than the glider in wooded areas where there are few clearings. But its high cost and short range make it a luxury.

No one has tried jet-glider tows for military or commercial long-haul operations. The thought will raise all sorts of objections. Nonetheless, technology could produce such a combination, and it would have many applications. Industry and government alike will ridicule a jet-glider tow combination, but they are satisfied that a glider-rocket combination being designed into the orbital space laboratory—through the glider return vehicle program—provides an economical way to handle manned rocketry. Blessed with the dollar sign, this glider has industry's blessing, and it will be built and used.

Gliders still have military uses. They are still the only aircraft that can haul heavy cargo thousands of miles and land it on any kind of open area that is a few hundred feet long. They can be released at a high enough altitude and far enough away not to be discovered until they are on the ground. Gliders can fly as large a force and carry as much heavy equipment as the military want. The failure to see this stems from psychological, philosophical, emotional and mental obstacles—better called the conventional-thinking, establishment-minded, hierarchical-orientated military mentality found in all armies.

Land warfare still has many places where gliders can be used. Wherever there is an extensive land mass, as in Eurasia or the Western Hemisphere, or large water areas to bridge, gliders can be useful. The threat to an army of glider armadas descending on its lines of communications is not to be taken lightly. Certainly, U.S. doctrine calls for no such imaginative use of a discarded weapon, but who can speak for the military innovators of other nations to whom the glider could give cheap transportation? Certainly, the Soviet Union, which successfully employed the glider in guerilla operations, has not discarded its glider guerrilla-support doctrine. With what other weapon would they replace it? There is none.

For a time after World War II, the U.S. Army Air Corps and the Army maintained an active but wary interest in gliders and glider operations. Until the early 1950's, officers and men in some of the courses at Fort Benning, Georgia, were still being given glider orientation rides.

By this time, the U.S. Air Force had developed transport aircraft that could land on rough landing strips and in open fields. Better aircraft for dropping parachutists were being produced. Artillery and tanks, which gliders might have flown into operation, were being carried in huge cargo aircraft and dropped by parachute over objectives. The need for the glider as a support aircraft for parachute operations had disappeared, at least as far as the parachutists or airborne-minded generals and staff planners were concerned.

Hamilcar gliders ready for take-off with Handley Page Halifax tow-planes.

After the war—Horsas waiting to be salvaged.

Soon, the helicopter had appeared as a transport for troops—much to the dismay of the paratroopers—and as a weapon carrier, doing much the same job as gliders had previously done at far less cost and which the powered troop transports could not do as well as had been hoped.

Canada held on to many of her gliders into the 1950's. Australia continued experimental work with its de Haviland for some years after the war. It is reported that the Indian armed forces were flying transport gliders left there by the U.S. until some time in the 1950s. England disposed of hers in the late 1940's.

Several sources claim that the Soviets have not dispensed with the military glider. They state that the Soviets have a small, but select, group in their air force that is composed of trained glider pilots, a group that will serve as a cadre if the Soviets decide on a rapid expansion of their glider fleet. To facilitate such expansion, these sources claim, a substantial number of gliders are available in storage.

Few vestiges of these gallant, misunderstood, often maligned aircraft now exist. One forms part of the airborne museum at Sainte Mere Eglise, the wing protruding through the wall of the museum to form a cover for the entrance. The Caproni Museum in Milan displays a Caproni transport glider. The U.S. Air Force Museum at Wright-Patterson Air Force Base, Ohio, has a CG-4A that someday may be displayed. The 101st Airborne Division Museum at Fort Campbell, Kentucky, has one exhibited, and the 82nd Airborne Museum at Fort Bragg, North Carolina, displays the fuselage of a CG-15A. The cockpit of a Horsa is exhibited at the Airborne Museum at Aldershot in England. The Museum of Army Flying at Middle Wallop has a Hamilcar on display.

These are the final tributes to a once great glider armada, now all but a memory.

BOOK TWO

Fighting Gliders
of World War II

To My Wife, Thelma

CHAPTER 1

Fighting Gliders:
The Secret Weapon

This section tells the heretofore little-known technical facts about the assault and transport gliders that so heroically served the fighting forces of Germany, Great Britain, the Soviet Union and the United States during World War II. It also reveals for the first time little-known facts about the gliders other nations produced.

Not before or since that cataclysmic conflict has the world used the glider in war. The appearance of this aircraft in war was destined to be but once. Technological shortcomings, production, supply and delivery problems and less than far-sighted military leadership combined to prevent its potential from becoming fully realized before the end of the war swept this formidable tool of warfare from history's stage.

The glider introduced the world to a new kind of airborne warfare.

On 10 May 1940, ten German gliders carrying 78 glidermen assaulted the enormous Fort Eben Emael, pride of the Allied defenses. Twenty-five minutes later, the fort and its 750 defenders had been rendered ineffective by the audacious glidermen's attack. This led to tremendous interest in the military glider in Great Britain, Japan and the United States. Later on, the Allies used gliders in Normandy, at Arnhem, along the Wesel and at a forgotten jungle strip in Burma, to list but a few of the glider's stirring feats.

Few realize that America produced 14,000 combat gliders—more than any type of its famed fighter or bomber aircraft—with the possible exception of one or two fighter models. At one time, America planned to build 36,000 gliders, and training was scheduled for more than that number of glider pilots to man the projected indomitable glider armada that might have swarmed over and inundated the Reich.

What advantages did gliders have that made them a useful weapon in combat and a desirable cargo carrier? There were many. Gliders gave mobility to ground units. Using gliders, forces could leap rivers, mountains and enemy defenses to make vertical envelopment possible. Field armies could operate in a third dimension. Gliders made airborne warfare not only a possibility, but also a reality. Gliders could carry a squad, a platoon or a company in a single load. They discharged units ready to fight, not scattered over a landscape in the way paratroopers landed.

Glider flight serial skimming the landscape. Waco CG-4A gliders in double tow behind Curtis Commando C-46s.

Gliders were also cheap to manufacture, in contrast to the cost of a powered aircraft. According to the number of gliders an aircraft towed, they could double or triple the amount of men or cargo a single aircraft could move through the air.

Most important of all, the glider was silent. Stealth was its trademark, and the terror it spread was a psychological advantage of unsurpassed importance.

Fighting gliders were a breed apart, different from any aircraft heretofore known. Their forerunner, the sailplane or sports glider, could use winds and thermal currents efficiently in "sail flight" and remain aloft for hours and travel many miles.

Sailplanes differed considerably from war gliders. Sailplanes have long, narrow wings and a pencil-like fuselage. They appear almost translucent against the sky and sun and maneuver gracefully with swallow-like intricacy. Gliders have stubbier wings and large bodies. Most of them look much like a powered aircraft without an engine.

Unlike the sports glider, the fighting, transport, cargo, assault or combat glider could not use atmospheric thermals to remain aloft. Once a military glider was released and its speed diminished to a critical point, its weight, design and construction prevented it from obtaining lift from air currents or thermals to keep it up. It began to glide down to the earth. Most of the craft produced during World War II had about a one-to-ten glide ratio; that is, in free flight they glided down at the rate of one foot for every ten feet they flew forward. The sailplane of that period had a one-to-twenty ratio. (Today, sailplanes are being built that have as much as a one-to-fifty ratio, so great have been the technological advances since the war.)

To get into the air, the sports glider was either towed by aircraft or automobile until it got up enough speed to lift it off the ground or it could be rolled down a slope to get enough speed to take off or be "winched" into the air, shooting like a missile from a slingshot to gain enough speed to fly.

The combat glider had to be towed off the ground behind a powerful aircraft. To be recovered, it had to be "snatched" from the ground by an aircraft in flight. A long rope, usually of nylon, stretched from the nose or wings of the glider to the tail of the powered tow plane. The glider was towed all the way to a point just short of or above its target. In many airborne assaults in World War II, gliders flew behind tow planes in "serials" of aircraft and gliders that stretched out in the sky for hundreds of miles, an awe-inspiring sight to frontline troops over whose heads they flew.

Once on their mission, gliders flew through rough weather and sheets of flak. Those that survived the trip unhitched above the enemy and glided down into battle. There was no escape on the winds; the commitment was irrevocable. Once an aircraft and glider took off with cargo, glidermen or weapons of war, only the aircraft returned.

CHAPTER 2

German Gliders

The development of Germany's military transport gliders dates from the early 1930's. Interest sprouted from a widespread national enthusiasm for sports gliding and soaring, an outcome of the restrictions imposed on Germany on the development and production of powered aircraft by the World War I Treaty of Versailles, signed in 1919.

As a result of the treaty, the energies of a nation noted for a strong interest in aviation, evidenced by the production of Fokker and other fighter aircraft and of dirigibles, were now restrictively channeled into gliding and soaring, the only outlet remaining for aviation enthusiasts. German achievements in gliding and soaring laid the foundation for Germany's later air power.

By 1932, something new was taking place: the Germans were visualizing potential in the frail sailplane as more than a recreational air vehicle. While the earlier gliders and sailplanes had been slung or thrust into thermals to obtain a few moments of exhilarating pleasure in the air for their pilots, aircraft started towing gliders for hundreds of miles. Pilots were also learning to tow two or more gliders—in fact, a train of gliders—behind a single aircraft. (Someone in America had also delivered mail by glider.)

By 1932, the Germans had also produced a glider large enough to carry meteorological equipment, a pilot and one or two scientists to man the equipment and conduct meteorological tests.

This glider was designed by Dr. Alexander Lippisch, in collaboration with Professor Walter Georgii, at the *Rhön-Rossiten-Gesellschaft* (RRG) Research Institute in Munich. The actual construction of the glider took place in the workshop of Alex Schleicher in Poppenhausen. This glider was ideal for meteorological readings at high altitudes. When released, it produced no noise or vibration, and it was free from electrical emanations usually found in aircraft that were likely to disturb sensitive instruments. The "flying observatory," as it became known, flew many research flights.

According to an article in *Air Enthusiast* (March 1972), Adolf Hitler took an interest in the "flying observatory" in Munich, when he went to visit an exhibition at the airport. At that time, he conferred with Professor Georgii and discussed the possibility of still larger gliders for military transport tasks.

How closely the Germans followed Soviet glider development is not precisely known. The few published facts are revealing and significant, however. Years before the Germans developed their "flying observatory" glider, the forerunner of their transport glider, the future DFS 230, German and Soviet military collaboration had been a matter of historical fact. *Hauptmann* Kurt Student, who later headed the German airborne forces during the war and became the highest-ranking proponent of glider warfare among the armies of the world, visited the Lipetsk airfield, a German base in the Soviet Union, in the years from 1924 to 1928. It is also known that *General* Ernst Udet, the German World War I fighter ace, visited the Soviet Union many times. That Student and other high-ranking officers gleaned data about Soviet glider activities is virtually certain.

Udet was involved in the German glider research and development program from its inception. It was he, according to William Green in his *Warplanes of the Third Reich*, who suggested that the flying observatory should be modified to carry soldiers. Along with *General* Udet, some of the more visionary members of the *Luftwaffe*, *General* Jeschonnek in particular, began to press for a combat model. The design and development of the project was given a "secret" classification right from the start and was turned over to the *Deutsche Forschungsantalt für Segelflug* (DFS), an affiliate of the RRG. An aircraft engineer, Hans Jacobs, assisted by glider pilots on the staff of the company, took the problem in hand. Green, who is a leading authority on world aircraft, states that the DFS 230, a successor to the flying observatory, "began flight tests late in 1937." Assuming Green to be correct, the Germans were at least two years, and perhaps as much as four years, behind the Russians in developing a transport glider as such.

The Germans were most likely first, however, in conceiving of the glider as an opportunity to develop new and unorthodox means of waging warfare. This concept was either Udet's or Student's. Udet thought of the glider as the modern equivalent of the Trojan Horse, landing soldiers in stealth and silence behind enemy lines. Student's approach was more aggressive. He saw gliders as a direct attacking and fighting weapon. He was to see his theory vindicated when Hitler ordered him to capture the Belgian fort, Eben Emael, in the opening attack on the West in May 1940. Eleven gliders carrying seventy-eight glidermen landed on the world's most "impregnable" fort and neutralized its 780-man garrison within twenty minutes. The next day, the fort capitulated. With this feat, glider warfare was born.

The Germans rated all their gliders as combat aircraft. Germany was the only country to arm every glider with machine guns. The DFS 230 carried one, the Go 242 eight, and the Me 321 two or more. In Germany, gliders were definitely considered to be fighting aircraft, whereas other nations considered

Obs, meteorological observation glider, forerunner of German military attack and transport gliders

DFS 230 attack glider. In history's first airborne assault, seventy-eight German glider troops in ten DFS 230's attacked and captured Fort Eben Emael on 10 May 1940.

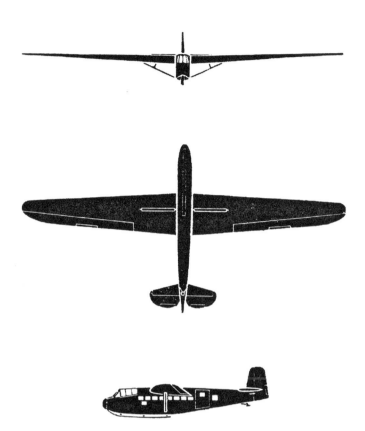

DFS 230, three-view section.

DFS 230 **Technical Data**

Crew: Pilot
Weight
    Empty: 1,800 lb
    Cargo: 2,800 lb
    Total with cargo: 4,600 lb
Dimensions
    Wingspan: 72'
    Wing area: 444 square feet
    Fuselage length: 37.5'
Cargo compartment
    Length: 13.2'
    Width: 3.6'
    Height: 4.5'

Payload: Nine fully equipped soldiers
    or the equivalent in cargo
Armament: A 7.92-mm machine gun
    in some versions
Towing speed: 120 mph
Tow planes: He 111, He 126, Ju
    52/53, Ju 87 and Bf 110

DFS 230 and Bf 109 *Mistelschlepp* ("pick-a-back") combination.

DFS 230 laden with electronic components, illustrating one of the many purposes for which the German gliders were used. This DFS was one element of an experimental airborne communications system.

them rather as military transports. Later on, the other nations took advantage of German experience and used gliders operationally in much the same way as the Germans had done.

DFS 230

As already discussed, the DFS 230 was an outgrowth of the RRG "flying observatory" of the early 1930's. The DFS 230 was designed by Hans Jacobs, chief engineer at the institute. It was first tested by Hanna Reitsch, the famous diminutive aviatrix, who also test-piloted the V bombs that later rained on Britain.

The wings of the glider were set high and braced. The fuselage was a framework of steel tubing covered with fabric with a rectangular cross-section. The wings were of stressed plywood with spoilers fitted on the upper surface to steepen the angle of glide. The wheels could be jettisoned. The glider then landed on a single central ski that extended from the nose to about the middle of its belly.

The DFS 230 was flown by one pilot and carried nine passengers. The seats in the first model were in a straight line, with six facing forward and four to the rear. The rear seats could be taken out to allow for cargo. The glider weighed 1,800 pounds and could carry up to 2,800 pounds of cargo. It had a wingspan of 72 feet and was 37.5 feet long. It was normally towed at 120 miles per hour.

The initial model was later modified. Loading doors had to be changed to accommodate a greater variety of loads, such as bicycles, antitank guns and motorcycles.

A light machine gun was fixed externally to the starboard side and manned by the occupant of the second seat who fired through a slit in the fuselage. A later model had the machine gun just aft of the canopy. Navigation lights were operated by a generator fixed to the nose of the glider. Clamps along the seats held carbines and submachine guns.

Large-scale production was launched under the supervision of the Gotha works. Many different companies ultimately participated in the production endeavor, including the Hartwig toy factory at Sonnenberg in Thuringia. In all, 2,230 DFS 230's were built.

Models B-1 and B-2 had dual controls and could carry more weight.

Designers also incorporated braking rockets and parachutes for deceleration in landing.

This glider was used to open the German invasion of the West during the assault on Eben Emael. It was used in the invasion of Crete and flew urgently needed men and supplies to the *Deutsches Afrika Korps*. Later, valiant efforts were made to get supplies to German field armies fighting in the Soviet Union by this glider, and it also stood by to participate in a gigantic, desperate, last-minute attempt to launch an airborne assault against the Soviet forces at Stalingrad.

DFS 230's were fitted out as workshops containing lathes and other machine tools, welding equipment and cabinets with an assortment of spare parts for fighter and other combat aircraft. One squadron of each fighter group on the Eastern Front towed these fighter maintenance and repair gliders to each base from which the group operated so that the group had immediate maintenance facilities available.

DFS 230 V7

A DFS-230 V7 was also developed. As William Green explains so aptly in *Warplanes of the Third Reich,* it "bore no relationship to the basic DFS 230 design." Its designation was a way of getting around bureaucratic intransigence so as to permit designers to build a new and better glider than the DFS 230 without raising resentment or objections.

Completed in 1943, it carried fifteen passengers, six more than the original DFS 230, or the equivalent weight of 4,180 pounds of cargo. Its cargo compartment was longer, its wingspan shorter and the length of the fuselage more than three feet greater. A novel feature was that a panel on the top was removable to enable loading through the roof.

Despite the fact that the DFS 230 V7 was a marked improvement on the DFS 230 in the weight and number of men it carried and had many new features, it was not accepted for production.

DFS 230 V7 Technical Data
Crew: Pilot and co-pilot
Weight
    Empty: 3,820 lb
    Cargo: 4,180 lb
    Total with cargo: 7,700 lb
Dimensions
    Wingspan: 63.6'
    Wing area: 425 square feet
    Fuselage length: 41'
Cargo compartment
    Length: 14.9'
Payload: 15 fully equipped soldiers or the equivalent in cargo
Armament: Three machine guns
Towing speed: 180 mph (maximum)

DFS 230 V-7, three-view section.

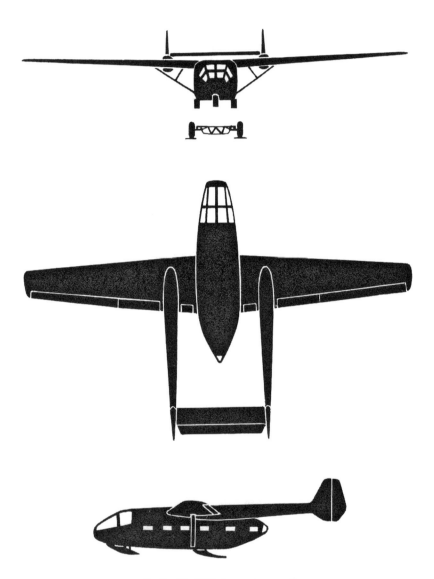

Gotha Go 242, three-view section.

Go 242

This versatile glider was used extensively for supplying air and ground formations fighting on Germany's widely separated fronts. It was produced by *Gothaer Waggonfabrik AG* of Gotha.

The design and development of the Go 242 stemmed from a demand for a cargo glider larger than the DFS 230, which could rush large amounts of critically needed bulky cargo, trucks, guns and other equipment to the front. Its design was the result of preliminary studies made by Albert Kalkert, an engineer at *Gothaer Waggonfabrik*. The *Luftwaffe* received the first Go 242 in mid-1941.

The craft was a high-winged, twin-boom monoplane, with a central cargo nacelle. Lift spoilers were fitted to the top surface of the wings. The wings, booms and tail were of wood; the cargo compartment had a framework of tubular steel. The wing was strut-braced and tapered in chord and thickness. The rear of the fuselage was hinged at the top and could be raised to load cargo. Early models had a droppable undercarriage, with skids in front and in the middle for landing.

Although the basic design remained unchanged, nine different revisions were made to the basic Go 242 in its production history. Two of them were made to allow *Fallschirmjäger* to jump from the glider, and a number of changes were made in the landing gear. One incorporated a plough that could be released by the pilot when landing in an effort to brake the glider quickly. Another important innovation was the attachment of a bank of four rockets to the rear of the fuselage to give the glider thrust in takeoff.

Provision was made for mounting eight machine guns for protective purposes, although not more than four were fitted at any one time. The glider carried twenty-two men, a pilot and a co-pilot. The pilot's and co-pilot's seats and the floor just below their legs were armored with eight millimeters of steel.

Some of the gliders were equipped as transportable maintenance shops, with lathes and other machinery permanently installed. Others had staff or command operations rooms. They were flown from location to location, as the need arose for their equipment.

The chief tow aircraft for the Go 242 were the He 111 and the Ju 52.

In all, *Gothaer Waggonfabrik* and its affiliates built 1,528 Go 242's. Of those, 133 were modified to become aircraft by the addition of two engines, and the were designated as the Go 244.

The Go 242 was used extensively for personnel and supply missions between German bases in Europe and North Africa to supply the *Deutsches Afrika Korps*. In the Soviet Union, they were used to help maintain the mobility of the forces in the field by flying supplies to extended ground force columns.

They flew critical supplies to beleaguered German forces at Kholm early in 1942 and to an encircled *Panzer-Armee* around Podolsk. They also assisted in evacuating German forces from the Crimea.

Go 242 Technical Data

Crew: Pilot and co-pilot

Weight

    Empty: 7,000 lb

    Cargo: 8,000 lb

    Total with cargo: 15,000 lb

Dimensions

    Wingspan: 79'

    Wing area: 700 square feet

    Fuselage length: 52.5'

Cargo compartment

    Length: 20'

    Width: 7'

    Height: 6'

Payload: 23 fully equipped soldiers or the equivalent in cargo

Armament: Four to eight machine guns

Towing speed: 150 mph (maximum); 130 mph (sustained)

Tow planes: Ju 52 and He 111

A personnel carrier—*Kübelwagen*—being loaded into a Gotha Go 242.

Gotha Go 242 parked at Wright Army Air Field, Ohio. This captured German glider was brought to the United States, assembled and extensively studied and tested.

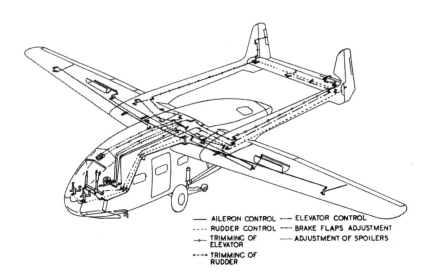

AILERON CONTROL ――― ELEVATOR CONTROL
---- RUDDER CONTROL ――― BRAKE FLAPS ADJUSTMENT
――― TRIMMING OF ――― ADJUSTMENT OF SPOILERS
ELEVATOR
――― TRIMMING OF
RUDDER

Gotha Go 242 control system, exploded drawing.

Gotha Go 242 fitted with bank of four Rheinmetal RI 502 solid-fuel rockets to assist in take-off.

A close-up of the RI 502 solid-fuel rocket propulsion system.

A Walter RI 202b rocket slung beneath wing of a Gotha Go 242.

Me 321

The *Gigant* (Giant), as the Me 321 was christened, was the world's largest operational glider and one of the largest aircraft built until recent years. It had a wingspan of 181 feet, was 93 feet long, and carried 24 tons. It has frequently been confused with the Ju 322, another enormous German glider.

An urgent requirement for a large glider developed when German military leaders concluded that any airborne assault on England must be backed up by air-landed tanks, self-propelled guns and the indispensable 88-mm flak. They felt that without these weapons, the invasion of England would be doomed.

The idea for a large glider for this strategic mission may have originated at Messerschmitt. According to Waldemar Voigt, who was head of the office of configuration design and aerodynamics at the company, Professor Willy Messerschmitt discussed the feasibility of building such an enormous aircraft with Voigt early in November 1940. Apparently, it was an idea first broached to Messerschmitt a month earlier by Josef Fröhlich, a department head. A few days after design studies had begun, Voigt assured Messerschmitt that it was not only possible to design such a glider, but also to tow it.

Messerschmitt had an audience with Rudolf Hess, the Deputy *Führer*, and made the proposal to build such an aircraft. Hess went to Hitler, who, intrigued with the idea, gave the go-ahead in a few days. Hess then turned the details over to the Air Ministry.

Voigt went on to produce the configuration design and aerodynamic layout. Fröhlich was given the mission of implementing the concept. He set up a sizable task force of engineers and assorted supporting staff at Leipheim to initiate the construction. Meanwhile, the Air Ministry issued a production order. Assembly of the gliders took place at Leipheim and Obertraubling. The first test flight was made at Leipheim on 25 February 1941, about fifteen weeks after the construction order had been given.

Flight tests were first carried out without loads, the glider being towed by a Ju 90, the only aircraft powerful enough to get the *Gigant* into the air. It took 4,000 feet of runway to get the wheels off the ground. The Germans encountered extreme difficulty in getting the glider airborne when it carried a load. Since they had few aircraft as powerful as the Ju 90 and it was evident that even this aircraft was not powerful enough to tow a fully loaded Me 321, they resorted to the "Troika tow," a Messerschmitt concept, which was a combination of three towing aircraft each independently hitched to the glider by a tow rope. The "Troika tow" proved successful. The aircraft used for this purpose was the Bf 110C fighter-bomber.

Ultimately, the "Troika tow" became costly in aircraft and pilots lost in experimentation and in the number of aircraft that it took from critical operations, so a special tug, the He 111 Z, was built. The product of the imagination of *General* Ernst Udet, it consisted of two He 111 H-6 twin-engine bombers, attached by a constant-chord wing section with an engine mounted at the center, making the five-engine He 111 Z, christened the *Zwilling* ("twin"). Full controls were in the port-side fuselage. The second pilot sat in the other fuselage and had full controls but no throttles. The total crew was five. It had a wingspan of 116 feet.

Eight auxiliary rockets were used to assist the tow plane at take off when there was a maximum payload. Each rocket developed 1,200 pounds of thrust. They were suspended from the lower surface of the glider's wings. When expended, the rockets were dropped by parachute. Landing gear could be dropped, and landing accomplished on four spring skids.

The fuselage was made of steel tubing covered with fabric. Wings were made of steel tubes giving a rectangular cross section and interconnected, as in a girder structure. Plywood covered the wing forward of the spar. Fabric covered the wing aft of the spar.

Once airborne, the *Gigant* handled well but proved a tremendous physical strain for one pilot to fly. This caused the designers to modify the glider to provide for a co-pilot.

Most Me 321's were first based in France in preparation for a German invasion of Great Britain. When the invasion did not occur, these gliders were transferred to the Eastern Front, where many of them were used to fly men, materiel and equipment. The glider carried 200 fully equipped men. When it carried troops, the storage space was divided into an upper and a lower compartment to carry a full company of men and their equipment.

Two hundred of these immense gliders were built. As the war progressed, a large number were converted into six-engine Me 323 aircraft.

Some aviation experts and historians doubt the Me 321 could actually carry 200 soldiers. However, according to Waldemar Voigt, its designer, there was no question of this capacity and the ability to transport even heavier loads. This was dramatically proven. The heavier Me 323 aircraft evacuated 220 men of Rommel's forces from North Africa to Italy on at least one flight. Eighty sat in the wings and 140 in the cargo compartment.

Messerschmitt Me 321, the largest glider ever built. Compare the Me 321 to the Go 242 beneath its wing.

The cavernous interior of the Messerschmitt Me 321.

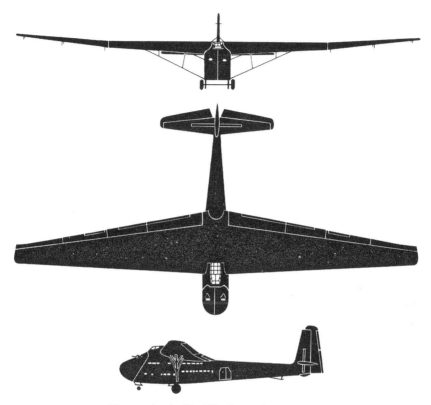

Messerschmitt Me 321, three-view section.

Me 321 Technical Data
Crew: Pilot, co-pilot and mechanic
Weight
    Empty: 26,000 lb
    Cargo: 44,000 lb
    Total with cargo: 70,000 lb
Dimensions
    Wingspan: 181'
    Wing area: 3,230 square feet
    Fuselage length: 93'

Payload: One heavy tank or one 88-mm flak or 200 fully equipped soldiers or the equivalent in cargo
Armament: Several machine guns
Towing speed: 110 mph (maximum)
Tow planes: Three Bf 110 C's or one He 111 Z

Messerschmitt Me 321 in tow behind the five-engined Heinkel He 111Z.

He 111Z .

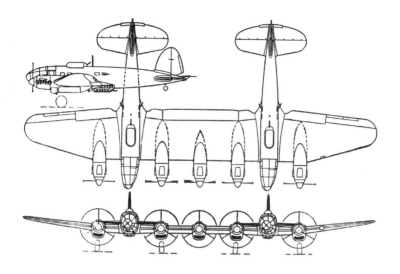

Heinkel He 111Z, three-view section.

Messerschmitt Me 323 powered aircraft.

Ju 322

This was the real mystery glider of World War II and one about which few details are known to this day. It was one of Germany's super gliders, sometimes referred to by the Germans as the *Goliath* and officially christened the *Mammut* ("Mammoth"). British intelligence dubbed it the Merseberg (see Me 321). It had a checkered history.

The belief was long held that Junkers went into the production of the Ju 322 to compete with Messerschmitt's 321 and get a share of the large-cargo transport-glider market. Actually, this was not the case.

The Ju 322 was the result of almost frantic efforts to build gliders capable of lifting tanks and heavy equipment for the invasion of England. When the Reich Air Ministry instructed Messerschmitt to design a glider—ultimately, the Me 321—it placed the same requirement on Junkers. The only difference in the instructions issued was that Messerschmitt was allowed to use steel. Junkers was directed to use wood, in anticipation of a critical shortage of steel, in which case the Air Ministry could fall back on Junkers's product to meet future requirements for large cargo gliders.

In every sense of the word, the Ju 322 was a "flying wing," a rare design in aircraft at any period in history. It was absolutely extraordinary that this should have been the basic design for such a huge aircraft. It was a design concept that had not been thoroughly tested at the time, even in the sporting glider, except perhaps by the Soviet Union.

The glider was to carry twenty tons of cargo, somewhat less than the amount the Me 321 carried. The wing was 203 feet long and constructed of wood throughout except for fittings, instruments and the like. The reinforced middle beam was actually the fuselage. The fuselage part of the wing had a leading edge that could be detached to open the immense interior for cargo. The cockpit was on the left side of the cargo compartment and above it.

Designing and developing the landing gear and the undercarriage proved one of the most difficult problems. The fully loaded glider weighed close to forty-five tons. Despite the original ruling against its use, eight tons of steel had to go into the construction of the various parts to give them the necessary rigidity and strength.

The undercarriage had to be under the glider as it was being loaded. The glider then had to be towed to flying speed, jettisoning the undercarriage as it was taking off or was airborne. The design engineers decided on the latter course. The gear was so heavy, however, that the engineers calculated it could not be dropped from too great a height or it would be destroyed when it hit the ground. If it were dropped at too low an altitude, it would bounce up and hit the glider. Many different kinds of gear were tested, using from eight to as many as thirty-two wheels (sixteen in tandem on each side).

Problems were also encountered with the wooden structure. It was found that parts were weakened by rot because of poor manufacturing techniques. The first tank loaded into the glider fell through the floor. (This was due in part to faulty ramp design.) This incident led to the reinforcement of the floor, whereby the problem of loading future tanks and similarly heavy equipment was solved, but at the expense of useful payload. It took an additional eight tons of material to effect the reinforcement, reducing the payload to fourteen tons. Other changes and some cautionary calculations caused the designers to reduce the payload to twelve tons.

In time, two prototypes were ready for tests. Even before flight tests began, Udet expressed his doubts that the glider would really fly while visiting Junkers. Junkers officials were so confident of the outcome of their daring venture, however, that they launched into the construction of ninety-eight more *Mammut* gliders.

The first test took place in April 1941. Reports state that the Ju 90 bomber, which was towing the Ju 322, could not get up enough speed at full throttle to lift the glider off the runway. In a subsequent try, the glider managed to get off the ground but could make no change in direction and had to cut off from the Ju 90 and land only a short distance from the takeoff field. In the test, the glider had so little vertical stability that its wings rotated in minor arcs, swinging the tow plane dangerously.

No other tests were made. Already facing a huge financial loss and with no assurance the Ju 322 would be successful, Junkers decided to terminate the project. The hulls of the existing prototypes and those under construction were cut up, and the wood obtained was used in automobile gas generators.

Junkers planned to build a yet larger glider, the Ju 488, at Toulouse, France. However, Allied bombings of the Toulouse industrial sites destroyed the factory where the glider was to be built and it was decided to terminate the project.

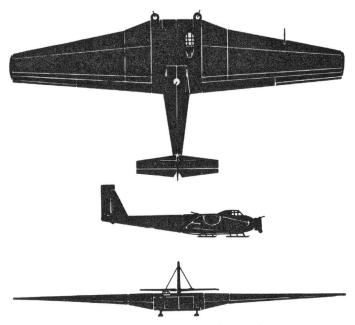

Junkers Ju 322, three-view section.

Ju 322 Technical Data
Crew: Pilot and co-pilot
Weight
    Empty: 56,000 lb
    Cargo: 24,000 lb
    Total with cargo: 90,000 lb
Dimensions
    Wingspan: 203'
    Wing area: 6,400 square feet
    Fuselage length: 95'
Cargo compartment
    Length: 38'
    Width: 30'
    Height: 10.1'

Payload: One Panzer IV or 100 fully
    equipped soldiers
Armament: Two 7.92-mm machine
    guns
Tow plane: Ju 90 V7

Junkers Ju 322.

DFS 331.

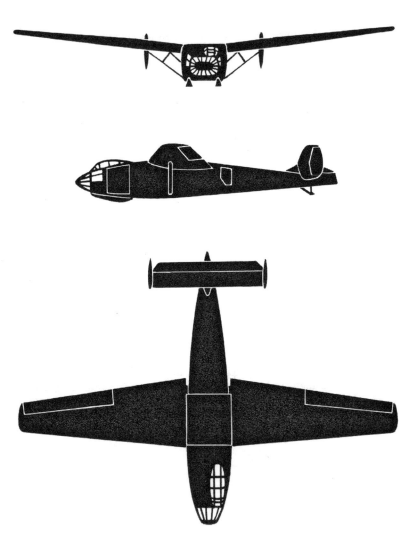

DFS 331, three-view section.

DFS 331

This glider was designed by Hans Jacobs, designer of the DFS 230. It was built by *Gothaer Waggonfabrik* in 1941 at about the time the manufacturer was also proceeding with the design and construction of the Go 242. Although the DFS 331 possessed some features novel to gliders of the time—excellent visibility in the cockpit, a wide cargo compartment and a superb airfoil longitudinal section of the fuselage—it did not go into production. This was primarily due to the progress of the Go 242, which had equally suitable characteristics and a larger cargo capacity.

Only one was built. It carried 4,500 pounds, approximately half the load of the Go 242.

DFS 331 Technical Data

Crew: Pilot and co-pilot
Weight
    Empty: 5,500 lb
    Cargo: 4,500 lb
    Total with cargo: 10,000 lb
Dimensions
    Wingspan: 71'
    Wing area: 646 square feet
    Fuselage length: 51.9'
Cargo compartment
    Length: 20'
    Width: 8.3'
    Height: 5.3'
Payload: 18 fully equipped soldiers or 4,500 pounds of cargo
Flight performance: 168 mph (maximum).

Go 345

Two models of the Go 345 were produced by the *Gothaer Waggonfabrik.*

The Go 345A, built in 1944, was a high-wing monoplane assault glider with a high-set braced tail. Both wings and tail fins had trim tabs. The landing gear was a semi-detachable tricycle gear of simple design. It could be loaded through detachable side doors. The design also permitted rapid exit of troops. The frame was made of steel tubing and covered with plywood.

The Go 345A carried a pilot and co-pilot, side by side, and had dual controls. Two Argus-pulse thrusters could be attached, one under each wing; these were designed to be started after the towline was dropped, when the glider had reached its destination, to give the pilot more flight range and thus more options in the choice of landing sites. They also helped him to avoid hostile fire.

A second model, the Go 345B, was built to carry cargo. Instead of side doors, it had a short nose which, along with the pilot compartment in it, could be swung up to permit loading. Wheels were used instead of skids. Neither glider was produced in quantity.

Go 345A Technical Data

Crew: Pilot and co-pilot
Weight
    Empty: 5,450 lb
    Cargo: 3,500 lb
    Total with cargo: 8,950 lb
Dimensions
    Wingspan: 67'
    Wing area: 537 square feet
    Fuselage height: 15.5'
    Fuselage length: 41.3'
Cargo compartment
    Length: 13'
    Width: 4.3'
    Height: 5.1'
Payload: 12 fully equipped soldiers.

Ka 430

This glider was the result of one of the more ambitious tactical designs. It was developed in the summer of 1944 under the auspices of Albert Kalkert, technical director of the Reporaturwerke in Erfurt, in conjunction with the Gotha design bureau. It was to have been mass-produced during the winter of 1944–45. Subsequent developments in the war made this impossible.

The Ka 430 was both an assault and transport glider. It was a high-performance aircraft, specially constructed for towing speeds up to 220 miles per hour. It was towable by almost any aircraft, including the Bf 109 and the FW 190, and had provision for the use of the *Starrschlepp*, a non-flexible towing bar, by which it was attached to the tow plane, or of a "V" tow cable, attached to the forward wing surfaces on either side of the fuselage.

The glider had a composite wood and metal frame construction. It had a tricycle landing gear for landings in prepared areas. If a landing in rugged terrain or an unprepared landing zone was anticipated, this could be dropped and the glider could land on skids. There was a parachute brake as well as rocket deceleration devices.

Loading could be carried out from the rear on a ramp formed by dropping a rear portion hinged to the glider. One side of the fuselage had detachable panels that could be taken off for loading or rapid unloading. The glider could carry twelve glidermen. A later modification introduced floor hatchways through which six *Fallschirmjäger* at a time could drop to the ground on a cylindrical platform shaped like a top. The *Fallschirmjäger* sat in seats around the platform, facing inward, attached to their seats by safety belts. The platform was attached to a chute. This concept was never tested, however.

The glider was armed with a machine gun mounted to a manually operated gun turret, which protruded forward from the top of the cockpit. It also had an armor-plated cockpit floor to protect the pilots.

A total of twelve Ka 430's were manufactured.

Ka 430 Technical Data
Crew: Pilot and co-pilot
Weight
    Empty: 3,750 lb
    Cargo: 3,750 lb
    Total with cargo: 7,500 lb
Dimensions
    Wingspan: 64'
    Wing area: 435 square feet
    Fuselage height: 15'
    Fuselage length: 44'
Cargo compartment
    Length: 12'
    Width: 5.6'
    Height: 5.3'
Payload: 12 fully equipped soldiers (*Fallschirmjäger* or glidermen) or cargo
Armament: One machine gun
Tow planes: Bf 109, FW 190 or other, slower aircraft

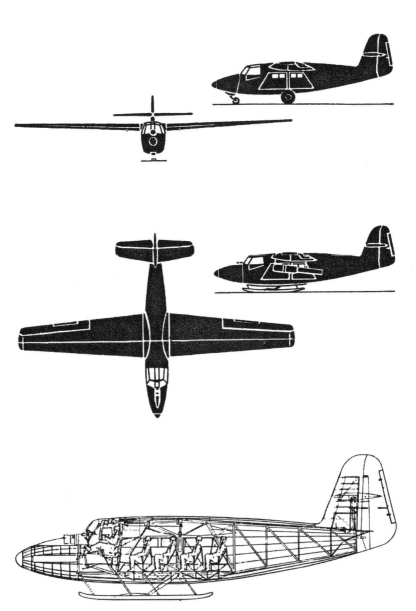

Gotha Go 345A, three-view section and exploded, drawing.

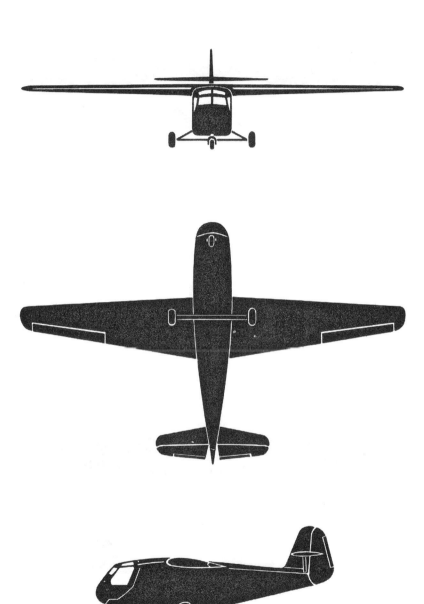

Gotha Go 345B, three-view section.

Gotha-Kalkert Ka 430.

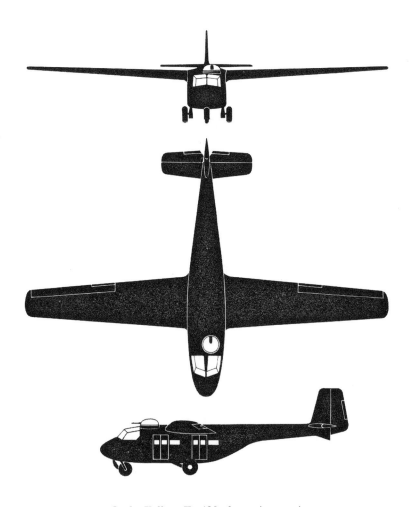

Gotha-Kalkert Ka 430, three-view section.

BV 40

As World War II progressed, Allied bombers became more difficult for the *Luftwaffe* to cope with. German officers frantically searched for a method to counter the tightly knit U.S. B-17 formations flying almost untouched by German fighters. Dr. Richard Vogt, chief designer and technical director of *Blohm und Voss*, proposed the idea to the Air Ministry of an unpowered glider—a "glide-fighter"—to intercept them. The idea was that a fighter would tow the interceptor to a height well above the bomber formations and release it when bombers came within glider range, letting the glider swoop into the Allied bombers. Its head-on attack would be so fast that it would be invisible to a bomber's gunner, until the glider pilot had fired his 30-mm cannon and had vanished.

The Reich Air Ministry thought Dr. Vogt's proposal worth exploring, and *Blohm und Voss* was given an order for the BV 40, which was to become the world's only interceptor glider.

It was a remarkably small glider with a wingspan of 25.96 feet and a length of 18.7 feet. The pilot was positioned prone on padded mats, his chin resting on a short padded post, in a compartment of welded sheet steel armor plate, the front panel more than 20 millimeters thick. The windshield was made of 120-mm non-fragmenting glass. Two steel panels could be slid forward overhead to give additional protection. The armament consisted of two 30-mm MK 108 cannon.

The glider was towed by a Bf 109G. It took off on a two-wheeled trolley, the trolley being jettisoned as soon as the craft was airborne. It landed on skids. It was flight tested in late May 1944. Several models were produced over the next several months.

There were many different concepts for the glider's usage. Pulsejets and rockets for emergency thrust were considered. It was suggested that it might carry small bombs to be dropped on enemy formations, be made into a towed fuel tank or be used as a bomb-glider, releasable from the wing of a large bomber.

Tests showed it could dive at speeds of 292 miles per hour, and it was felt that a 560 mile-per-hour speed could be attainable. Nineteen prototypes were produced.

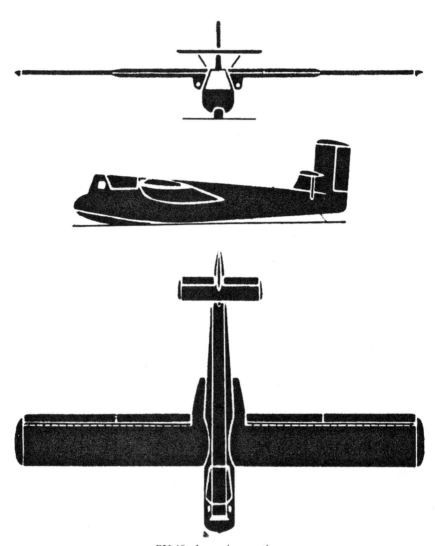

BV 40, three-view section.

BV 40 Technical Data
Crew: Pilot
Weight
    Empty: 1,844 lb
    Cargo: 250 lb
    Total with cargo: 2,094 lb
Dimensions
    Wingspan: 25.96'
    Wing area: 93.6 square feet
    Fuselage length: 18.7'

Armament: Two 30-mm MK 108
    cannon
Flight performance: 560 mph
Tow planes: Bf 109 G or FW 190

The BV 40 interceptor glider. The pilot flew in the prone position.

The small size of the BV 40 is evident in this photograph.

OTHER DEVELOPMENTS

As the Germans continued to use gliders on their many fronts, their experience provided them with a fund of data pointing to technical improvements which would give gliders greater operational effectiveness and pilots a greater margin of safety, thus creating newer and better gliders. Some of the technical innovations got nowhere, excellent though they were. Others were developed, like the V-1 and V-2 powered glide-bombs, which were an outgrowth of the glider.

One of the early German experiments with gliders was known as the *Mistelschlepp*. It consisted of securing a fighter aircraft to the top of a glider, so that the power of the fighter assisted the tow plane in lifting both into the air. The combination flew successfully many times. The Germans saw a way of getting gliders to targets quickly by means of this method; once released, the fighter would stand by overhead to provide protective cover. Designs were also on the board for an explosive-laden glider as a missile, guided by radio to its target by the pilot of the fighter. Why this combination was not further exploited is not fully known. It is reported reliably that it had a long history, having been seen in flight over Czechoslovakia after the Germans seized that country but before World War II started.

Rockets were also extensively used to give gliders their own propulsion, thereby helping the tow plane get the glider into the air. Rocket-assisted take-offs were common practice with all models of gliders used in combat in the latter stages of the war. Rockets were also used for braking gliders when they made their landings. The Germans were the first to have a parachute brake, a deployable parachute at the end of the fuselage that the pilot could activate to allow him to bring his glider into a small or constricted landing area.

To give gliders greater maneuverability and to extend their gliding range once released from tow planes near their targets, the Argus impulse thruster was available, but it was never extensively used.

As a result of the problem that confronted the *Luftwaffe* in providing fighter escort for long-range bombers, a series of experiments started in 1940 with aircraft tow combinations intended to increase the operational range of the fighters. The towed glider carried fuel for the fighter. This was the starting point of a number of tests on towing possibilities, which led to the *Starrschlepp*, the non-flexible tow-bar. It consisted of a metal rod from one to ten meters in length with a ball-and-socket joint at both ends. It was wired internally or externally between tug and glider for intercommunication. The bar was releasable by either the towing aircraft or the glider. By using this system, the disadvantage of blind glider flying was reduced, the strain of night flying was eased and intercommunication was made superior to that of any other system of tow. The *Starrschlepp* failed to be exploited more because each Ju 52 used with it required modification for its installation. The rapidly changing war situation made the demand for these aircraft so great that time for making the alterations could not be afforded. Nonetheless, the *Starrschlepp* was extensively used for towing at night in the latter part of the war when Allied control of the airspace over Germany during daylight hours made it suicidal to use gliders in daylight missions.

Through its intelligence, the *Luftwaffe* learned of the system of glider pick-up used by the U.S. and conducted considerable research to develop such a system, but it was unsuccessful.

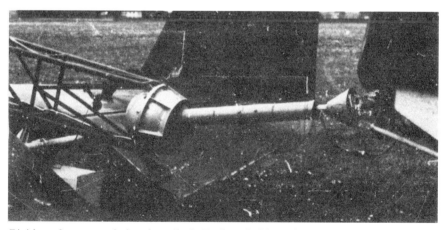

Rigid tow bar appended to the tail of a Junkers Ju 52 used primarily in rigid-tow flight with the DFS 230.

A close-up of the glider-to-tow-plane coupling mechanism.

The rigid-tow combination in flight with a He 111 towing a DFS 230.

CHAPTER 3

The British Glider Effort

When the British realized that the road to Dunkirk had begun with the crushing defeat at Eben Emael in Belgium by a small German gliderborne force, they quickly took stock of their airborne doctrine and resources. Not surprisingly, their strategy was completely devoid of any reference to the use of airborne forces, and there was absolutely no aircraft designed for dropping paratroopers. The British oversight before Dunkirk had been so flagrant that the term "transport glider" had not even been coined.

Winston Churchill got the matter off dead center in his characteristic way, by ordering the creation of a 5,000-man airborne force. This order led to a glider-construction program since the British did not have enough powered aircraft to carry 5,000 paratroopers. Some of the lift had to come from another source, and obviously this source had to be the glider.

The amount of airborne lift Britain had mustered some three years later was phenomenal. Glider production in Britain—until then practically nonexistent—was one of the extraordinary achievements of British industry, calling for prodigious efforts at all levels. In its glider production effort during World War II, British industry showed itself at its best and produced in quality and quantity, under great hardships and handicaps, what no other nation could hope to exceed.

HADRIAN

The British Hadrian glider was actually the U.S. Army Air Corps' Waco CG-4A, described in detail under the heading of U.S. gliders. While pilots of the British Glider Pilot Regiment generally preferred to fly the Horsa, the Hadrian proved a valuable adjunct to British transport glider resources. From the British standpoint, the Hadrian was definitely considered to be primarily a troop-transport glider. Trucks and artillery would be transported in the Horsa or the Hamilcar. The Royal Air Force procured 740 CG-4A's from the United States, and these were given the name Hadrian.

HAMILCAR

The Hamilcar was the largest glider built by the Allies, a true monster of an aircraft and a daring gamble. It prompted Colonel Frederick R. Dent, chief of the U.S. Army Air Corps' glider procurement program to remark while

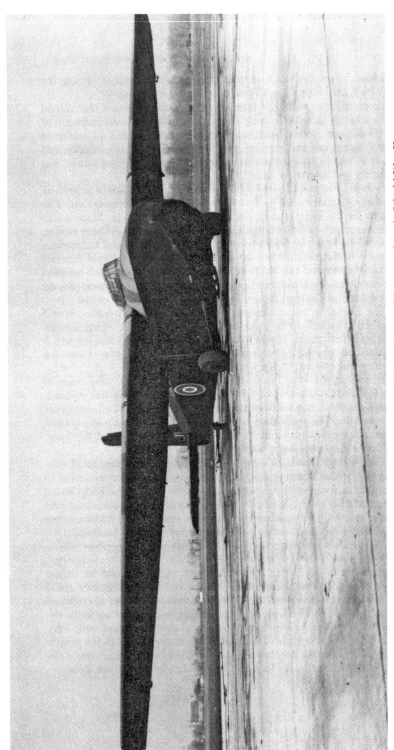

The Hamilcar, the largest all-wood production glider to be used in operations in World War II.

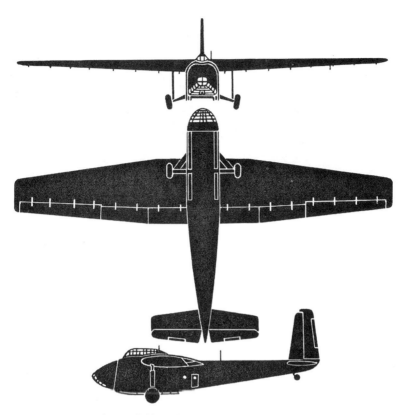

General Aircraft Hamilcar, three-view section.

Hamilcar Technical Data

Crew: Pilot and co-pilot

Weight
    Empty: 19,000 lb
    Cargo: 17,000 lb
    Total with cargo: 36,000 lb

Dimensions
    Wingspan: 110'
    Wing area: 1,657 square feet
    Height: 20.3'
    Fuselage length: 68.5'

Cargo compartment
    Length: 25.5'
    Width: 8'
    Height: 7.5'

Payload: One Tetrach Mark IV tank or one Locust tank or two armored cars or forty fully equipped men or equivalent.

Towing speed: 150 mph

Maximum airspeed: 187 mph

Aspect ratio: 11.5

Tow planes: Halifax, Lancaster and Stirling bombers

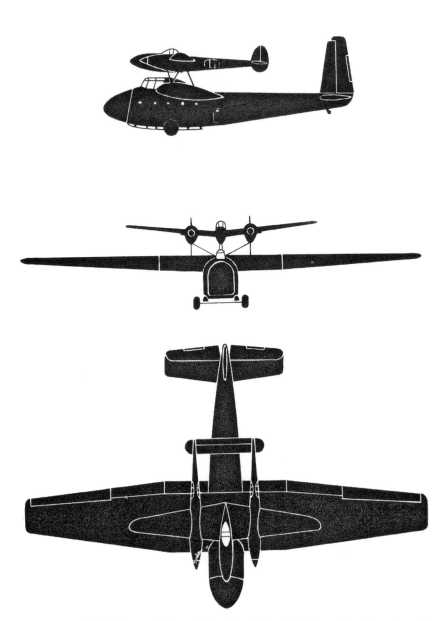

The concept of P-38/General Aircraft Hamilcar "piggy-back" combination, three-view section.

visiting British glider activities: "It was the biggest hunk of airplane I have ever seen put together!"

In deciding to build the Hamilcar, the British reasoned that upon commitment of large airborne forces, such a glider would be needed to transport tanks, large guns and vehicles and huge amounts of ammunition and other stores to give the airborne forces not only holding power, but a strong and aggressive punch.

General Aircraft Limited designed and built the Hamilcar at their Railway Carriage and Wagon Company plant in Birmingham. The design for the glider was finally approved in early 1941. Since it was considered advisable to design and construct a half-scale flying model, a team of a 100 draftsmen and 20 engineers and technicians jumped to the task, backed up by the facilities of the Royal Aircraft Establishment and the National Physical Laboratory, which handled the development of structural and wind-tunnel data. The model proved successful, and General Aircraft soon built the full-scale glider.

The Hamilcar was the largest wooden aircraft built during World War II. To carry the weights it had to lift with structural and aerodynamic efficiency, it was necessary to select a wing loading much greater than anything previously contemplated for a glider. This wing loading came to 21.7 pounds per square foot.

It was a high-wing, cantilever monoplane with a wingspan of 110 feet and a wing area of 1,657 square feet. The wing was of wood, with a center section and two tapering outer sections. The inner structure had two box spars with laminated plywood booms and plywood webs, augmented with ribs. A thin plywood sheet covered the wing, and there was a fabric cover over it.

The wooden fuselage was rectangular in shape and constructed in two separate main sections, which could be separated to facilitate its transport by ground to assembly points. The body was constructed to enable its plywood surface to carry a substantial part of the stresses developed from whatever source. The bulbous nose was hinged on the starboard side and swung open for loading.

The decision to design the craft as a high-wing monoplane with a nose-opening door was made to ensure that armored tracked vehicles could be driven straight out without the need for special ramps when the aircraft was lowered onto its skids. As a result, the vehicles could be in action in as little as fifteen seconds after the aircraft had come to rest. To speed its exit, the vehicle was started up while the glider was still in the air. The vehicle's exhaust pipes had temporary extensions to the outside of the glider; these disengaged as the vehicle moved forward. As the forward motion continued, a mechanical device freed the nose-door lock and automatically opened the door.

Although the craft was initially constructed with wheels that could be dropped, leaving it to land on skids, the technique was changed to keep the

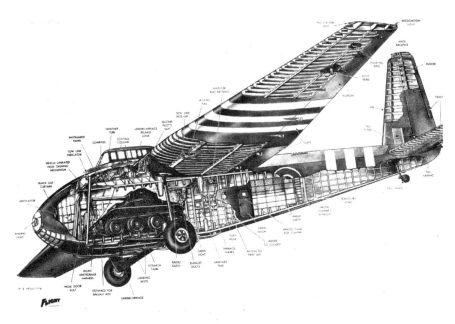

A General Aircraft Hamilcar transporting a Tetrarch light tank, exploded drawing.

Loading a Locust light tank into a General Aircraft Hamilcar.

wheels for landing. This allowed pilots to taxi some distance to get clear of landing strips. When the glider came to rest, the high oil pressure in the chassis shock-absorber struts was released, causing them to telescope and permitting the glider to sink onto its skids so that the vehicle inside could drive out.

Two pilots, each with controls, sat in tandem in splendid isolation in the cockpit. A bulletproof windshield protected them from the front and sides, while armor plating protected them from the rear. They had telephone communication with the crews of vehicles below and the pilot of the towing aircraft.

The Hamilcar could carry the following loads: one Tetrarch Mark IV or a Locust armored fighting vehicle; two Bren gun universal carriers; two armored scout cars; one 25-pound gun with prime mover; or similar payloads.

Because of its "all-up" weight of 36,000 pounds, it needed an enormously powerful aircraft to tow it. During early tests, a Halifax with souped-up engines was used. Later, as the Halifax bomber was modified to increase its engine power, a standard Halifax became the tug for the Hamilcar, although the Lancaster and Stirling four-engined bombers were also used on occasion.

The first full-size prototype flew on 27 March, 1942. During the course of the war, 412 Hamilcars were built. They saw yeoman service in Normandy, along the Wesel and at Arnhem.

One Hamilcar was procured by the U.S. for test and evaluation at its Air Force Materiel Command at Wright Army Air Force Field near Dayton, Ohio. Design studies were made to determine the feasibility of operating the Hamilcar in a "piggy back" system, using the P-38 fighter.

A later British development was the Hamilcar X, which was a two-engined powered Hamilcar. It proved a very successful aircraft.

HENGIST

The Hengist was designed and built by Slingsby Sailplanes. It was designed to carry fifteen fully equipped soldiers. The Ministry of Aircraft Production placed the order at a time when the feasibility of constructing and producing anything as large as a twenty-five-place glider in quantity was in doubt.

Slingsby delivered the first model in the latter part of 1942 to the Airborne Forces Experimental Establishment at Sherburn-in-Elmet in Yorkshire, near Leeds. As described by Lawrence Wright in *Wooden Wings*, it was "a pretty aircraft, high-winged, slab-sided, obviously from the Slingsby stable."

It incorporated some unique technical innovations. Made of wood throughout, except for some fittings, it had a wingspan of 80 feet, and a length of 56.6 feet. The wings had flaps along the trailing edges and spoilers. The flaps were actuated by opening a scoop on the under surface of the wing. This drove air into the bellows within the flaps, forcing them to open downward. The flaps were raised while in flight by closing the scoop and opening a vent in the upper surface of the wing. This induced suction which, along with pressure of the air on the underside of the flaps, caused them to close. Lift spoilers were manually operated by lever from the cockpit, which caused the spoilers to open out from the upper surfaces of the wings.

The undercarriage had brakes and could be jettisoned, after which the glider landed on a pneumatic skid running the length of the cabin and on a small pneumatic skid at the tail. No flight test was conducted using the skids, however. The pilot and co-pilot had a full system of dual controls for flaps, spoilers and wheel brakes between their seats, as well as an elevator wheel, which was also between the seats.

Tests showed that in towed flight, control was good, though a slight stiffness in the ailerons was reported. The glider flew comfortably with the rudder free and with the pilot using only one hand. It also performed well in free flight, with no tendency to snatch, oscillate or take charge. The flaps were very effective, but test pilots reported fluttering at all free-flight speeds and some tail heaviness when flaps had been activated.

Slingsby built eighteen Hengists. One was soon to be written off, when a rigger omitted a wing-root pin, and the glider shed a wing near Dishforth. Fortunately, the pilot, John Nielan, survived, although he had to spend several months in a hospital.

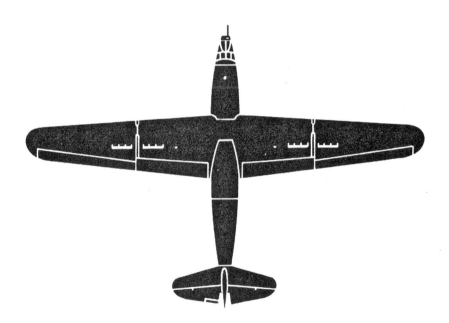

Slingsby Hengist Technical Data
Crew: Pilot and co-pilot
Weight
    Empty: 4,666 lb
    Cargo: 3,667 lb
    Total with cargo: 8,333 lb

Dimensions
    Wingspan: 80'
    Wing area: 780 square feet
    Fuselage length: 56.6'
Payload: 15 fully equipped soldiers
Towing speed: 160 mph
Aspect ratio: 8.21

Slingsby Hengist.

The Slingsby Hengist glider in flight.

HORSA (MARK I AND II)

Without a doubt, the Horsa was the most ungainly looking glider ever produced and the ugly duckling of all World War II gliders. It prompted the remark that the inside of its long fuselage looked like a section of the London Underground in miniature.

Intent on conserving critical metals as well as drawing upon woodworking industries not yet heavily involved in wartime production, the Air Ministry called for the glider to be of wooden construction in specifications issued to the Airspeed Aviation Company in December 1940. So well did the design team headed by Hessell Tiltman comply, that H. A. Taylor, in *Airspeed Aircraft since 1931*, was prompted to say it "must have been the most wooden aircraft ever built. Even the controls in the cockpit were masterpieces of the woodworker's skill."

According to Taylor, Tiltman carried out his design efforts at the de Havilland Technical School at Hatfield and, later, at Salisbury Hall, London Colney, after he had been bombed out of the technical schools. Airspeed assembled the first two prototypes at the Great West Road airfield, now part of Heathrow Airport. Five more were built at Airspeed's Portsmouth works, and they went on to build 700 production models there. By 10 September 1941, only nine months after the specification was issued, G. B. S. Errington test-flew the first Horsa at the Great West Road aerodrome.

Airspeed built two Horsa models, the Mark I and the Mark II.

They were similar in external appearance. The Horsa was a high-wing monoplane with a large Plexiglas nose and a tricycle landing gear that could be jettisoned. The Mark I had a wing span of 88 feet and fuselage length of 67 feet. To the top of the fin, it stood 19.5 feet high. The fuselage was circular in cross-section, its plywood skin attached to stout circular wooden ribs. Light wooden benches ran down each side, with a three-seat bench across the rear.

The Mark I was originally conceived as a paratrooper transport to drop paratroopers over target while under tow and then be towed back to friendly territory to land. For the use of paratroopers, it had two passenger doors, one on either side of the fuselage, which were widely separated for simultaneous exits and were designed to be slid upward to enable paratroopers to jump out or fire guns at attacking aircraft. Other firing points were an aperture in the roof aft of the main spar and a trap door in the tail. The firing points, however, were never used in action. The parachutist's static line was attached to a short rail just over each parachute door; the paratrooper would hook his line to this rail on approaching the door just before making his exit. Supporting arms and supplies were to be dropped in containers.

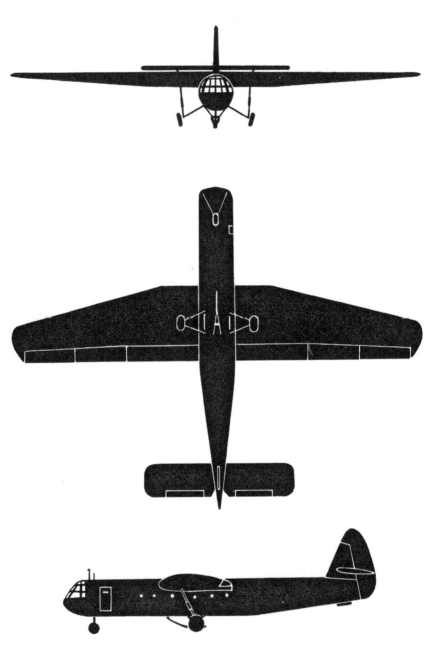

Airspeed Horsa, three-view section.

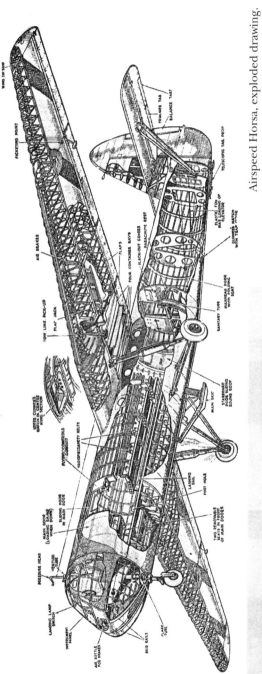

WING TIP SKID

PICKETING POINT

AIR BRAKES

FLAPS

FOUR CONTAINER BAYS

BLACK-OUT COVERS

PARACHUTE SEAT

TRIMMER TAB

BALANCE TAB

TELESCOPIC TAIL PROP

PLASTIC FOR PILOT LOADING OF ELEVATOR

GUNNER'S PATCH WITH TEAR MODE

TOW LINE PICK-UP

FLAP JACK

SANITARY TUBE

BULKHEAD DOOR WITH FOLDING SEAT

UPPER GUNNER'S MANOEUVRING FLYING SECTION

FLYING CONTROLS CONDUIT

SEATS/SAFETY BELTS

STARBOARD DOOR SLIDING SOUND ROOF

MAIN SKID

MAIN DOOR (LOADING RAMP WHEN DOWN)

SLIDING DOOR IN MAIN DOOR

LASHING RAIL

POST HOLE

TWO REMOVABLE SEATS IN FRONT OF MAIN DOORS

PRESSURE HEAD

VENT TUBE

LANDING LAMP SWITCH

INSTRUMENT PANEL

AIR BOTTLE FOR BRAKES

SKID RAILS

FLARE TUBE

Airspeed Horsa, exploded drawing.

An Airspeed Horsa with
U.S. markings in flight.

The Mark I also had a rectangular loading door in the port side just aft of the nose. This measured 7.8 by 5 feet and was hinged at the bottom edge so that it could be lowered and used as an unloading ramp. The ramp was rarely used for loading because of its rather steep angle to the interior of the glider and also because it might be damaged in loading and thus ground the glider. For loading vehicles, troops could use ramps in lieu of the door. They were each 11.8 feet long.

Originally, the only vehicles carried with the glidermen were motorcycles, although jeeps could be loaded with difficulty. With the necessity of maneuvering heavy equipment such as a jeep around the corner of the cargo door, loading time proved excessively long and means were sought to reduce it. Airspeed carried out experiments in early 1944 to remove the tail by means of a band of demolitions placed along the rib at the end of the cargo compartment. On landing, a designated soldier blew off the rear of the Horsa; the ramps were then placed from the floor of the rear of the compartment to the ground and vehicles were driven out of the rear of the glider. Although a drastic solution, it worked successfully, and this "surcingle," as it was termed, was used in the Normandy landings. In the meantime, the RAF devised a means of making the tail a separate unit, bolted to the main fuselage by eight bolts with ingenious quick-release nuts. As standard equipment, Horsas carried powerful wire cutters. When the tail came off to unload equipment in combat, one of the pilots or an airborne trooper had the responsibility of cutting the glider control cables leading to the empennage control surfaces with the wire cutters. Airspeed modified many Horsas before the Normandy invasion with the quick-release nut system, but the "surcingles" were still carried in those gliders for emergency use. The Mark I's without the later modification were termed "white" Horsas, while those with it were "red" Horsas.

The Mark II Horsa was designed to resolve the inconvenient problems of loading and unloading heavy equipment inherent in the Mark I. It had a hinged nose that could be swung open to enable the loading of jeeps and other heavy equipment. It was realized that the nose of a glider is particularly vulnerable in a combat landing to damage that might jam the nose door and prevent it from opening or otherwise prevent unloading from the front of the cargo compartment. Correspondingly, the rear unloading system of the "red" Horsas was built into the Mark II's, which became known as "blue" Horsas.

The Mark II carried twenty-eight fully armed soldiers and a pilot and co-pilot. In lieu of an equivalent weight of men, it could transport two jeeps, a 75-mm howitzer and a one-ton truck, or an assortment of other gear or ammunition weighing up to 7,380 lb. The Mark I carried 250 pounds less.

The Mark II was towed using a "Y" tow rope with the top ends of the Y hitched on the forward edge of each wing; the rope for the Mark I hitched

The components of an Airspeed Horsa.

just forward of the nose wheel. The normal flying position of the Horsa was immediately behind and slightly higher than the tug plane.

In early models, a telephone system provided a means for the tug pilot and the glider pilot to talk to each other. Telephone conversation terminated when the glider cut away from the aircraft, to the disadvantage of the glider pilot. Later in the war, the RAF had radios placed in all Horsas, enabling aircraft pilots and glider pilots to communicate with each other even after the glider had landed.

Despite its ponderous appearance, the Horsa performed well. It towed at a maximum speed of 160 miles per hour. Extra large "barn-door" flaps permitted a steep angle of descent. At the same time, they throttled the speed build-up during glider descent. The Horsa landed on concrete runways or ploughed fields with almost equal ease. When pilots used the enormous flaps and the pneumatic wheel brakes, the ungainly craft could be brought successfully into surprisingly small fields.

In addition to the Mark I and II, Airspeed built a Horsa bomber and a powered Horsa for experimental purposes. The former had a bomb bay built to carry either 2,000, 4,000 or 8,000 lb bombs. The powered glider was fitted with two 375-horsepower Armstrong-Siddeley Cheetah X radial engines. A much larger model of the Horsa was also built, but it remained in the experimental class with the bomber and powered versions.

Horsas carried British and American airborne forces into Norway, Sicily, Normandy, Arnhem, Yugoslavia and across the Rhine at Wesel. They also served in Palestine, and numbers of them were shipped to India and Canada.

Horsa Mark II Technical Data
Crew: Pilot and co-pilot
Weight
    Empty: 8,370 lb
    Cargo: 7,380 lb
    Total with cargo: 15,750 lb
Dimensions
    Wingspan: 88'
    Wing area: 1,104 square feet
    Height: 20.3'
    Fuselage length: 68'
Cargo compartment
    Length: 34'
    Width: 7.5'
    Height: 10.5'

Payload: 28 fully equipped soldiers or 2 one-ton trucks (Jeeps) or 1 U.S. 75-
   mm howitzer with prime mover (jeep), ammunition and crew.
Towing speed: 160 mph (100 mph with flaps)
Stalling speed: Flaps up 58 mph, flaps down 48 mph
Aspect ratio: 7.2
Tow planes: Albemarle, Halifax or C-47

Some General Aircraft Horsas had cordite explosive between the tail and main fuselage sections. After landing (and after passengers were clear of the the glider), the
cordiate as exploded to sever the sections and enable the rapid unloading of equipment through the opening created. This photo was taken after the D-Day landings.

HOTSPUR (MARK I, II AND ILL)

The Hotspur was the first transport glider produced by the Allies. From a design standpoint, it was a graceful craft that was the stepping stone from the frail, swallow-like sailplane to the enormous transport gliders that were soon to be on the drawing boards. As a matter of fact, it retained enough of the characteristics of the sailplane to indicate that the aircraft industry had not yet grasped the concept of what form a transport glider should take or just how to attain the objective of carrying tons of equipment on glider wing.

The original concept was for an eight-seater glider with a very long landing approach and a glide angle not steeper than 1:24. The craft was to be used for one flight only; in other words, to be completely expendable.

The General Aircraft Company got the requirements for the glider in June 1940. Surprisingly, General was able to produce the first aircraft in little more than four months, and the first flight took place on 5 November 1940.

The Hotspur Mark I had a wing span of sixty-two feet. The top of the fuselage could be detached and cast off by the troops inside to allow them to jump over the sides of the boat-shaped bottom half.

The Mark II was a pronounced departure in design from the Mark I. This change came for two reasons. First, it was determined that the glider should be used to drop paratroopers. Secondly, tow craft were to take the glider right into the landing zone at low altitude, so the glider would need a steep, fast approach to land.

As a result, the Mark II had a reduced wingspan measuring forty-six feet—sixteen feet shorter than the Mark I. This raised strength factors by 50 percent and permitted a 20 percent increase in the gliding angle. Doors were introduced to enable paratroopers to jump from the glider.

A third Hotspur, the Mark III, was designed for training. The main difference between the Mark II and III was that the former was towed from the keel and had an unbraced tailplane, whereas the latter was towed from the nose and had a braced tailplane.

The Hotspur models were mid-wing cantilever monoplanes. They had an oval fuselage of wooden structure with a stressed plywood skin. Pilots sat in tandem, each at his controls. There were two cabins, one fore and one aft of the wing structure, each with its own access door. Access to the pilot's compartment was by a hinged canopy. The wheels could be jettisoned.

Eighteen Mark I's were built and 997 Mark II's. Fifty Mark I's were converted into Mark III's. Although extensively used for training by the Glider Pilot Regiment, Hotspurs were never used in combat.

Hotspur Mark II Technical Data
Crew: Pilot and co-pilot
Weight
     Empty: 1,755 lb
     Cargo: 1,880 lb
     Total with cargo: 3,635 lb
Dimensions
     Wingspan: 45.9'
     Wing area: 272 square feet
     Height: 10.8'
     Fuselage length: 39.7'
Payload: Seven fully equipped soldiers
Tow planes: Hawker Hector or Auda

TWIN HOTSPUR

This glider was conceived as a method for lifting greater loads, using components of the Hotspur. It consisted of two Hotspur fuselages, secured to each other by a special centre section. It was an innovative design and more than doubled the effective cargo capacity of the Hotspur. It could carry the pilot, co-pilot and fourteen glidermen, eight in each fuselage. The pilots were in the port fuselage, from which they controlled the glider.

The Twin had a wingspan of 58 feet, a length of 39.7 feet and a height of 10.5 feet. The wing area was 262 square feet. It weighed 3,025 pounds empty and carried 3,525 pounds. It was towed at 150 mph.

Although it transported considerably more than the original Hotspur, this glider was soon discarded, since it had some of the Hotspur's disadvantages: difficulty in getting out when the glider landed and less than desirable cargo capacity. Although the cargo capacity had been increased in the Twin, motorcycles and light trucks could not be loaded even if they met weight limitations, because of the design of the glider.

Only one was built.

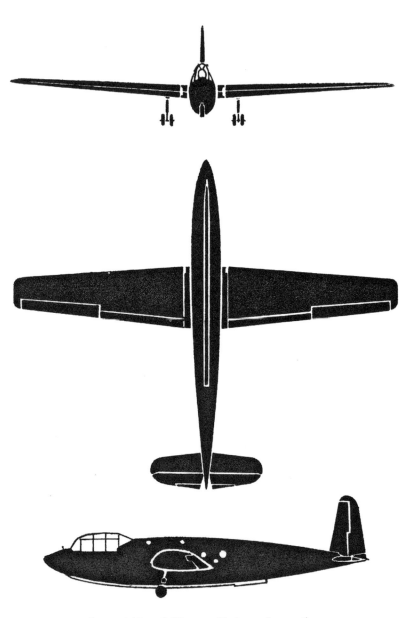

General Aircraft Hotspur II, three-view section.

General Aircraft Hotspur about to land.

Troops loading into a General Aircraft Hotspur.

Interior of a General Aircraft Hotspur looking aft.

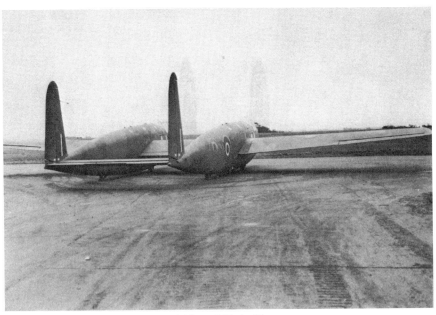

General Aircraft Twin Hotspur.

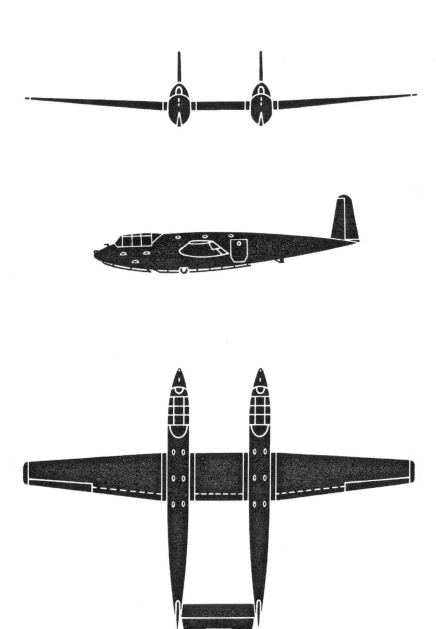

General Aircraft Twin Hotspur, three-view section.

CHAPTER 4

Japanese Transport Gliders

During the Sino-Japanese War in 1937, the Japanese ordered three test gliders built: the Tachikawa Ki-23 and Ki-25 and the Fukada Ki-24. The Ki-23 was a single-place glider, the others were two-place models. The Fukada proved an excellent glider and was produced in a civilian version as the Hikara-6-I.

When World War II started, news filtered through to Japan that transport gliders had been used by the Germans in their invasion of the West. Based on this information and their experience with the Ki-series gliders, the Army launched a transport glider program. Work on the first glider began in June 1940, one month after the German glider assault on Fort Eben Emael in Belgium.

The Army designated its series Ku from the word *kakku* ("to glide"). The Japanese Navy, in a parallel action, launched a glider development program of its own.

Ku-1

The first Japanese glider to be built was the Ku-1. Professor Hiroshi Sato of the Imperial University's engineering school of Kyushu designed the glider, and the Maeda Aircraft Corporation manufactured it.

The first model was a shoulder-wing, twin-boom, twin-fin glider with a wing-span of more than fifty-five feet. Maeda completed it in the summer of 1941 and tested it at the Tachiarai military airfield in Kyushu on 1 September 1941.

The Army soon accepted it. It carried six to eight fully equipped soldiers and a pilot.

The Ku-1 was succeeded in the series by the Ku-2, with the major modification being that the new glider had a transparent nose, a single boom and a longer fuselage. It did not go into production.

The final development in the series was the Ku-3, a model whose fuselage resembled a wing cross-section. The wing was tapered and had spoilers. It could seat eight men in the absence of other cargo. It also did not go into production.

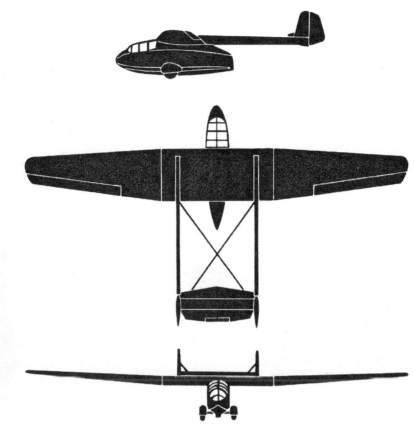

Maeda Ku-1-I, first Japanese transport glider, three-view section.

Ku-1 Technical Data
Crew: Pilot and co-pilot
Weight
    Empty: 1,540 lb
    Cargo: 1,320 lb
    Total with cargo: 2,860 lb
Dimensions
    Wingspan: 55'
    Wing area: 324 square feet
    Fuselage length: 32'

Payload: 8 fully equipped soldiers
Towing speed: 80 mph (110 mph maximum airspeed)
Aspect ratio: 9.7
Tow planes: Mitsubishi Ki-51 (Sonia) or Ki-30

Maeda Ku-1-I

Ku-1-I.

As larger gliders were produced, the Ku-1 was relegated to training use. Approximately 100 were produced.

Ku-6

After the Ku-1 series, the Maeda Aircraft Corporation produced the Ku-6, one of the most interesting concepts in aircraft created by any nation during World War II. The Aeronautical Institute of the Imperial University in Tokyo did the actual design for Maeda. They designed it to the requirements set forth by the Army's Troop Transport Command.

The Army needed a quick means to move armored fighting vehicles long distances over the main islands of Japan to resist seaborne invasion. It conceived the idea that this could be done by equipping the vehicle with wings, empennage, and take-off carriage. Once landed, the items needed to make the vehicle airborne could be rapidly detached to allow it to go into action as a ground vehicle. This is a concept not unlike that ordered by General "Hap" Arnold of the U.S. Army Air Corps.

By late 1939, the Japanese Army Air Force Examination Department initiated Special Tank Project Number 3 that took the code name *Sora-sha* ("air vehicle"). This later became *Kuro-sha* ("black vehicle"). The Aeronautical Institute of the Imperial University in Tokyo designed the glider while *Maeda Koken Kogyo* (Maeda Air Research Industry) constructed the wing and empennage and Mitsubishi built the special tank and major structural components of the fuselage. The *Sora-sha* became the Ku-6, its glider series number.

The total weight of the Ku-6 was 7,712 lb, of which 6,174 lb were attributable to the weight of the light tank. Maeda completed the prototype in January 1945.

Ku-6 Technical Data
Winged Air-Transportable Armored Fighting Vehicle
Crew: Pilot and co-pilot
Weight
    Empty: 1,538 lb
    Cargo: 6,174 lb
    Total with cargo: 7,712 lb
Dimensions
    Wingspan: 72'
    Wing area: 649 square feet
Payload: 1 armored fighting vehicle

Ku-7

The Ku-7, christened the "Buzzard," was also more popularly known as the *Manazuru* ("Flying Crane"). It was the Japanese Army's most noteworthy large-size transport glider. It filled the need for greater tactical and strategic mobility and striking power for army elements by enabling the quick movement of armored fighting vehicles and large numbers of soldiers. Although the doctrinal reasons for launching into the design and construction of this large glider were sound, it never went into mass production as a glider, and there is no record of its having been used in any operation.

The Kyoto branch of the Kokusai Aircraft Company built the glider and the Aviation Research Laboratory of Tokyo University assisted in designing the wing. The wing was tapered and highly efficient aerodynamically. The design was based on the Japanese "B" series wing section and was patterned after the very successful Ki-77 long-range aircraft.

The glider had twin booms, each surmounted by vertical fins and connected by an elevator assembly. The fuselage pointed upward at the rear. In appearance, it was very similar to the Go 242 glider. It had a tricycle landing gear, consisting of a nose wheel and two main wheels on each side placed in tandem.

Undertaken as a project in late 1942, the glider was first tested in August 1944. Standard towing aircraft for this large glider were the Nakajima Ki-49-II ("Helen") or the Mitsubishi Ki-67-I ("Peggy"). Loading was carried out via the rear of the cargo compartment, which had a swinging door made of the rear of the fuselage.

Nine Ku-7's were built; testing was not entirely completed when the war ended. So promising were the glider models, however, that it was decided to produce a powered version of the glider. This became known as the Ki-105. Forty Ki-105's were built and became known as the *Ohtori*.

Ku-7 Technical Data
Crew: Pilot and co-pilot
Weight
    Empty: 10,000 lb
    Cargo: 16,455 lb
    Total with cargo: 26,455 lb
Dimensions
    Wingspan: 114'
    Wing area: 1,288 square feet
    Fuselage length: 64'

Cargo-compartment dimensions
    Length: 17'
    Width: 10'
    Total with cargo: 7'
Payload: 32 fully equipped soldiers or 1 eight-ton tank or a 7.5-mm howitzer
    plus 4-ton prime mover
Towing speed: 125 mph (220 mph maximum airspeed)
Aspect ratio: 10.8
Tow planes: Nakajima Ki-49-II or Mitsubishi Ki-67-1

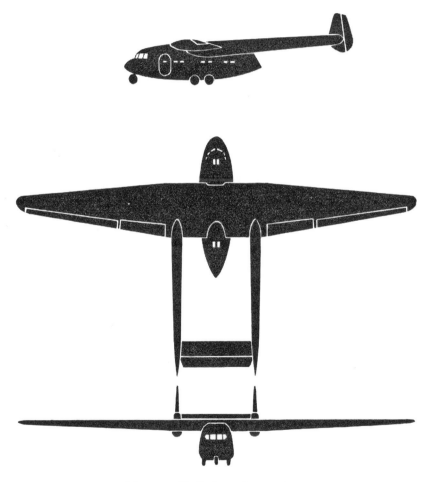

Manazuru Ku-7, three-view section.

Manazuru Ku-7. Note the similarities to the German Gotha Go 242.

Twin-engined Ki-105, a powered Ku-7 glider.

Ku-8

In December 1941, a Ki-59 ("Theresa") transport aircraft was modified to transform it into a glider. The modifications were not extensive. They consisted primarily in removing the two engines, converting the undercarriage into one that could be dropped and adding skids to the bottom of the fuselage. The new aircraft became the Ku-8-I experimental glider. It carried eighteen fully equipped troops. Later, this model was drastically modified to effect an almost complete redesign of the original. The wing shape was changed as well as the fuselage.

In April 1943, this new version entered production as the large-size transport glider, the Ku-8-II ("Gander"). It was built at the Hiratsuka plant of the Kokusai Koku Aircraft Company and accepted after a round trip flight between Fussa and Okinawa in August.

The wing was seventy-six feet long and constructed with two main spars. Plywood covered the wing forward of the lead spar, and the whole wing was covered with fabric. One of the most unconventional features of this glider and one that makes it unique among all aircraft is that its spoilers were separate: four-foot-long wings set a foot above the main wing on either side of the fuselage and along the wings' trailing edge. To reduce lift, the spoilers could be rotated as much as ninety degrees from the horizontal. The fuselage was of welded tubular steel. The nose was of Plexiglas and had no framework structure that would obstruct the pilot's ability to see the tow rope and tow plane.

The glider had dual controls, and a unique arrangement whereby the pilot had a wheel control and the co-pilot a stick. The length of the glider was forty-five feet. It had landing wheels that could be dropped, enabling the glider to land on skids. Tie-down devices were part of the floor structure; vehicles and other gear could be lashed to these devices to prevent them from shifting in flight. The nose of the fuselage opened sideways to permit cargo to be loaded.

The Ku-8-II was towed by a Mitsubishi Ki-21 ("Sally") heavy bomber. In tests, wings began to flutter at speeds greater than 225 miles per hour. Pilots took the view that the glider was a clumsy aircraft and difficult to handle.

However, one reliable report indicates the Japanese Army had 700 Ku-8-II's built. A number of Ku-8-II's were found by American forces at Nichols Field near Manila on the island of Luzon in the Philippines after the Japanese surrendered.

Ku-8 Technical Data
Crew: Pilot and co-pilot
Weight
    Empty: 3,750 lb
    Cargo: 3,950 lb
    Total with cargo: 7,700 lb
Dimensions
    Wingspan: 76'
    Wing area: 544 square feet
    Fuselage length: 45'
Cargo-compartment dimensions
    Length: 10'
    Width: 6.3'
    Total with cargo: 5.6'

Payload: 18 fully equipped soldiers or miscellaneous cargo or 1 small mountain artillery piece
Towing speed: 120 mph (150 mph maximum flight speed)
Tow planes: Mitsubishi-2I-II, Ki-57-II or Ki-67-I

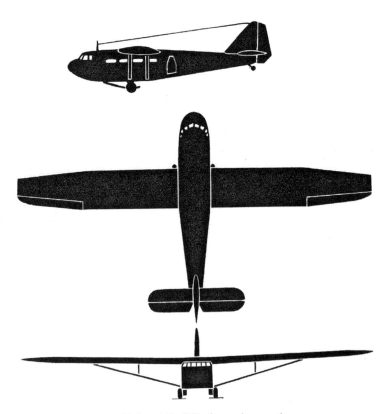

Kokusai Ku-8-II, three-view section.

Kokusai Ku-8-II.

Spoilers of a Kokusai Ku-8-II.

Kokusai Ku-8-II with ramps in position for loading a vehicle or artillery piece.

Nihon Kogata Ku-11.

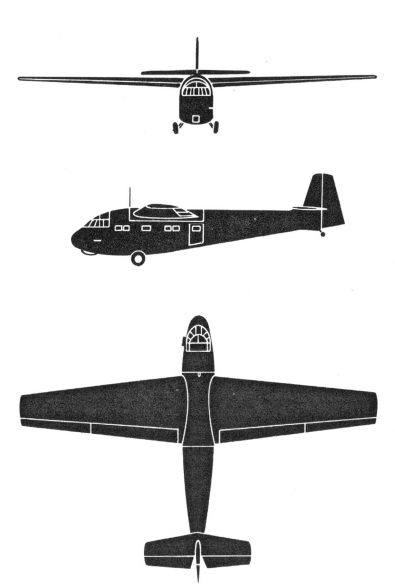

Nihon Kogata Ku-11, three-view section.

Ku-11

There is very little information available about the Ku-11. The Nihon Small Plane Manufacturing Company produced it as an experimental glider, and it became known as the Nihon Kogata Army Experimental Transport Glider Ku-11. Mr. Miyahara designed it.

It was a high-wing transport glider intended for landing personnel at strategic locations to counter enemy invasion efforts. It carried twelve fully equipped troops.

The Ku-11 was to have been built in small subcontracting woodworking shops. It never went into production because the Army was indecisive about its use and suspended further developments.

Ku-11 Technical Data

Crew: Pilot and co-pilot
Weight
    Empty: 2,800 lb
    Cargo: 2,600 lb
    Total with cargo: 5,400 lb
Dimensions
    Wingspan: 60'
    Wing area: 475 square feet
Payload: 12 fully equipped soldiers

MXY-5, MXY-5A

In August 1941, the Japanese Navy ordered its Experimental Aeronautics Board to produce a towed glider transport for airborne forces. The specifications required that it should be manned by a pilot and copilot and carry eleven personnel, that it should be towable by either a Mitsubishi G3M ("Nell") or a G4M ("Betty") bomber and that it should be capable of becoming airborne under tow in a distance of 2,700 feet. Further, either of the tow craft should be able to tow two gliders.

The Japan Aircraft Corporation built the MXY-5, with a Mr. Yamamoto, a civil engineer, as its chief designer. The glider incorporated the most advanced ideas in aircraft design and employed the latest techniques in manufacturing and metallurgy.

The result was an exceptionally fine aircraft. The wing was a high cantilever, with a tapered design 59.4' long. The main wing spar was of duralumin. The wings had flaps and spoilers. The ribs were of wood, and the whole wing was covered with plywood, featuring cloth over the plywood. The fuselage had a tubular steel framework and was also covered with plywood and fabric.

There were dual controls, droppable landing wheels and a single skid running from the nose to midpoint on the bottom of the fuselage. The wheels were retractable and were retracted when the glider was used for training. They could be dropped after take-off when the glider was on an operational mission.

The glider was tested in 1942 at the Kasumiga-Ura Air Base, a naval training center northeast of Tokyo, where it successfully passed all tests. Between 1942 and July 1945, the Navy had nine MXY-5's and three MXY-5a's built. The glider was never used operationally.

MXY-5 and MXY-5a Technical Data
Crew: Pilot and co-pilot
Weight
    Empty: 3,530 lb
    Cargo: 2,240 lb
    Total with cargo: 5,940 lb
Dimensions
    Wingspan: 59.4'
    Wing area: 475 square feet
    Fuselage length: 43'
Payload: 11 fully equipped soldiers or 2,240 lb of cargo
Tow planes: Mitsubishi G3M or G4M

Japanese Navy Kugisho MXY-5.

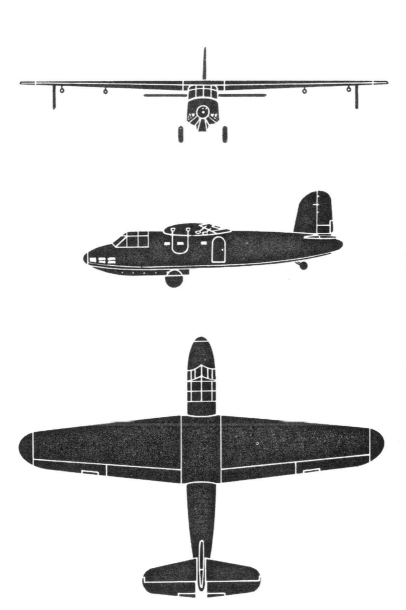

Japanese Navy Kugisho MXY-5, three-view section.

CHAPTER 5

The United States Glider Program

In February 1941, the U.S. Army Air Corps found that in "view of certain information received from abroad" that a study should be initiated on developing a glider that could be towed by aircraft. General Henry H. "Hap" Arnold, chief of the Army Air Corps, directed the initiation of this study on 25 February and requested his staff should prepare a statement recommending the desirable characteristics of a military transport glider by 1 April 1941.

Arnold was the first American military leader to demonstrate interest in the possible worth of a transport glider in a military capacity. Shortly thereafter, the United States set a breathtaking pace in glider development and procurement, involving countless companies in design and construction. Specialized aircraft companies, furniture factories, piano companies, a casket maker and even a pickle company entered into the massive effort.

Almost 16,000 transport and training gliders were produced for the military services. 13,909 of these were CG-4A's; there were more CG-4A's manufactured during the war than any other single model of aircraft except for the B-24 heavy bomber, the P-47 and the P-51.

The procurement of all gliders involved twenty-three companies in ten states in the development of experimental models; it involved twenty-two companies in fourteen states in eleven production models. In the effort, almost 500 million dollars was expended, a considerable amount for the 1940's.

The U.S. Army Air Forces shipped 5,991 CG-4A's, 87 CG-15A's and 81 CG-13A's to the European theater of operations. It sent 2,303 CG-4A's to the Mediterranean and six to China-Burma-India from the United States, additional numbers later being shipped there from other theaters. Army Air Force flight elements in the South Pacific received 504 CG-4A's and 5 YCG-13A's and Great Britain 740 CG-4A's and six CG-13A's, making a grand total of 9,723 U.S. gliders shipped overseas.

Shortly after the program began, the U.S. Army Air Corps (soon to be designated the Army Air Forces on June 1941 and assume the status of an independent service) set up a Glider Branch in the Materiel Command at Wright Field near Dayton, Ohio. The glider branch became the focal point for the development and procurement of transport gliders for the Army Air Forces. The Materiel Command carried out many research and testing projects at the Clinton County Army Air Field near Wilmington, Ohio. The counterpart for the development of Navy gliders was the Naval Aircraft Factory in Philadelphia, Pennsylvania.

The AAF applied its standard aircraft nomenclature to transport gliders. As an example, the combination XCG-3 stood for (X) experimental, (C) cargo, (G) glider and the (3) for the third new glider model in the series of glider aircraft being produced. (T) meant training, and (B) stood for bomb in the training and bomb gliders, respectively. The (A) in CG-3A meant that this glider was no longer experimental and had been accepted for production. When the (A) was changed to (B), as will be found with the CG-4B (see section on the CG-4A), the (B) indicated a major modification of the production glider. When a glider went from the experimental to the production stage and was approved except for minor tests, the (X) was replaced with a (Y), thus XCG-13, became YCG-13. By this production action the AAF enabled companies to manufacture urgently-needed gliders without awaiting the completion of trials.

ARMY AIR CORPS AND AIR FORCE GLIDERS

XCG-1, XCG-2
The Army Air Corps launched a glider development program in May 1941 by signing a contract with the Frankfort Sailplane Company, located in Joliet, Illinois, that called for Frankfort to build the XCG-1, an eight-place glider, and the XCG-2, a fifteen-place glider. The company was to build static-test and flight-test models of each.

At that time, Frankfort was achieving recognized success in the construction of the XTG-1 Frankfort Utility Glider for the glider pilot training program, which was just getting under way. Because the company was already committed to the XTG-1, progress on the design and construction of the XCG-1 and XCG-2 moved slowly. In December 1941 the company finally brought a static-test model of the XCG-1 to the Army Air Force Materiel Command at Wright Field, Troy, Ohio, for test and evaluation. The model failed structural tests, and the AAF cancelled the XCG-1 and XCG-2 contract.

CG-3A
The AAF meanwhile negotiated for the construction of other experimental gliders with the Waco Aircraft Company of Troy, Ohio. A contract, approved in June 1941, provided that they would build one static-test and one flight-test model of an eight-place XCG-3 glider, and one static-test and two flight-test models of a fifteen-place glider.

The company moved rapidly into design and construction of the wind-tunnel model. By September, Waco reported they had completed wind-tunnel tests. By 26 December 1941, they delivered a static-structural-test model and

Frankfort XCG-1 under construction.

Waco XCG-3.

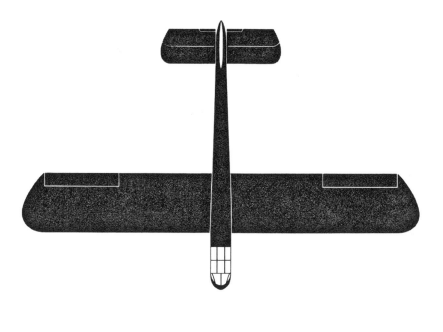

Waco CG-3A, three-view section.

a flight-test model were produced just one month later. Both models tested satisfactorily, and the Army Air Forces accepted the XCG-3 as satisfactory for quantity production in April 1942.

The XCG-3 was a high-wing monoplane with strut braces, wooden wings and empennage construction. The fuselage was a frame of welded steel tubing covered with fabric. Like most early gliders, it could be fitted with either of two landing gears: a semi-fixed one that was attached and used for training and a gear that could be jettisoned by the pilot from the cockpit after the glider was airborne. The latter was available for combat operations and airborne maneuvers. If the wheels were dropped, the glider landed on plywood skis attached to its underside.

The Army Air Forces made the decision to go into quantity production of an enlarged XCG-3 that would carry nine equipped soldiers. It was designated the CG-3A, and the Commonwealth Corporation of Kansas City, Missouri, was awarded the contract. But within a short time, the U.S. military substantially reduced the procurement of the glider, turning instead to the more suitable XCG-4, which was well under way at Waco. Commonwealth built 100 CG-3A's before the contract's termination. The company then turned its technical knowhow, gained from the CG-3A experience, to the building of the CG-4A.

The CG-3A's were shipped to many glider-pilot training bases in America, where the gliders were extensively flown in transition phases of training before the pilots began to fly the larger and heavier CG-4A.

CG-3A Technical Data
Crew: Pilot and co-pilot
Weight
    Empty: 2,400 lb
    Cargo: 2,000 lb
    Total with cargo: 4,400 lb
Dimensions
    Wingspan: 73'
    Wing area: 420 square feet
    Fuselage length: 48.5'
Payload: 7 fully equipped soldiers
Towing speed: 120 mph (maximum)

CG-4A
The CG-4A was probably the most awkward-looking glider produced by the U.S. during the war and, at the same time, the one that handled best. One pilot, accustomed to the lines of graceful sailplanes, described the CG-4A as a "ghastly sight!" Another remarked: "It's all right to fly a box car, but why fly it sideways!"

On the credit side of the ledger, the CG-4A carried a large amount of cargo for its weight and could be flown safely by pilots lacking comprehensive training. This latter factor was a decided advantage in the early phases of planning glider operations, when the need for more than 30,000 trained glider pilots was projected.

Waco delivered the static-test model on 28 April 1942 and the flight-test model on 14 May 1942. So urgent was the need for an acceptable transport glider that both were submitted to an accelerated test schedule. In a significant test, an aircraft towed the XCG-4 from Wright Field to Chanute Field, Illinois, a distance of 220 miles.

Except for a minor change needed in the rudder and fin, the XCG-4 passed the test phase successfully, and it was declared acceptable on 20 June 1942. The Army Air Forces found the solution to the urgent need for a reliable, easily manufactured combat glider in this aircraft.

In effect, the CG-4A was an enlarged version of the CG-3. General Arnold wrote in a directive: "I would like very much to have a small light jeep constructed . . . to carry two men and have light armor and guns. This jeep should be designed and constructed with a view to fitting wings to it so that we can take off as a glider and drop it as a glider. Having dropped as a glider, it lands on a field somewhere, sheds its wings and goes around as a jeep." Consequently, the designers made the fuselage of the CG-4A commodious enough to carry the army's quarter-ton truck. To permit the truck to enter the glider, they conceived of a unique design whereby the entire nose, containing the pilots' seats and controls, was hinged at the top of the fuselage. The nose could be swung upward, thereby creating an opening into which the truck could be driven. To carry personnel, box-like plywood three-man passenger seats were added, two on each side of the cargo area.

As other experimental gliders showed little promise of supplying an acceptable fifteen-place glider, the U.S. military entered into mass production of the CG-4A. Eleven companies were awarded contracts for a total of 640 of these gliders.

The CG-4A was a strut-braced, high-wing monoplane that could carry more than its own empty weight. The wings, two spars and ribs were made of wood, with the surface a thin sheet of plywood covered with fabric. The elevators were fabric-covered only. The wings had elliptical tips and little or no dihedral.

The fuselage was a welded steel tube frame covered with fabric.

The floor was honeycomb plywood, a fabricating technique that gave strength and rigidity with little weight. The plywood structure was reinforced under the areas of the floor that bore the load of the one-ton truck wheels. As simply constructed as it appeared, it nonetheless had more than 70,000 parts. Before the last CG-4A came off the production line, its original design had been altered more than 7,000 times.

100 Waco CG-3As, as manufactured by Commonwealth, parked at Kansas City airport awaiting shipment to glider pilot training centers in the U.S.

Waco CG-4A (Commonwealth forces Hadrian), workhorse of the American glider-force worldwide.

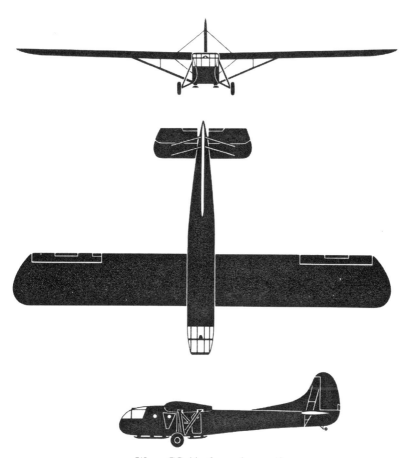
Waco CG-4A, three-view section.

CG-4A Technical Data
Crew: Pilot and co-pilot
Weight
    Empty: 3,440 lb
    Cargo: 4,060 lb
    Total with cargo: 7,500 lb
Dimensions
    Wingspan: 83.6'
    Wing area: 852 square feet
    Height: 7.3'
    Fuselage length: 48'
Cargo compartment
    Length: 13.2'
    Width: 5.8'
    Height: 7.2'

Payload: One ¼-ton 4 x 4 truck with radio, driver, radio operator and one other soldier or one M3A1 75-mm howitzer plus crew of three; or 13 fully equipped soldiers
Towing speed: 120 mph (maximum)
Stalling speed: 50 mph
Aspect Ratio: 8.21
Tow planes: C-47, C-46, C-54, A-25, B-25 or P-38

Cockpit of the Waco CG-4A. Note the tow rope release lever (center, left).

Waco CG-4As under construction.

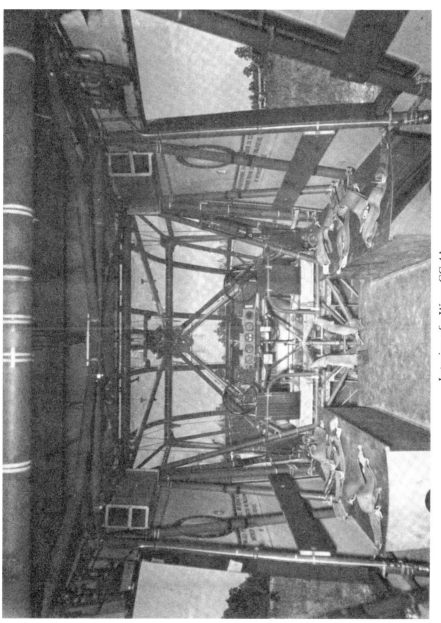

Interior of a Waco CG-4A.

Waco CG-4A, brake parachute released, coming in for a landing.

Waco CG-4A glider with Ludington-Griswold nose modification to give pilots added protection. Of the Wacos that flew in the Holland invasion, 700 had this modification, which saved many lives in those fields in which the Germans had erected antiglider posts (Rommel's asparagus).

Waco CG-4A in rigid tow behind a Douglas C-47.

A Waco CG-4A drops take-off wheels.

A powered Waco CG-4A, the XPG-1.

A rare photograph of a Waco CG-4A glider "mock-up" in a glider and transport mock-up training area. To save the CG-4As wear and tear in the ground phases of airborne training, hundreds of wooden mock-ups were constructed in wooded areas and fields adjacent to airborne divisions. Troops practiced loading and lashing quarter-ton trucks, artillery and other equipment in them. Note the Curtis Commando C-46 mock-up in the background.

Water-landing a Waco CG-4A at Lauvinburg-Maxton Air Base, North Carolina, to test it in water landings and also to determine its ability to float. One of the many tests made with this glider to duplicate diverse landing situations.

Waco designed a unique system to allow the jeep to go into action quickly, using the vehicle to raise the nose of the glider. After the jeep had been loaded into the glider, a cable was hitched to the pintle of the jeep. When the glider had landed and come to a halt—or even while yet airborne—the driver of the jeep started its motor. Glidermen cut or untied lashings holding the vehicle in place. The glider pilots hastily got out of the nose. The driver then drove slowly forward. As he did this, the cable pulled the nose up. The vehicle's wheels pushed the ramps, causing them to fall forward to the ground so the vehicle could drive out of the glider. When the nose had been fully raised, it automatically locked, and when the jeep had driven a few more feet, the cable automatically unhitched from the pintle of the jeep. The total procedure took but a few seconds to accomplish.

Early models of the CG-4A took off on wheels which were jettisoned above the take-off field to be recovered later. They landed on plywood skids.

The CG-4A had dual wheel controls, placed side by side. It could be trimmed in respect to all three axes with three separate trim tab controls located above and between the pilots' seats. Instruments included the air-speed indicator, a "sensitive" altimeter, a bank-and-turn indicator, and a rate-of-climb indicator. These were typical aircraft instruments of that period. They were manufactured for use in aircraft where engine vibrations kept gauges from sticking. Since they were not sensitive enough for the vibration-less gliders, wary pilots had to tap them from time to time to be certain they were registering accurately.

Later models had a two-way radio to enable the pilot to talk to his tow pilot. Until then, glider and plane were connected by telephone. This was unsatisfactory, since the telephone wire, which was wrapped around the tow rope, was often damaged or even cut.

On 13 May 1942, the Material Command at Wright Field signed a contract with the Timm Aircraft Company of Los Angeles for the construction of a plywood fuselage for one CG-4A glider, thus ensuring a satisfactory all-wood design for the CG-4 fuselage in the event of a shortage of steel tubing. In April 1943, Timm delivered the XCG-4B, containing a wooden fuselage. In external appearance, the glider was exactly like the CG-4A. It performed satisfactorily, but no need ever arose to place it in production.

In all, 13,909 CG-4A's were produced, enough to meet all operational needs. The Ford Motor Company turned out 4,190, while the Northwestern Company of Minneapolis, Minnesota, the second-largest producer, built 1,509 gliders. The cost of a CG-4A averaged $18,800.

The Army Air Forces built five models of powered gliders: XPG-1, XPG-2, XPG-2A, PG-2A and the XPG-3. One each of the experimental models was built and ten PG-2A's.

XCG-5

The XCG-5 was developed to serve as a model in the investigation of the effect of light-wing loading characteristics. The Army Air Forces gave the job to the St. Louis Aircraft Corporation in June 1941, specifying that two glider models be developed. One was the eight-place XCG-5, the other a fifteen-place XCG-6.

Early in 1942, the company delivered a static-test model of the XCG-5 to the Materiel Command. Structural tests showed a serious failure at 90 percent load. Tests on the flight-test model, delivered in October 1942, proved no more successful. Testers found unsatisfactory balance that would have required a complete redesign of the glider, if development were to be continued. The military decided not to ask the company to undertake the task and terminated the contract. Subsequently, the XCG-6 was also cancelled.

No technical details are available.

XCG-7 AND XCG-8

To encourage more companies to develop gliders, the Army Air Forces awarded a contract to Bowlus Sailplanes of Los Angeles, California, for two each of an eight-place glider (XCG-7) and a fifteen-place glider (XCG-8).

The XCG-7 was delivered to Wright Field, where the Materiel Command subjected it to tests during February 1942. It failed the structural test. After repairs, the glider again failed tests.

The company encountered serious problems in producing the larger XCG-8 and prevailed upon the Douglas Aircraft Corporation to render assistance in the project. Despite Douglas's intervention and the enthusiastic endorsement of Dr. Wolfgang Klemperer, the former German sailplane and glider designer and pilot (then a Douglas aeronautical engineer), Bowlus made no appreciable progress towards acceptance of the XCG-8 as a production glider. It also proved faulty in tests.

The Army Air Forces finally concluded that there would be no procurement of any Bowlus gliders, since the XCG-7 had proved of "limited military utility" and that the XCG-8 had failed structural tests.

Both gliders were of wood and fabric construction and had a designed towing speed of 120 miles per hour. The XCG-7 was to weigh 5,000 lb and the XCG-8 was to weigh 7,450 lb, without loads.

The XCG-7 flight-test model, which had handled well according to some reports, was sent to the High Voltage Laboratory of the National Bureau of Standards for use in tests in protecting wooden aircraft from lightning. The XCG-8 flight model was destroyed in a storm at Wilmington, Ohio, in June 1943.

XCG-7 Technical Data

Crew: Pilot and co-pilot

Weight

    Empty: 5,000 lb

    Cargo: 2,000 lb

    Total with cargo: 7,000 lb

Dimensions

    Wingspan: 80'

    Wing area: 600 square feet

    Fuselage length: 36'

Payload: 7 fully equipped soldiers

Towing speed: 120 mph (maximum)

XCG-8 Technical Data

Crew: Pilot and co-pilot

Weight

    Empty: 7,450 lb

    Cargo: 3,600 lb

    Total with cargo: 11,050 lb

Dimensions

    Wingspan: 90'

    Wing area: 880 square feet

    Fuselage length: 45'

Payload: 13 fully equipped soldiers

Towing speed: 120 mph (maximum)

YCG-10A

Late in 1941, Colonel Frederick R. Dent, Jr., head of the Glider Branch at the Materiel Command, who had just returned from a visit to England to observe Britain's glider activities, expressed the opinion that America must build gliders that could carry substantially more than the CG-4A. If the five U.S. airborne divisions then being formed were to be adequately supplied, they needed gliders that could transport trucks larger than the jeep, larger-caliber artillery pieces, heavy tonnages of ammunition and other bulky supplies and equipment.

With this objective in mind, the Army Air Forces awarded a contract to the Laister Kauffman Aircraft Corporation of St. Louis, Missouri, in April 1942 for the XCG-10, a thirty-place glider. Three were to be built, constructed from wood as far as was practical.

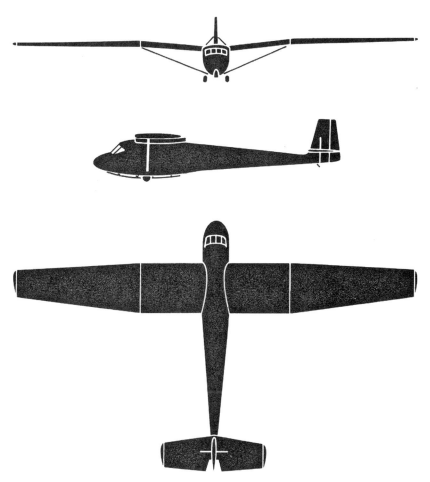

St. Louis XCG-5, three-view section.

The gull-wing St. Louis XCG-5.

Bowlus XCG-7, three-view section.

Bowlus XCG-7.

Bowlus XCG-7, showing nose detail.

Bowlus XCG-8.

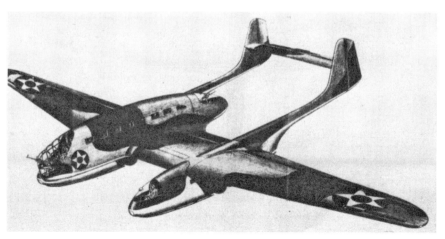

Design concept of the AGA XCG-9.

In October, the company delivered a static-test model to Wright Field. (By then, Waco had made substantial progress on the large XCG-13, a glider with characteristics comparable to those specified for the XCG-10.)

When the Waco XCG-13 was approved for production, the military dropped work on the XCG-10 and asked Laister Kauffman to develop a somewhat larger glider, the XCG-10A. The XCG-10A specifications called for a troop/cargo glider that would transport a combat load of 8,000 lb and a have a gross weight not to exceed 15,980 lb. Its wingspan was to be 105 feet and the fuselage 68.5 feet. Air speed was set at 150 miles per hour. This was an increase over the 120 miles per hour established for earlier models, designed to take advantage of faster C-46 and C-54 tow aircraft, which had become available for airborne operations. On 30 April 1944, the company delivered a flight model to the Clinton County Field. It had the distinction of being the only large wooden aircraft to pass military testing successfully in many years.

The XCG-10A was a high-wing, full cantilever, monoplane glider. Tail surfaces were supported by a boom attached to the upper rear portion of the fuselage. It had a tricycle landing gear, with a retractable nose wheel. Spoilers on the upper surface of the wing were operated manually by a lever in the cockpit. Slotted flaps covered one half of the wing length and were operated hydraulically. The glider had dual control; the pilots sat side by side. To comply with the original contract, the entire craft, with the exception of fittings, was of molded plywood.

The outstanding feature of the glider was its enormous cargo compartment, 30 feet long, which extended from the pilot's compartment to about four feet aft of the rear edge of the wing. The exterior of the cargo section cleared the ground by only 20 inches. It had clamshell doors and a ramp that could be lowered at the rear of the compartment to load a two-ton truck.

As large as the glider was, it proved suitable for "snatch" pickups. These were accomplished by the B-17 and the C-54.

There was pressure for the production of large gliders as quickly as possible. As a result, the Army Air Forces negotiated a production contract with Laister Kauffman in August 1942 for ten YCG-10A's—the designation for the production model—even though the XCG-10A had not been accepted as a standard piece of equipment. By 1945, the company had manufactured ten of the gliders.

In early 1945, William S. Knudsen, head of the War Production Board, summoned Jack Laister of the manufacturing firm to Washington. Knudsen grilled Laister on technical details and operational characteristics of the company's glider as well as its production qualifications. Concluding the conference, Knudsen stated he was entirely satisfied with the YCG-10 program.

Shortly afterwards, the company received instructions to gear up for the production of 1,000 CG-10A's. These gliders were to participate in the invasion of Japan. To be built in St. Louis, they were to then be shipped by barge down the Mississippi, loaded on freighters in New Orleans and shipped via the Panama Canal to islands in the Pacific to be readied for the assault.

This program was not immediately terminated when the war against Japan ended as were other glider contracts, a testimony to the confidence the Army Air Forces had in the company and the transport. Manufacturing continued into 1946 before the contract was closed.

YCG-10A Technical Data
Crew: Pilot and co-pilot
Weight
    Empty: 12,150 lb
    Cargo: 10,850 lb
    Total with cargo: 23,000 lb
Dimensions
    Wingspan: 105'
    Wing area: 1,180 square feet
    Height: 26.3'
    Fuselage length: 67'
Cargo compartment
    Length: 30'
    Width: 8.5'
    Height: 6.7'
Payload: 1 2.5-ton truck or 2 105-mm howitzers (M2) or 1 M1 155-mm howitzer or 1 M2 howitzer and a prime mover (jeep) or 40 fully equipped soldiers
Towing speed: 180 mph (maximum) (140 mph with flaps)
Stalling speed: 75 mph (flaps up) (70 mph flaps down)
Aspect Ratio: 8. 15
Tow planes: C-47, C-46 or C-54

CG-13A
Because of the success of the Waco Company with the CG-4A, the Army Air Forces decided to apply Waco's experience to designing and developing a glider of larger capacity. As a result, they were asked to develop the XCG-13 on 23 September 1942. It was a thirty-place transport glider with a towing speed of 175 miles per hour at 12,000 feet altitude, a gross weight of 15,000 pounds and a useful military load of 8,000 lb.

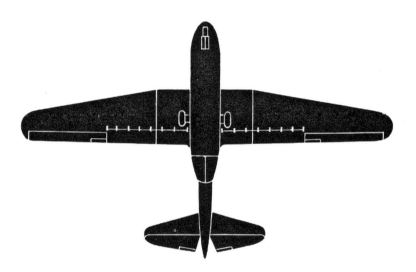

Laister-Kaufmann XCG-10A, three-view section.

Laister-Kaufmann YCG-10A, Trojan Horse. America's largest all-wood glider and the pride of her glider fleet. The Laister-Kaufmann YCG-10A was loaded from the rear.

Snead XCG-11 wind-tunnel test model.

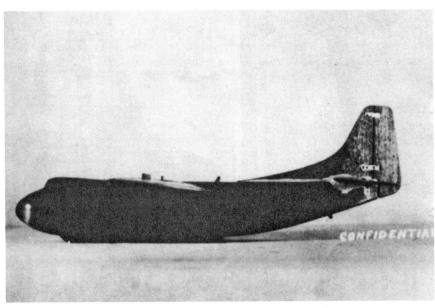

Read-York, XCG-12 wind-tunnel test model.

Testing began in March 1943 of the first XCG-13 prototype at Wright Field in Ohio. The glider passed preliminary tests successfully, with a few modifications.

On 7 July, after a tornado had wrecked the second flight-test model, a static-test model was tested and approved. By the end of the summer of 1943, the military had its first large glider ready for production. Since actual production orders went out before tests were completed, the early-production models were designated the YCG-13A. Later, in full production, the glider became the CG-13A.

The fuselage framework was made of welded steel tubing covered with fabric. Wings were of wood and externally braced. Flaps were hydraulically operated. Like that of the CG-4A, the nose of the CG-13A was hinged at the top and could be elevated by means of a pair of hydraulic actuating cylinders. Ramps were then dropped and vehicles driven into the interior. It was possible to release four aerial delivery containers or "parapacks" through doors at the rear of the cargo compartment while the glider was in flight. Pilots sat side by side at dual controls. Despite the size of this glider, it could be picked up with ease by a tow-craft in the glider-snatch technique developed midway through the war.

The glider was given clear approval and went into production. Ford produced eighty-five; Northwestern, forty seven.

CG-13A Technical Data
Crew: Pilot and co-pilot
Weight
    Empty: 8,700 lb
    Cargo: 10,200 lb
    Total with cargo: 18,900 lb
Dimensions
    Wingspan: 86'
    Wing area: 873 square feet
    Height: 20'
    Fuselage length: 54'
Cargo compartment
    Length: 24'
    Width: 7.5'
    Height: 6'
Payload: 1 M2 105-mm howitzer with 1 jeep prime mover, ammunition, and gun crew; one 1 2.5-ton 6x6 truck or fully equipped soldiers
Towing speed: 135 mph (sustained); 195 mph (maximum) (150 mph with flaps)
Stalling speed: 83 mph (flaps up) (79 mph flaps down)
Aspect Ratio: 8.41. Tow planes: C-47, C-46, C- 54, B-17 or B-24

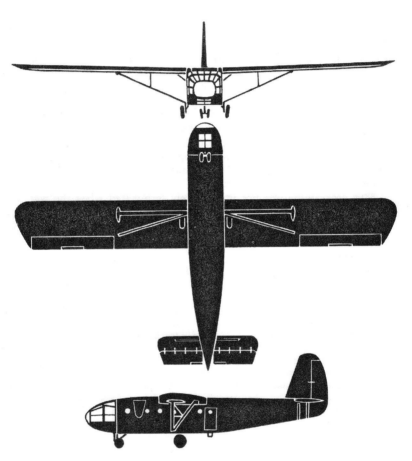

Waco CG-13A, three-view section.

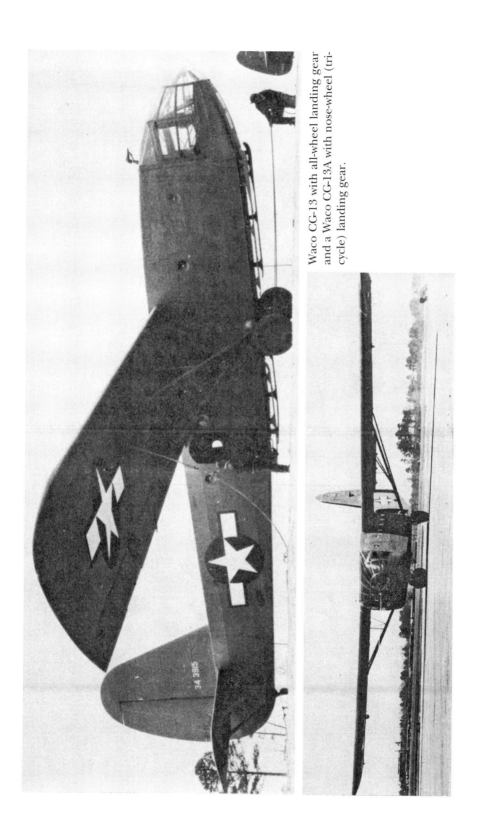

Waco CG-13 with all-wheel landing gear and a Waco CG-13A with nose-wheel (tricycle) landing gear.

Loading a tracked weapons-carrier in a CG-13A.

Interior of a Waco CG-13A.

XCG-14 AND XCG-14A

The XCG-14 was the last of the fifteen-place gliders produced by the Army Air Forces. It was designed and developed to meet new concepts in the tactical use of gliders. Faster and more powerful tow planes, such as the C-54, were being produced, and this meant that the slower transport gliders would no longer be suitable for tow by the newer generation of transporters. Some glider proponents in the Army Air Forces also saw an expanded role for gliders in using them as fighter air-support vehicles, ferrying aircraft components, built-in workshops or other facilities. They were to be towed by fighters in close support of fighter bases. The Germans were already doing this, particularly with their Go 242's. Finally, one school of thought held that a glider was needed that could be towed to a high-altitude release point beyond the reach of enemy sensors for missions requiring great secrecy or a high degree of tactical or strategic surprise. Such a glider needed to withstand stresses not expected of existing gliders.

The glider produced to meet these requirements was the XCG-14. The Army Air Forces negotiated a contract with the Chase Aircraft Company of New York on 30 October 1943. The Soviet-born engineer and architect, Michael Stroukoff, builder of railroads, bridges and theaters and part owner of Chase, designed the XCG-14, applying his knowledge of hydrodynamics to the problem of obtaining the highest performance from a wing. The result was a surprisingly good glider with a high, full cantilever wing. It had the highest aspect ratio that had heretofore been recorded in the files of the U.S. National Advisory Committee on Aeronautics, the repository for all airfoil design.

The XCG-14 was built in the loft of an old building in lower Manhattan, then disassembled, moved out in sections to a garage in the Bronx near Bailey Avenue, and there reassembled.

The XCG-14 had a maximum designed airspeed of 200 miles per hour. The fuselage had a natural marine plywood skin and was wood braced, as were the wing and tail. Its rich, polished mahogany surface made it a superb product of the woodworker's art, but it was soon painted over with aluminum paint. The rear part of the fuselage pivoted upward on a horizontal hinge to provide access to the cargo compartment. The glider had a fixed main landing gear, retractable nose, manually operated wing flaps, and dual controls. It had a large Plexiglas "greenhouse" nose, giving an unexcelled field of vision to the pilots, although it was later found that some pilots experienced optical distortion, a result of light rays being bent by the molded glass.

A modified second model was designated the XCG-14A. Although the wing was the same, other modifications were substantial, such as the increase in the number of passengers from fourteen to twenty-four fully equipped

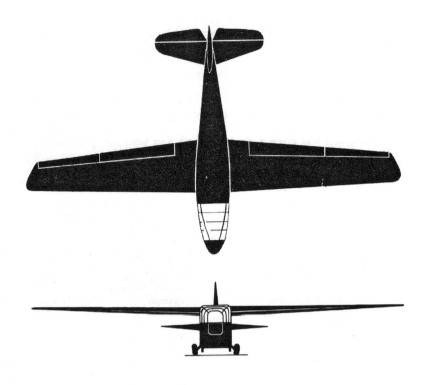

Chase XCG-14, three-view section.

XCG-14 and XCG-14A Technical Data

Crew: Pilot and co-pilot

Weight
    Empty: 3,237/7,500lb
    Cargo: 4,368/8,000lb
    Total with cargo: 7,605/15,000lb

Dimensions
    Wingspan: 71.8'/86.25'
    Wing area: 507/706.5 square feet
    Height: 6.8' (approximately)

Cargo compartment
    Length: 24'/38'
    Width: 5.5'
    Height: 5.8'

Payload: One ¼-ton 4x4 truck plus 3 soldiers; 1 M3A1 75-mm howitzer plus crew or 15 fully-equipped troops; or 24 fully-equipped troops

Towing speed: 170 mph (maximum)

Stalling speed: 60 (flaps down)

Aspect Ratio: 10.18

Tow planes: P-38 or other fighter aircraft

soldiers. The molded glass was replaced by flat glass panels, and the cargo compartment was made more commodious. The tail in the XCG-14A was also raised to permit the cargo compartment to be opened for loading purposes.

Both models of the glider proved satisfactory in tests. The XCG-14A was at one time towed at 275 miles per hour by a Republic P-47 (Thunderbolt) fighter. These two gliders and other gliders produced by Chase came to be known as "Avitrucs."

CG-15A

By the autumn of 1943, enough data had been collected to indicate that it was time to either make major modifications in the successful CG-4A or to launch into the design and development of a new glider with comparable cargo capacity but with better flying characteristics. Thousands of CG-4A's had flown in training, maneuvers and operations in a variety of weather conditions, towed by many different aircraft. In preparation for airborne operations in the Mediterranean theater and for the cross-channel invasion, a build-up of glider forces was under way in Africa and England. The decision was made to build a new glider, the XCG-15, incorporating the needed changes.

Major Floyd Sweet, a design and development engineer and chief test pilot, who had become head of the Glider Branch when Colonel Dent was assigned to a bomber command overseas, became project engineer for the XCG-15. Conferring with Francis Acier, the chief aeronautical engineer of Waco, who had been instrumental in the design of the CG-4A, Sweet soon made a few but important modifications to the CG-4A design to produce the XCG-15. Consequently, the transition to the XCG-15 by companies already producing the CG-4A was relatively simple to accomplish.

On 14 October 1943, Waco changed over to construction of the CG-15A. The new glider had a 40 percent shorter wingspan than the CG-4A, its most distinguishing characteristic. Other differences included the addition of flaps and new ailerons, crash protection for passengers and crew, a somewhat higher towing speed, improved landing gear and better visibility for the pilot. Although the glider was 400 lb heavier than the CG-4A, it carried some 500 lb more in men or cargo. Because the CG-15 had flaps, it had a higher sink rate when the flaps were used.

Three months after the contract for production gliders was signed, the first of the CG-15A's was delivered to Wright Field.

XCG-15A Technical Data
Crew: Pilot and co-pilot
Weight
 Empty: 4,000 lb
 Cargo: 4,000 lb
 Total with cargo: 8,000 lb

Dimensions
    Wingspan: 62.1'
    Wing area: 623 square feet
    Height: 12.7'
    Fuselage length: 48.8'
Cargo compartment
    Length: 13,1'
    Width: 5.9'
    Height: 5.5'
Payload: 1 1-ton 4x4 truck, plus a driver and two other soldiers; one M3A1
    105-mm howitzer with crew; or 13 fully equipped soldiers
Towing speed: 180 mph (maximum) (100 mph with flaps)
Stalling speed: 62 mph (flaps up) and 53 mph (flaps down)
Aspect Ratio: 6.21
Tow planes: C-47, C-46, C-54, A-25, B-25 or P-38

XCG-16

The XCG-16 was an interesting departure from the single-fuselage design that had been common to American gliders. It also introduced the twin boom. In it, the trend towards better aerodynamic characteristics for transport gliders could be seen, a trend that was to reach its apogee in the XG-20, a post-war development. It is worth noting that the XCG-16 had some of the same aerodynamic design elements as the German *Mammut*.

    The story of its development is extraordinary. In February 1942, William Hawley Bowlus of Bowlus Sailplanes began the design and construction of a flying wing glider. A half-size prototype of the glider was completed later that year. In October 1942, Bowlus and an associate, Albert Criz, began a campaign to secure a government contract. They organized the Airborne Transport Company in Los Angeles, California, which finally became the General Airborne Transport Company.

    An inspection of Airborne Transport's facilities disclosed that the "factory" was a small store building formerly used as a dry cleaning shop. It was just large enough for the half-sized glider they had constructed to be fitted into the building sideways.

    The company then launched into the construction of a full-scale model, looking for support in Washington. They were stimulated by self-deception or possible political support and believed that a contract for 1,000 of their gliders was in the offing.

    After completing the glider, Airborne Transport Company offered it to Wright Field for test and evaluation, with the company concurrently conducting its own tests. On 11 September 1943, Richard DuPont, the glider specialist

Chase XCG-14.

Chase XCG-14A.

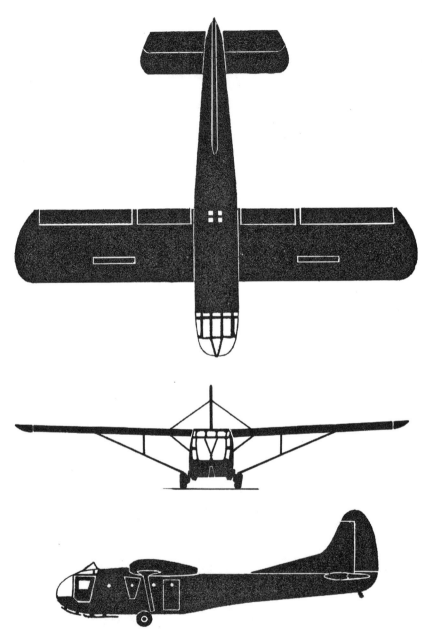

Waco CG-15A, three-view section.

on the staff of the chief of staff of the Army Air Forces, and Colonel Ernest Gabel of the same office were killed when the glider crashed at March Field, California. Bowlus, without authority from military officials, had arranged for a test flight. The glider took off with some passengers and loaded with bags of lead shot or sand to bring the load up to capacity. Unfortunately, no one had the forethought to lash in the deadweight bags, and they shifted in the turbulence. The glider began "porpoising," endangering the tow plane. The tow plane's pilot cut the test glider loose. By then, the glider was so off balance that it was uncontrollable, and it went into a dive. Bowlus and one other passenger managed to parachute to safety. All others were killed.

This tragedy did not deter the company, and a contract was approved on 13 November. They finally delivered one glider, some six months later than promised and at three times the original cost estimate. This glider became the XCG-16.

It was a high wing, cantilever monoplane with twin booms to support the empennage. Unique from an aerodynamic standpoint was the airfoil-shaped fuselage between the booms, looking much like the Brunelli aircraft introduced in the early 1930's. The front of the wing on each side of the loading nacelle opened like a jaw, the top swinging on horizontal hinges along the leading edge of the airfoil and the bottom swinging on hinges on the bottom of the fuselage to rest on the ground and form a loading ramp. The glider had dual controls and the pilots sat in tandem. The landing gear was retractable. The outer wing panels had slotted wing-flaps, and the center section of the fuselage also had a split flap. The flaps were actuated by electrical power. The glider was constructed largely of plywood, and the movable surfaces, such as flaps, were covered with fabric. Because the cargo area tapered to zero at the rear, the seats at the rear of the fuselage allowed little headroom for passengers.

The glider was tested at the Clinton Army Air Field and at Orlando, Florida, by the Army Air Forces Board. It concluded that the glider had inadequate crash protection, unsatisfactory loading ramps, insufficient personnel exits, awkward location of flight equipment, critical lateral loading and restricted pilot visibility. The contract was terminated on 30 November 1944.

XCG-17

The XCG-17 represents one of the later and certainly more innovative developments in wartime gliders. In the fall of 1944, the Army Air Forces was faced with the problem of delivering large quantities of supplies from India to China. This meant flying over the so-called "hump" in Burma. Since sufficient cargo aircraft were not available for the task, it was proposed that transport gliders might be used to improve the supply situation. Glider development took a unique turn. The military decided to see if the C-47 aircraft, the reliable workhorse of the military and civilian transport services, could be saddled with yet another task.

With reasonable modifications, it was found possible to produce a glider version of the C-47 that could carry up to 15,000 lb of cargo when towed by a C-54.

To attain the maximum cargo capacity, the C-47 was stripped of radio and navigator's equipment, and the space turned into a part of the cargo compartment. Bulkheads were removed, creating a space 30.4 feet long. Engines were also removed and the nacelles covered with spun-aluminum caps. Wing outer panels and the vacant nacelles were converted into fuel storage tanks to carry fuel as cargo. By these various actions, cargo capacity was ultimately boosted to 15,000 pounds to make the XCG-17 America's largest cargo-carrying glider of the war.

The man-hours needed to make the conversion proved surprisingly few for the results achieved, and later tests confirmed the feasibility of converting a C-47 into an efficient cargo glider. It was determined that the XCG-17 could be reconverted to a C-47 in equally few hours.

While development and testing were taking place, however, the supply situation in the China-Burma-India theater improved, and there was no longer a requirement for the conversion of substantial numbers of C-47's.

XCG-17 Technical Data
Crew: Pilot and co-pilot
Weight
     Empty: 11,000 lb
     Cargo: 15,000 lb
     Total with cargo: 26,000 lb
Dimensions
     Wingspan: 95'
     Wing area: 987 square feet
     Height: 17'
     Fuselage length: 63.8'
Cargo compartment
     Length: 30.3'
     Width: 8'
     Height: 6'
Payload: 3 1-ton 4x4 trucks with drivers; miscellaneous cargo, including fuels; or 27
     fully equipped soldiers
Towing speed: 190 mph (maximum) (112 mph with flaps)
Stalling speed: 75 mph (flaps up) and 66 mph (flaps down)
Aspect Ratio: 9.15
Tow planes: C-54 or 2 C-47's in tandem tow

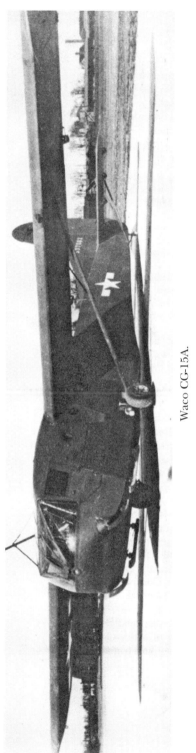

Waco CG-15A.

General Airborne XCG-16

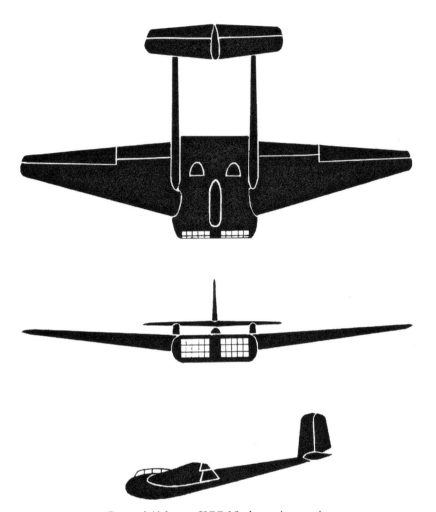

General Airborne XCG-16, three-view section

XCG-16 Technical Data

Crew: Pilot and co-pilot

Weight
    Empty: 9,500 lb
    Cargo: 10,080 lb
    Total with cargo: 19,580 lb

Dimensions
    Wingspan: 91.8'
    Wing area: 1,140 square feet
    Height: 18.3'
    Fuselage length: 48.3'

Cargo compartment
    Length: 15'
    Width: 7'
    Height: 5'

Payload: 2 M2 105-mm howitzers; 1 M2 105-mm howitzer and 1 1-ton 4x4 truck with gun crew; or 42 fully equipped soldiers

Towing speed: 220 mph (maximum) (120 mph with flaps)

Stalling speed: 62 mph (flaps up) and 58 (flaps down)

Aspect Ratio: 7.4

Tow planes: C-47, C-46 or C-60

Unloading the General Airborne XCG-16.

Two Douglas C-47s in tandem towing an XCG-17, the glider counterpart of the Douglas C-47, in experimental towing tests.

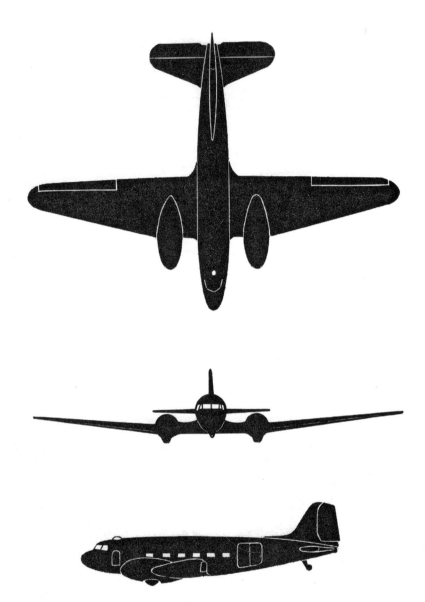

XCG-17, three-view section.

XCG-17 glider.

Chase XCG-18A.

XCG-18A

As the war progressed, most of the existing glider fleet started to become obsolescent. Moreover, the deputy chief of the Air Staff declared that "all present types of gliders are considered to be obsolescent, because they deteriorate rapidly and are inflexible in that they can be used only as gliders." This set the stage for a new U.S. glider program, although it only went into full swing after the war had ended.

In the spring of 1945, two new gliders were proposed: one was to have a useful military load of 8,000 lb and a cargo compartment 24 feet long; the second one was to have a 16,000 lb load capacity with a cargo compartment 30 feet long. Up to that time, the largest artillery piece a U.S. glider could carry was the 75-mm howitzer, which was too small a weapon for expanding airborne needs. In the future, the weight of the equipment a glider could transport was to be the governing factor, rather than the number of personnel it could carry. Also important in the design of gliders was the stipulation that they could readily be converted into powered aircraft with the addition of engines.

Chase Aircraft received a contract in January 1946 for the manufacture of the XCG-18A. Although it looked strikingly similar to the XCG-14A, it was much different in that it had an all-metal steel-framed fuselage covered by light sheet aluminum. Other features were an aluminum-covered wing and tail surface, tricycle landing gear and a retractable nose wheel.

Loading and unloading were accomplished by raising the entire tail section, which afforded an opening 7.7 feet high by 6.5 feet wide. It was designed to have a top speed of 180 miles per hour.

Because specifications were changed midway in production, the glider was not completed until 1948. The designer, Michael Stroukoff, demonstrated his axiom that to be successful as an aircraft, an aircraft must be a good glider first. He added two Wright R-1850 engines and provided the U.S. Air Force with a sister ship, the XC-122, to the XCG-18A. The former could carry cargo and act as a tow ship for the XCG-18A. Later on, the reliable XCG-18A transformed into the powered C-122.

XCG-18A Technical Data

Crew: Pilot and co-pilot
Weight
    Empty: 14,700 lb
    Cargo: 8,000 lb
    Total with cargo: 22,700 lb
Dimensions
    Wingspan: 71.8'
    Wing area: 507 square feet
    Fuselage length: 53'

Cargo compartment
  Length: 24'
Payload: 30 fully equipped soldiers or a mix of soldiers and equipment to
  maximum load of 14,700 lb

XCG-19

Because of the interest of the Army Air Forces in the all-metal glider, it was
decided to construct an 8,000 lb metal monocoque glider in essentially the
same design as the XCG-18. Whereas the stress was taken by the steel-tubing
framework in the XCG-18 and the sheet aluminum was used as fairing only,
the aluminum covering of the fuselage was structured to take the stress in
the XCG-19. Bell, Douglas and Hughes responded to the solicitations for
proposals.

Douglas received the contract in 1946 and, by March 1947, had a mock-
up 60 percent complete. However, because of Defense Department budget
limitations that year, the U.S. Air Force determined to cancel either the
XCG-18 or the XCG-19. Since the former was near completion, the Air Force
decided to cancel the Douglas contract for the XCG-19.

The XCG-19 was considered a light assault cargo glider. It had an 85 foot
wingspan and was 61 feet long. Its cargo compartment measured 24.7 x 7.7 x
6.5 feet. It loaded from the rear with the cargo doors opening out and down.
Its loaded weight was 14,380 pounds, and it carried 8,000 pounds of cargo.

XCG-20

An unusually symmetrical aircraft, the XCG-20 was a high-wing glider of
all-metal monocoque construction, equipped with fully retractable tricycle
landing gear and hydraulically operated slot flaps. The hydraulic pump was
electrically driven, the power plant supplied by a gasoline-driven auxiliary
motor. It met the requirement for a glider that could carry a useful military
load of 16,000 lb. It had a combination door and loading ramp at the rear of
the cargo compartment that provided easy access for loading bulky cargo. It
could seat sixty fully equipped soldiers or accommodate fifty litter patients.

Chase Aircraft received the contract to manufacture the all-metal XCG-
20 on 2 December 1946. In the tradition of the XCG-18A and the XC-122, the
XCG-20's sister ship, with reciprocating engines, was the XC-123. Surprisingly,
the glider was equipped with two twin J-47 jet pods "borrowed" from a B-47
in 1951. It was flown in and out of short fields and had a maximum speed of
more than 500 miles per hour and became America's first jet transport.

XCG-20 Technical Data
Crew: Pilot, co-pilot and crew chief/mechanic
Weight
    Empty: N/A
    Cargo: 16,000 lb
    Total with cargo: N/A
Dimensions
    Wingspan: 110'
    Wing area: 880 square feet
    Fuselage length: 77'
Cargo compartment
    Length: 30'
    Width: 12'
    Height: 10'
Payload: 60 fully equipped soldiers; 50 litter patients; vehicles, including armored ones, up to the load limit of 16,000 lb

XFG-1
In October 1943, the Army Air Forces wished to test the feasibility of extending the range of cargo and bomber aircraft through the use of a trailing glider carrying fuel. The Cornelius Aircraft Corporation of Dayton, Ohio, developed the glider, which was to test an unusual aerodynamic configuration that might also be used for a fighter plane.

The glider, decidedly nonconventional in design, had forward-swept wings, and no horizontal tail surface as found in conventional aircraft. It carried 764 gallons of fuel and had a total loaded weight of 8,000 lb. The wings swept forward fifteen degrees at 25 percent chord line position. The undercarriage could be jettisoned.

The Spartan Aircraft Company of Tulsa, Oklahoma, constructed the glider under subcontract. Wind tunnel and structural tests were made during the summer of 1944, and the XFG-1 made its first flight test on 11 October. Later that year, a Spartan test pilot checking for spin recovery was unable to bring the glider out of a spin and was killed in the ensuing crash.

Captain Adam J. Stolzenberger took charge of the project of building a quarter-scale, free-flight, radio-controlled model. It was built at Wright Field and taken to the Naval Air Station at Lakehurst, New Jersey, where a Navy blimp lifted it to the desired release altitude. The model was put into a spin and successfully recovered by opening a safety parachute.

In the meantime, a new test model XFG-1 had been built. The test pilot spun the glider on the first test, recovering successfully by employing what he

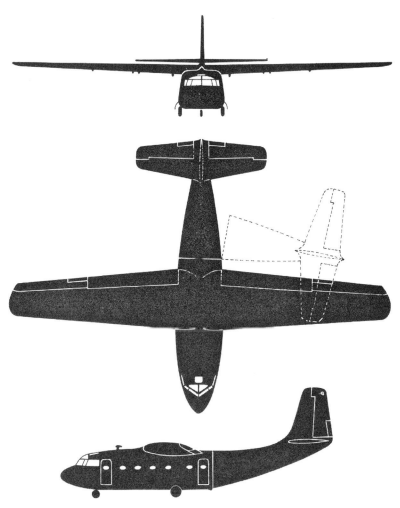

Douglas XCG-19 design concept.

Cargo: 4,638 lb
Total with cargo: 8,000 lb
Dimensions
Wingspan: 54'
Wing area: 356 square feet
Payload: 764 gallons of fuel

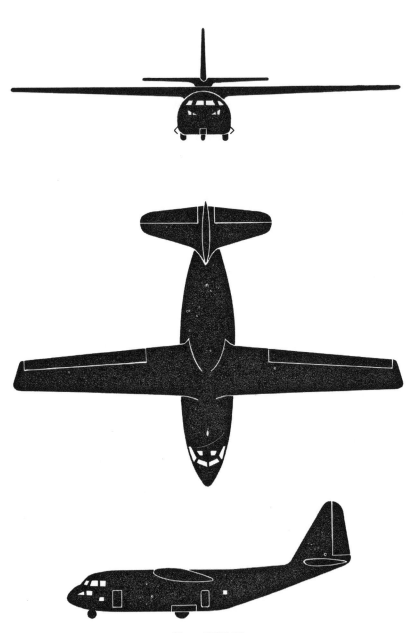

Chase XCG-20.

Chase XCG-20, from which the aircraft industry borrowed many design innovations, which were incorporated into some of America's most advanced aircraft.

Cornelius XFG-1.

Cornelius XFG-1 fuel glider, three-view section.

termed "a critical sequence and trimming of controls." On the second test, a spin-recovery parachute was used.

The military decided that using a spin-recovery parachute with the XFG-1 was the only effective way to recover the glider from a spin. It was never accepted for production.

XFG-1 Technical Data
Crew: Pilot
Weight
    Empty: 3,362 lb

THE NAVY PROGRAM

In April 1941, Captain Marc A. Mitscher, then the assistant chief of the Bureau of Naval Aeronautics, directed the production of a "personnel and equipment"–carrying glider for the Navy. A program was developed to produce two float-wing gliders that could land on water. It was hoped that large numbers could be used in the Pacific theater of war. One glider was to carry twelve passengers; a second, a twin-hull model, was to carry twenty-four passengers.

The Marine Corps expressed great enthusiasm for the project. They envisioned gliders being effective attack transports in their island-hopping campaigns. The Navy continued the glider production program until the end of 1943. Because of problems encountered in production and uncertainties that were beginning to develop about the feasibility of using gliders in the Pacific area, the program was then discontinued.

XLRQ-1

The Naval Aircraft Factory in Philadelphia negotiated a contract with the Bristol Aeronautical Corporation of New Haven, Connecticut, for the twelve-man glider. The first static-test model was delivered in October 1942 under the designation XLRQ-1.[1] After static tests, controls and instruments were installed, and the glider was prepared for limited test flights. These took place during January 1943. The J2F-5 and the PBY-5A were used as tow planes.

A flight-test model was delivered on 5 May 1943. This glider had a tricycle landing gear and a wheel-control system for the pilot. Testing continued into the latter part of the year.

The XLRQ-1 had excellent visibility for passengers and crew. A transparent paneled Plexiglas cover extended from the nose to a point midway in the fuselage.

---

1. X (experimental), L (glider), R (transport). The last letter designated the manufacturer, e.g., N (Naval Aircraft Factory).

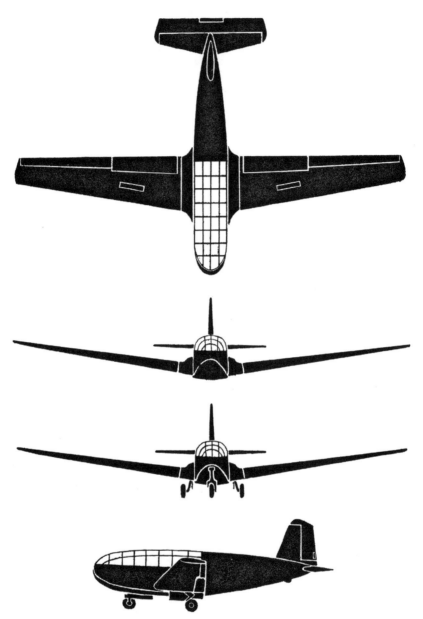

Navy Bristol XLRQ-1, three-view section.

Only two gliders were constructed, although optimistic supporters had talked in terms of producing 12,000 of them at one point in the early stages. The twin-hull, twenty-four-place model was never built.

XLRQ-1 Technical Data
Crew: Pilot and co-pilot
Dimensions
    Wingspan: 71'
    Wing area: 500 square feet
    Height: 16'
    Fuselage length: 43.5'
Payload: 10 fully equipped Marines
Tow planes: J2F-5 or PBY-5A

XLRA-1 AND XLRA-2
The Navy contracted with Allied Aviation of Baltimore, Maryland, for XLRA float-wing gliders. In configuration and construction, they were similar to the XLRQ-1, differing primarily in landing gear. The XLRA-1 had a dual center wheel and wingtip skids. The XLRA-2 had a conventional two-wheel, landing gear that could be jettisoned.

Each were constructed primarily of wood, with fuselage and wing skin of impregnated plywood and a two-step planing hull. Wingspans were 70.5 feet and fuselage lengths 40 feet.

Although the Navy contracted for 100 LRA's, contracts were cancelled before any but the prototypes were built.

XLRG-1 AND XLRH-1
Two contracts were let for twenty-four-place gliders. Prior to letting contracts for either of these gliders, the Navy contracted the AGA Aviation Corporation of Willow Grove, Pennsylvania, for the construction of a 40 percent scale model of what was later to become the XLRG-1. Exactly thirty-five days later, AGA produced the glider and delivered it to Philadelphia. The head of the glider development program in the Navy, Captain R. S. Barnaby, flew the glider successfully on a number of test flights.

On 23 December 1941, the Navy awarded a contract to AGA, later to become G&A Aircraft Inc., for the construction of the XLRG-1. This configuration was to be of "twin-float" design. Each float was to be designed to carry five fully equipped men. The center nacelle was to carry the pilot, a co-pilot and twelve men.

Shortly thereafter, the Navy negotiated a contract with Snead and Company to produce a "twin-hull" model, the XLRH-1. Although the Navy had

Navy AGA float glider, forty-percent scale model.

Navy Allied XLRN-1.

Navy bomb glider.

Timm AG-2 assault glider.

sufficient confidence in this model to contract for a production run of fifty, it terminated the contract with Snead and AGA before either prototype was completed.

XLRN-1

Designed and built in tight secrecy at the Naval Aircraft Factory at Johnsonville, Pennsylvania, the all-wood XLRN-1 was one of America's two largest gliders and is its least known. It had a 110 foot wingspan and a rated payload of 18,000 lb. Two documents differ on loaded weights, with one indicating 33,160 lb and the other 37,764 lb. Its overload weight was 40,000 lb.

Its contemplated use was as a troop transport, a 3,000-gallon fuel glider and, most spectacularly, as a bomb-glider to fly into the mouth of a German submarine pen and explode on impact. For this last use, it had a television-like sensor in the nose.

It was test-flown many times and reportedly heavy at the controls. A Navy four-engine Douglas R5D towed the XLRN-1.

XLRN-1 Technical Data
Crew: Pilot and co-pilot
Weight
    Empty: 15,160/19,764 lb
    Cargo: 18,000/18,000 lb
    Total with cargo: 33,160/37,764 lb
Dimensions
    Wingspan: 110'
    Wing area: 1,200 square feet
    Fuselage length: 67.5'
Payload: 80 fully equipped soldiers; 3,000 gallons of fuel; or high-explosive demolitions (with the glider serving as the delivery platform)
Towing speed: 180 mph (maximum)
Tow planes: R5D

BOMB-GLIDER
The Navy also had a bomb-glider development program. It relied on existing air frames using Taylorcraff, Piper and Aeronca aircraft, replacing engines with extended nose nacelles and a nose wheel, thus converting them to tricycle landing aircraft. Equipped with television cameras and radar, these systems proved highly reliable during extensive testing. They never were used operationally, however.

OTHER DEVELOPMENTS

In addition to the experimental and production gliders already discussed, the Army Air Forces signed contracts for the XCG-9, XCG-11, XCG-12, XCG-19, the XAG-1 and the XAF-2, which reached various stages of completion but were not accepted. Most contracts were cancelled. Some wind-tunnel models were built.

TRAINING GLIDERS

Less well-known than the transport-glider program, but nonetheless important, was the production of the one-, two- and three-place training gliders, designated XTG's and TG's. Many companies participated in the design and manufacture of the 10 different training glider models. Of these, 7 went into production and 1,210 were built.

POWERED GLIDERS

The Army Air Forces experimented with a number of twin-engine CG-4A gliders. Originally, many Army Air Force leaders had gliders in mind that were to be expendable, one-mission aircraft. Later, maneuvers and operations proved gliders to be durable beyond expectation, and this viewpoint changed. In addition, it was considered poor economics to build gliders as large as were being constructed and then to use them for just a single mission. For this reason, the idea was conceived of placing a "package" engine installation in the gliders, thus producing an aircraft capable of carrying bulky loads over short distances. The idea was to be able to convert a glider into a powered aircraft within a few hours. Power in a glider would also be used to assist in takeoffs, extend gliding range and to provide a means of recovering a glider after it had landed and returning it to friendly lines.

Three powered gliders were developed. The CG-4A, powered by two 125-hp Franklin engines, became the XPG-1. The CG-4A, powered by two 175-hp Ranger engines, became the XPG-2. The CG-15A was powered by two Jacobs R-755-9 engines. All tested satisfactorily. However, it was determined that there would be no tactical use for them. If the need arose, however, they were available for production.

BOMB GLIDERS

In 1942, the Army Air Forces procured ten XBG-1 bomb-gliders. These gliders were to have an explosive warhead and released from under the wing of a bomber. An operator in the bomber was to direct the glider to its target by radio control. They never became operational.

ASSAULT GLIDER

An idea that tantalized the Army ground forces but drew heavy fire from the Army Air Forces was that of an assault glider—an armed glider suitable for landing on fields that had not yet been secured by parachute forces.

The Army visualized a glider that was to be a sort of flying pillbox and would land before the main serials of transport gliders and parachute forces. This assault glider would protect the landings against enemy infantry, small-arms fire, and antiaircraft fire. Two .50-caliber and two .30-caliber machine-guns mounted behind armor plate and manned by glidermen would give the glider substantial firepower. In addition, there were to be two rocket launchers, Tow planes for the attack glider were to be either bombers or fighters.

On 22 May 1943, the Materiel Command awarded contracts to Timm Aircraft Company and Christopher Company for an XAG-2 and an XAG-1, respectively. Each glider was to have a gross weight of 8,500 lb and a towing speed of 240 miles per hour. Each was to be a low-wing cantilever monoplane, with room for six glidermen and a pilot and co-pilot. The gliders were to be of all-wood construction. Christopher delivered a wind-tunnel model, but General B. W. Chidlaw, who oversaw its development in the Office of the Assistant Chief of Air Staff for Materiel, criticized the glider as a "damned fool idea." The assault-glider project was "spiked" in September 1943.

GLIDER "SNATCH" PICK-UP TECHNIQUE

Numerous suggestions for using gliders came from the front as America gained combat experience. One idea was to land gliders on packed snow to resupply ground units in the arctic. Another was to land them on water where suitable landing areas were not available. Still another idea was to use gliders in the routine supplying of weapons, ammunition, food and personnel to fixed and mobile ground and air-force elements. It was pointed out that the latter method of supply would be especially useful for armored operations. Another suggestion was to drop airborne maintenance repair shops, housed in gliders, behind armored units to maintain the armored vehicles. It was also recommended that gliders should move airborne field hospitals from one location to another or evacuate wounded from combat areas.

At first, many of these suggestions might have been far beyond the scope of the glider to accomplish, but they were made feasible by the development of a pick-up device. It enabled a flying tow plane to whisk away a loaded glider from a standing position. In July 1943, Major Louis B. Magid, Jr., on the staff of the Airborne Command at Fort Bragg, North Carolina, tested the device and its associated technique. In these tests, a C-47 flying at 140 miles per hour snatched a glider off the ground with ease. Within seconds from the time the C-47's tow-hook seized the glider tow rope slung between two upright poles, the glider was in the air and flying at 120 miles per hour. Major Magid reported that the engines of the aircraft showed less strain during the pick-up than during a conventional take off. The technique was used with a fully-loaded glider with equally good results. Soon, successful tests were being made in snatching gliders equipped with skids as takeoff gear. Snatch tests were conducted with the CG-13A and were successful.

This technique was soon being used in training and after maneuvers to recover gliders. It saved dismantling thousands of gliders, which would have had to be hauled out from constricted areas by truck without this new technique. The snatch technique was also soon being used after combat operations to transport flyable gliders back to home bases. It was used to evacuate wounded in the European theater and in Burma.

DOUBLE TOW

After tests held at Camp Mackall, North Carolina, in September 1943, it became commonplace for C-47's to tow two gliders in a staggered V formation. This double-tow arrangement had the advantage of decreasing the air space taken up by flights delivering airborne elements into combat. It also had additional benefits: it delivered soldiers in a more concentrated mass and doubled the towing capacity of the aircraft.

Parachutists also jumped from gliders in double tow. The results were more successful than had been expected, causing Colonel Ward S. Ryan, who had conducted the tests, to recommend that gliders be modified for the use of parachute forces. This was not done, however, as the Army Air Forces found that using gliders in this way would prove less efficient than using them to carry the regularly constituted glider infantry and other glider-trained ground units.

HAMILCAR "PIGGYBACK"

During 1949, the Army Air Forces procured a British Hamilcar glider for test and evaluation. They also began studies to determine if the Hamilcar or another glider could be carried "piggy back" as the Germans had done with the DFS 230. They used the P-38 fighter aircraft attached to the top of the Hamilcar, although consideration was also given to using the P-38 with the CG-10A.

Piggyback glider delivery had several advantages over standard glider-tow techniques. The combined aircraft was piloted en route to its objective by the pilot of the P-38. This would ease the problem of flying the glider hundreds of miles, sometimes just with instruments, as experienced in standard towrope flight. After releasing the glider, the P-38 would provide it with protection overhead against hostile air attacks. If the glider could be loaded with fuel for the combined aircraft, long-range flights could take place, enabling the shipment of gliders to distant theaters of war. This last point was important in view of the fact that glider operations overseas had had to be curtailed because there was inadequate shipping space for the enormous crates that gliders required.

However, there were serious disadvantages to the piggyback system. It was time-consuming to arrange the coupling of the two craft. Furthermore, it meant that the much-needed fighter would be grounded for unacceptable periods of time. Once airborne, there would be difficulty in releasing the glider in the event of a power failure in the P-38 (the release mechanism was to be electrically operated). It was envisioned that wing-loading differentials would make the combination difficult to fly. Although the study concluded that the idea was aerodynamically feasible—structurally and from the standpoint of weight and balance—the disadvantages were too many, and the idea was allowed to die.

TOW PLANES

In the spring of 1942, General Arnold directed the Materiel Command to determine the suitability of the various combat and transport aircraft as tugs for towing gliders. Wright Field conducted extensive tests from then until late in 1944. The results showed that the C-47, C-46, C-54 and C-60 transport aircraft, the A-25 attack bomber, the B-25 bomber, the P-38 fighter and any four-engined bomber or transport were all suitable for towing the CG-4A and the CG-15A. If the P-38 were used, however, it would be necessary to place sandbags in the nose of the glider.

The CG-13A could be towed by a C-46, a C-54, a B-17 or a B-24, in addition to the favored C-47. However, by the end of 1944, the C-47 became the most widely used tow aircraft, due to its performance and availability in all theaters of war.

Pick-up hook folded to the fuselage of a Douglas C-47.

Waco CG-4A's ready for take-off. Note the radio-telephone wire attached to the tow rope for pilot-to-pilot communication.

Preparing the "clothes-line" for a glider snatch.

A Douglas C-47 "picking up" a Waco CG-4A.

CHAPTER 6

Gliders of the Soviet Union

A-7

The Antonov A-7, also known as the Red-Front (Rot-Front) RF-8, was one of the early Soviet military transport gliders. It won a design award for Oleg K. Antonov, the famous aeronautical engineer. The first models were built about the time World War II started (1939). In its high aspect-ratio, its 62.2-foot wing, and its fuselage, it preserved many of the excellent flying characteristics of a sailplane. It was 37.7 feet long and carried eight equipped soldiers.

It had a retractable landing gear and all the latest instruments necessary to enable the pilot to handle the glider in all flyable weather; 400 were manufactured.

The Army used the A-7 extensively to support Soviet guerrillas operating against the Germans. The glider was towed by the Il-4, the SB-3 and the Il-2.

A-7 Technical Data
Crew: Pilot
Dimensions
    Wingspan: 62.2'
    Wing area: 335 square feet
    Fuselage length: 37.7'
Weight
    Cargo: 2,000 lb
Payload
    Pilot, 8 equipped troops
Tow-planes: Li-2, SB-3

A-11 (G-11)

While some sources doubt that the A-11 was ever built, there is substantial evidence to prove its existence. The evidence shows that the A-11 was an improved version of the A-7 glider. It was similar in appearance to the A-7, except for the fact that it had a strut-braced wing.

Vladimir Gribovskii collaborated with Oleg K. Antonov in its design and development. It had a wing span of 82 feet and a length of 42 feet.

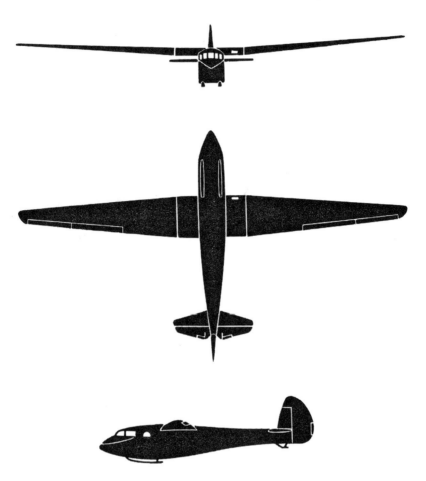

Antonov A-7, three-view section.

Groshev GN-4, the world's first military transport glider.

Antonov A-7.

Polikarpov BDP (S-1).

Ilyushin Il-32.

Reports also exist of a G-11 glider. In view of the fact that Gribovskii was the co-designer of the A-11, it is possible that the A-11 and the G-11 (Gribovskii-11) were one and the same glider, the A-11 at some time taking the G-11 designation for unknown reasons.

A-11/G-11 Technical Data
Type: Transport
Crew: Pilot and co-pilot
Payload:
    Pilot, co-pilot, 20 equipped troops
Dimensions
    Wingspan: 82'
    Fuselage length: 42'
Weight
    Cargo: 4,400 lb

BDP (S-1)
In July 1941, the Bureau of Special Construction, OKB (Osoboe Konstruktorskoe Buro), ordered the production of a battle transport-glider, BDP (Boevoi Desantnyi Planer). The first model was built within a month, and the first test flight was made before the end of the summer.

The BDP (S-1), as it became, had a high cantilever wing 65.7 feet long, of wooden construction, with a high aspect ratio. It was tapered and had a wing-root dihedral. Trailing edge flaps were fitted.

The monocoque fuselage was oval shaped and accommodated a pilot and 20 fully-equipped troops. Gun-ports were built into the fuselage, from which glidermen could shoot at attacking aircraft or, while landing, at enemy troops. The wheel under-carriage was dropped after take-off and the glider landed on plywood runners.

The government stopped production shortly after the first gliders were manufactured, deploying the factory to the east in Russia to escape destruction by the advancing Nazi armies. Production of the BDP (S-1) was not resumed because the government turned all aircraft production resources toward the construction of combat aircraft.

BDP (S-1) Technical Data
Type: Battle glider
Crew: Pilot
Payload: 20 soldiers, equipped, or equivalent weight in other cargo.
Towing speed: 100 mph (maximum)
Dimensions
    Wingspan: 65.7'
    Wing area: 481 sq ft

Weight
>   Total with cargo: 7,700 lb
>   Empty: 5,070 lb
>   Cargo: 2,630 lb

MOTOR-GLIDER MP-1

The motor-glider MP-1 (Motoplaner-1) showed the wartime continuation of Russian hopes to develop a satisfactory powered glider—long a dream of glider advocates. This development took place in 1943 just before the deployment of the factory to the east. The MP and the BDP (S-1) differed only in minor detail, except for the installation of two 140-hp five-cylinder engines on the leading edge of the wing of a standard BDP (S-1). A fixed-wheel landing gear was installed, also hoops at the ends of the wings to protect the tips on landing. A trim tab was fitted to the rudder, and a small window at the bottom of the nose to give the pilot better visibility.

The MP-1 had to be assisted at take-off when carrying a full load, but when empty could take off without assistance. It was released by its tow-plane once airborne and flew at 100 miles per hour, having a range of close to 500 miles.

GLIDER-BOMBER PB

During 1942, the OKB considered building a single-seat glider bomber, the PB (Planer Bombardirovshchik) and produced plans for it. These called for the glider to have an internal bomb bay that would allow for a variety of loads, including supply containers and a 4,400 lb bomb. The project was dropped, however, perhaps because of the urgent need for facilities and materials to build combat aircraft.

G-31

The G-31 military glider was a daring experiment far ahead of its time. It was designed by Pavel Ignat'evich Grokhovskii, military pilot, parachutist, inventor, and head of the special design bureau of the Leningrad Institute.

It was a mid-wing all-wooden monoplane. The fuselage was a narrow plywood monocoque construction that used wood-fabrication techniques advanced for that day. The pilot and co-pilot sat above the wing in a plexiglass enclosure. The forward edge of the wing, which was 91.9 feet long, was transparent for approximately sixteen feet on each side of the fuselage. Eighteen passengers, nine on each side, lay flat in the wing behind the transparent window.

The G-31 glider-plane or powered glider, Yakov Alksnis, followed the development of the G-31 glider. A 700-hp M-25 9-cylinder radial engine, placed in the nose, powered the Yakov Alksnis.

After flight tests of these gliders had been conducted at Moscow, it became clear that the design did not allow for quick enough abandonment of the glider by its passengers in an emergency or when landing under fire in combat. For this reason, the G-31 and G-31 Yakov Alksnis were abandoned.

G-31 Technical Data
Type: Transport glider
Crew: Pilot and co-pilot
Dimensions
    Wingspan: 91.9'
    Wing area: 753 sq ft
Weight
    Total with cargo: 7,054 lb
    Empty: 3,086 lb
    Cargo: 3,968 lb
Payload
    18 troops fully-equipped.
Flight performance
    Maximum airspeed: 84 mph

GN-4

The GN-4 (Croshev No. 4), designed by G. F. Groshev, was built at the Moscow Glider Factory shortly after the factory's establishment. It was first revealed to the public in the 1934 all-union glider meeting.

This was the world's first transport glider. In design, it stood between the sailplane and the wartime transport glider, although in configuration it was much like a large sailplane. Although designed to be towed throughout its flight, except for the few minutes after its release from its tow-plane, it is reputed to have flown as a sailplane under suitable wind conditions. It was primarily designed for flying as one of a combination of gliders in a glider train, and was normally towed by the commercial version of the R-5.

The GN-4 was a strut-braced high-wing monoplane with a narrow oval fuselage. It had an enclosed pilot's compartment with five passenger seats behind the pilot. The 60-foot wing had a straight leading edge and a trailing edge tapered from the centre section. It had a very high aspect ratio. The R-5 towed it at close to 100 miles per hour. The empty weight of the glider was 1,000 pounds.

GN-4 Technical Data
Type: Transport glider
Crew: Pilot

Dimensions
    Wingspan: 60'
    Fuselage length: 27'
Weight
    Total with cargo: 1,992 lb
    Empty: 1,000 lb
    Cargo: 992 lb
Payload
    5 passengers
Flight performance
    Towing speed: 100 mph

Il-32

The Il-32 was designed by S. V. Ilyushin and a single glider, a prototype, was finished in 1948. No others were built.

It was an all-metal, high-wing, cantilever monoplane. A unique feature was that both the nose and the rear of the cargo compartment were hinged to permit the loading of heavy or bulky equipment. The glider had built-in ramps for loading wheeled cargo.

It carried a crew and thirty-five fully equipped soldiers.

KT-20

Conceived in 1944 by D. I. N. Kolesnikov and P. V. Tsybin, well-known in the Soviet Union as pioneers in glider design, the KT-20 (named after the designers) was a large transport glider. A few were built in the Yakovlov factory. It had a sharply tapered strut-braced wing 72.6 feet long and a tapered fuselage 49.4 feet long.

The KT-20 was loaded from the rear. The section beyond the trailing edge of the wing lifted upward to open the cargo compartment. It was constructed of wood and metal and carried twenty-four troops or 4,410 pounds of cargo. It was towed by the Il-12.

KT-20 Technical Data

Type: Transport glider
Crew: Pilot and co-pilot
Dimensions
    Wingspan: 72.6'
    Fuselage length: 49'
Weight
    Cargo: 4,410 lb
Tow-plane: Il-12

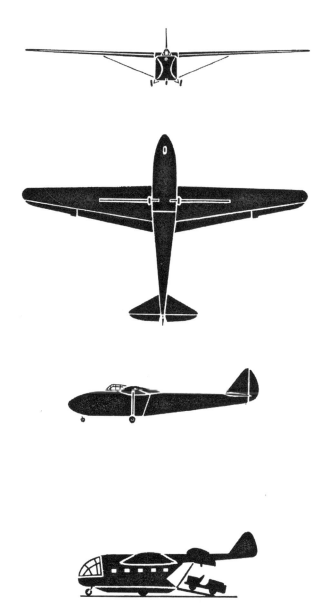

Tsybin KT-20, three-view section, and Moskalyev SAM-23.

SAM-23

In 1943, in addition to the KT-20 and the BDP (S-1), the Soviets produced the SAM-23. It was a high-wing, twin-boom, sturdily built monoplane resembling the U.S. YCG-10A. A. S. Moskalev, its designer, conceived a "gondola" fuselage, and so designed the SAM that it efficiently loaded and carried bulky cargo, including Jeep-sized vehicles. The pilot and co-pilot sat in the nose behind a large concave plexiglass window which allowed excellent observation.

The glider had an integral ramp that was lowered when the rear of the cargo compartment was raised, and was propped up between the booms for loading. It could carry sixteen men or a jeep, or an equivalent weight in other cargo.

The Soviets produced a number of SAM-23's. Moskalev also proposed a motorized SAM, but the project never developed beyond the design stage.

SAM-23 Technical Data

Type: Battle transport glider
Crew: Pilot and co-pilot
Weight
    Cargo: 3,600 lb
Payload:
    16 equipped troops or a jeep or the equivalent of other cargo.

JAKOVLEVA-CYBINA GLIDER

This glider was reportedly shown at the Moscow Soviet Aviation Day exhibitions in 1949. Six were designed and built under the direction of A. S. Jakovleva, and another six under the direction of aeronautical engineer P. V. Cybina.

It is possibly the same craft as the medium-sized Tshibin cargo glider, since the likelihood of two new gliders appearing at this date is questionable. On the other hand, descriptions of the Jakovleva-Cybina—and the fact that there appears to be no question that one glider was designed and built by these two engineers and the other by Tshibin (in his own right a prominent aircraft designer)—lead to the conclusion that there were, in fact, two new and different models. It is interesting that descriptions of the Jakovleva-Cybina glider and the American World War II CG-4 are similar; and it is quite evident that the Jakovleva-Cybina and the CG-4 are alike in appearance.

The Jakovleva-Cybina glider had a large "greenhouse," giving the pilot and co-pilot excellent visibility relatively free from interference from structural bracing. It carried troops or cargo, and could be used for parachute drops. It was fabric covered and opened from the front for loading. The towing aircraft was the Il-12.

WINGED TANK "KT"

Around 1941, it was rumored in Soviet circles that the Soviet Army was in the process of developing a glider transport system that could carry a small battle-tank. More recently available reports about this project tend to confirm the fact that such a project did exist.

Assisted by a staff of engineers, Oleg K. Antonov was charged with the development and construction of what came to be known as the transport glider KT (Kryliatyi Tank or Winged Tank). The project apparently started in 1939 or 1940 and was completed in 1941, when the system was tested.

The KT was a new departure in transport glider design in several major respects. One very interesting feature is that it was a biplane glider. Second, Antonov used the T-60 tank as the fuselage of the glider; this combination could be towed into the air and released while in flight to glide down to a pre-selected spot behind enemy lines. The six-ton T-60 tank, its gun pointing to the rear, was secured between the twin booms of the glider and attached to the under surface of the lower wing. A substantial part of the tank protruded ahead of the lead edge of the lower wing. The system was so designed that the controls for the glider were inside the tank.

In view of the shortage of metal in the Soviet Union at the time, the glider frame was made of wood, and the wings and empennage were covered with fabric.

With the test pilot Sergei Anokin at the controls of the winged tank, Pasha Jeremejew, at the controls of a four-engined Tlf-3 bomber, towed the enormous weight into the air. Although the take-off and early stages of the flight went well, the bomber's engines began to overheat, and the glider had to be released. Anokin started the tank's engine and then let the tank treads start to move slowly. At about 200 feet above the ground, he accelerated the treads; they reached their maximum land speed just before the treads touched the ground. The system landed smoothly, and Anokin brought it to a stop. The tank was quickly disengaged from its wings, and it raced off.

Despite the success of the first flight, no others took place, reportedly because there was a shortage of towing aircraft with enough power to tow the winged tank, such planes then being urgently needed at the front.

KT Technical Data

Type: Battle-tank transport glider
Crew: Pilot
Weight
    Empty: 4,800 lb
    Cargo: 13,200 lb
    Total with cargo: 18,000 lb

Dimensions
    Wingspan: 49.2'
    Wing area: 732 sq ft
    Fuselage length: 37.7'
Payload: 1 six-ton T-60 tank
Flight performance
    Lift off speed: 100 mph
Tow-plane: TB-3 bomber

TS-25

First seen by the public in 1948 at the Soviet Aviation Day exhibition in Moscow, the TS-25 was one of the largest of the postwar Soviet gliders to go into production. At the time of the exhibition, six had been manufactured. It had many of the design characteristics of the wartime KT-20, for which Tsybin was a co-designer, and in one way can be considered a technologically sophisticated successor to the KT-20.

Designed by P. V. Tsybin, the TS-25 was a heavy cargo-glider. It had a braced high wing and a pilot's compartment sitting above the cargo compartment. The nose was hinged to facilitate loading. The wheels could be dropped, after which the pilot landed the glider on skids fitted to the bottom of the craft. The glider appeared to be constructed largely of wood, with wing and fuselage exteriors of stressed plywood.

The Soviets furnished a number of the TS-25's to the Czechoslovak military forces, who called it the NK-25.

TS-25 Technical Data

Crew: Pilot and co-pilot
Weight
    Empty: 5,115 lb
    Cargo: 4,806 lb
    Total with cargo: 9,921 lb
Dimensions
    Wingspan: 82.8'
    Wing area: 830 sq ft
    Fuselage length: 54.1'
Payload: 25 troops, equipped, small vehicles, light artillery, or miscellaneous cargo.
Towing speed: 155 mph (maximum)

Yak-14

The Yak-14, a large, bulky, square-shaped wooden glider was designed by A. S. Yakovlev and produced shortly after the war. This glider and the TS-25 caused

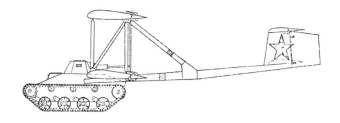

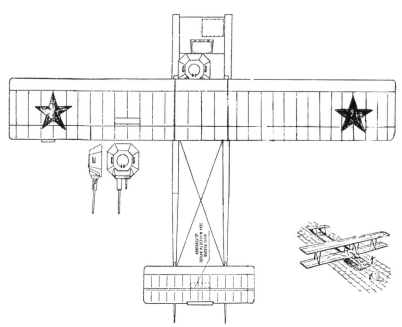

Antonov Kryliatyi tank KT "winged tank," three-view section.

Tsybin TS-25.

a sensation at the Soviet Aviation Day Show held at the Tushino Airport near Moscow in 1949, when six of each flew overhead in what was described as "spectacular glider-trains."

The Yak-14 had a high-aspect-ratio braced wing with a span of 85.8 feet. The wing was built from three sections, a rectangular center section and two tapered outer sections that were square at the ends. The wing had no dihedral. Fowler flaps and slotted ailerons extended over the whole of the trailing edge.

The nose opened sideways to permit the loading of cargo. The pilot and co-pilot sat in the nose, which featured a large "greenhouse", giving the pilot excellent visibility relatively unobstructed by structural bracing.

The Yak-14 carried small vehicles or other cargo to the extent of 7,716 lb, or could transport thirty-five fully-equipped soldiers, and it could be used to drop parachutists. The cargo compartment measured 26.3 feet in length by 7.6 feet in height and was 7.4 feet wide. The maximum towing speed was 186 miles per hour.

The Soviet Union supplied several of these gliders to the Czechoslovak military forces.

Yak-14 Technical Data
Type: Transport glider
Crew: Pilot and co-pilot
Weight
    Empty: 6,825 lb
    Cargo: 8,056 lb
    Total with cargo: 14,881 lb
Dimensions
    Wingspan: 85.8'
    Wing area: 1,050 sq ft
    Fuselage length: 60.5'
    Cargo compartment
        Length: 26.3'
        Width: 7.4'
        Height: 7.6'
Payload: 35 fully-equipped troops
Towing speed: 186 mph (maximum)

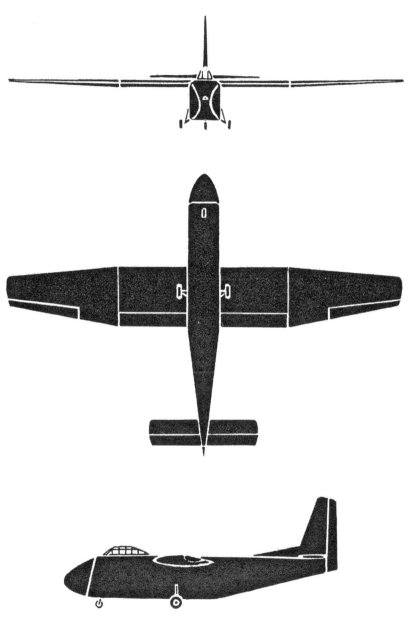

Yakovlev Yak-14, three-view section.

Yakovlev Yak-14.

Yakovlev Yak-14.

CHAPTER 7

Some Lesser-known Developments

A number of other nations produced gliders during World War II or shortly thereafter as a result of the extensive use of gliders in combat operations by the belligerents. It is a little-known fact that Australia, France, Italy, India, Yugoslavia and others designed and manufactured gliders. Canada, on the other hand, procured several models from the United States and England. Czechoslovakia received some of the latest models produced in the Soviet Union.

ARGENTINA: I-AE-25

Built by the Instituto Aerotecnica de Cordoba, the I-AE-25, also known as the *Manque* ("Vulture"), looked very much like the American Waco, CG-4A. Built of wood, it more closely resembled the Timm, CG-4B, a CG-4A configuration but of all-wood construction.

As with the CG-4A, the nose of the I-AE-25 could be raised for loading of vehicles or artillery. It had a wingspan of 83.7 feet and a length of 48.2 feet.

The I-AE-25 had a lower cargo capacity than the CG-4A, 2,474 pounds as against 4,460 pounds, undoubtedly the result of the weight of the wood used for its construction. Its empty weight was 5,423 pounds—or some 1,983 pounds more than its American counterpart. Only one I-AE-25 was built.

AUSTRALIA: DHA-G1, G2

In 1942, when the Japanese were advancing towards Australia, the Royal Australian Air Force decided to develop a transport glider. According to Merv Waghorn of de Havilland, these gliders were for fighter support. They were to land at forward Spitfire bases with cargoes of engines, guns and crews, which were to maintain the Spitfires. Other sources state the gliders were to fly troops to attack Japanese forces landing at remote beaches. The small troop capacity of the gliders make this latter use questionable.

The de Havilland factories at Bankstown were awarded the contract, established under Specification 5/42, and produced two prototypes under the company's designation DHA-GI and the registration numbers EG-1, 2 (Experimental Glider-1, 2). The gliders were made largely of wood, with a 60-foot wingspan and a fuselage 33 feet long. These prototypes were given RAAF

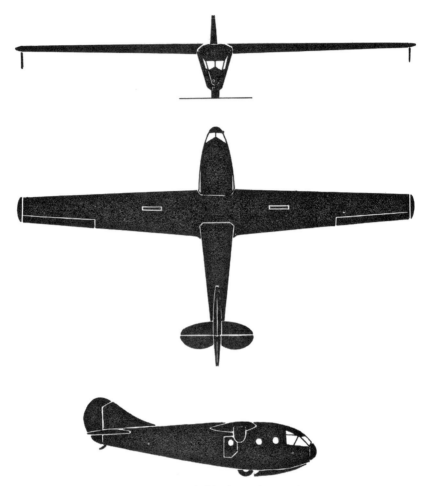

De Havilland DHA-G1, three-view section.

De Havilland DHA-G1.

designations A57-1001 and A57-1002 in December 1942 and were tested at Laverton.

In mid-1943, under a subsequent contract calling for a somewhat modified version with a wingspan of 50.5 feet and slightly larger fuselage, de Havilland built six DHA-G2's (RAAF's A57-1/6's). The empty weight was 1,450 pounds and the glider carried 1,800 pounds.

With the exception of one DHA-G2, which after the war was converted to a Griffith suction-wing test-glider using a centrifugal fan driven by a Mercury 59A, 96-hp engine, the gliders had an indifferent career. They were used in limited operations with the School of Land and Air Warfare.

DHA-G1, G2 Technical Data

Type: Transport glider
Crew: Pilot
Weight
    Empty: 1,240 lb, 3,250 lb
    Cargo: 1,550 lb, 1,800 lb
    Total with cargo: 2,790 lb. 3,250 lb
Dimensions
    Wingspan: 59', 50.5'
    Wing area: 300 sq ft
    Fuselage length: 33'
    Height 7'
Payload: Six fully-equipped troops.
Towing speed: 130 mph (maximum)
Maximum airspeed: 200 mph

CANADA

In 1942, the Royal Canadian Air Force contemplated purchasing thirty Hotspur gliders from the United Kingdom to use in training a cadre of Canadian glider pilots in a school then being considered by the Air Staff. Thought was also given to organizing a glider operational training unit. None of these plans materialized, however.

Later that year, apparently modifying its plans, the Air Force did purchase twenty-two Hotspur II's, and presumably many Canadians did learn to fly them. Canadians piloted gliders in some of the most important glider operations in Europe. In one of the most daring glider flights in history, with one Canadian and one RAF pilot at the controls, a CG-4A carrying medical supplies and other critical items was towed across the Atlantic Ocean from Canada to England.

After the war, the RCAF obtained three Horsas, thirty-two Hadrian Mark II's (CG-4As), a CG-15A and one PG-2A. RCAF inventories carried these gliders for as long as ten years after the war.

CHINA

Shortly after World War II, the Nationalist Chinese Air Force ordered the production of an assault glider. The Institute of Aero Research at Chengtu in Szechwan-Province completed the first prototype in 1947. It carried a pilot, co-pilot and twelve passengers. It was one of the few low-wing transport gliders built during or after the war, possessing a surprisingly. streamlined appearance. It was of wood construction, doped with aluminum. Although twelve were ultimately produced, the glider remained experimental, and there were no production orders placed.

CZECHOSLOVAKIA

Gliding and soaring long have been popular sports in Czechoslovakia. Although during the war, while dominated by the Nazis, little took place in glider development, after the war, particularly in the late 1940's, that country's armed forces took a serious interest in transport gliders. By the early 1950's, the country had two under construction, the AE-53 and the LD-605.

The AE-53 had much the appearance of the American Laister Kaufmann YCG-10A; the LD-605 resembled the CG-4A. Each had comparable loading ports to their American counterparts. Before the two had reached completion, the Soviets turned over numbers of the TS-25's and Yak-14's to the Czechoslovakian Air Force, and the construction of the AE-53 and LD-605 was discontinued.

FRANCE: CASTEL-MAUBOUSSIN CM-10

After the invasion of France by the Allies and the recapture of Paris, the soon-reorganized French Air Ministry determined to investigate the possibility of using the transport glider for military operations. French military leaders had been impressed by the Allied assault-glider operations in various phases of the war against Germany.

The ministry requested the *Etablissement Fouga*, headed by Pierre Mauboussin (a company that specialized in designing and building sports gliders), to design and build a military glider similar to those used by the Royal Air Force and the U.S. Air Force. The glider initially took the name *Castel Mauboussin*, "Castel" being derived from "Castello," the Spanish name of Robert Castello, the technical design manager of the company. It was he who had proposed a high-wing monoplane with a high lift-to-drag ratio.

The ministry ordered two prototypes. The first was delivered in 1947 (although its design and construction had begun before the end of the war). Despite the fact that the French had just been liberated from German occupation and the economy was weak and materials in short supply, the glider turned out to be a superb aircraft.

Chinese glider.

Czechoslovakian NK-14 (Soviet Yak-14).

Aerodynamically, the *Mauboussin* was a clean aircraft of all-wood construction. It had a wing-span of 87 feet and a length of 60 feet. It loaded from the front, the nose swinging open at the side to permit loading to take place. It could carry two quarter-ton trucks or a quarter-ton truck and a howitzer with trailer as well as gun crew and driver.

The first test-flight took place at Mont-de-Marson with test-pilot Leon Bourriau at the controls. The flight was successful, as was the program of evaluation-testing, until the final phases when Bourriau unknowingly exceeded stress limits set for the glider. The CM-10 disintegrated, and although Bourriau managed to eject and came to the ground by parachute, he was severely injured.

The glider, nevertheless, was considered an unquestionable success, and before testing was completed, the ministry placed a pre-production order for twenty-five gliders with the Societe National de Construction Aeronautiques du Nord. Later, the number was increased to 100. The Societe National had been called in because the Fouga facilities were inadequate to meet the production requirements. Before production had really got under way, however, budget changes made it necessary to cut production, and only six were ever manufactured.

Several production models were later converted into powered aircraft. One was fitted with two piston engines, another with jets. However, neither project succeeded, despite its attractive performance as a glider, and later in its powered 100 and 101 versions. The demise of the CM-10 was the result of the change of French military thinking, which gave priority to paratroops over gliderborne forces. In addition, there was a surplus of powered aircraft in France after the war, including the Ju 52 and the C-47. Budgetary cutbacks also played an important role in reducing the chance of the CM-10 taking a solid place in the military and civilian aviation industry.

CM-10 Technical Data
Type: Heavy transport glider
Crew: Pilot and co-pilot
Weight
    Empty: 6.400 lb
    Cargo: 9,000 lb
    Total with cargo: 15,400 lb
Dimensions
    Wingspan: 87'
    Wing area: 770 sq ft
    Fuselage Length: 60'
    Height: 19'

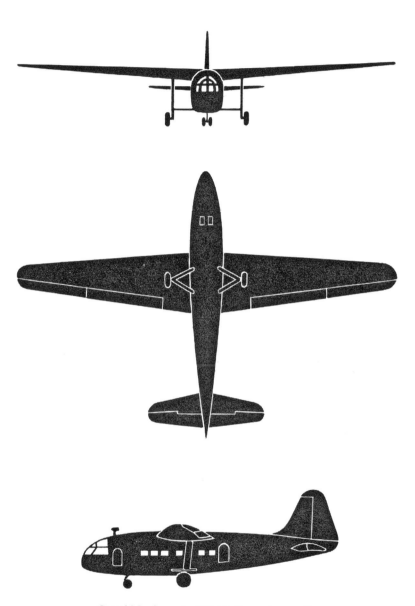

Castel Mauboussin CM-10, three-view section.

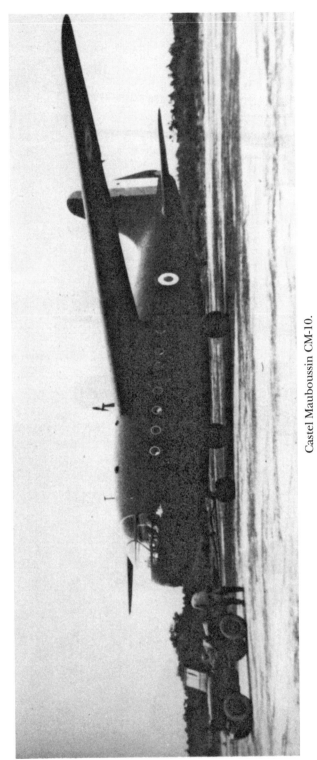

Castel Mauboussin CM-10.

Cargo compartment
    Length: 26'
    Width: 5.8'
    Height: 7'
Payload: 35 troops, equipped; two 1/4-ton trucks; or military equipment to
    load capacity
Towing speed: 180 mph (maximum)
Tow-planes: Ju 52, Halifax, SO 161, C-47

INDIA

Strangely, India in 1941 and 1942 was one of the first nations to produce a military transport glider, even though the centers of World War II conflict were still fairly removed from her borders. It was not until early 1944 that General Orde Wingate launched imperial glider forces against the Japanese in Burma in the most innovative airborne campaign of the war. U.S. gliders piloted by Americans transported these troops on more than ten glider missions of that campaign.

Anticipating extensive airborne operations in the eastern theater, Britain negotiated to build forty Horsas in India, but a contract was never signed. Lawrence Wright, in *The Wooden Sword*, points out high costs as the major factor, since bids showed it would cost ten times as much to produce the Horsa there as it was then costing in England.

The British shipped some Horsas to India, but the idea of sending quantities was shelved, since four-engine tow-planes necessary for towing the heavy glider in the tepid climate and to the heights necessary to cross mountain ranges on future missions were not available in quantity in India.

Lawrence Wright also reports the Indians did use and apparently took over some CG-4As for training their own glider pilots.

G-1

Engineers V. M. Ghatage, F. M. Crane and M. C. McCarthy, Jr., of Hindustan Aircraft Limited designed the G-1 transport glider during 1941 and 1942. It was a semi-monocoque wood glider that carried eight passengers, a pilot and a co-pilot. A two-ply molded plywood with wood grain at 45 degrees to the longitudinal axis of the glider covered the fuselage.

The cockpit enclosure was of molded, framed, transparent plastic panels, designed to give the pilots excellent visibility. It could be raised to allow pilot entrance and in case of emergency could be jettisoned to permit rapid escape. It had a large passenger door on the right side just behind the last passenger seat.

Plywood covered the built-up truss ribs of the 56.7-foot single-spar wing. The wing had spoilers on the upper surface near the leading edge midway in the semi-span. The rudder and elevators were covered with fabric.

The glider had dual controls, and pilots sat in tandem. It had jettisonable wheels and a single hardwood ski.

G-1 Technical Data

Crew: Pilot and co-pilot
Type: assault/transport glider
Weight
    Empty: 1,500 lb
    Cargo: 2,500 lb
    Total with cargo: 4,000 lb
Dimensions
    Wingspan: 56. 7'
    Wing area: 300 sq ft
    Fuselage length: 30.5'
    Height: 11.1'
Payload: 8 passengers or cargo
Towing speed: 160 mph (maximum)
Aspect ratio: 10

Unique among Allied gliders and in keeping with German glider doctrine that the glider should be a fighting weapon as opposed to just a passive transport vehicle, plastic windows had gun ports through which occupants could fire their rifles while in flight. The G-1 weighed 4,000 pounds and could carry 2,500. Hindustan Aircraft produced a single prototype and parts for ten more. In *The Wooden Sword*, Lawrence Wright reports wing warping on the prototype, a probable reason that the ten were never assembled, and the glider never went into production.

Hindustan Aircraft G-1.

Ambrosini AL-12P.

ITALY

Italy formed its first glider transport organization in June 1942. Initially, the Italians flew the German Go 242 and the DFS 230. As the war progressed, the military leaders determined to build their own gliders, and several models were ultimately produced.

Italian gliders and glider pilots were marshaled for the Malta operation as part of the total of a more than 500-strong glider operation planned by the Axis.

AL-12P

The Ambrosini AL-12P was built in 1942 by the Aerolombardi Corporation at the "Cantu" (Como Province) works. Its designer was A. Ambrosini, and its project engineer Ermengildo Preti.

A cantilever high-wing monoplane glider designed for attack and transport purposes, its tubular, 47-foot-long, wood-ribbed fuselage was covered with stressed molded plywood secured to the ribs. The 70-foot wing had a "double-box" foliated spruce plywood spar; plywood covered the wing surface, although ailerons were fabric-covered. Large slotted spoilers could be activated to stand perpendicularly above and below the wing and were one of the advanced features of this very well-designed glider.

AL-12P Technical Data
Type: Attack and transport glider
Crew: Pilot and co-pilot
Weight
    Empty: 3,500 lb
    Cargo: 2,700 lb
    Total with cargo: 6,200 lb
Dimensions
    Wingspan: 70'
    Wing area: 630 sq ft
    Fuselage length: 47'
Payload: 12 fully equipped troops or equivalent weight

The nose of welded steel tubing was covered with plywood into which large Plexiglas windows were set. Pilots sat side by side in the nose, which was hinged on the right side to open for the loading of cargo. There was a side door from which paratroopers jumped. The fuselage had seven equally-spaced windows on each side. The empennage was plywood-covered.

The glider carried twelve fully equipped troops or 2,700 lb of other weight. It was test-flown in 1943 and proved to be an excellent glider. Aerolombardi produced sixteen of these gliders for the Italian Army, and some were used

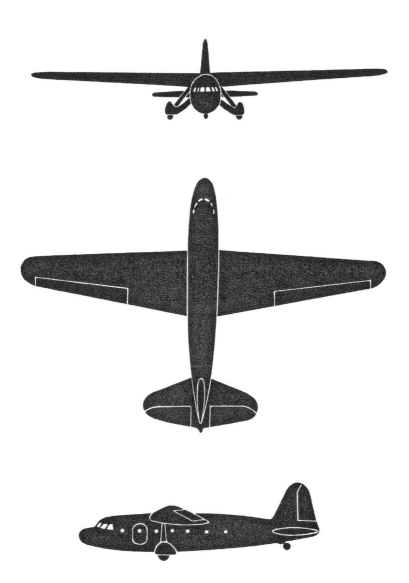

Ambrosini AL-12P, three-view section.

in operations fitted with 195-horsepower Alfa-115 four-cylinder, air-cooled engines, it became the P-512.

TM-2 (CATTM-2)

Designed by Caproni's Ing. Del Proposto, the TM-2 (CATTM-2) made its first flight in 1943. It was a large glider that had a loaded weight of 8,800 pounds and carried twenty passengers.

It was all-wood construction with plywood and fabric covering.

Four large doors opened into the cargo compartment, facilitating loading. It had a wingspan of 74.8 feet and was 42.5 feet long.

In one of the early test flights, the TM-2 went into a spin, killing the pilot. The glider was still not accepted for production at the time of the armistice.

The Caproni Corporation planned to equip the glider with motors but did not go through with the idea. The prototype, one of the few World War II gliders still in existence, is in the Milan Museum.

TM-2 (CATTM-2) Technical Data

Type: Transport glider
Crew: Pilot and co-pilot
Weight
    Empty: 4,400 lb
    Cargo: 4,400 lb
    Total with cargo: 8,800 lb
Dimensions
    Wingspan: 74.8'
    Wing area: 496 sq ft
    Fuselage length: 42.5'
    Fuselage height: 15.5'
    Payload: 20 fully-equipped troops or equivalent weight in cargo

SWEDEN: FI-3

The A. B. Flygindustri, Halmstad, Sweden, received a requirement from the Swedish Air Force for a transport glider in 1941. From this period until the end of World War II, the company produced five FI-3 gliders.

They were of wooden construction and had fabric covering. Doors were quickly detachable panels on each side of the fuselage.

The FI-3 had a wingspan of 54.6 feet and a length of 30.8 feet.

Fully loaded, the glider weighed 3,970 pounds.

At the end of World War II, the Swedish Air Force terminated the program.

Ambrosini AL-12P fuselage interior.

The spoilers of an Ambrosini AL-12P.

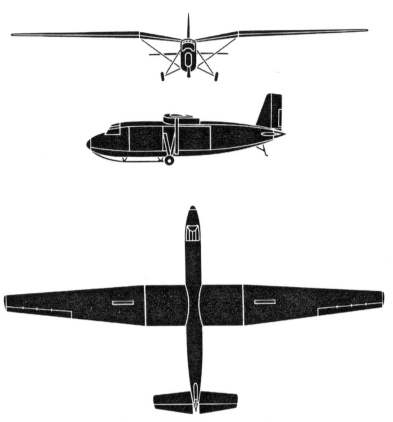

Caproni TM-2, three-view section.

Caproni TM-2.

FI-3 Technical Data
Type: Transport glider
Crew: Pilot and co-pilot?
Weight
    Empty: 1,742 lb
    Cargo: 2,228 lb
    Total with cargo: 3,970 lb
Dimensions
    Wingspan: 54.6'
    Wing area: 344.5 sq ft
    Fuselage length: 30.8'
    Payload: 11 fully equipped troops

TURKEY: THK-1

In 1941, alert to new developments in aviation, the Turkish Air Force decided to examine the potentialities of the transport glider. It issued a requirement for a transport glider to the *Turk Hava Kurumu* (Turkish Air League, or THK).

By 1943, the League had produced the THK-1, an all-wood glider that carried a pilot and eleven passengers.

Although some tests were conducted, the Turkish Air Force lost interest in the project, and the development of the glider was terminated.

YUGOSLAVIA

After World War II, Yugoslavia decided to investigate the possibilities of the transport glider as a military weapon that would fit into her armament requirements. It carried a single small vehicle or twelve passengers in a pod-like fuselage that opened at the rear to enable loading of bulky equipment. Its high braced wing was set well back over the fuselage. It had a single boom and a fixed tricycle landing gear. Only one such glider was built. It was designed by Ivo Sostaric.

A. B. Flygindustri FI-3.

Ivo Sostaric glider.

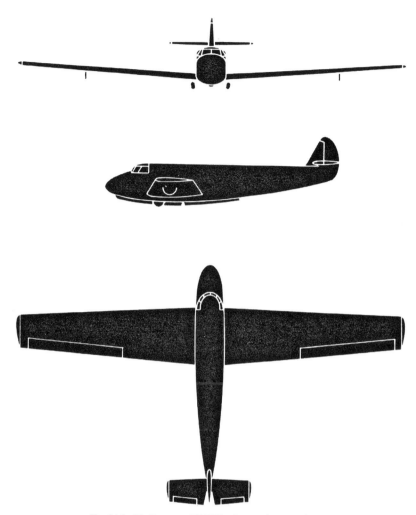

Turkish Air League THK-1, three-view section.

Turkish Air League THK-1.

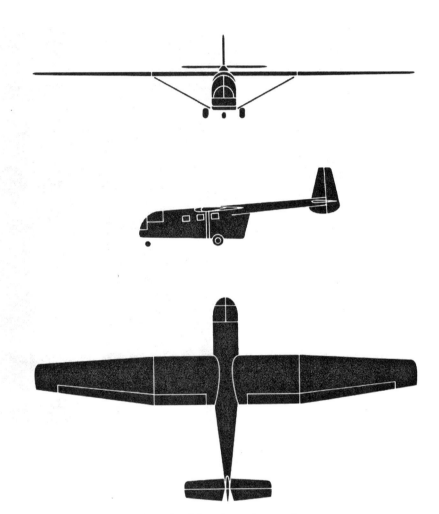

Ivo Sostaric glider, three-view section.

Loading, Flight and Landing Plans of the U.S. 82nd Airborne Division for Operation "Market Garden"

Tables and landing patterns in this appendix are abstracted from the operations report of the U.S. 82nd Airborne Division for "Market-Garden," the airborne invasion of Holland. They show the detail in which the operation was planned and consummated by tracing elements of Company A of the 325th Glider Infantry Regiment from their loading plan to the area in which they landed.

Tables B, C, D and E are representative tables taken from the glider loading, flight and landing plan taken from the invasion report of the 82nd Division. Company A is found in Table B. This and the others, as well as landing-pattern charts, show in minute detail the fortunes of the various gliders that took off on that eventful mission.

Fortunately for Company A, it fared better than some of the others.

Twenty-four of its twenty-five gliders landed in LZ O, where they were supposed to land according to Table B. Examination shows that many gliders carrying other units of the 82nd had serious mishaps, and some landed sixty miles away from the zone, a long hike through enemy saturated country.

Most equipment shown on Table E lifted by the gliders landed in serviceable condition. Casualties, despite the misfortunes to the gliders evident in Table D, were surprisingly few, although the fate of some of the passengers was not reported since they landed so far from the designated zone.

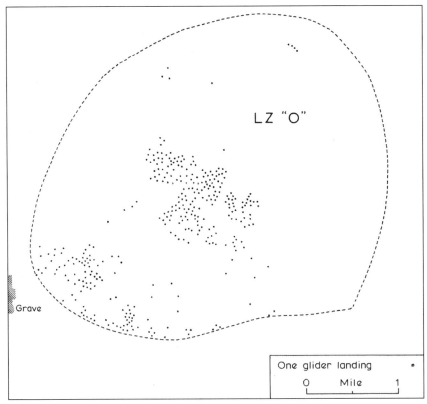

Glider landings of the U.S. 82nd Airborne Division in Operation "Market Garden."

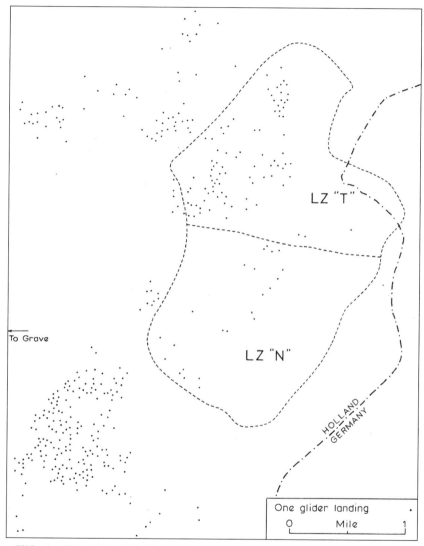

Glider landings of the U.S. 82nd Airborne Division in Operation "Market Garden."

TABLE A

Abstract from the Glider Loading Plan of Company A, 325th Glider Infantry Regiment, 82nd Airborne Division

Glider No. 1

1 Wpns Plat Sgt T/Sgt	240
3 Basics	720
1 Sgt LMG Sq Ldr	240
2 Amm Bearers LMG	480
1 Gunner LMG	240
1 Supply Sgt	240
1 Officer FA Fwd Obs	240
2 EM FA Fwd Obs	480
1 Asst Gunner LMG	240
	—— 3120

Equipment:

1 Litter w/2 Blankets	26
1 Can Water	50
1 Box K Rations	46
1 LMG	50
2 Shovels	10
2 Picks	14
22 Chests MG .30 Cal Am	440
	—— 636

Total	3756

Glider No. 2

1 Mortar Sqd Ldr Sgt	240
2 Amm Bearers Mortar	480
1 Gunner 60mm Mortar	240
1 Asst Gunner 60mm	240
1 Mortar Sec Ldr S/Sg	240
1 Mortar Sec Msgr	240
1 Wpns Plat Ldr Lt	240
3 Basics	720
2 Msgrs Wpns Pl Hq	480
	—— 3120

Equipment:

1 Litter w/2 Blankets	26
1 Can Water	50
1 Chest MG .30 Cal Am	20
4 CLs 60mm Amm	416
2 Shovels	10
1 Box K Rations	40
1 Axe	7
1 Mortar	50
1 Pick	7
	—— 626

Total	3746

Glider No. 3

2 Sqd Ldrs 60mm Mor Sgt	480
2 Gunners 60mm Mor	480
2 Asst Gunners 60mm	480
4 Amm Bearers 60mm	960
2 Basics	480
1 Arm Arti	240
	—— 3120

Equipment:

1 Litter w/2 Blankets	26
1 Can Water	50
2 Shovels	10
1 Box K Rations	40
3 CLs 60mm Amm	312
2 Mortars	100
3 Chests MG .30 Amm	60
2 Picks	14
1 Axe	7
	—— 619

Total	3739

Glider No. 4

1 Capt Co Comdr	240
1 Sgt Comm	240
2 Msgrs (Co)	480
7 Riflemen (Pl)	1680
2 Basics (Rad Op)	480
	—— 3120

Equipment:

1 Litter w/2 Blankets	26
1 Can Water	50
2 Boxes K Rations	86
3 CLs 60mm Amm	312
1 Axe	7
83 Sandbags	28
2 Shovels	10
1 Radio SCR 300	40
3 Picks	21
1 Box K Rations	40
	—— 620

Total	3740

SERIAL Nº A-14   TIME of DROP- 1617   FIELD- BARKSTON HEATH   LZ- O   ROUTE- S   GP Nº 61ST

ORGANIZATION	TAIL NUMBER	GLIDER INTACT	DAM	DES	MISS	OK	KIA	EVAC	MISS	JEEP SER	UNSER	TRAILER SER	UNSER	GUN SER	UNSER	DISTANCE FROM LZ
Co "B" 325 GLI INF	43-42638	X				14										LZ
"	43-39947	X				14										"
"	43-40510		X			14										"
"	43-41466	X				14										"
"	42-56514	X				13										"
"	43-26947	X				14										"
"	43-41074		X			14										"
"	43-340463	X				15										"
"	341525	X				14										"
"	43-40562	X				12		/								19 mi SW LZ
"	43-42108		X			13										"
"	341536	X				13										"
"	43-41539	X				14										"
"	43-37388	X				13										"
"	43-41710	X				13										"
Co "A" 325 GLI INF	327282		X			14										"
"	43-41217	X				14										"
"	336703	X				14										"
"	319879	X				14										"
"	339657	X				15										"
"	265283		X			15										"
"	43-41484	X				15										"
"	279393	X				13										"
"	341942	X				14										"
"	319832	X				15										"
"	341583		X			14										"
"	319865	X				14										"
"	340390	X				14										"
"	265551	X				13										"
"	256336	X				13										"
"	42-43657		X			13										"
"	43-19105	X				14										"
"	42-73566	X				14										"
"	43-19761	X				14										"
"	43-40389	X				14										"
"	43-77545	X				14										"
"	43-19811		X			14										"
"	341395	X				14										19 mi SW LZ
"	256344	X				14										"
TOTAL		31	9			550		1								
PERCENTAGE		77.5	22.5			95.82		.18								

TABLE B

SERIAL Nº A-16   TIME OF DROP-1631   FIELD-FULBECK   LZ-0   ROUTE-S   GP Nº 440 TM

ORGANIZATION	TAIL NUMBER	GLIDER				PERSONNEL				JEEP		TRAILER		GUN		DISTANCE FROM LZ
		INTACT	DAM	DES	MISS	OK	KIA	EVAC	MISS	SER	UNSER	SER	UNSER	SER	UNSER	
Ha & Ha Co 325	339987	X				7							X			17 mi SW
"	336728		X			13										19 mi SW
"	42-77594	X								X						30 mi SW
"	339675	X			X	9			3	X						28 mi SW
"	274065															LZ
"	341903	X								X						"
"	340094	X			X	4										
"	339661			X		4			11			X				28 mi SW
"	342631			X		6			1							LZ
"	42-77762					16										
Co "C" 325 GLI INF	341202	X		X		13										"
"	339729	X				14										"
"	336428	X		X		14										"
"	342133	X				12	1									"
"	272511	X				12										"
"	372285	X				13										"
"	274083	X		X		13										"
"	279167					11										"
"	256221	X				12										"
"	273070	X		X		13										"
"	340430	X				13			1							ENGLAND
"	277564	X				12										LZ
"	327454	X				13										12 mi SW
"	271495	X				15										13 mi SW
"	336958	X		X		14										ENGLAND
Ha & Ha Co 1st Bn 325	42-77780	X				11										LZ
"	341053	X				3			1	X						13 mi SW
"	279183	X				7										19 mi SW
"	277509	X														
"	274061				X	4				X		X				
"	343095				X	3					X					
"	246492															
"	342141	X				4			1							19 mi SW
"	277959				X	2								X		LZ
"	341159					5								X		
"	341864				X	6										
"	339914															
"	277449	X				5						X				19 mi SW
"	341496	X				7						X				
"	341059	X				3										
TOTAL		26	5	3	6	333	4	4	33	6	4	5	2			
PERCENTAGE		65	12.5	7.5	15	89.7	1.1		9.2	60	40	71.4	28.6			

TABLE C

SERIAL N° A-8 ORGANIZATION	TIME OF DROP-1442 TAIL NUMBER	GLIDER INTACT	DAM	DES	MISS	FIELD-FOLKINGHAM PERSONNEL OK	EVAC	KIA	MISS	LZ-N JEEP SER	UNSER	ROUTE-N TRAILER SER	UNSER	GP N° 313 GUN SER	UNSER	DISTANCE FROM LZ
BTRY "B" 320 FA BN	43-41489	X				3					X					3 MI NE
"	43-41683	X				3					X					4 MI NE
"	43-41089	X				7										"
"	43-41421	X				13										"
"	43-41502			X		2					X					
"	43-41440						1								X	3 MI NE
"	43-41412			X			1	2			X				X	4 MI NE
"	43-??3??			X			1									
"	42-77818	X		X		2					X				X	3 MI NE
"	43-20131			X		2				X					X	3 MI NE
"	43-19801		X						X							LZ
"	43-40093		X						X							"
"	43-40546		X											X		"
"	43-41579			X					X					X		"
"	43-36937		X						X							"
"	43-41373		X	X					X			X				"
"	43-41459		X	X					X			X				"
"	43-40212			X		4							X			"
"	43-42154	X		X		4							X			"
"	43-41905			X						X			X			"
"	43-42127			X						X			X			"
"	43-41684			X						X			X			
"	43-41677			X		5				2	X					
"	43-40219			X		5				2	X					
"	43-42007	X	X	X		5				2	X					
"	43-40162			X		5				2	X					
"	43-40085	X		X		5					X					
"	43-47829			X			1									
"	43-41146	X														
"	43-40641		X			5										LZ
"	43-40213		X			5										"
"	43-40461		X			5										"
"	43-37390					5										"
"	43-41964	X				3										"
"	43-41994	X	X			4										"
"	43-36791		X			4	1									"
"	43-40554		X													"
"	43-41607		X													"
TOTAL		101	9	13		93	2	1	40	4	11	2	5	2	4	
PERCENT		25	20	22.5	32.5	69.7	1.3	.9	.28	26.6	73.6	28.5	71.5	33.4	66.6	

TABLE D

SERIAL N° A-II   TIME OF DROP - 1503   FIELD - FULBECK   LZ - T   ROUTE - N   GP N° 440TH

ORGANIZATION	TAIL NUMBER	GLIDER				PERSONNEL				JEEP		TRAILER		GUN		DISTANCE FROM LZ
		INTACT	DAM	DES	MISS	OK	KIA	EVAC	MISS	SER	UNSER	SER	UNSER	SER	UNSER	
Hq d Ho Btry Dv Arty	43-40150	X				2	1			X						LZ
"	43-40153	X	X			4	1					X				"
"	43-40376	X				2				X		X				"
"	43-40138	X				4				X						"
"	43-19831		X			3			2							60 mi SW
"	43-41705	X				3				X						LZ
"	43-37304	X				5						X				"
"	43-40141	X				3				X						"
"	43-40393		X			3				X						"
"	43-40523		X			5				X		X				"
"	43-40220		X			2	1			X		X				"
	341340			X		5										"
	40139		X			2				X		X		X		"
Btry "B" 456 FA Bn	42-77900	X				5								X		"
"	43-42094	X				4								X		"
Btry "C" 456 FA Bn	42-7499	X				2				X						"
"	43-41309	X				8								X		"
"	43-27375	X				9				X				X		"
"	43-36826	X				9										"
"	43-41791	X				5				X				X		"
"	43-39738	X				9								X		"
"	42-77660	X				2								X		"
"	43-41398	X				10				X		X		X		"
"	43-41181	X				3										"
"	43-40240	X				9										"
"	43-36946	X				2				X						"
"	42-70454	X				5				X				X		"
"	42-56358	X				10								X		"
"	41-40236	X				2				X						"
"	43-40241	X				6								X		"
"	43-41520	X				7				X		X		X		"
"	42-56120	X				2				X		X				3 mi SW LZ
"	42-56226	X				4		2								"
"	43-43090		X			5						X				"
"	43-41969	X				2								X		"
"	43-39233	X				4										"
"	43-36917	X				3										"
"	43-41863	X														"
TOTAL		31	8	1		171	5	2		17		10		11		
PERCENTAGE		77.5	20	2.5		96	2.2	1.8		100		100		100		

TABLE E

Glider Data

	Wing		Weights			Troops*	Built
	Span (feet)	Area (sq. ft.)	Empty	Cargo	Total		
Argentina							
I.AE.25	83.7	851.42	5,423	2,474	7,897	13	1
Australia							
DHA-G1 (EG-1, 2)	59	300	1,240	1,550	2,790	6	2
DHA-G2 (A57-1/6)	50.5		1,450	1,800	3,250	6	6
Canada							
Horsa	88	1,204	8,370	7,130	15,750	25	3
Hotspur I	62				3,600	8	22
Hadrian Mark II (U.S. CG-4A)	84	852	3,440	4,060	7,500	13	32
CG-15A (U.S. CG-15)	62.1	623	4,000	4,000	8,000	13	1
China							
No designation				2,800		12	12
Czechoslovakia							
NK-25	same as data on Ts-25 (see *Soviet Union*)						
Yak-14	(see *Soviet Union*)						
France							
CM-10	87	770	6,400	9,000	15,400	35	6
Germany							
Assault/transport							
DFS 230	72	444	1,800	2,800	4,600	9	2,230
DFS 230 V7	63	425	3,520	4,180	7,700	15	1
Go 242	79	690	7,000	8,000	15,000	23	1,528
Me 321	181	3,230	26,000	44,000	70,000	200	200
Ju 322	203	6,400	56,000	24,000	90,000		2
DFS 331	71	646	4,500	5,500	10,000	18	1
Go 345A	67	537	5,450	3,500	8,950	12	2
Assault							
Ka 430	64	435	3,750	3,750	7,500	12	12
Fighter							
BV 40	26	94	1,844	250	2,094	1	19
India							
G-1	56.7	300	1,500	2,500	4,000	8	1
Italy							
AL-12P	70	630	3,500	2,700	6,200	12	16
TM-2	74.8	495	4,400	4,400	8,800	20	1
Japan							
Army							
Ku-1	55	324	1,540	1,320	2,860	6–8	100

	Wing Span (feet)	Area (sq. ft)	Weights Empty	Cargo	Total	Troops*	Built
Ku-6	72.3	649	1,538	6,174	7,712		1
Ku-7	114	1,288	10,000	16,455	26,455	32	9
Ku-8	76	544	3,750	3,950	7,700	18	700
Ku-11	60	475	2,800	2,600	5,400	12	3
Navy							
MXY5	59.4	475	3,520	2,240	5,940	11	12
Soviet Union							
A-7	62.2	335		2,000		8	400
BDP (S-1)	65.7	485	5,070	2,630	7,700	20	7
A-11, (G-11)	82	440		4,400		20	1
G-31	91.9	753	3,086	3,968	7,054	18	1
GN-4	60		1,000	992	1,992	5	1
IL-32				8,000		35	1
KT-20	72.6	840		4,410		24	2
SAM-23				3,600		16	1
Tank-delivery							
(Winged Tank)	49.2	732	4,800	13,200	18.000		1
Ts-25	82.8	830	5,115	4,806	9,921	25	6
Yak-14	85.8	1,050	6,800	7,716	14,900	35	413
Sweden							
FI-3	54.6	344.5	1,742	2,228	3,970	11	5
Turkey							
THK-1				2,400		11	1
United Kingdom							
Hadrian	84	852	3,444	4,060	7,500	13	746
(U.S. CG-4A)							
Hamilcar (half scale prototype)							1
Hamilcar	110	1,657	18,000	17,500	36,000	40	412
Hengist	80	780	4,666	3,667	8,333	15	18
Horsa I	88	1,104	8,370	7,130	15,500	25	2,302
Horsa II	88	1,104	8,370	7,380	15,750	28	1,490
Hotspur I	62			3,600		7	18
Hotspur II	45.9	272	1,755	1,880	3,635	7	997
Hotspur III	45.9	272	1,660	1,940	3,600	7	50
Hotspur twin	58	262	3,025	3,525	6,550	14	1
United States							
Army Air Force							
XCG-1						7	0
XCG-2						13	0
CG-3A	73	420	2,400	2,400	4,400	7	100
XCG-4	83.6	852	3,440	4,066	7,500	13	1
CG-4A	83.6	852	3,440	4,060	7,500	13	13,909
XCG-4B	83.6	852				13	1
XCG-5						7	1
XCG-6							0
XCG-7	80	600	5,000	2,000	7,000	7	1
XCG-8	90	880	7,450	3,600	11,050	13	1
XCG-9						23	0
XCG-10			7,980	8,000	15,980	28	0

	Wing Span (feet)	Area (sq. ft)	Empty	Weights Cargo	Total	Troops*	Built
XCG-10A	105	1,180	12,150	10,850	23,000	40	1
YCG-10A	105	1,180	12,150	10,850	23,000	40	6
XCG-11						28	0
XCG-12			9,349	8,282	17,631	28	0
XCG-13	86	873	7,000	8,000	15,000	28	2
YCG-13	86	873	7,000	8,000	15,000	28	2
YCG-13A	86	873	7,000	8,000	15,000	28	3
CG-13A	86	873	8,700	10,200	18,900	40	132
XCG-14	71.8	507	3,237	4,368	7,605	15	1
XCG-14A	71.8	507	7,500	8,000	15,500	24	1
XCG-15	62.1	623	4,000	4,000	8,000	13	1
XCG-15A	62.1	623	4,000	4,000	8,000	13	2
CG-15	62.1	623	4,000	4,000	8,000	13, 14	427
XCG-16	91.8	1,140	9,500	10,080	19,580	42	2
XCG-17	95	987	11,000	15,000	26,000	27	1
XCG-18A	71.8	507	8,000	8,000	16,000	30	1
XCG-19	85		6,380	8,000	14,380	38	0
XCG-20	110	880	24,000	16,000	40,000†	60	1
XFG-1	54	356	3,362	4,638	8,000		2
Assault Glider							
XAG-1					8,500		0
XAG-2					8,500		0
Navy-Marine							
XLRA-1	70.5	495	2,800			12	1
XLRA-2	70.5	495	2,800				1
XLRN-1	110	1,200	15,160	18,000	33,160‡	80	1
XLRQ-1	71	500	2,800			12	2
XLRG-1 (40 percent scale flight model)							1
XLRG-1	109		4,800			24	0
XLRH-1	110		4,800			24	0
Yugoslavia							
No designation			2,800			12	1

*For crew, see technical data.

† Although maximum take-off weight was 70,000 pounds, tow planes were not available that would tow a glider of this loaded weight. Thus, 40,000 pound limit was established.

‡ Overload weight was 40,000 pounds.

Powered Gliders

	Glider	*Powered adaptation*
Australia	DHA-G2	Glas II suction-wing
France	CM-10	CM 100
	CM-10	CM 101R jet
Germany	Go 244	Go 244
	Me 321	Me 322
Italy	AL-12P	P-512
Japan	Ku-7	Ki 105
Soviet Union	G-31	G-31 Yakov Alksnis
	BDP (S-1)	MP-1
	SAM-23	SAM-23
	IL-32	IL-34
United Kingdom	Hamilcar	Hamilcar X
	Horsa	Horsa
United States	CG-4A	XPG-1
	CG-4A	XPG-2
	GG-4A	XPG-2A
	CG-4A	PG-2A
	XCG-15A	XPG-3
	XCG-18A	C-122
	XCG-20	XC-123
	XCG-20	XC-123A

APPENDIX D

CG-4A Production Data to October 31, 1944		
Contractor	Average Cost	Delivered
Ford	14,891	2,418
Waco	19,367	999
Gibson	25,785	1,055
Commonwealth	24,232	950
Northwestern	24,543	887
G & A	25,144	464
General	31,010	1,013
Ridgefield	38,209	155
Robertson	39,027	147
Pratt, Read	30,802	925
Laister-Kauffmann	29,437	210
Cessna	30,324	750
Babcock	50,906	60
Timm	51,123	433
Ward	379,457	7
National	1,741,809	1

Performance Data

Horse-power Required for Operational Gliders at Sea-level

Glider Type	CG-15	CG-4A	CG-4A	CG-16	CG-13A	CG-13A	CG-10A	Two CG-4As	Horsa
Gross Weight	8,000 lb	7,500 lb	9,000 lb	19,500 lb	16,500 lb	18,580 lb	24,000 lb	Each 7,500 lb	15,000 lb
Load	4,100 lb	3,600 lb	5,100 lb	10,080 lb	8,000 lb	10,080 lb	12,000 lb	7,200 lb	6,800 lb
Airspeed	H.P.	H.P.	H.P.	H.P.	H.P.	H.P.	H.P.	H.P.	H.P.
100	185	268	292	350	480	520	545	525	440
110	220	293	315	370	520	555	570	550	500
120	260	340	364	425	575	600	610	635	650
125	285	375	395	455	610	630	645	710	740
130	313	415	425	490	650	675	680	800	840
135	345	458	Max Speed	527	700	720	735	900	945
140	375 *.092	506 .141		567	750	775	800	1000	1040
150	450	650		650	875	895	965	1150	1200

Note: *Data calculated by Glider Branch, Aircraft Laboratory from Wind Tunnel and/or Flight Test Data.*

Performance of the CG-4A in Approved
Tow-Plane Combinations (One CG-4A with cargo = 7,500lb)

Aircraft	One glider				Two gliders
	C-47	C-60	C-46	B-24	B-17
Ground roll (ft)	2550	1950	3300	3000	3,750
Distance to clear 50ft obstacle (ft)	3950	2950	5100	3750	5750
Climb (fpm)	275	600	275	530	300
Cruising speed (mph)	120	120	125	144	140
Range (miles)	830	990	950	1360	720

470

Select Bibliography

AAF Historical Office, Headquarters Army Air Forces, Army Air Forces Historical Studies: No. 47 (unpublished); *Development and Procurement of Gliders in the Army Air Forces 1941–1944.*

Air Enthusiast for March, April and May 1972.

Chatterton, George. *Wings of Pegasus* (London, MacDonald, 1962).

Greene, William. *Warplanes of the Third Reich* (Garden City, Doubleday, 1970).

Headquarters US Army Air Forces in Europe, AAF Sta. 197, APO 633, U.S. Army 15 Oct. 1945. Air Staff Post Hostilities Intelligence Requirements on German Air Force, *"Tactical Employment Troop Carrier Operations, Section IV, F, 1, 2, 3, 4, 5, 6, 7 and 8."*

Management Control Central District-ATSC, September 1945. *The History of the Glider Program at Northwestern Aeronautical Corporation.*

Masters, John. *Road Past Mandalay* (New York, Harper, 1961).

Ministry of Information, Great Britain. *By Air To Battle* (London, His Majesty's Stationery Office, 1945).

Morzik, Fritz-Gerhard. *Himmelchen, Die deutschen Transportflieger im Zweiten Weltkrieg* (Frankfurt am Main, Bernard & Graefe Verlag für Wehrwesen, 1966).

Nemecek, Vaclav. *Sovetska Letadla* (Prague, NV).

Otway, T. B. H. *Airborne Forces*, from the series, *The Second World War, 1939–1945, Army* (The War Office, 1951).

Seth, Ronald. *Lion with the Blue Wings* (London, Victor Gollancz, Ltd., 1955).

Taylor, William H. *Glider Operations on Two Fronts.* AAFSAT Special Intelligence Report, No. 54, September 1944.

USAF. Historical Division Liaison Office, March 1962. *USAF Airborne Operations World War II and Korean War.*

USAF. Historical Study No.1. *The Glider Pilot Training Program, 1941–1947.*

Warren, John C. *Airborne Missions in the Mediterranean, 1942–1945* (USAF. Historical Study 74).

———. *Airborne Operations in World War II, European Theater* (USAF Historical Study 97).

Wright, Lawrence. *The Wooden Sword* (London, Elek, 1967).

Acknowledgments

BOOK ONE

I am indebted to many people for their contributions and for their assistance in preparing this exhaustive (and exhausting) work. Ever since I served as a gliderman during World War II—where I collected some of the first data about transport gliders—I have gradually compiled material from many sources and had the help of many people. I trust that I have not omitted attributing contributions from any person or source whatsoever, but if I have inadvertently done so, it has not been intentional.

Regrettably, some German material I had used in the manuscript was lost when I mailed it to the U.S. from England, where I had been working with the publisher. The data from the material had already been used, but the names of individuals and archives in Germany who had so generously provided the information were recorded in the correspondence lost with the material. Thus, I may not have given credit to those sources.

United States

General John R. Alison, wartime deputy commander, 1st Air Commando Group

The late Captain Homer Ambrose, U.S. Navy, Ret., editor

Captain R. S. Barnaby, U.S. Navy, Ret., test pilot and wartime chief engineer, Naval Aircraft Factory, Philadelphia

Robert Bovey, wartime glider pilot

Richard M. Bueschel, author and Japanese and Chinese aviation historian

Eleanor M. Burdette, reference librarian, National Aeronautics and Space Administration (NASA), headquarters library, Washington, D.C.

Jack Coogan, actor and wartime transport glider pilot

Colonel Carl F. Damberg, U.S. Air Force, wartime chief, Aircraft Laboratory, Wright Field, Ohio

Major Fred Demousse, U.S. Army, linguist who assisted in translating of Russian material

The late Major General Frederick R. Dent, U.S. Air Force, wartime chief, Glider Branch, Wright Field, Ohio

Dr. Cortez F. Enloe, Jr., military surgeon on the staff of General Orde Charles Wingate

Marcia Frances, U.S. resident of Vienna, Austria, who translated German material

Rene Francillon, Ph.D., author of *Japanese Aircraft*

Royal Frey, curator, U.S. Air Force Museum, Wright-Patterson Air Force Base, Ohio

Virginia G. Fincik, archives technician, 1361st Photo Squadron, Aerospace Audio Visual Service, U.S. Air Force

Colonel John R. Galvin, U.S. Army, author of *Air Assault*

Elsie L. T. Goins, Office of Naval Aviation History

Jane S. Hess, head, General Reference and Cataloguing, NASA Langley Research Center Library, Hampton, Virginia

Colonel Joe A. Hinton, U.S. Army, wartime chief, Airborne Section, General Staff, G-3, Supreme Headquarters, Allied Expeditionary Force (SHAEF)

Chief Warrant Officer Michael Lansing, U.S. Army, German linguist, assisted in translating German materials

Lieutenant Colonel Robert C. Mikesh, U.S. Air Force, assistant curator, aeronautics, also Louis S. Casey, curator of aircraft, National Air and Space Museum, Smithsonian Institution, Washington, D.C.

Rose F. Mrazek, author's mother, translator of Czech material

Colonel Mike C. Murphy, U.S. Air Force reserve, wartime glider pilot and glider staff officer, AAF, the Pentagon

Lieutenant Colonel Dan Harris, U.S. Army, Ret., Japanese linguist

Thomas E. Holman, archivist, Military Archives Branch, National Archives, Washington, D.C.

Colonel O. W. Howland, U.S. Air Force Reserve, Ret., wartime commander, 435th Transport Carrier Group

Key K. Kobayashi, assistant head, Japanese Section, Orientalia Division, Library of Congress, Washington, D.C.

Colonel Edward H. Lahti, U.S. Army, Ret., wartime commander, 511th Parachute Infantry Regiment, 11th Airborne Division

Charles B. MacDonald, author of *Company Commander* and deputy chief of history, Office of Army's Chief of Military History, Washington, D.C.

General Anthony G. McAuliffe, commander of the 101st Airborne Division
at Bastogne

Leeds Mitchell, author and wartime transport glider pilot

Dr. Hector Nadal, wartime surgeon, glider-borne medical unit

Herbert Naylor, multilingual linguist

Colonel Virgil Ney, U.S. Army, Ret., author and military historian

Rudolf Opitz, wartime *Luftwaffe* assault/transport glider pilot residing in
Stamford, CT.

C. Parker, president, Northwestern Aeronautical Corporation, Minneapolis,
MN. During World War II: partner, Auchincloss, Parker and Redpath

Lady Alice Pennington, linguist, widow of Sir John Pennington, concert
orchestra conductor

John A. Powers, wartime transport glider pilot

Colonel Robert Rentz, U.S. Air Force, Ret., wartime transport aircraft pilot

Michael Rosen, historian

Max Rosenberg, deputy chief of history; Carl Burger, chief, Histories
Division; David Schoen, chief, Support Division; Mary Ann Cresswell,
archivist; Office of U.S. Air Force History, Washington, D.C.

William T. Sampson, wartime transport glider pilot

Lloyd Santmyer, wartime test pilot

Paul Schweizer, president, National Soaring Museum, Elmira, NY, and
president of Schweizer Aircraft Corporation

Albert F. Simpson, Historical Research Center, Maxwell Air Force Base,
Alabama

Ted Solinski, editor of *Nashville Tennessean* and wartime transport pilot

Michael Stroukoff, Jr., son of the designer of XCG-I4, -14A and the XCG-20

Colonel Floyd J. Sweet, U.S. Air Force, Ret., NASA Headquarters,
Washington, D.C., wartime commanding officer for a period, AAF
Training Detachment, Twenty-nine Palms, CA, and later glider project
officer and test pilot then chief, Glider Branch, Wright Field, Dayton,
OH

Dorothy Taylor, manuscript typist

Major General Louis A. Walsh, U.S. Army, Ret., contributor, information on
Japanese transport gliders

Paul L. White, archives technician, National Archives

Arthur A. Whiting, wartime aeronautical engineer for Curtis Wright Aircraft Corporation

Robert Wolfe, chief, Captured Records Branch, Military Archives Division, National Archives; also George Wagner, reference specialist, same office.

and

Thelma, my wife and editor, who assisted me immeasurably during the writing

Germany

Edmund Auer, *Luftwaffe* test pilot, engineer

D. C. Consbruch, *Zentralstelle für Luftfahrtdokumentation und Information (ZLDI)*

Hans-Karl Becker, wartime assault, transport glider pilot

Werner Davignon, historian, *Luftwaffe* chief navigator, air transport group

Wilhelm Fulda, *Luftwaffe* assault, transport glider pilot and captor, the bridge at Corinth, Greece

Generalmajor Walter Gericke, *Bundeswehr*

Oberst Walter Hornung, *Luftwaffe* air transport group commander

Heiner Lange, *Luftwaffe* assault, transport glider pilot

Alexander Lippisch, aeronautical engineer, pioneer German aircraft designer

H. J. Meier and W. A. Thurow, Vereinigte Flugtechnische Werke GMBH

Generalmajor Friedrich Morzik, *Luftwaffe*, wartime commander of Germany's air transport on the Eastern Front

Eugen Moser, *Luftwaffe* assault, transport glider pilot

Dr. Sack, *Zentralbibliotek der Bundeswehr der Leiter*

Hanna Reitsch, wartime *Luftwaffe* test pilot

Dr. Friedrich Stahl, *Bundesarchiv-Militararchiv*, Freiburg in Breisgau

Generaloberst Kurt Student, *Luftwaffe*, pioneer in the use of the glider as a military weapon

Dipl. Ing. Heinz Trautwein

Woldmer Voigt, head of the Departments of Advanced Design and Hardware Design, Messerschmitt, Augsburg

Oberstleutnant i.G. Volker, *Militärgeschichtliches Forschungsamt*, Freiburg

Helmut Wenzel, wartime paratrooper, key figure in capture of Fort Eben Emael

Oberst Rudolf Witzig, German Armed Forces, captor of Fort Eben Emael

and

Messerschmitt-Bolkow-Blohm and Hamburger Flugzeugbau GMBH ein internehmensberger der Messerschmitt; Heinkel Flugzeugbau, Vereinigte Flugzeug Werke (Speyer)

United Kingdom
Jean Alexander, author of forthcoming work on Russian military aircraft

Jack Beaumont, aviation authority, proprietor Beaumont Aviation Literature

J. M. Bruce, deputy keeper, aircraft collection, RAF Museum

Brigadier George Chatterton, author of *Wings of Pegasus* and wartime commander of the Glider Pilot Regiment

Edmund Creek, collector of German aircraft data, collaborator on several works on aircraft

Colour-Sergeant T. Fitch, Airborne Forces Museum, Aldershot

S. Lucas, senior museum assistant, Photographic Library, Imperial War Museum

A. Mundey, historian, RAF Archives

Major G. G. Norton, honorary curator, Airborne Forces Museum, Aldershot

Lieutenant-Colonel Terence B. H. Otway, DSO, wartime commander of the 9th Battalion of the Parachute Regiment

C. W. Prower, coordinating engineer, Hawker-Siddeley Aviation Ltd., formerly on the staff of General Aircraft

Gladys Puddock, my typist in the UK, whose spirits never flagged and who had an uncanny ability to interpret my illegible scrawl

Anne Tilbury, archivist, photo collection, *Flight International*

Hessel Tiltman, head of team that designed the Horsa glider

W. J. P. Wigmore, general secretary, Glider Pilot Regiment Association

K. G. Wilkinson, managing director, Mainline, BEA

Lawrence Wright, author of *The Wooden Sword* and wartime transport glider pilot

Public Archives

Australia

Warrant Officer A. H. McAulay, Australian Army, historian and sailplane pilot

W. A. Smither, Department of Air, Canberra

Belgium

Henri Lecluse, Liege, Belgium

Jean-Louis Lhoest, editor, *Le Peuple*

Canada

F. Wise, Director, Directorate of History, Department of National Defence, Ottawa

France

M. Henri Michel, Directeur de recherche au Centre national de la recherche scientifique

Raymond Danel, aeronautical engineer, historian

India

Squadron Leader B. S. Hatangade, assistant air attaché, Indian Embassy, Washington, D.C.

Italy

Ing. Angelo Ambrosini, designer and builder of transport glider AL-12P

Colonel S. SM Vittoria Castiglioni, Army Office of Military History

Japan

Lieutenant Colonel Hideo Aoki

Ikuhiko Hata, chief historian, Ministry of Finance, Tokyo

Commander Sadao Seno

Yoshisuke Yamaguchi

Sweden
Rudolf Abelin, aircraft designer and test pilot, president and general
manager of Saab-Scania, Malmö

Kjell Lagerstrom, SAAB, New York

BOOK TWO

Artwork
Thomas Kliment, artist, who did some of the silhouettes
Robert Vilseck, artist for *National Geographic* who did a portion of glider sil-
houettes

Picture Credits
U.S. Air Force
Fritz Stamer
Institut fur Flugausrustung
U.S. Air Force in U.S. National Archives: Wright Field Collection in U.S.
National Archives
E. J. Creek
Bundesarchiv
Smithsonian Institution
Messerschmitt Archives
Hamburger Flugzeugbau (GmbH)
Flight
Planet News
Imperial War Museum
Luftfahrtarchiv
Navy Department in U.S. National Archive
U.S. Army
Roger W. Griswold
William K. Horn
U.S. National Archives
M. B. Passingham
J. P. Alcxander
Royal Australian Air Force
Peter Selinger
Giorgio Evangelisti
Skane-Reportage
Air Enthusiast

Index

Page numbers in italics indicate illustrations

Stackpole Military History Series

Real battles. Real soldiers. Real stories.

Stackpole Military History Series

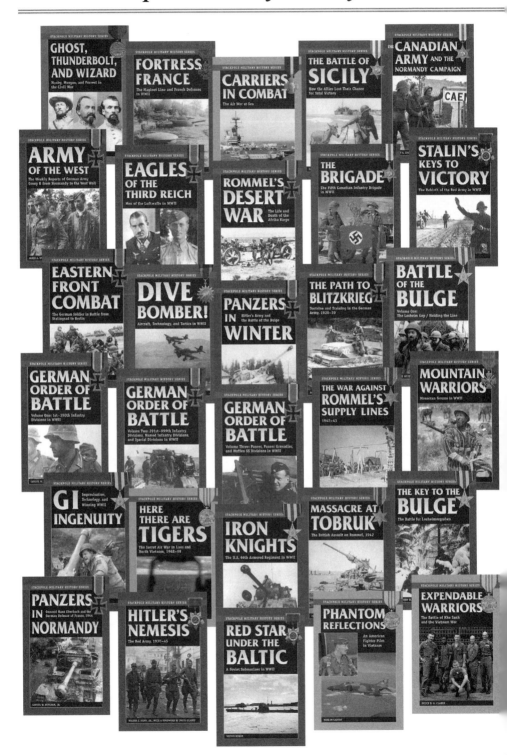

Real battles. Real soldiers. Real stories.

Stackpole Military History Series

Real battles. Real soldiers. Real stories.

STACKPOLE MILITARY HISTORY SERIES

LUFTWAFFE FIGHTERS & BOMBERS
The Battle of Britain
CHRIS GOSS

STACKPOLE MILITARY HISTORY SERIES

NIGHT FLYER / MOSQUITO PATHFINDER
Night Operations in WWII

STACKPOLE MILITARY HISTORY SERIES

POLAND BETRAYED
The Nazi-Soviet Invasions of 1939
DAVID G. WILLIAMSON

STACKPOLE MILITARY HISTORY SERIES

THE SIEGE OF KÜSTRIN
Gateway to Berlin, 1945

STACKPOLE MILITARY HISTORY SERIES

AIRBORNE COMBAT
Glider Wars / Fighting Gliders of WWII

NEW for Spring 2011

STACKPOLE MILITARY HISTORY SERIES

ARNHEM 1944
The Airborne Battle
MARTIN MIDDLEBROOK

STACKPOLE MILITARY HISTORY SERIES

EUROPE IN FLAMES
Understanding WWII
EDITED BY HAROLD J. GOLDBERG

STACKPOLE MILITARY HISTORY SERIES

FIGHTING IN VIETNAM
The Experiences of the U.S. Soldier
JAMES WESTHEIDER

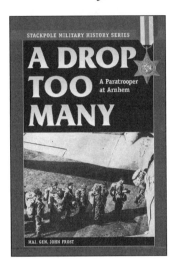

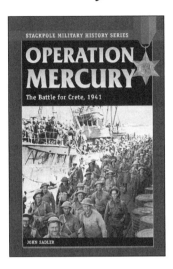

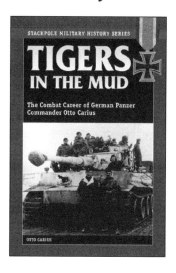

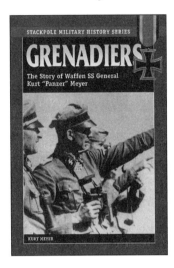

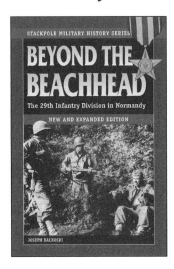

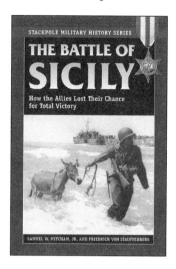

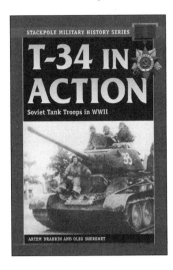

Stackpole Military History Series

DIVE BOMBER!
AIRCRAFT, TECHNOLOGY, AND TACTICS IN WWII
Peter C. Smith

It is a dive bomber that provides one of the most dramatic images of World War II: a German Stuka screaming toward the ground as part of the blitzkrieg that opened the war. Almost all the major combatants developed dive bombers, from the Japanese Val to the American Dauntless and Soviet Pe-2. In this illustrated history of Allied and Axis dive bombers, military historian Peter C. Smith traces these formidable aircraft from the earliest test runs to their emergence as devastatingly effective weapons in the Pacific and Mediterranean, on the Eastern Front, and in Western Europe.

$19.95 • Paperback • 6 x 9 • 400 pages • 69 photos, 26 diagrams

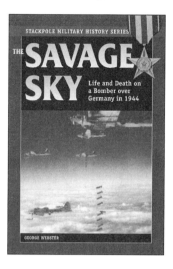

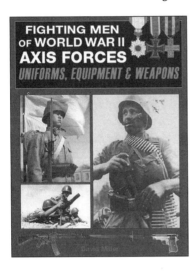
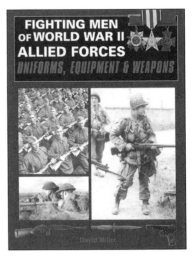